THE OTHER BATTLE OF BRITAIN

THE OTHER BATTLE OF BRITAIN

1940 BOMBER COMMAND'S FORGOTTEN SUMMER

PAUL TWEDDLE

The History Press

Frontispiece: A Few of the Many. The crew of a
102 Squadron Whitley.

First published 2018

The History Press
The Mill, Brimscombe Port
Stroud, Gloucestershire, GL5 2QG
www.thehistorypress.co.uk

British Library Cataloguing in Publication Data.
A catalogue record for this book is available from the British Library.

ISBN 978 0 7509 8706 6

Typesetting and origination by The History Press
Printed and bound in Great Britain by TJ International Ltd

Contents

Introduction

In April 2010 my wife Caroline and I, with our two boys Benedict (aged 6, very nearly 7) and Theo (just 20 months) took a short break to the south Kent coast. Feeling very democratic, as the general election had just been called, we each chose a place to visit. Wakehurst Place for Caroline (she holds a PhD in Plant Biochemistry), the seaside at Hastings for Benedict and the magnificent castle at Dover for me and for Benedict. Theo did not seem to care where he went and was duly disenfranchised. Having just come out of the fascinating secret wartime tunnels cut through the famous white chalk cliffs beneath the castle, we stopped to admire the panoramic view over the port and English Channel. It was a bright, crystal-clear spring day and the coastline of France was clearly visible on the horizon. I pointed it out to Benedict and remarked that that was just how close the Germans came to invading Britain in the summer of 1940, following the evacuation of Dunkirk brilliantly organised in the damp rooms we had just visited. Glancing down, my eyes came across a photograph on one of English Heritage's information boards, more than a little faded by the sun. It was the famous photograph of Goring with his full entourage gazing over the Channel at the White Cliffs of Dover. Jabbing my finger at the photograph, 'That's them there,' I said, pointing at the French coast, 'looking at us, here,' indicating the place we were standing. 'Not far, is it? But they never managed to get here.' Now Benedict, a curiously well-informed 6- nearly 7-year-old, nodded sagely and said, 'That was the Battle of Britain, wasn't it? The Spitfires and Hurricanes and all that stuff.' Indeed it was and we strolled on.

Later that afternoon as we headed back to our hotel, we called at the under-visited Battle of Britain Memorial at Capel-le-Ferne. We wandered along the propeller-shaped footpaths to the beautiful statue of the lone pilot sitting with arms wrapped around his drawn-up knees, his young face serene and untroubled, lifted slightly towards the sky. Having looked at the squadron crests on its plinth, we all walked slowly back to the immaculate memorial wall to read a few of the 2,900 names perfectly inscribed upon it. Benedict had heard of some of the more famous names and, having read some others, asked, 'Are these the names of all the men who fought in the Battle of Britain?' I thought about it for a minute and replied, 'Well, no, not really. These are the names of the famous Few, the brave pilots and aircrew of Fighter Command, but there were lots of others who helped too.' Benedict did not even pause for breath, 'Ah, they'll be your bomber men again, daddy,' and ran off to catch up with Theo, who was toddling around on the grass.

His initial views that day, though those of a young boy, are the ones that are widely held, in so far as they are held at all, by the general public in Britain. The Battle of Britain was all about Spitfires, and maybe Hurricanes, roaring about the skies over London and the South-East, shooting down loads of German Messerschmitts. As someone who teaches a bit of history, I do know that this is the line most textbooks take, sketchily covering these events before hurrying on to the Blitz and its effects. The general media certainly follow suit and each summer several newspapers run a feature or two on The Few and on TV another documentary repackages the archive film to tell the story once again.

I should make it absolutely clear here and now that I am in the first rank of those who insist that the Battle is a story worth telling. Indeed, as I point out to the boys and girls I teach, the Battle is arguably the most important in Britain's long and unparalleled military history. The Few deserve, without reservation, their place at the very top of the lengthy roll of British military heroes – and I mean heroes in the full and proper sense of the word. However, that small group of men from Britain, its Empire and beyond, were not alone in seeking to defend the people of these islands in the summer of 1940. Indeed, they were not even alone within the RAF itself. The men of Coastal Command and Bomber Command also fought tirelessly and bravely by day and by night to prevent invasion and to reduce the weight of attack being unleashed on this country. It is revealing and sobering to recall that in the Lady Chapel in Westminster Abbey, originally added by Henry VII, damaged by military action in 1940, restored and rededicated by King George VI on 10 July 1947, there lies, beneath the magnificent stained-glass Battle of Britain memorial window, a Roll of Honour. Illustrated magnificently, its beautiful script records for future generations the names of the 1,497 pilots and aircrew who made the ultimate sacrifice in defence of Great Britain between 10 July and 31 October 1940. Listed by Command, one stands out as being by far the longest, comprising some 732 names. It is that of Bomber Command. In many ways, the forgotten heroes of that Command's forgotten summer.

Acknowledgements –
Proud Words on a Dusty Shelf

I have run up a number of debts during the long and tortuous process of writing this book. I would like to thank the few survivors of The Many who took the time to meet or correspond with me to share their experiences of the tumultuous summer of 1940. Likewise, my family and friends who have encouraged me and taken an interest in the progress of the project, however slow it was at times. The girls and boys in my Latin and Greek classes, most recently at Holmewood House, have also taken my digressions into military history with remarkably good grace. I would particularly like to thank The History Press for its support with this book, especially Amy Rigg, Alex Waite and Martin Latham, who have guided both it and me through the entire production process with consummate professionalism, patience and no little good humour. However, the special award for supreme patience and tolerance in the face of this book must go to my lovely wife Caroline and our boys Benedict and Theo, who, once again, have lived in the shadow of the bombers for so long. Maybe one day they will get their way and we will move on into the twenty-first century!

All images courtesy of ww2images.com. Many thanks to the Battle of Britain Memorial Trust for allowing the use of *The Wall* by Flight Lieutenant William Walker, which is inscribed on a plinth at The Battle of Britain Memorial, Capel-le-Ferne, Kent – the inspiration for this book on The Many in Bomber Command.

Chapter 1

A New Kind of War

By the time the War Cabinet assembled at 11 a.m. on 15 May, rumour was rife and a heady mix of anticipation and foreboding hung heavy in the air. At 7.30 that morning Prime Minister Churchill, disgruntled to be awoken at such an hour, had received a telephone call from a shocked and despondent Paul Reynaud, his French counterpart, who informed him that the Germans had smashed through French lines and were decimating the remaining French forces, leaving the road to Paris wide open. His conclusion was that the battle was over and the war was lost. Churchill begged to differ and sought to reassure his near hysterical ally, pointing out that the War Cabinet was to meet within a matter of hours and would act swiftly. There were no fewer than fifteen items on the wide-ranging agenda. Item two was air policy and to add their expertise to the discussion were the new Secretary of State for Air, Sir Archibald Sinclair; Air Chief Marshal Sir Cyril Newall; Chief of Air Staff and his deputy Air Marshal Sir Richard Peirse; and Air Chief Marshal Sir Hugh Dowding, Air Officer Commanding, Fighter Command. The item, which had largely been prompted by Reynaud's grave warnings, was divided into two parts – firstly, whether Britain should send more fighters to France and secondly, whether Britain should launch attacks on military objectives in the Ruhr and elsewhere in Germany east of the Rhine.

Mindful of the perilous position in France and the manifest and direct consequences of their decision, the Cabinet declined to sanction the deployment of further fighters to the Continent. History rightly makes much of this momentous decision but tends to overlook the one that followed. The French government had set its face firmly against such a move, deterred by near certain retaliation by the Germans, but the motion drew a far warmer reception from the War Cabinet, now absolute in their determination to act in Britain's interests. Sinclair opened the discussion by pointing to the wide range of military and industrial targets available and the significantly detrimental effect attacking them would have upon Germany's war effort on land, sea and air. Newall spoke next, fully endorsing Sinclair's views, as did Peirse, Dowding, Admiral of the Fleet Sir Dudley Pound and General Sir Edmund Ironside, Chief of the Imperial General Staff. The discussion then turned to those with political responsibilities and here too the unanimity was astonishing, especially given the tense and menacing conditions in which the discussion was taking place. Eden, Alexander, Atlee, Halifax and Duff-Cooper all concurred, each stating the positive benefits, military and political, at home and abroad, as they saw them; even Neville Chamberlain, the recently deposed Prime Minister, so long an advocate of less martial means, now advocated this overtly offensive course, considering that 'this battle had reached so critical a stage that … it would therefore be wrong to stay our hands any longer from the proposed night bombing operations.' The avalanche of support no doubt pleased the pugnacious Churchill, who added his thoughts thus, considering 'that the proposed operations would cut Germany at its tap root'. He also hoped it would have an effect on the current land battle, bolster French morale, have a salutary effect on Italy (then lurking menacingly in the wings of the war) and believed that this was the psychological moment to strike at Germany proper and 'convince the German people that we had both the will and the power to hit them hard.' The proposal was carried unanimously and without further debate. Never one to procrastinate, Churchill suggested operations should begin that night. Thus began the longest and most intense single campaign of the war, the strategic air offensive against Germany, waged by Bomber Command. It would involve more than 125,000 highly trained air crew, with several times that number of specialists acting in support of them, the loss of more than 55,000 young men from Britain and the Empire, take up a large proportion of the nation's industrial production and cost the economy millions of pounds. In return, it would devastate Germany from end to end, significantly hamper and constrain the development and growth of German war production, weaken the offensive spirit of the general population, cause the deaths of well over 500,000 Germans, compel the deployment of more than 1 million men and considerable military hardware and expertise to the defence of the Reich, pave the way for the invasion of Occupied Europe and take the war right to the heart of Germany, thereby increasingly sparing Britain the full horrors of war.

In the desperate days during the summer of 1940, with a powerful, ruthless and rampant enemy only a matter of miles away and the fate of the country and its Empire hanging in the balance, it also played a crucial and largely overlooked role in the defence of the United Kingdom in the Battle of Britain.

It had barely been twenty-five years since the first bomb dropped from a Zeppelin had landed on Norfolk on 15 January 1915, killing two civilians and wounding thirteen more. Britain's island inviolability had been breached and, as the raids continued, it rapidly became clear that every citizen – young and old, male and female, rich and poor – was potentially in the front line. The profound implications of this development were immediately crystal clear. Writing in response to the first daylight attack made upon London by an aircraft on 28 November 1916, *The Times'* leader writer noted, 'If I were asked what event of the year had been of the most significance to the future of humanity, I should reply … the appearance of a single German aeroplane flying at high noon over London.'

Lord Rothermere, the influential newspaper magnate and Chairman of the Air Board, immediately led the strident calls for retaliation. By the end of the war in November 1918, some 1,414 British citizens had lost their lives and a further 3,416 had been seriously injured by aerial bombardment, but in reply more than 12,000 bombs, totalling 553 tons, had been dropped on German targets in 578 separate raids. Had the war lasted a day or two longer, the RAF's new super-heavy bomber, the Handley Page V/1500, would have carted its half-ton load from its base in Nancy to Berlin.

The threat of attack from the air hung heavy over the heads of the British people in the 1920s and '30s in the same manner as nuclear war would later in the century, and the question of air attack was one of the very few aspects of the Great War to be actively pursued by successive inter-war governments. As early as May 1924 an Air Raids Precautions Committee was set up under Sir John Anderson to consider ways to ameliorate the effects of bombing upon the civilian population. Evidence from the Air Staff painted an apocalyptic picture. Air raids on London would kill 1,700 and injure 3,300 in the first twenty-four hours, decreasing to 1,275 and 2,475 respectively the next day and then 880 and 1,650 for each twenty-four-hour period thereafter. Great thought was given to the means of preventing such an unprecedented slaughter but the problem was an intractable one. Aircraft development, particularly that of fighters, was stagnant as defence spending was slashed in the face of economic recession and widespread anti-war sentiment. Anti-aircraft protection was equally woefully inadequate, with a shortage of suitable weaponry and effective technology: an air exercise in 1926 revealed that, of the 2,935 shells expended, only two succeeded in hitting the target and that in broad daylight and clear conditions.

It is no wonder, then, that a sense of doom and gloom prevailed. Successive governments concluded that there was little that could be done to prevent such cataclysmic slaughter and devastation, which could continue for days on end. The public long remembered Prime Minister Stanley Baldwin's chilling statement made in the House of Commons on

10 November 1932: 'No power on Earth can protect the man in the street from being bombed. Whatever people might tell him, the bomber will always get through.' The Air Raids Precaution Committee had already concluded that, even with mass evacuation and the best defensive measures available, 'It may well be the nation whose people can endure aerial bombardment the longer, and with the greatest stoicism, will ultimately prove victorious.' There seemed to be just two possibilities to prevent the 'knock-out blow' – disarmament and rearmament. When the lengthy disarmament talks held in Geneva, upon which so many hopes were riding, inevitably fell foul of national prejudices and vested interests and failed to produce a suitable formula for policing the skies, the viable options were down to one. The only protection against the bomber was the bomber. In essence, to have the capacity to bomb your enemy harder and more often than he could you, an early form of Mutually Assured Destruction. Thus, it came as no surprise when, as if acting on cue, the moment Chamberlain had finished his sombre and lugubrious declaration of war on the morning of 3 September 1939, the air raid warning sounded in London.

The appalling horrors of the trenches and the scale of the losses suffered had inflicted a deep and unhealed scar upon the British consciousness. Especially as the joy of victory faded, people from all walks of life vowed that the mass slaughter should never be allowed to happen again and new ideas that seemed to hold out the promise of making this heart-felt aspiration a reality were instantly attractive and appealing. One such idea was put forward by the newly formed Royal Air Force, with at least half an eye on justifying its continued existence as a separate entity – strategic bombardment from the air, effectively the removal of an opponent's capacity and, indeed, will to wage war. In the light of the real moral and economic pressure to save lives and cut costs, the Strategic Air Offensive had much to recommend it and quickly became the cornerstone of RAF policy. By its threatened use or its thoughtful and skilful deployment, a comparatively small force could achieve disproportionally large goals and put an end to a war quickly and conclusively, without the need for a prolonged and bloody campaign on the ground. 'It may,' the Air Staff declared, 'in itself be the instrument of victory or it may be the means by which victory can be won by other forces. It differs from all previous forms of armed attack in that it alone can be brought to bear immediately, directly and destructively, against the heartland of the enemy.' Sir Hugh Trenchard, the highly influential Chief of Air Staff and 'Father of the Royal Air Force', was a forceful proponent of the approach and made a strong case for devastating attacks upon legitimate military and economic targets directly related to the war effort. There were, however, significant limits as to what he considered legitimate and these would have profound effects upon the deployment of the RAF in 1939–40. He wrote in May 1928:

> What is illegitimate as being contrary to the dictates of humanity, is the indiscriminate bombing of a city for the sole purpose of terrorising the civilian population. It is an entirely different matter to terrorise munitions workers (men and women) into absenting themselves from work or stevedores to abandoning the loading of a ship with munitions through fear of air attack upon the factory or dockyard concerned. Moral effect is created by the bombing in such circumstances but it is the inevitable result of a lawful operation of war – the bombing of a military objective.

The thrust of his argument gained ground and became the widely accepted wisdom. By the time Bomber Command was finally formed as a separate entity in July 1936 as part of the rapid reorganisation and rearmament programme belatedly initiated in response to events unfolding in Germany, planning was under way for what became the Western Air Plans, a blueprint for the Strategic Air Offensive against Germany. The sixteen detailed plans strove to undermine Germany's capacity to wage war by attacking targets critical to its offensive war effort, such as Luftwaffe bases and aircraft factories, naval bases and dockyards, industrial war material production sites – especially in the Ruhr – oil storage and refineries, rail, waterway and communications targets and administrative centres of government. Italy was to be subjected to similar attack if necessary and both countries were also to be deluged by a massive propaganda leaflet campaign, warning the population of the dire consequences of continued hostilities. Bomber Command, therefore, entered the war with clear aims and objectives – to protect Great Britain by destroying the enemy's capacity to conduct a war effectively.

Having clear and effective planning is one thing, executing it is quite another. The parsimonious and languid approach of successive governments to military spending after the war had a significant deleterious effect upon the RAF and the years slipped by with precious little investment in new aircraft, equipment and training. Indeed, an RFC veteran returning to the colours in, say, 1934 would have needed nothing more than a light refresher course before becoming fully operational once more. At the end of that year, there was still not a single bomber in service that could from an airfield in Britain reach the nearest point in Germany, deliver more than a paltry 500lb bomb load and return. If an attempt had been made in daylight there was little chance of survival lumbering along at about 90mph in an unwieldy, lightly armed aircraft such as the Handley Page Heyford, fully in range of modern anti-aircraft guns and in the face of the Nazi regime's rapidly improving fighter opposition. If the attempt had been made by night, the problems of navigation and target location in hostile skies almost precluded success and a safe return. The matter did not end there for a similar degree of stagnation and paralysis had inevitably affected most other aspects of the service. In terms of defensive armament, a key factor in a bomber's ability to operate unescorted in a hostile environment, little had changed and the aircraft still relied on the Great War stalwart, the slow-firing light Lewis gun, mounted on metal rings in open turrets. The bombs too belonged to a bygone era, the standard 112lb and 250lb bombs had only limited destructive capability and then only when the crew had used basic navigation techniques, still largely based on visual sightings and map reading, to locate the target. Quite simply, as there had been little progress in the performance of the bombers themselves, there was little imperative to develop and enhance the skill set of the crews. Things were clearly not as they should have been.

The RAF expansion programme was belatedly put into place and accelerated in the mid-1930s to meet the increasingly obvious threat posed by the new National Socialist government in Germany, unencumbered by many of the niceties of democratic government and society and backed by almost unlimited financial resources. The Air Ministry put out new specifications for a medium bomber and Vickers-Armstrongs set out to meet it with the help of an innovative designer, Barnes Wallace. The resultant Wellington, which first flew from the firm's airfield at Brooklands in Surrey on 15 June 1936, was a quantum leap forwards. Capable of 250mph, it had a service ceiling of about 20,000ft, four .303 machine guns mounted in pairs in power-operated turrets in the nose and tail (often two more manually operated guns in the beam position), a maximum load of 4,500lb and a range well in excess of 1,000 miles fully loaded. The Air Ministry immediately placed orders and the first operational Wellingtons were delivered to 99 Squadron at Mildenhall in October 1938. Handley Page also aimed to meet the original specification B9/32 and its chief designer Gustav Lachman came up with the Hampden. Major J.L.B.H. Cordes lifted the prototype off the runway at Radlett for the first time on 21 June 1936 and was immediately impressed by its manoeuvrability. So was the Air Ministry and orders were swiftly placed. A little faster than the Wellington, it had a similar ceiling and top speed and could take a 2,000lb load almost 1,900 miles, dropping to 1,200 miles with a 4,000lb bomb load. For defence, it packed just a single .303 Vickers K gas-operated machine gun in the nose, dorsal and ventral positions and one Browning .303 in the wing – hardly a serious deterrent to a hard-hitting Me 109 or Me 110. By a happy chance, it was also found that two 1,500lb parachute sea mines could be squeezed into its bomb bay, thereby creating a particular and highly successful niche for the bomber.

The third mainstay of Bomber Command's force, and the only one designed *ab initio* to operate at night, was the Armstrong Whitworth Whitley.

Sleek, if not especially stylish, its modern lines were a mile away from its predecessors when it first flew on 17 March 1936. Put into service with 10 Squadron based at Dishforth in March 1937, it could lug a 4,000lb bomb load well over 1,500 miles at a theoretical cruising speed of 185mph, though most crews rarely saw those figures in practice. Armed with a revolutionary Nash and Thompson power-operated quadruple .303 machine gun in the rear turret, with further armament in the nose, the Whitley gave the Command its first real capability to launch an offensive against Germany. It and the other two were supported in their roles by two light bombers, the Fairey Battle and the Bristol Blenheim. By 1940 both aircraft were, and were known to be, little more than obsolescent death traps, making the selfless determination of the crews that flew them that summer – and beyond – all the more remarkable and poignant. Initially a private venture backed by Lord Rothermere, in April 1934 the Air Ministry was impressed by the Blenheim's capabilities, especially its top speed of 280mph, then well over 100mph faster than any fighter in service. By the time the first aircraft reached 114 Squadron in March 1937, its advantage had been lost and even an upgraded Blenheim IV, which reached the front-line squadrons in January 1939, found itself outpaced and out-gunned by its opposition. The Fairey Battle fared even worse and its service history is one of bravery beyond reason. Designed to meet specification P.27/32 issued in August 1932 for a monoplane to carry 1,000lb of bombs over a range of 1,000 miles with a top speed of 200mph plus, its first flight was not until 10 March 1936, by which time it was already obsolescent, too slow, too lightly armoured and too lightly armed to survive in combat. Nevertheless, by the outbreak of war, there were more than 1,000 of these three-man light bombers in service and they formed the bulk of the Advanced Air Striking Force (AASF), sent to and ultimately fought almost to extinction over France.

These then were the aircraft at the disposal of those in command of the Strategic Air Offensive, the means by which established thought believed the enemy's heartland would be crushed, removing his capacity and will to wage war, thereby protecting those at home and bringing the war to a rapid end. Reality, however, lagged far behind, although the Air Ministry did have a new generation of heavy bombers – the Short Stirling, the Handley Page Halifax and the Avro Lancaster – being developed as quickly as possible, aircraft far more capable and effective. The new generation of fighters could outstrip and run rings around the bombers, in daylight at least, throwing into doubt the maxim that the bomber would always get through. If and when it did, the crews were faced with the grave problem of locating and hitting a target, something taken for granted in the inter-war years, using means that differed little from those used when flight was in its infancy. Great strides forward had been taken in recent years but the Strategic Air Offensive was Bomber Command's *raison d'etre* and that it was not better prepared for its long-awaited campaign reflects badly on all those at the top of government and the service.

Nevertheless, the men and women throughout the Command were absolutely committed to their task and set about it with a professional determination, fully aware of what was at stake. In a directive sent by Air Vice-Marshal (AVM) Sholto Douglas, Deputy Chief of Air Staff, to Air Marshal Charles Portal, Air Officer Commanding-in-Chief (AOC-in-C) Bomber Command on 4 June, in the wake of the Dunkirk evacuation, it was acknowledged that, 'in present circumstances when the initiative rests with the enemy, our strategical policy is liable to be deflected by the turn of events from the course we should like it to follow'. It went on, 'you should regard your primary aim as being to complete the offensive against German oil resources', and, given the recent developments, 'it is desirable as far as is consistent with your primary aim, to dislocate the German aircraft industry by attacks on such bomber and fighter assembly factories as may be within your range'. When conditions were inadequate to do this 'you should continue as at present to bring about continuous interruption and dislocation of German war industry, particularly in those areas within range where the aircraft industry is concentrated, the Hamburg, Bremen, Ruhr and Frankfurt areas', before a chilling reminder, 'You should bear in mind throughout that the bomber force and particularly the medium bombers, may have to play a most important part in repelling an invasion of this country.' The task was quite clear and prescriptive, and not in any way indiscriminate, and Portal was explicitly warned to have 'due regard for avoiding as far as possible, undue risk to the lives of French, Dutch or Belgian civilians', and even over German targets 'in no circumstances should night bombing be allowed to degenerate into mere indiscriminate action, which is contrary to the policy of His Majesty's Government.' It was a heavy burden that had been placed on the Command and one that was to change emphasis repeatedly throughout the summer in the face of a fast-changing and increasingly menacing threat. On 13 July Portal was instructed that his 'main offensive should be directed towards objectives the destruction of which will reduce the scale of the air attack upon this country.' Portal tried to inject an air of realism, pointing out that many of these worthwhile targets were in either sparsely populated areas or isolated districts and that few could 'be found with any certainty in moonlight by average crews. Expert crews may be expected to find the remainder on clear nights with a full moon and average crews will sometimes find them after a good deal of time has been spent in the searching' and, as a result, 'a very high percentage of the bombs which will inevitably miss the actual target will hit nothing else of importance and do no damage and the minimum amount of dislocation and disturbance will be caused by the operations as a whole.' Portal, a highly intelligent and experienced airman, had come to a simple and profound conclusion pretty well from the outset; if the bombers, which were limited in both raw numbers and destructive capability, had serious difficulties in locating and destroying specific targets, then they might as well aim for valid targets in locations in which every bomb would count, whether on target or not, a blueprint for area bombing. Portal reminded his superiors that 'we have the one directly offensive weapon in the whole of our armoury, the one means by which we can undermine the morale of a large part of the enemy people, shake their faith in the Nazi regime and at the same time and with the very same bombs, dislocate their heavy industry and a good part of their oil production.' With the Luftwaffe stepping up its attacks in preparation for the expected invasion and Churchill at the same time demanding in a letter to Lord Beaverbrook, 'an absolutely devastating, exterminating attack by very heavy bombers from this country upon the Nazi homeland', Portal's views seemed to have captured the mood of the day: those in charge in the Air Ministry begged to differ, at least for the moment.

At least Germany was being bombed and, by all accounts from crews, reconnaissances, fledgling aerial photographic evidence and neutral observers and press reports, hit hard by the steadily, if slowly, increasing momentum of the attacks. These attacks took a new direction in late August when Portal and his staff took full advantage of Churchill's bullish response to the first Luftwaffe bombs to fall on London proper to mount a series of attacks upon military and industrial targets in Berlin. By 3 September Churchill, in a paper to the War Cabinet to mark the first anniversary of the war, was describing the bombers as 'the means of victory' and concluded:

> We must, therefore, develop the power to carry an ever increasing volume of explosives to Germany, so as to pulverise the entire industrial and scientific structure on which the war effort and economic life of the enemy depend … In no other way at present visible can we hope to overcome the immense military power of Germany … The Air Force and its action on the largest scale must therefore claim the first place over the navy or the army.

This long-term plan set in stone the military and economic direction of Britain's war effort for several years to come and opened the way for the long-awaited attritional contest, pitting the fortitude and resolution of the British people against those of the German population. Hitler lost no time in making clear his response when he addressed a near hysterical mass rally in the Berlin Sportspalast. Skilfully employing his well-honed rabble-rousing techniques, he steadily built up to his familiar high-pitched yet controlled shriek, declaring:

When the British Air Force drops two or three or four thousand kilograms of bombs, then in one night we will drop one hundred and fifty, two hundred and fifty, three hundred or four hundred thousand kilograms. When they declare that they will increase their attacks on our cities, then we will raise their cities to the ground … The hour will come when one of us will break and it will not be National Socialist Germany!

Fighting for its very survival in the face of apparently insuperable odds and with a ruthless and hugely powerful enemy hammering on the door and poised to break in, Britain, in full cognisance of what it meant, had chosen to play the only card it had left: unrestricted air warfare.

On 9 September, just two days after the Luftwaffe's first massed raid on London, Portal presented a paper to the Air Staff in which he listed the top twenty cities in Germany ripe for attack and urged that a force of 150 aircraft, a maximum effort at the time, should hammer each in turn to cause the greatest dislocation and destruction possible. The Air Staff, with more than half an eye on maintaining the Command's crucial anti-invasion attacks, went no further than saying that attacks could be made, for example, upon Berlin 'from time to time when favourable weather conditions permit'. Whether Portal knew it or not at the time is unclear, but he was soon to get the chance to put his ideas into practice for on 4 October he was promoted to the highest post in the RAF, Chief of Air Staff. His appointment was surely no coincidence and Churchill lost no time in blasting a series of broadsides in his direction urging higher bombing tonnages, concluding, 'It is a scandal that so little use is made of the enormous mass of material provided. The discharge of bombs on Germany is pitifully small.' Spurred on by this, Portal put the finishing touches to a new directive, which landed on the desk of the new supremo at Bomber Command, Air Marshal Sir Richard Peirse, on 30 October. It confirmed that, 'the enemy has, at least temporarily, abandoned his intention to invade this country' and that, 'the time seemed particularly opportune to make a definite attempt with our offensive to affect the morale of the German people when they can no longer expect an early victory and are faced with the approach of winter and the certainty of a long war.' The change of direction was clearly spelled out: 'Your first aim should be to continue your attacks on Berlin whenever conditions make it probable that the aircraft will get through,' and that, 'You will undertake similar attacks upon towns in central and western Germany,' when such deep penetrations were not possible. The emphasis was to remain on oil, communications, war industries, power sources and transport but now, 'where primary targets such as oil and aircraft objectives are suitably placed in the centre of towns or populated districts, they might also be selected'. In case there was any remaining doubt, the directive called for heavy attacks: 'It is desired that regular concentrated attacks should be made on objectives in large towns and centres of industry, with the primary aim of causing very heavy material destruction which will demonstrate to the enemy the power and severity of air bombardment and the hardship and dislocation which will result from it.' For the first time, an attack on morale was laid out as an objective as heavy attacks, 'should be spread over the widest possible area so as to take advantage of the fear induced by concentrated attacks to impose ARP measures with the resulting interruption of work and rest and the dislocation of industry.' It was a coherent, logical, practical and ultimately deliverable plan, a true Strategic Air Offensive, and its authors were well aware of what it entailed. There was little room for sentiment or compassion among the British people for an enemy still at the gates, especially one blasting cities the length and breadth of the country night after night. At the end of October 1940, as the Battle of Britain drew to a close but with the future still very much uncertain, it was clearer than ever that the bomber after all was the sole means of taking the war to the enemy, the very heart of the enemy, and by doing so it protected the men, women and children of Britain and offered them, and the wider world, a tiny speck of light at the end of a very long and dark tunnel.

Chapter 2

The Other Battle of Britain: Phase One

The Battle of Britain, arguably the most important battle in British history, appears far more clear-cut in history books than it ever did to those taking part. To them, without the benefits of hindsight, it was a sequence of frenetic days in which momentous events were played out and the uncertain future unfurled with the passing dawns and sunsets. In the history books and the official record it has a definite start date, 10 July, and an end date, 31 October. For example, these are the dates where pilots who took part in an operational sortie with Fighter Command qualified for the prestigious Battle of Britain clasp. They cover the period from the time when the Luftwaffe began to intensify its attacks upon the shipping in the English Channel to the time when the momentum and scale of its daylight attacks pretty much faded away as autumn slipped into winter. Traditionally, it is divided into four phases, though the duration of each is often a matter of debate. The first covers the initial period of preparation for Operation Sea Lion and the necessary 'intensive air warfare against England'; the second, the beginnings of the attempt to gain the vital air superiority over the Channel and southern England; the third, the damaging attacks on the RAF airfields and the onslaught to destroy Fighter Command in the air and on the ground; and the fourth, the assault on London and the final attempts to bring Fighter Command to battle en masse. Much of this was intended to pave the way for Sea Lion and even when it was called off, Hitler considered it vital to maintain the 'political and military pressure on England' and kept the door ajar on the invasion, intending to review the situation in the spring of 1941. There really was, on both sides, no knowing how things would turn out. What was clear though was that these were crucial days upon which much, and perhaps everything, depended and it is against this menacing and uncertain background that the grinding and remorseless work of Bomber Command must be placed in its forgotten summer. As the days lengthened into high summer, the hopes of a nation and Empire rested on the shoulders of a select band of young airmen.

It was a dull and damp morning in North Yorkshire as a watery sun struggled to penetrate the thick, grey, low cloud and illuminate the lush green countryside beneath. Picturesquely situated adjacent to the Great North Road in the heart of the beautiful Vale of York, with the North York Moors clearly visible to the east and the magnificent Pennine Dales to the west, RAF Leeming, a new bomber airfield only opened a few weeks before on 3 June 1940, was calmly setting about its daily routine. A few drab vehicles were moving sedately around the airfield as individual and small groups of airmen going on or coming off duty made their way to one building or another, either way shaking the sleep from their tired eyes and weary limbs. One young man, who was not there to see the new day beginning but sincerely wished he was, was Sergeant (Sgt) Peter Donaldson of 10 Squadron. While he was there in his mind's eye, his body was on board a train bound for Frankfurt in the company of two armed guards and a powerful and ever vigilant Alsatian dog. Passing through the blossoming countryside, villages and towns en route, keenly looking out for bomb damage but in vain, he had plenty of time to reflect upon the manner in which his fighting war had come to such an abrupt end, just as the main struggle over Britain was gaining momentum.

The sight of the dawn breaking, however dully, over Leeming would, in fact, have been quite novel for him as he had only been there for a matter of hours before embarking upon what turned out to be his final sortie. He had, since the previous December, been based a little further north at Dishforth and had racked up an impressive number of operations flying as a navigator in a Whitley V. Thoroughly experienced and settled, he had been awoken by an orderly that morning, certainly one after a particularly good night before, and greeted with the news that he and his squadron was to proceed straightaway to Leeming, a few miles along the A1. Somewhat dismayed, he packed his things and joined the transport, only to be even more dismayed upon arrival to find his name on the ops board for that night; target Kiel, take-off 21.00. There was barely enough time to unpack and complete the necessary preparations for the sortie before climbing on board and confirming the route details with his pilot, Flt Lt Ffrench-Mullen.

As navigator, it was not the easiest of flights for Donaldson as thick cloud blanketed both the North Sea and the hostile lands beyond. With no hope of locating even the general target area and having gone well beyond the Estimated Time of Arrival (ETA), the experienced captain decided enough was enough and called for a course home. As the Whitley slowly ground its way back over the North Sea through the ever-lightening sky, the fuel situation was fast becoming critical. Still within range of enemy fighters, Ffrench-Mullen reluctantly ordered the precious bomb load to be jettisoned and warned the crew to be extra vigilant. With luck, they decided as the miles ticked off agonisingly slowly, they might just about make it home. Their luck was out. The rear gunner's urgent voice reported the rapid approach of two Me 109s out on an early morning patrol. Ffrench-Mullen reacted at once, slamming the Whitley's nose down and heading for sea level with all available speed. It was an unequal race and the nimble fighters soon reeled in the lumbering bomber and took turns to close and strafe the British aircraft, their shells and bullets raking it from end to end. A triumphant yell from the rear gunner that he had hit one of the attackers raised the crew's spirits briefly but a glance at the flames streaming from the starboard engine soon snuffed out any spark of optimism. Although Ffrench-Mullen did give the order to abandon the aircraft, there was no more than a few seconds before the Whitley hit the water, hard but on an even keel. Donaldson picked himself up and managed to open the hatch, untied and threw out the dinghy, which resolutely refused to inflate until the pilot, still standing on the port wing, was able to reach down and activate the compressed air bottle. Unusually, all five men in the crew succeeded in clambering aboard the dinghy more or less intact before the Whitley wearily slid beneath the waves.

Their good fortune, not available to many others in a similar plight, continued and after just two hours, wet, cold and miserable as they were, two small, coastal fishing boats came into view and headed directly towards them. The only aspect of bad luck was that they were German but at that moment, none of them worried too much about that. Pulled on board and plied with steaming hot black coffee and great hunks of heavy rye bread, Donaldson was allowed on deck to try to dry off in the gentle breeze and strengthening sun. Rummaging around in the dinghy that the fishermen had hauled on board, he came across the standard jack-knife and flare gun and, to the horror of the young helmsman, picked up both as he rapidly assessed his chances of taking control of the boat in daring fashion. Reality reasserted its grip as he glanced at the nearby shore of the heavily militarised German island of Heligoland. He put the items down and waited patiently for the boat to dock. Once ashore, the British crew were searched and then put on another boat for transfer to Wilhelmshaven and from there they were taken by train to the Dulag Luft in Frankfurt, an interrogation and transit camp for aircrew. In spite of a number of escape attempts, the final one being successful and involving a lively spell with a number of tough Russian former prisoners of war, it was to be the best part of five long years before Donaldson would see the sun rise over an RAF airfield.

Other young men were waking up, rather groggily, on airfields across eastern England that morning, rather like Donaldson should have been. At RAF Waddington in the flat Lincolnshire countryside, several crews were coming to after a busy and eventful night. No. 44 Squadron of 5 Group had taken off as soon as it was growing properly dark around 10 p.m. in order to make the most of the short summer nights. It was due to carry out a task in which 5 Group had come to specialise, Gardening, the code name for the dropping of sea mines, generally known as vegetables. By a happy coincidence, 5 Group's commander, AVM Arthur Harris – later Air Officer Commanding, Bomber Command – was a strong advocate of such offensive action and the Group's main aircraft, the Handley Page Hampden, proved to be well suited to this effective but unglamorous form of attack. In the summer of 1940, with invasion looming, any disruption to German sea traffic had to be good news.

Flying Officer (Fg Off) J. Crossley and his crew hurtled down the runway into the darkening sky a few minutes after 22.00 hours and headed east for their target area off the Dutch coast. Flying undisturbed through the night sky, by midnight they were in position to drop their mine. Turning for home after releasing it, the crew spotted first one lightship, then another, sure signs of considerable nocturnal sea traffic. Crossley decided to attack and set course accordingly. The 250lb bombs, carried for just such an eventuality, undershot the first and fell some 100 yards to port of the second. Having expended all his ordnance, Crossley headed west and landed at RAF Waddington at 02.40 hours, tired but satisfied with his night's work. Sgt E. Farrands had also dropped his vegetable before coming across and attacking a 4,000-ton cargo vessel about 5 miles east of Wangerooge. His pair of 250lb bombs were claimed as near misses. Four other 44 Squadron crews were fired upon by a flak ship stationed specifically to intercept such night intruders and mine layers. The Hampdens of Pilot Officer (Plt Off) W.J. Lewis, C. Hattersley, E.J. Spencer and Sgt N.S. Herring attacked the ship independently about a mile or so south-east of Wangerooge. Possible hits and near misses were claimed but no definite results were seen. Squadron Leader (Sqn Ldr) J.G. Macintyre was also in the area and dropped his bombs upon anti-aircraft guns, situated on a concrete mole, which had opened fire on his low-flying aircraft. All the crews returned safely in the early hours of the morning after a typical night's work, carried out without fanfare or particular recognition. Its results might have been hard to quantify, but it had certainly showed that Bomber

Command was willing and able to interfere with German preparations and movements and that darkness offered no immunity from attack.

The weather was a little better further south on the first day of the Battle of Britain, with patchy cloud and sunny spells. At RAF Wattisham, in the heart of rural Suffolk, preparations were well under way to carry out 2 Group's operations for the day attacking targets scattered across occupied Europe. No. 107 Squadron's Blenheim IVs were tasked to attack the former French airfield at Glisy near Amiens, thereby reducing the scale of the air attack upon the United Kingdom. Although such relatively low-level daylight raids upon well-defended targets were widely understood to be extremely dangerous – no fewer than nine Blenheims had been lost on similar operations the previous day, for example – they were deemed vital to the national interest at this critical time. Any damage and disruption they could cause would be worthwhile. Working from early morning, six of the light bombers were made ready for take-off shortly before midday. The eighteen young crewmen made their way across the grass and climbed aboard the waiting aircraft. Circling the airfield, five Blenheims took up their station behind their leader, Sqn Ldr H.P. Pleasance, and headed south towards France. Two hours later the small force was well over enemy territory and, on its final approach at 7,000ft, coming under heavy fire. A perfect target at that height for all types of flak, the formation, a little more ragged now as the sky all around them erupted into a storm of explosions and deadly splinters, pressed on and succeeded in dropping their bombs across the airfield. Their job done, the Blenheims turned for home, keen to get out of range of the flak. Scant minutes later, nine Me 109s were spotted bearing down on them and, although the British airmen knew there could only be one outcome, they steeled themselves for the onslaught to come. The fighters tore into the light bombers and, in spite of the best efforts of the pilots and gunners, blasted the Blenheims out of the sky one by one. Within fifteen minutes it was all over and the 109s broke off, leaving a single battered bomber to make its lonely way north to a still uncertain future. After what seemed a lifetime later, Sqn Ldr Pleasance gently eased his Blenheim on to the ground at Wattisham. Exactly half of the young airmen who had taken off a matter of hours earlier lay dead, with another, Sgt G. Hawkins, destined to die in tragic circumstances just three weeks before the end of the war when Allied aircraft strafed a column of prisoners of war on the march.

For one of the survivors it was the beginning of an arduous and dangerous odyssey that ended with the award of the Military Medal. Sgt Robert Lonsdale, the observer in Plt Off J.P. North-Lewis' Blenheim R3916, escaped from the blazing bomber and found himself in the pretty countryside near Airaines in the Somme region of northern France. The whole area was still very much in a state of confusion and there was a considerable number of British servicemen hiding and wandering around the local farms and roads. Lonsdale fell in with three gunners from the Royal Artillery and later managed to acquire some civilian clothes. A few days later, the party was stopped, questioned and arrested by some suspicious and alert German soldiers at Oisement, having been given away by their incongruous footwear. Five days later, while being transported by truck, Lonsdale managed to jump out and make his escape. Sleeping rough and scavenging whatever food he could, he kept moving and headed south, crossing the demarcation line into Unoccupied France at Chabris on 11 August. Once again, he fell in with several British soldiers who were under the loose control of the Vichy authorities. Like many others at that time, he ended up in Fort St Jean in Marseille, whiling away his time, often despairing of securing a passage home. In the city, Ian Garrow, a captain in the Seaforth Highlanders ,and a Presbyterian Minister of the Church of Scotland, the Reverend Donald Caskie – better known as the Tartan Pimpernel – had set up a fledgling escape line based at the Seamen's Mission at 46 Rue de Forbin to help men just like Lonsdale. Playing a deadly game of cat and mouse with the ambivalent Vichy authorities and having obtained some financial and practical help from Donald Darling of MI9, based in Lisbon, plans were made to get men across the border and into Spain, then neutral but very much pro-German. Lonsdale and five others, including Gordon Instone, who later recounted his escape in his book *Freedom the Spur*, left Marseille for Perpignan by train on Boxing Day 1940. From there the party was taken by hired smuggler-guides across the Pyrenees – no easy task in mid-winter – and into Spain, where they were soon spotted and arrested by the Spanish authorities. Transferred from one cell to another and seemingly worse off than ever, Lonsdale ended up in the notorious prison at Miranda del Ebro. Eventually released into the care of British embassy officials, he finally crossed into Gibraltar on 11 April 1941 and from there was taken home, later completing a tour of forty-five operations.

Thursday 11 July, nominally the second day of the Battle, turned out to be a dismal day; the low cloud, driving rain and thunderstorms being the very antithesis of the traditional image of the gloriously hot and sunny summer of 1940. Indeed, the weather was bad enough to seriously disrupt the Command's operations. As a force of approximately fifty Luftwaffe aircraft headed north from the recently occupied Channel Islands towards Portland on the south coast, a slightly smaller force of Blenheims was heading south and east to attack targets in the Low Countries, France and Germany. Such were the flying conditions that thirty, some three-quarters of those despatched, were forced to turn for home without releasing their bomb load. The remainder, scattered and buffeted, managed to locate enemy airfields at Boulogne, Schiphol and St Omer through gaps in the storm clouds and put in determined attacks without, however, being able to see any significant results. Plt Off J.H.T. Palmer's crew from 82 Squadron based at Watton met with an undeserved end to their devotion to duty, being shot down near St Omer by a pair of Me 109s from III/JG51. The crew were quickly captured, though Palmer died on 6 December 1942.

Conditions were not significantly better that night when Bomber Command despatched sixty-four aircraft to attack a number of targets across Germany. Long before the advent of the bomber stream and the drive towards concentration, Groups and indeed squadrons and individual crews, were largely left to their own devices to set routes and timings to suit themselves, with only the sketchiest of guidance and operational orders.

No. 3 Group had drawn up and circulated its latest instructions to stations just the previous day. It advised the squadrons that their aim was, 'to destroy the targets outlined in paragraph C above and cause as much dislocation as possible to German industry during the hours of darkness'. Routes were to be, 'at the station commander's discretion, but avoiding defended areas,' and with regards to timing 'aircraft are not to cross over territory occupied by the enemy 75 minutes after sunset at that position and are to be clear of territory occupied by the enemy 75 minutes before sunrise', leaving just a small window for operations during the short summer nights. Similar operational orders were in force throughout the Command, with the accent undoubtedly upon the professionalism of the individual crews.

The men of 58 Squadron at RAF Linton in North Yorkshire were already damp by the time they were settling nervously into their seats, well aware that they had a stormy and dangerous night ahead of them. Taking off shortly after 21.00 hours, the heavily laden Whitley Vs soon ran into thick cloud, electrical storms and pockets of heavy icing, which made flying difficult and accurate navigation all but impossible. En route to Leverkusen, Fg Off Cribbs was, perhaps, relieved to have to turn for home when Sgt Harris repeatedly kept passing out; the station medical officer diagnosed excessive nasal catarrh hampering the unfortunate airman's attempts to breathe at altitude. Most of the other crews failed to locate anything identifiable at all and headed back westwards with their bomb loads intact. Flt Lt Aikens had a lucky escape when his aircraft became suddenly and dangerously encased in ice. Plunging earthwards out of control, the ice had been torn off the bomber by the increased speed and warmer air, enabling Aikens to regain control, though only after plummeting through several thousand feet of storm-darkened sky. Levelling out at 7,000ft, his crew managed to pick out the glow of, perhaps, a blast furnace, somewhere south east of Cologne. Considered an SEMO, or self-evident military objective, the pilot immediately ordered his bombs to be released in a single stick while this fortuitous and fleeting opportunity still existed. What, if anything, was hit, he never found out. Indeed, of the squadron's aircraft operating that night, only one claimed to have located and positively identified the target area. Sgt Archer and his crew had also had to plough through heavy, ice-bearing cloud before they reached Leverkusen. Putting the Whitley's nose down for a diving attack, a method popular with crews at the time, Archer ordered the bombs to be released at just 5,000ft. As all but three were delayed action ones, there was little to see for their efforts.

This was a situation that was to become all too familiar, frustrating and unsatisfactory for both the crews who had risked their lives to carry out the attack and for those staff and intelligence officers who were desperate for accurate information and hard evidence upon which to base and assess their plans. Unusually at this stage of the war, when photographic reconnaissance was still largely a twinkle in some enlightened senior officer's eye, 38 Squadron had been ordered to provide a Wellington to carry out a recce over the Baltic port of Stettin. The squadron had not been the first choice. A Wellington of 115 Squadron, also based at RAF Marham, had been assigned to the sortie but as it was being prepared, the photoflash was accidently set off, with devastating results. Three ground crew were injured by the blast and subsequent blaze that engulfed the aircraft. So it was the rapidly briefed Fg Off Cross and his crew who found themselves taking to the air at 20.45 hours and, heading further north than his colleagues, flew into slightly clearer conditions. Nevertheless, with the cloud base at 8,000ft, Cross was compelled to come down lower than he would have liked in order to pick up the coast and follow it along to Stettin. On arrival he found the port thoroughly alerted to his presence and could only just make out the outline of the well blacked out city and harbour. A photoflash succeeded in illuminating the dock area, enabling a number of good photographs to be taken but also served as the signal for the waiting ground defences to open up on the sole intruder. After a very uncomfortable few minutes Cross and his crew regained the security of the darkness and began the long haul home. It was a rare success that night, as nineteen of the aircraft despatched failed to locate anything at all and many others were reduced to trying their luck on bombing whatever they were able to find. Three aircraft failed to return, a Hampden of 144 Squadron, a Whitley of 58 and a Wellington of 149; there were no survivors.

The unseasonably stormy weather continued the next day. Although the Luftwaffe managed to attack a convoy codenamed 'Booty' off the Essex coast and the shipyards a few hundred miles further north in Aberdeen, the dreary conditions were regarded as prohibitive and 2 Group's light bombers remained grounded throughout the day, apart from an unproductive reconnaissance of the Belgian coast carried out by the Blenheims of 107 Squadron. The murky conditions in the south persisted after dark and 3 and 5 Groups scrubbed all operations, giving the increasingly hard-pushed air and ground crews a welcome night off. Things were marginally better further north and 4 Group ordered two dozen Whitleys to be bombed up for sorties to Kiel and Emden. Although Met reports, always taken with a pinch of salt by the crews, suggested that conditions would be clear enough for a damaging attack to be made, the docks at Kiel were all but invisible beneath an almost unbroken blanket of cloud. Seven of the dozen aircraft failed to locate the target and, in accordance with standing orders, returned with their bomb load intact. The remainder bombed what they could discern but without identifiable result. The second batch took off shortly after 22.00 hours and headed towards Emden's dockside petrol and oil tanks. Ironically, conditions in the target area were better than the Met reports had suggested, enabling all but two of the Whitleys to locate and attack the target, igniting fires reported by the crews as still being visible more than 70 miles away.

Sgt R. Langton was flying over the port at a steady 11,000ft and had just dropped his load when his Whitley rocked and shuddered, hit by flak that mangled the port engine. Hauling the stricken bomber around and out of the danger zone, he and his second pilot, Sqn Ldr C.S. Bryan, who was there to gain operational experience, quickly assessed the situation and realised they were unlikely to make it home. Even with the thought of the North Sea, inhospitable even in the height of summer, between them and safety, they nonetheless resolved to give it a go. While the pilots battled to keep the aircraft in the air and under control, the navigator, Sgt Coad, checked and re-checked his course, well aware that he could ill afford to make an error. Little by little the bomber lost height and over the next three and a half hours, as their confidence ebbed and flowed, the five men on board willed the aircraft over the sea. Eventually, the force of gravity overcame the efforts of the overworked and overheating starboard engine and at 04.25 hours Langton gave the order to prepare for ditching. A final SOS was sent as the crew apprehensively braced themselves for the severe impact of a fast-moving aircraft colliding with the North Sea. Langton successfully guided the Whitley down in level flight, belly flopping on to the water and skidding to an abrupt halt. As was often the case with this type of aircraft, it stayed in one piece and afloat, giving the crew vital time to scramble out. The dinghy had self-inflated but was upside down and the men were thoroughly wet and exhausted by the time they had righted it and hauled themselves on board. As daylight strengthened, the Whitley slid gently beneath the surface, having brought its crew to a position some 38 miles off the Norfolk coast. Mostly uninjured, the men were confident of rescue and within an hour a trawler appeared on the horizon and headed straight for them. Having been picked up and taken to Great Yarmouth, the crew made their way back to Driffield and further operations. For this and other actions that summer, Langton was awarded a DFM and commissioned, later losing his life flying with 76 Squadron on 8 October 1944 over Westkapple.

The light fog and cloud prevalent over much of Britain on Saturday 13 July was sufficient to encourage those in charge at 2 Group to launch another series of daylight raids across France, Belgium, Holland and even northern Germany. Twenty-two Blenheims were made ready, their three-man crews anxiously scanning the sky for signs that the cloud, upon which they would rely for protection, was about to break up. As the crews headed out over the sea, to their dismay, the murk began to clear, revealing blue sky and sparkling sunlight, affording unlimited visibility. A dozen crews in accordance with their orders, weighed up their chances and promptly turned back. The remainder pressed on to attack the invasion barges already moored in Bruges, the airfield at Evere and the oil refineries at Monheim. Such small and scattered attacks caused little material damage but did create disruption and remind the Nazi regime, its jubilant people and those in occupied countries that there was still a war on. Once again, however, there was a price to be paid for such defiance and two Blenheims, some 20 per cent of the attacking force, failed to return: of the six men two, Sgts Adams and Avery, survived to become POWs but four did not.

Undeterred, throughout the day, the heavy bomber force was being prepared to take the offensive to the enemy that night. Long before the doctrine of concentration of force held sway, the ninety-seven-strong force was directed to a number of widespread, pinpoint targets. The Air Ministry press release noted that, 'Fourteen enemy aerodromes in Holland and Germany were bombed; other objectives included docks at Hamburg, Wilhelmshaven and Emden; Focke-Wulf and Junkers 53 factories at Bremen and Deichshausen; oil refineries at Monheim and Hamburg; supply factories at Grenvenbroich, Gelsenkirchen and Hamburg and goods yards at Hamm, Osnabrück and Soest.' It went on to make clear that all these targets had been chosen in relation to the enemy's probable plans for the invasion of Britain and that, 'the success of the RAF's attacks is contributing effectively to a reduction in the striking power of the German Air Force.' Whilst this was indeed the intention and to some degree the case, such sweeping and positive statements told only part of the story.

No. 49 Squadron formed part of the forty-three-strong force of Hampdens tasked to attack the vital Dortmund–Ems Canal, Hamburg and Deichshausen. Taking off into the darkening sky a little after 21.00 hours, the broad and sweeping Lincolnshire countryside stretched out amid the lengthening shadows far beneath the heavily laden bombers. This bucolic idyll of summer did not last long and as the Hampdens headed east towards the darkening horizon, they flew into dense low cloud and squally showers.

Fg Off Roderick Learoyd, who within a month would win a Victoria Cross (VC) for his outstanding and calculated courage, try as he might, could not locate his target in the dismal flying conditions. Stooging around over enemy occupied territory in the hope of eventually spotting a target worthy of being attacked was not too pleasant a task, but Learoyd finally stumbled across Eelde airfield and let go his stick of bombs. One was observed to burst near the edge of the airfield but the impact point of the others remained unseen. Sgt Hills had a similar experience as he located and attacked the Nordeney seaplane base; the bomb bursts were visible through the rainy murk but their precise location was anyone's guess. At least Hills was marginally better off than some others in 49 Squadron. Plt Off Campbell saw nothing of his attack on Borkum, likewise Fg Off Burnett over Wismar and Fg Off Haskins over Stade airfield. They in turn were better off than Plt Off Pinchbeck and Plt Off McClure, who failed to identify any target and returned with their bomb loads still firmly onboard. Flt Lt Forsyth and his crew were simply thankful to have made it back to base at all, as it had looked for a while as if they would not. An electrical storm had rendered all the aircraft's instruments and wireless unserviceable while over enemy territory, compelling them to jettison their bombs to save fuel and grope their way westwards through the murk and darkness, relying on little more than luck and good judgement. Fortunately, conditions improved significantly and they were able to make their way back home relatively easily.

The Hampdens of 44 Squadron, based nearby at RAF Waddington, fared a little better, several at least identifying a target. Sqn Ldr D. Parker claimed to have located the aircraft factory at Lemwerder and his crew observed the bombs bursting in and around the various factory buildings. Plt Off W.M. Smith observed his stick of bombs burst across Nordeney airfield and Sgt E. Collins and Flight Sergeant (Flt Sgt) J. Clayton did likewise at Borkum, both crews reporting a particularly large and impressive explosion on the airfield. Plt Off C.P. Price had an especially successful night, having also found and attacked the factory at Lemwerder. Running in from east to west at just 500ft, Price guided the bomber over the factory, releasing six 250lb bombs and sixty 4lb incendiaries as the buildings flashed by beneath, though low patchy cloud and ground mist prevented an accurate assessment of this daring attack. En route home, Price and his crew noticed two Me 110s coming in to land at Borkum. Pushing the throttles forward to swiftly close the gap, Price bored in to attack the unsuspecting German aircraft with machine gun fire. One immediately caught light and plunged into the sea below, the other banked hard and was swallowed up by the darkness. It was a very satisfied and elated crew that landed back at Waddington to tell their tale in the wee small hours. For five other 44 crews the night ended in familiar fashion, with a flat, dull feeling of weariness and frustration, having risked all but achieved nought, after being unable to locate the primary or any alternative target.

The Whitleys of 4 Group were also out and fared comparatively well. Nos 10 and 51 Squadrons despatched three aircraft apiece to raid the oil plants in Mannheim and all but one succeeded in carrying out the attack. The fierce anti-aircraft fire damaged one bomber, that of 51's Fg Off G.A. Lane, who thought it prudent to put down at RAF Honington, the first airfield he came across. Two of 77 Squadron crews also had narrow escapes, following a mauling by flak over the same target. Plt Off R.B. McGregor was approaching the target area when his Whitley was caught in the glare of a searchlight. Immediately, more dazzling beams locked on to the bomber, turning it into a perfect target for what seemed like every flak gunner in the city. McGregor threw the aircraft wildly around the sky and managed to break free of the searchlights but not before the aircraft had sustained severe damage. It was a long and fraught flight westwards and as soon as the crew spotted RAF Duxford, a 12 Group fighter station in Cambridgeshire, McGregor lost no time in reuniting the bomber with terra firma. His fellow squadron member, Fg Off J. Piddington, had an equally torrid time of it. His Whitley too was hit by flak over the target, damaging an engine, which duly packed up somewhere over Holland. Slowly but surely losing altitude, the crew anxiously counted down the miles over the North Sea and as soon as the English coast came into sight, Piddington gave orders for his crew to prepare to bail out. Once it had passed beneath them, three of the crew parachuted to safety, though the second pilot bravely elected to stay to help Piddington locate an airfield and land the valuable bomber. It turned out to be another 12 Group station, RAF Martlesham Heath, and the pair pulled off a textbook single engine landing on an unfamiliar airfield.

Others too had shown the determination to press on in the face of significant opposition from both the enemy and the elements. Sgt Jones of 58 Squadron had lifted his heavily laden Whitley off the ground at RAF Linton in the heart of Yorkshire that evening and had turned east, bound for a town he had probably never heard of, nor was able to pronounce, Grevenbroich. It was not difficult to find the already alerted target area and Jones, still hidden in the darkness, swung his Whitley into line to pass through the flak bursts and searchlights at a steady 7,000ft. Once over the target, the dazzling glare from the lights ruined the crew's night vision and no one on board was able to pinpoint the primary or indeed secondary targets. Having passed through the maelstrom, Jones then hauled the sluggish bomber around to repeat the process. With only a handful of aircraft involved in the raid, the ground defences were able to give the bomber their undivided attention. Staring hard into the inky blackness, punctuated by blindingly white searchlights and the flashes of explosions, the crew failed again. Still not ready to give up, Jones circled out of range in the hope of lulling the defenders into a false sense of security before sweeping in for another run. The result was the same and this time, with the bomber resembling a colander, having had the windscreen and various parts of the fuselage holed, one propeller damaged and the trailing aerial shot away, the pilot finally decided to give it up as a bad job. However, even then he did not head directly for home but, having identified an airfield near Antwerp, turned and held the bomber straight and level at 6,000ft to carry out the attack. As the crew resumed their course, the weather conditions began to deteriorate and it was with great relief that an airfield finally came into sight. Jones touched down well off track at RAF Abingdon at 04.15 hours after a shattering seven hours in the air, much of it spent damaged, over hostile territory or inhospitable sea. After a short rest and emergency repairs, Jones and his crew flew back to Linton, arriving a little after midday. Although quite extraordinary, at the time such a sortie was considered quite par for the course and the names of Jones and his crew appeared, as they expected, on the ops board next time.

Sunday might well have been the traditional day of rest but it was now just another day in an increasingly intense and deadly war. The day dawned a perfect July day but according to the weather experts, it would not be over the Continent, and therefore six Blenheims of 114 Squadron, based at Horsham St Faith, were readied to carry out intruder raids upon the heavily industrial and well-defended Ruhr area. Squinting up at the clear, bright sky and feeling rather sceptical of the Met Men's predictions, the eighteen airmen climbed into their swelteringly hot aircraft and prepared to take off. Not at all to their surprise, the sky over the North Sea and beyond remained resolutely clear and the crews came to the conclusion that to press on would be tantamount to suicide and turned for home. A lone 110 Squadron Blenheim on a photoreconnaissance sortie to Kiel did likewise, ending Bomber Command's effort by day.

By night it was a different matter, with eighty Whitleys, Hampdens and Wellingtons attacking targets scattered across Germany – Diepholz, Paderborn, Gelsenkirchen, Wezendorf, Hamm, Hamburg, Bremen, Soest and Cologne. No. 38 Squadron, based at RAF Marham, for example, was split between targets in Bremen and Cologne and the favourable conditions, with only light, patchy cloud, enabled the crews to locate both cities quite easily and to identify the docks and industrial areas accurately. In spite of the lethal combination of flak and searchlights, especially around Cologne, the attacks were pressed home and a number of large fires were left burning, their glow lighting up the night sky for miles around. These also acted as a beacon for prowling night fighters and Sgt Giles' Wellington was stalked and attacked by an unseen aircraft. The encounter was shockingly brief but brutal and Giles was lucky to shake off his assailant before a second and, perhaps, fatal, pass could be made; it was several long hours before the damaged bomber touched down safely. No. 37 Squadron's Wellingtons had been at readiness for anti-invasion sorties since 10 July, broken only by two unsuccessful sweeps of the North Sea in search of downed aircrew. Now they were assigned the vast dockyards at Hamburg and the equally vast marshalling yards at Hamm, both playing significant roles in the invasion build-up, as their targets for the night, with any SEMO in the Ruhr and Bremen areas as their alternatives. Mindful of the day fighting and imminent invasion, any airfield was designated a target of last resort.

The five-strong Hamm force was led by Wing Commander (Wg Cdr) Merton, though as usual each crew made its own way to and from the target area. The Wellington 1Cs lined up and took off into the darkening sky over RAF Feltwell just after 22.00 hours, just in time for those left behind and released from duty to nip down to the local for a well-earned pint and to relax. It was very different for those over enemy territory, scanning the sky for hostile aircraft and the ground for the target. The clear conditions meant that the crews were able to locate and positively identify the sprawling acres of tracks and sidings. Approaching at a steady 9,000ft and 160mph, Merton pushed the nose of his aircraft down in a shallow dive and released his stick of nine bombs at 7,700ft before swinging around and opening the throttles to clear the area. The bombs were observed bursting within the yards and igniting two major fires, which were visible for some miles. A second aircraft, under the command of Sqn Ldr Rivett-Carnac, came in a little higher and also tried to confuse the sweating gunners below. Cutting his engines, he guided the Wellington into a silent, shallow, diving approach, a tactic that was popular among crews at the time. Dropping down to 7,500ft, his load was released in a single stick across the tracks and warehouses, a little to the east of a small lake. The crew was rewarded by a series of large, bright green flashes which followed the bursting of the bombs and left behind an enormous conflagration, estimated to be at least 500 yards long and spreading rapidly, still visible against the blackness for many miles distant. The other crews also reported successful, if less spectacular, attacks and all the Wellingtons made it home safely, landing in dribs and drabs between 03.20 and 04.20 hours.

The other section of the squadron was not so fortunate with their final run-up to the target in Hamburg. Thundering towards the dockyards at between 10,500 and 12,000ft, the crews were dismayed to see a thick blanket of cloud beginning to spread inexorably over Germany's second city. Plt Off Parsons dropped a stick over the docks but was able to observe the explosion of only the first bomb before the impenetrable cloud-shield slid into place. He and his crew, however, remained confident that the rest were also on target, as were the three other crews, which had at least been able to establish they were in the right area. Reports of the defensive activity, which were inevitably based upon other experiences and individual comparisons, ranged from intense and accurate to moderate and sporadic but all crews agreed on the silent and menacing presence of a balloon barrage at 8,000 to 9,000ft. One of the crews, that of Sgt J.F. McCauley, failed to return, thereby initiating the career of one of the most determined and courageous prisoner-escapers of the war, Sgt George Grimson.

Born in the London suburb of Putney, Grimson was one of those downed airmen who from the start was bent on escape and set about it with single-minded determination. Often considered by his peers as uncommunicative and somewhat dour, the pipe-smoking 25-year-old did not suffer fools gladly and was not beyond imposing his trenchant views upon others. Peter Donaldson, a 10 Squadron navigator shot down less than a week before Grimson, first met him in Stalag Luft I in Barth in the summer of 1941. Donaldson was heavily committed to an escape plan with his friend Ali Stamford and had been boosting his meagre stocks of food ready for the break out by some illicit trading with a compliant guard. Grimson, unaware of the purpose behind this apparently friendly and collaborative relationship, suggested loudly in a crowded room that anyone who behaved in such a manner with the enemy should have his block knocked off. All eyes turned to Donaldson who, far lighter and slighter than the tough and muscular Grimson, felt he had no option but to take up the challenge, if for no other reason than to protect the secrecy of his almost complete preparations for escape. The pair moved out into a corridor and faced each other warily. Grimson suddenly reached out and grabbed Donaldson by the lapels and butted him viciously in the face, knocking him to the ground. He followed up at once, pulling his dazed opponent on to his back, his arm drawn well back ready to deliver a crushing blow. Donaldson managed to wriggle sideways out of the haymaker's path and to his surprise managed to turn and land one of his own on the off balance Grimson. Before matters could come to a conclusion, the lights went out and the camp's air raid siren began to wail. Unable to see to carry on the fight, the pair separated and Grimson roared that they should conclude the proceedings behind the cookhouse the next morning. Grimson was indeed where he said he would be but Donaldson was not and was alone drinking a cup of mint tea when Grimson not unexpectedly burst into his room. Grinning to reveal a broken tooth, Grimson approached Donaldson with his hand outstretched and wished him a happy holiday – clearly now aware of the escape plans under way. Though he and Stamford succeeded in escaping from a working party based at a nearby gas works and were out for several days, the pair were recaptured and sent to different camps.

It was at Stalag Luft III that Donaldson next came across Grimson and the two became good friends before the latter's escape in May 1943. By now a fluent German speaker, Grimson had kitted himself out in a belted boiler suit overall, complete with Luftwaffe side cap, an impressive and realistic ammeter/voltmeter, complete with a large dial and trailing leads, a capacious tool bag and ladder, borrowed from the camp theatre. He brazenly approached the guard tower and shouted that he had been sent to repair the seismograph near the wire. Given permission, he fiddled about for some time before dropping his pliers by accident in the German compound on the other side of the wire. He swore loudly and announced to the bored guard that he could not be bothered to walk all the way around to get them but would just climb over the wire using his ladder. He proceeded to do just that, even asking the guard to keep an eye on the ladder so that no prisoners could steal it. Having retrieved his pliers, Grimson set about his work again before, with a cheery wave, he told the guard he was off for his coffee break and would be back for the ladder shortly. Grimson strode purposely through the German compound and, having found a quiet spot, removed his overalls to reveal civilian clothes beneath. Dressed smartly, talking volubly and waving the apparently appropriate passes, he proceeded to walk straight out of the camp and to the local station, boarding a northbound train. Sadly, he was recaptured trying to get on board a Swedish ship on the Baltic coast.

Transferred to Stalag Luft VI at Heydekrug, Grimson was undeterred and set about a new and audacious scheme not only to escape but, realising that breaking out was only the first step to freedom, use his experience to set up an escape line for others. Putting his fluent German to good use, he discovered that the camp interpreter Adolph Munkert was favourable to the Allied cause and that he was in contact with a Pole of German origin called Sommers who had links with the Polish resistance. On 21 January 1944, Grimson once again talked his way out of a POW camp, clad in a bona fide German uniform provided by Munkert, before making his way to a forester's cottage some distance away, as advised by Sommers. From there he moved on to Danzig, where he recruited a group of Polish men who were willing to escort prisoners to the port and hide them until arrangements could be made to smuggle them on board ships bound for Sweden. Coded messages providing progress reports were smuggled into the camp by Munkert.

Within a couple of weeks the line was in business, in spite of the obvious risks and penalties involved. Warrant Officer (WO) Paddy Flockhart was the first to try his luck, breaking out of the camp and making his way to Danzig, where he met Grimson. After a frustrating and anxious few days, Grimson provided him with a workman's outfit and a route into the heavily guarded dock area. Flockhart managed to sneak on board one of the ships unchallenged and, hiding himself in the hold, succeeded in avoiding the thorough German searches carried out prior to sailing. Well out to sea, he revealed himself to the crew and upon landing in Sweden was put in contact with the British embassy, returning to Britain a short while later. Elated by this success, Grimson continued to work on the line, even making a number of highly dangerous trips back to Heydekrug to meet Munkert, who passed on the information to those in the camp. Security was tight and on one such trip Grimson was questioned and asked for identification no fewer than twenty-seven times. Two more men broke out, WO R.B.H. Townsend-Coles and Sgt Jack Gilbert, and followed the route to Danzig. Once again, Grimson looked after the men and found a way into the heavily patrolled dock area. Leading them, Grimson made his way furtively to a Swedish freighter that was guarded by a German soldier who noticed some movement in the shadows and issued a challenge. In the ensuing scuffle, Gilbert was able to sneak aboard unseen, subsequently arriving safely in Sweden and later Britain. Townsend-Coles was far less fortunate, being arrested, beaten and later shot. Grimson managed to extricate himself and melt away into the darkness but, though hopes amongst those back in the camp remained high for some time, he was never heard of again. The Germans began to suspect that there had been help from within the camp and Munkert was questioned, tortured and shot. Sommers was arrested and hanged himself in his cell to avoid further brutal treatment. Prominent British prisoners were questioned, roughly handled and transferred to different camps.

The new working week began like many others in a British summer, cool and dull. A thick layer of low, dark cloud threatened and delivered steady and persistent rain for much of the day, dousing people going about their business and hampering flying over most of the country and near Continent. Neither side, however, could afford a day to go to waste. While the Luftwaffe mounted small-scale attacks over the south-west and south Wales, the Thames estuary and the Isle of Wight, a total of seventeen Blenheims from 107, 110 and 18 Squadrons were assigned the airfields of northern France and Belgium and several industrial plants in the Ruhr as targets. Standing on the sodden airfields, beneath a leaden sky, the young crews did not hold out much hope of a successful operation. True, the crews were grateful for the protection afforded by the cloud for these daylight incursions, but this was too much; they had little confidence in the Met men's 'pukka gen' that it would break up a little over the target areas. Getting to those areas in such conditions would in itself be no easy task and thirteen of the crews gave up trying and gingerly groped their way home through the murk. One pair pressed on to reach and bomb the airfield at Evreux, without noticeable effect, and a second pair the airfield at Liseux, where incendiary bombs were recorded as bursting around an unidentified twin-engine aircraft. Scant reward for the effort expended.

That night, as the conditions had not improved beyond the marginal, only 5 Group, under the redoubtable and pugnacious AVM Harris, chose to mount operations. Thirty-two Hampdens were made ready and loaded up, twenty with a mixed bomb load and the remainder with mines. No. 44 Squadron's night is representative of the Group as a whole. Taking off as night fell, the twin-engine bombers had to plough through dense cloud, driving rain and electrical storms en route to their targets. Surprisingly, six crews did manage to locate and attack the Misburg oil refinery near Hanover and were satisfied to note that they had left several sizable fires blazing in their wake; as was so often the case, that was as much as could be said about the raid's effectiveness. Plt Off W. Walker and his crew made it to the Hanover area but, frustratingly, could not locate the primary target, in spite of dropping down to the perilously low altitude of just 700ft and repeatedly criss-crossing the well-defended city. Eventually, the crew managed to discern a train chuffing slowly along a line near the Dummer Sise lake to the east of the conurbation. A little further along, there was a factory-like building so Walker brought the Hampden around and streaked at low level over it, the train and the line, releasing his load as he went. The engine was seen to come to an abrupt halt, wreathed in a billowing garland of smoke, steam and sparks, although the fate of the building remained uncertain. Two other crews were in a similar predicament and, again, sought out targets of opportunity, one an illuminated flightpath at Mavern and the other the vast and busy marshalling yards at Osnabrück. Another crew, hampered even further by a defunct intercom system, failed to locate any suitable target and headed home with the bomb load intact for use another day.

The other two crews from 44 Squadron on ops that night, those of Flt Lt F.E. Eustace and Sgt D. Parker, were gardening with ten more Hampdens in the Sound of Copenhagen. Far less spectacular and with no immediate result to be seen, the mining campaign was waged by Bomber Command throughout the war and formed an important component of its unfaltering strategy of steadily grinding down the enemy. In the early days of the war, 5 Group, under AVM Harris, came to specialise in such sorties that, for obvious reasons, required high standards of navigation in a dark and often hostile environment. Flying with an altimeter showing hundreds rather than thousands of feet over the sea, often just off the enemy-held coast, the prospects for survival were bleak for those who sustained damage from shore-based batteries or heavily armed flak ships, stationed on well-known navigational routes and markers off regular and important target areas. Flt Lt Lewis 'Bob' Hodges, destined for both a knighthood and air rank, a pilot with 49 Squadron, based at Scampton, in the summer of 1940, described the kind of sortie undertaken by Eustace and Parker:

Mining was a major role, particularly for the Hampdens squadrons of 5 Group. The magnetic mines that were used fitted very neatly into the bomb bay of the Hampden and they carried out the majority of the early mining missions. These magnetic mines, which were relatively new, were dropped by parachute at low altitude, about 1,000ft. They came down on to the surface of the sea by parachute and then the effect of the seawater on a soluble plug enabled the parachute to be released. The parachute floated away and the mine itself became active and sank to the sea bed where it rested until a ship passed over the top. The laying of the mine was critical. They had to be dropped in relatively shallow water in order to be activated. So navigation was a problem as the operations were mainly carried out at night. They were carried out to the Baltic in great numbers, along the sea lanes of the Frisian Islands, the north German coast and the entrance to the Kiel canal. We had to fly low over the

North Sea, which was not pleasant, particularly when you had low cloud and rain and static electricity building up on the aeroplane, which caused what was called St Elmo's Fire, like a blue flame flashing on the windscreen. It was not dangerous but very disconcerting. Then in bumpy conditions you had to find the enemy coastline, assess your position and then do a run to find the actual spot in the sea where the mine had to be actually dropped.

In spite of the short hours of darkness and the prevailing poor flying conditions, Eustace and Parker successfully carried out their task and returned to Waddington safely; unusually, all the bombers operating that night did too.

As day dawned on Tuesday 16 July a glance out of almost any window in the country at the dull, misty and rainy scene, would have revealed that this was not an ideal day for flying. No. 2 Group decided otherwise and fifteen Blenheims from 18 and 82 Squadrons were given orders to carry out early morning spoiling attacks on several coastal airfields and ports in northern France and Belgium where the shipping and barges needed for the expected invasion were already being gathered. No fewer than eleven of the crews gave up the ghost in the face of appalling conditions but the remainder pressed on, one locating and attacking a significant number of barges, estimated to be 200–300, moored three abreast in the canals between Armentieres and Merville. Several were claimed as damaged and one, at least, was noted as sunk; the intelligence gathered was probably more valuable. The sorties were not without cost, however. Plt Off A.B. Jones wrote off his Blenheim in a forced landing near Welwyn Garden City, injuring one of the men on board. His fellow 18 Squadron members, Sgts Bunker, Harris and Hatch, fared far worse, losing their lives when shot down into the sea north-east of Bruges by Feldwebel Georg Kiening of 6/JG54. With little or no improvement in the weather expected, all operations were called off by early evening.

Nothing much had changed by morning and 17 July saw little activity on either side of the Channel. Once again, however, a baker's dozen of

Blenheim crews took to the leaden skies to keep up the disruptive pressure upon the airfields and ports along the enemy-held coastal strip. Only two managed to get through the murk and locate a suitable target, bombing a barge concentration near Enkhuizen on the Bruges canal before turning around and groping their way homewards through the squally showers and thick clag. Once again, most of the nocturnal operations were axed but seven Wellingtons were despatched to attack the oft-visited oil plant at Gelsenkirchen. It had, at best, an outside chance of success and it was no great surprise that only three of the crews succeeded in locating a target of any sort, releasing their bombs to no visible effect. One 149 Squadron aircraft rounded off a particularly difficult and unsatisfactory night by crashing on landing at Mildenhall. Of the seven Blenheims sent to harass the airfields, only one reached its target, scattering its load over the airfield at Morlaix, again with no visible result. So much for summer flying.

The night did, however, see an important first, though as it turned out, without any spectacular consequence. For some time, it had been clear that the Luftwaffe was operating in significant numbers by night, both as an offensive and a defensive force. Any interference with this process could only be beneficial and as a result, Sqn Ldr Webster of 15 Squadron set off to the Caen area to carry out the RAF's first 'intruder' patrol of the war. Unfortunately, the weather had largely grounded the Luftwaffe too and Webster returned empty handed but having set a portentous precedent for operations that would carry on to the very last days of the war.

By the next morning, there was a marginal improvement in the weather, though low cloud and rain still dominated the weather charts. Marginal or not, it was enough to encourage 2 Group to mount its now customary raids to cause damage, dislocation and disruption to the attack upon the British Isles. The crews again struggled in the conditions but the airfield at St Omer, for example, was hit by several aircraft, causing visible and appreciable damage. Boulogne harbour and docks also received a hammering in the late afternoon. Sgt Moffat of 15 Squadron had been briefed to bomb the shipping in the harbour but, unable to locate any, switched to other targets and, as the official log records, 'made an excellent job on the harbour, planting his bombs in the centre of an extremely large warehouse and started a large fire'. Other crews followed his example but, as the log pithily comments, 'from the photos taken it appears that some people still need tuition in bombing.' Equally disturbing were the reports from the crews, which recorded the scale of the build-up of materials on the other side of the Channel; no fewer than 700–800 wagons were recorded as being lined up in the marshalling yards in Ostend, with a further 300 parked not too far away in Cassel.

Two more of 15's crews were allotted a German target, the oil plant at Sterkrade-Holten, where conditions were predicted to be tolerable. In fact, they were a little too tolerable and when Flt Sgt St John found his Blenheim flying in splendid isolation in an all but clear sky over Germany, he decided discretion was the better part of valour and turned for home, taking useful photographs of the heavy traffic on the Dutch and Belgian waterways as he went. He had, in fact, got further than his colleague, Fg Off Mahler, who had barely flown 10 miles from the English coast before he encountered three roving Me 110s. Whilst no match for the nimble Hurricanes and Spitfires, the Me 110 'destroyers', armed with machine guns and cannon, were formidable opponents for the lightly armed Blenheim. Mahler immediately banked away from his assailants but they were upon him in seconds, all forward-firing weapons blazing as soon as the range closed. The Blenheim jinked its way wildly through the sky, its .303 machine guns returning fire whenever the opportunity arose. One Me 110 was seen to break off the attack and turn away and a second was seen to shudder as the British bullets hit home at close range, before diving steeply towards the sea, seemingly out of control. The third, however, bored in unmolested and raked the Blenheim from end to end, causing considerable damage and setting the inner wing fuel tanks ablaze. Now just a few miles off the clearly visible Norfolk coast, Mahler rammed the stick forward and aimed for the long, flat sandy beach, coming up tantalisingly close. Struggling to line up and fighting to maintain control of the blazing aircraft, Mahler was grateful to be spared further attention from the Me 110, which had clearly decided his opponent was doomed and broken off the engagement. Mahler needed all his skill to lower the wallowing aircraft down on to the soft sand, raising high waves as it ploughed along the beach. As soon as it ground to a halt, the three largely uninjured crew members clambered out of the wreckage in double quick time. They had not put much distance between themselves and the burning bomber before it exploded in spectacular fashion as the flames ignited the bomb load, ammunition and nearly full fuel tanks. As a postscript, local army units reported observing two Me 110s crashing into the sea as a result of the combat; it was a remarkable outcome for the courageous crew.

Once again, the dreary conditions curtailed the Command's night operations, with the more northerly-based 4 Group cancelling all its sorties; however, the Wellingtons of 3 Group and the Hampdens of 5 Group were declared operational and a sizeable total of sixty-six aircraft took off to attack half a dozen dispersed targets. Many of the young crewmen might well have wondered why they had bothered, given that it was obvious that conditions for accurate navigation and bombing were just as woeful as before. Plt Off Fox, a pilot flying Hampdens with 49 Squadron at Newmarket, recorded a typical entry in his squadron's log, stating that his crew had failed to locate the primary target but had released their bombs on what they thought was a blast furnace that they thought was in the Krefeld area, noted for its heavy industry. The explosions were observed to be in the vicinity of the aiming point and several small fires were seen to have been ignited. The rest of the squadron fared no better; Fg Off Haskins attacked the most suitable target he could find, a searchlight battery about 10 miles south of Rotterdam, without any visible result, while Fg Off Burnett and Sgt Roberts failed to locate any target at all and headed home through the murk with bomb load intact. No. 44 Squadron fared slightly better with several crews managing to discern worthwhile targets, one Eschwege airfield where bombs were seen to burst on and around the airfield resulting in a number of fires and explosions, another Juist airfield, a third the marshalling yards at Münster and a fourth another SEMO, tentatively identified as a blast furnace at Oberhausen. Although no aircraft were lost, the squadron did not get away scot-free.

Plt Off Wilfred Walker, who had attacked a train so spectacularly only a few nights earlier, was passing over Wünsdorf airfield at 6,000ft in order to verify his identification of the target below and was on his second run when the now alert defences opened up with both heavy and light flak. In spite of all the 'muck' hurtling up and bursting all around him, Walker held the bomber steady and released his load of six 250lb HE bombs and sixty 4lb incendiaries, all of which were clearly observed by the gunner as exploding across the airfield. Just then, the aircraft bucked and shuddered from a near miss and almost immediately began to wallow and lose height. Anxiously scanning the aircraft around him for significant damage, the navigator, Plt Off David Romans, a Canadian who had joined the RAF in March 1939, was relieved not to find more than a few holes but puzzled as to why the aircraft was not responding properly. The reason became quickly and shockingly apparent. A piece of shrapnel had torn into his pilot's head and rendered him unconscious. Romans clambered forward and tried to heave Walker out of the way as gently as possible in the circumstances and take his place but, unable to do so, he had to make do with perching himself upon his pilot's knees. Trained in the rudiments of flying for just this sort of perilous eventuality, the navigator swiftly brought the bomber back under control and confirmed his earlier opinion that the aircraft was more or less intact. Following his own course home, the inexperienced and apprehensive pilot put the Hampden back on track and headed west through the dark sky. Having located Waddington without incident, Romans informed the station of his predicament and all emergency procedures were initiated. With dozens of anxious eyes following his every move, he lined up the Hampden with the runway and warily began his approach, acutely aware that the lives of the other men on board were in his hands. Hoping fervently that his assessment that the aircraft had not sustained serious flak damage was correct, he gingerly lowered the bomber towards the runway and, to everyone's surprise and delight, pulled off a slightly bumpy but perfectly acceptable landing. Almost before the wheels had stopped turning, an ambulance was alongside ready for the bloodied and still unconscious Walker. He was rushed the few miles to hospital in Lincoln but died from his wounds shortly after arrival and was later buried near his home in Staffordshire. Although Romans was awarded an immediate DFC, it was a sad and undeserved end to a highly skilful and courageous effort.

The Wellingtons were sent to attack mainly aircraft targets, the factories and depots at Diepholz and Rottenberg, together with the oil refineries at Hanover and Bremen, with the marshalling yards in Hamm thrown in for good measure. No. 37 Squadron's night was typical, despatching nine Wellingtons to various targets, with airfields being designated as targets of last resort. As night fell, around 22.00 hours, the heavily laden bombers took off, initially cruising through a relatively clear sky. It was not to last and the crews soon encountered an intense front with thick cloud billowing up to 14,000ft, forcing the bombers to climb higher than expected into the eerie moonlit world above. Fortunately, they outpaced the front to find the German landscape clearly visible in the bright and uninterrupted moonlight. Most pilots dropped down to 7,500–10,000ft over the target area and several employed the commonly used shallow diving glide approach, hoping to baffle the ground defences. It did not always work and Plt Off Fletcher encountered an intense barrage of light and heavy flak over Rottenberg in exchange for dropping his high explosive on and around several large hangars. The crews found different tactics being employed over Hamm, where the defences remained inactive until the bombers were directly overhead; then, a potent combination of light and heavy flak, supported by searchlights, opened up. Flt Lt Clayton's crew reported their bombs causing a series of massive explosions, resulting in a very large, concentrated fire. Fg Off Lemon decided the glare from all the pyrotechnics was too bright to identify the target accurately and swung away in search of another. Having located an airfield, thought to be Wesel, he was just lining up his run when he inadvertently switched on his landing lights, clearly illuminating his aircraft. Normally a lethal error to make, the Luftwaffe men a few thousand feet below, assumed the aircraft overhead was friendly, fired a green landing flare and illuminated the runway. Taking full advantage of this unexpected helping hand, Lemon put the Wellington's nose down and levelling out at just 500ft, streaked across the airfield, dropping his bombs and firing as he went. Almost at once a red flare was fired and the lights extinguished, but the damage had already been done. It was a very jubilant crew that headed home to tell their tale.

Perhaps the most conspicuous success of the night, however, was achieved by the crews attacking the Dortmund–Ems canal. Unlike Britain in 1940, the intricate network of navigable rivers and canals still played an enormous role in the German economy and transport system, carrying about one-third of the nation's freight. It was clear that if the use of these waterways could be impeded, the effect upon the economy in general and the preparations for invasion in particular would be significant. Bomber Command identified a significant bottleneck in the system, a double aqueduct where the canal crossed the river Ems. As such a pinpoint target was recognised as being especially difficult to hit, the area was thoroughly photographed in advance and detailed scale models made to help the crews identify the target and understand its importance. One pilot was widely reported as praising such support: 'If we had not seen the models beforehand, we could easily have made a mistake, for there were several places which more or less resembled our target.' The Hampdens were fortunate to encounter clear conditions with excellent visibility on account of the bright moonlight and comparatively little opposition on this occasion. For once, photographic reconnaissance was able to confirm the crews' jubilant reports and positive claims. Many newspapers and magazines carried officially released pictures, showing a long stretch of drained canal and a number of barges left high and dry, surrounded by bomb craters in the canal bed and banks, some measuring 30ft across. To top it all off, all the aircraft returned safely.

The following night the crews were not so fortunate as three of them failed to return, with twelve of the fifteen men losing their lives. It was the busiest night since the fall of France with eighty-six Wellingtons, Whitleys and Hampdens sent on operations; as was usual at the time, the targets were wide-ranging and varied. The latter once again headed off to the north German ports to attack naval-related targets with eight crews mounting an attack upon the 12,000-ton 'pocket battleship' *Admiral Scheer*, which with six 11in guns posed a potent threat as a high seas raider. The Hampdens successfully made it to Kiel but only one crew managed to locate and identify the warship lying at anchor. The large 2,000lb armour-piercing bomb load was released but landed harmlessly in the sea. The *Admiral Scheer* was not the only capital warship under attack, as the far larger *Tirpitz*, still being fitted out, was identified and four 250lb bombs were dropped. No results were observed from this audacious attempt, though it is doubtful whether such small bombs would have caused much damage had they hit the armoured giant. Five more Hampdens did a spot of gardening in the waters off Friedrichshafen and, as was standard practice, carried a number of 250lb HE bombs in addition to the mine in case of suitable targets of opportunity being located. Two crews from 44 Squadron did just that. Flt Sgt J.F. Clayton had already sown his mine and turned for home when he suddenly picked out several lights shining out of the inky darkness off Sanro Island. Upon wary investigation, it was found that they belonged to a sizeable cargo vessel that soon regretted its negligence. Clayton wheeled around and boring in at just 800ft, hurtled over the ship, releasing a pair of bombs which fell close enough to rock the vessel violently. Sgt T. Henderson's crew was also returning to base when they noticed the lights and explosions and hurried to investigate. Having identified the ship as a valid target, Henderson too made an attack, his bombs seen to land within a matter of yards of the ship, causing it to lurch wildly. Although no further results were seen by either crew, it seemed likely that the ship would have sustained some damage from the brief but unexpected onslaught. A third crew from 44 met with far less success; a call was received from Sgt E.L. Farrand's aircraft stating that it had been badly mauled by flak and that it was turning back east aiming to make landfall in Denmark, rather than risk crossing the North Sea. It never made it, crashing instead into the sea just short of Jutland, killing Sgts Nixon and Miller. For one of the survivors, Bernard Green, it was the beginning of another chapter in a long career. Commissioned into the Ox and Bucks Light Infantry, he went into the trenches near Ploegsteert in March 1915 and was wounded by grenades two months later. On his recovery, he was transferred to the Machine Gun Corps, promoted captain and served on the Somme, where he was Mentioned in Despatches; a spell at Passchendaele followed as did promotion to major and a Military Cross (MC) in June 1918. Wounded in the heel by a steel fragment in October 1918, one might have thought that Green had done enough in the service of his country but in 1939, with war looming, at the age of 52, he joined the Royal Air Force Volunteer Reserve (RAFVR) as a pilot officer and subsequently joined 44 Squadron as a rear gunner; his flying career was brief and came to an abrupt end on this night, shot down on his first operational flight. Green succeeded in making it ashore and, finding his bearings, strode off in the direction of Sweden, covering a number of miles before being captured. 'Pop' Green was not, however, ready to retire gracefully and earned his place working as a 'penguin', discreetly disposing of the tunnel spoil via heavy bags carried within his trouser legs, in the Great Escape from Stalag Luft III on 25 March 1943. Making it out of the tunnel, he was recaptured later on the same day. He was the first to be returned to the camp and was lucky not to be included in the fifty prisoners shot as a reprisal.

Flak also gave an almighty shock to Flt Lt D.D. Pryde and his 77 Squadron crew. Their Whitley N1384 had one of its engines smashed as it was still en route, forcing them to jettison their load and turn home. After a seemingly interminable and nerve-jangling flight across the North Sea, Pryde managed to land safely at the Fighter Command station at Duxford. Another Whitley from 102 was hit by flak over Bremen and had to force land at Bircham Newton. Night fighters too were busy that night, adding to the danger in the hostile night sky. A Wellington from 149 Squadron, based at Mildenhall, endured a prolonged combat with a pair of German aircraft. The battle ended inconclusively with slight damage to the bomber and its gunners filing unconfirmed claims for both the assailants. A Whitley from 78 Squadron was also attacked by two night fighters over the Ruhr but managed to break off the engagement and melt into the darkness unscathed.

Flt Lt S.E.F. Curry of 51 Squadron, based alongside 77 Squadron at Dishforth, was not so fortunate. Curry's Whitley had taken off at 21.45 hours bound for the oil refinery at Gelsenkirchen and at 02.00 hours encountered Oblt Werner Streib and Cpl Linzen of NJG1 on patrol. They first spotted a vague shape in the darkness to one side, which gradually transformed itself into a twin-engine aircraft. At first, they identified it as another Dornier, long and thin and known to be operating in the area, but as Streib nudged his aircraft a little closer, he caught sight of the RAF markings. Almost immediately there were vivid and dazzling flashes of light as the rear gunner of the Whitley opened fire. Streib replied with two long bursts and later recalled:

> His starboard engine was burning mildly. Two dots detached themselves and disappeared into the night. The bomber turned on a reciprocal course and tried to get away but the plume of smoke from its engine was still clearly visible. I attacked again, aiming at the port engine and wing, without meeting any counter fire. Two more bursts and the engine and wing immediately blazed up. The aircraft turned over and crashed into the ground.

This was at Ibbenburren, about 12 miles west of Osnabrück; there was only one survivor. A similar fate befell a Wellington of 9 Squadron. Sqn Ldr J.B.S. Moneypenny, an amiable and experienced pre-war regular, had taken off from RAF Honington a little after 20.00 hours bound for the Dornier factory at Wismar; nothing else is known of the bomber's fate beyond the fact that the body of gunner Plt Off H.F.A. Lees was later recovered from Eckernforder Bay, 25 miles north-west of Kiel.

The next twenty-four hours were to prove even more costly for Bomber Command; it would lose no fewer than eight aircraft. The first loss came early in the day. Twenty-five Blenheims from 2 Group were despatched to carry out what by now had come to be almost routine tasks, carrying out attacks upon airfields in the occupied countries, naval targets in northern Germany, industrial targets in the Ruhr and general and meteorological reconnaissance. Though dull and rainy over much of the country, over

Europe the sky was relatively bright and clear, compelling all but two of the crews to abort their missions. One carried out a daring attack upon the airfield at Flushing and returned safely; the other, piloted by Sqn Ldr J.F. Stephens, crashed into the sea off the Dutch coast, the victim of Lt Kinzinger of I/JG54 at 13.30, a bare ninety minutes after it had taken off from Wattisham bound for Vlissingen. Only one of the three-man crew escaped with his life, gunner Sgt E.C. Parker.

A few hours later the Command made another major effort, sending ninety-five aircraft to attack German targets, principally oil refineries and storage in Bremen, Hamburg and Gelsenkirchen, but also the Dornier factory in Wismar and the capital ships in Wilhelmshaven, not to mention a spot of gardening. Even this last, most routine of operations was not without its share of danger on this occasion. No. 49 Squadron's Sgt Stretton had laid his mines in the Daffodil area off the Danish coast when he located a merchant ship south of Copenhagen. Immediately, he made an attack with two 250lb bombs and was rewarded with misses near enough to cause some visible damage to the ship. Plt Off K.W. Mitchie from the same squadron was engaged in a similar task in the Baltic Sound. Having taken rather too long to locate his target area, Mitchie endured a nerve-wracking flight back across the North Sea, watching the needles on his fuel gauges heading inexorably towards zero. Eking out the fuel as long as he could, he eventually sighted the north Norfolk coast in the dawn light and immediately opted to get the Hampden on to the ground, near Hunstanton and still some way short of Scampton; the crew emerged from the wreckage shaken but substantially intact.

Nos 61 and 144 Squadrons, both based at RAF Hemswell in Lincolnshire, had been assigned especially difficult and hazardous targets, the *Admiral Scheer* and the *Tirpitz* at anchor in Wilhelmshaven, using 1,500lb M mines, a new form of mine designed by Barnes Wallace, who attended the briefing. The M mines had to be dropped at ultra-low level – between 30 and 80ft – and at a specific speed of 150mph and at an angle of 45 degrees, no mean feat of flying or courage in the pitch black over a heavily defended and alert enemy port, far from the safety of home. The mines were fitted with parachutes that opened immediately in order to slow the rate of descent before sinking to the bottom of the harbour, where they exploded on contact. The massive explosion was intended to damage the most vulnerable part of the ships, the bottom of the hull. Realising the dangers involved, the crews were briefed to approach the harbour from different directions and several were ordered to carry out diversionary attacks throughout the city area in an attempt to divide the defensive fire and cause as much confusion as possible in order to conceal the delivery of the mines. In spite of these precautions, the M bombers flew into an avalanche of flak of all calibres as they crossed the harbour. Only one would survive the onslaught. Flt Sgt Saunders was unable to locate the battleships and so gave orders to drop his mine near a group of ships lying alongside the mole before, damaged, he streaked at deck level away from the deadly pyrotechnic display and set course for home. Plt Off D.H. Davis' Hampden, smashed by flak, plunged into the Grosser Haven near to the Kaiser Wilhelm Bridge, killing three of the four men on board. Plt Off K. Jones managed to keep his badly battered Hampden in the air a little further, crash landing in open fields near Jever airfield; although the fuselage snapped in two, all the crew survived to spend the next five years as prisoners. Plt Off A.H. Gould's aircraft was reduced to an airborne bonfire by flak, with both engines ablaze, steaming long flames across the wings. Navigator Sgt J.F. Cowan politely asked if a course for home was required but Gould declined and gave orders for crash positions to be taken in readiness for a landing on a beach. The tide was out and the pilot managed to control the Hampden sufficiently to pull off a magnificent landing, slithering across what turned out to be mudflats, driving tidal waves of thick, evil smelling, salty mud high into the air. As soon as it ground to a halt, three men began feverishly to extricate themselves from the wreckage, more or less unhurt; the fourth man did not follow them and the mangled body of gunner Plt Off D.S. Carnegie was found nearby, beside him his unopened parachute. Low-level flying was an unforgiving and hazardous occupation.

No. 144 Squadron did not come away unscathed either. Flt Lt D.H. Edwards was presumably hit by flak at almost point blank range but managed to coax his aircraft out of range and enemy territory; at 03.22 he ordered a message to be sent stating that he was about to ditch about 90 miles east of Skegness, about thirty minutes flying time from safety. No more was heard and no trace of the aircraft and its gallant crew was found. In spite of this determined attack, the battleships remained unscathed.

The losses for the night did not stop there. The Wellingtons succeeded in igniting large fires at the oil targets at Bremen and Gelsenkirchen but a third of the thirty-six crews failed to locate their primary targets, instead seeking out self-illuminated targets, airfields and the catch-all targets of opportunity. Fg Off Lemon and Plt Off Watt of 37 Squadron, in spite of long searches, fell into this category; Lemon stumbled across another synthetic oil plant at Mors and with the defences on full alert, met with a very hot reception. Buffeted by the flak bursts all around him, Lemon held the Wellington 1C steady at 12,000ft and let go his load of high explosive only when over the target, although the results were lost amid the dazzling searchlight glare piercing the sky from 2 miles below. Watt had a quieter time when he made an attack upon a collection of large buildings a couple of miles south-west of Dulmen. His first stick was observed to straddle the target and several fires were started by his incendiary bombs. With the target now better illuminated, he decided to make a second run and confirmed his attack by releasing a flash bomb and taking several photographs. Over Gelsenkirchen itself, one aircraft, under the command of Flt Lt Clayton, had an unusual encounter. Approaching the bomber was an enemy fighter, fully illuminated by searchlight beams that skilfully tracked its progress. Unaware of the Wellington's presence in the darkness, the aircraft approached to within 300 yards before firing a coloured flare, at which point the searchlight was immediately shut down. Clayton judged discretion to be the better part of valour and sheered off, later bombing a railway junction at Recklinghausen.

A fellow 37 Squadron crew also reported a lucky escape; Fg Off Williams' Wellington was attacked by no fewer than three night fighters and one pass left his rear gunner mortally wounded and his aircraft more vulnerable. In the exchanges of fire, one assailant was claimed as destroyed but it was a subdued crew that landed at RAF Feltwell a few hours later. The crew of Plt Off G.H. Muirhead did not make it back to Feltwell at all, falling victim in the wee hours to the guns of Oblt Walter Ehle of 1/NJG1. Oblt Siegfried Wandam in the same unit made a claim for a Wellington a little later and this probably accounted for the loss of Fg Off S.M.M. Watson and his 75 Squadron crew, based at the same station, after attacking their target in Horst. The grim, grinding campaign of attrition that characterised Bomber Command's war was beginning to take shape.

In contrast, the next morning dawned bright and clear; it was going to be a lovely summer's Sunday. Unusually, the Blenheim crews in 2 Group were able to laze about and enjoy it as, perversely, the weather was far too good for their normal hit-and-run type of sorties. A lone 114 Squadron Blenheim was ordered to make a reconnaissance of the Wilhelmshaven area, an almost daily standing order, but followed orders and returned in the total absence of any cloud cover whatsoever. Even the inevitable, short-lived thunderstorms in mid-afternoon failed to dampen the crews' enthusiasm for a day off.

Nevertheless, the Command's daily routine continued unbroken and was not without its dangers, preparing the aircraft for another busy night's work, testing the aircraft and general practice flying. At RAF Honington deep in rural Suffolk, 9 Squadron's Plt Off P.R.B. Wanklyn had only recently been made up to captain of his Wellington 1C, having completed several operations as second pilot. Sunday 21 July was his day on the rota for additional flying practice. Twenty-year-old, 6ft 7in, Sgt Rupert 'Tiny' Cooling was in exactly the same position and recalled the evening clearly, many years later. Wanklyn approached him and asked if he would do him a favour, adding that he had something to do in the mess and asking him to take the first turn. Cooling saw no reason not to and duly finished his circuits about 21.30 hours. He met Wanklyn waiting in the crew room, passed a few pleasantries and added for good measure that the bomber was in fine fettle. He had not gone far when he heard the roar of the engines as the Wellington sped down the runway and shortly afterwards a 'God Almighty thump' and turned to see the typical ball of flame and thick black smoke already towering into the clear, evening sky. Neither Wanklyn nor the only other man on board, wireless operator Sgt D. Bennett, stood a chance. The cause of the crash was not discovered and it was attributed to pilot error; the raging inferno, in full view of all on the station, brought the full meaning of war home to all.

The Group commanders were keen to make the most of the favourable weather and planned another series of attacks, involving more than eighty aircraft. Eight Hampdens were on gardening duties and a further seventeen headed back to the Dornier factory at Wismar, with a number of direct hits claimed. Four of these from 44 Squadron arrived a little after the rest and reported several large fires burning in and around the target area. No. 3 Group's Wellington force attacked a number of targets and hits were claimed on the vast Focke-Wulf factory and the docks at Bremen, as they were at the oft-visited oil plant at Gelsenkirchen. The aircraft parks at Rotenburg and Gottingen were also reported as damaged and three specific claims were made for hits on large aircraft hangars, resulting in fires that were clearly visible from a number of miles away. Two trains were machine gunned from low level on the homeward leg of the journey and one was recorded as halted in a cloud of steam. The Whitleys of 4 Group were also busy, carrying out attacks upon the Fiesler aircraft factory at Kassel and the vital marshalling yards at Hamm and Soest. No. 2 Group's Blenheims, after their short-lived break, were back in action over the occupied airfields at Caen, Morlaix and Querqueville and the invasion ports. Even the Fairey Battles of 103 and 105 Squadrons were pressed into service for the first time since their hammering in the Battle of France to add their weight to the attack. The Air Ministry communique the following morning in cool, spare terms revealed the Command's work to a nation increasingly under lethal pressure and keen to hit back. 'Military objectives in Germany, France, Holland and Belgium, including oil depots and tanks, aircraft factories, goods yards, barges and aerodromes were bombed by the RAF in operations in which French airmen took part. Some idea of the havoc wrought is conveyed by the statement that a trail of blazing oil marked the course of the Ghent–Salzaete canal after the bombers had passed.' The general public was left in no doubt that Bomber Command was playing its full part in the defence of the country and the degradation of the planned assault upon it. Nor was it shielded from the price paid in doing so; it was revealed that one bomber had been lost on operations. It was a Whitley V flown by Sgt V.C. Monkhouse of 78 Squadron, the squadron's first loss since beginning operations a few days earlier after a period as the Group Pool Training squadron. All five men on board perished when the aircraft crashed upon German soil.

It was only a marginally better night for John Bowman, a pre-war regular gunner with 83 Squadron. His Hampden was coned by several searchlights over Kiel harbour and was given a particularly hard time by the flak crews, delighted to be given such a clear target. The aircraft was thrown all over the sky but remained starkly illuminated against the dark sky and increasingly buffeted by close shell bursts. In the belief that the aircraft's demise was nigh, the order was given to bail out and almost immediately the bomber was blasted into a steep, diving spin. Bowman heaved himself towards the hatch and it took a few, frantic, time-consuming kicks to free it, perhaps twisted and damaged. Sweating with the strain, he managed to hurl himself through it and into the night, automatically tugging open his parachute. Landing heavily, he realised at once he had broken his leg and resigned himself to capture. For many months he heard nothing of his crew and counted himself fortunate to be the sole survivor until one day his former navigator, Plt Off J. M. Muir, came into his POW camp. He revealed that the pilot had managed to bring the Hampden out of the spin and had coaxed the bomber home, with the rest of the crew on board. Bowman's initial bitterness quickly faded as he learned the pilot had lost his life flying with another crew.

Monday morning dawned fairly damp and dreary. Indeed, conditions were sufficiently poor down the eastern side of England to scrub all of the daylight operations; after that news, the Blenheim crews did not mind such a miserable summer's day. For the crews of 107, the respite proved to be briefer than expected as they were informed that they were 'on' that night. Their target was to be Creil airfield, a busy French base from which attacks were being launched against Britain. Weather conditions had, if anything, deteriorated as the day had gone on and they certainly did nothing to make the crews' lives any easier. The damp Blenheims took to the watery sky as daylight faded and, having circled their airfield at Wattisham watched by their anxious colleagues, headed south. As they crossed the Channel, the sky began to clear a little, enabling the crews to navigate more easily, each making their own way to the target area, the fires raised by the first crews acting as a beacon for those following behind. The fires caused by the high explosive took hold and were visible to the crews more than 40 miles away. It was not, however, all one-way traffic. The airfield was well defended and flak probably accounted for the loss of Blenheim L9414; perhaps the wireless had been damaged but nothing was heard about the fate of the aircraft until the body of the observer, Sgt C.J. Holland, was washed up on the Sussex shoreline, indicating it had crashed into that narrow strip of sea between enemy-held territory and the safety of home.

Elsewhere, Bomber Command spread itself thinly, attacking a dozen or so separate targets. The Battles of 103 and 150 Squadrons were again in the air harassing naval targets in the Rotterdam area. Eight Hampdens from 44 Squadron followed the well-worn aerial path to the oil plant at Gelsenkirchen and the seven crews that made it there reported a strong attack, noting several significant fires and several secondary explosions that hurled smoke and debris more than a mile up into the sky. The final crew instead located Horst airfield and offloaded their bombs but without visible results. A similarly sized force of Hampdens attacked two other priority targets, the gigantic marshalling yards in Hamm and Eschwege, in an attempt to hamper German military and industrial transportation.

One aircraft was picked up by a night fighter and in the brief and confused exchange over Texel, the gunner fired off 300 rounds but without any apparent effect. Seven Wellingtons from 38 Squadron were sent to attack industrial targets in Dusseldorf and, in the very heart of the Ruhr, Essen. There the local weather was atrocious and made the crews' task all but impossible. The squadron log recorded succinctly:

> Essen; bombed but results were not observed. Conclusion; not very successful owing to heavy cloud over the target area. Flak was intense but only fairly accurate.

Some consolation at least. The Whitleys, the largest force deployed that night at twenty-five-strong, met similar conditions over the Ruhr targets and the Focke-Wulf factory in Bremen. The crews did their best in difficult circumstances and succeeded in bombing their primary or alternative targets but with unknown results. One bomber, that of Sgt J.B. Jones of 58 Squadron, was hit by flak and at 02.00 hours came down near an inn, a little to the north of the village of Oesterholz, with the loss of all on board.

It was a little brighter the next morning and orders were soon whizzing around 2 Group arranging operations for that afternoon. The targets were, as usual, the airfields and ports along the Channel to keep the pressure on the invasion and strike forces. However, the weather once again blunted the attack with the conditions convincing eleven crews of the need to abort in line with their orders. A handful of others drew a different conclusion and pressed on in spite of the obvious dangers. One, from 15 Squadron, had a particularly narrow escape. The Blenheim had taken off from Wyton shortly before 16.00 hours and about an hour and a quarter later was running the gauntlet of the light flak over St Omer airfield. Flying at a steady 3,000ft an anti-aircraft shell burst directly beneath the bomber, tossing it about like a child's toy. At once the previously ordered aircraft became chaotic as the blast blew in the floor hatch and side window panels, allowing a 200mph gale to rip through the interior, scattering dirt, maps and equipment everywhere. The blast had also damaged the aircraft's elevators and sent it into a violent spin. Pulling out with a scant couple of hundred feet to spare, the badly shaken crew began to take stock and discovered that their wireless was also U/S, as were a number of the instruments. Following a generally northern course, the crew crossed the Channel and navigated their way home at low level, searching for well-known landmarks to guide them. Landing safely at 18.40 hours, the crew had a great story to tell their friends but it could so easily have been very different.

The Blenheims, along with a handful of Battles, were out again that night to cause as much dislocation as possible along the Channel coast. A combination of low cloud, fog and general murk hampered visibility and reduced the effects of the raids considerably but, unfortunately, not their cost, with one Blenheim coming down just off the Dutch coast; there were no survivors. Once again the rest of the Command's effort was divided by Group and aircraft type. The Hampdens were assigned the task of bombing the docks at Wilhelmshaven and an aircraft factory at Wenzendorf, with about half the crews claiming to have located and attacked the targets. One of these, Flt Sgt Apps of 49 Squadron stated his bombs had been observed falling directly on to the factory, resulting in a large explosion and outbreak of fire. The remainder attacked an array of alternative targets, especially airfields, along the enemy coast.

The Wellingtons of 3 Group were to keep up the pressure on aircraft production, attacking the well-established factory at Gotha and the vital fuel supply, or as pilot Tiny Cooling put it when he heard at the briefing, 'that bloody oil refinery at Gelsenkirchen. Again.' Ruefully he added, 'Nobody seemed to hit it.' Heading towards an oft-visited and important target held obvious and very real dangers as two bombers had brief but deadly encounters with patrolling Me 110 night fighters, one of which left a navigator mortally wounded. The confusion and shock caused by such short, violent and often unexpected engagements had a profound effect upon those involved. The darkness and lightning fast speeds at which they generally took place sometimes, for example, resulted in wildly differing reports of the actions; on this occasion, official records reveal that the Wellington gunners claimed one assailant shot down and another damaged while the German pair, neither of which was hit, made claims for both bombers being brought down. Such claims were normally made in good faith, but the disparity between reality and perception made it difficult for intelligence officers, gleaning their information second hand, to piece together an accurate picture of what was happening in the night sky.

It was the same for the assessment of the damage caused on the ground. An interview with a neutral Turkish businessman was widely reported in the press on 23 July 1940. He had just returned from a trip that had taken him to a number of German cities, such as Emden, Dusseldorf, Essen, Cologne and Hamburg. He categorically stated that there was scarcely a factory in these industrial powerhouses left unscathed and intact. Hamburg's docks, he declared, were in ruins after recent heavy attacks. Whilst taken with a pinch of salt by those within the Command, the picture painted fitted in well with the accounts given by the crews, whose assessments were made at night, at a distance and under fire, while dazzled and disorientated by the noise and blinding flashes of explosions all around. On this night the crews over Germany did not find matters easy. No. 77 Squadron's O-Orange, piloted by Plt Off Andy Dunn, already an experienced captain with a DFC to his credit, had taken off from Driffield at 21.00 bound for the Fiesler and Messerschmitt factories at Kassel. It ran into some murky conditions and, after flying around the target area for some time, searching for a break in the layer of thick cloud beneath them, Dunn decided to head west and seek out an alternative target. That lucky break in the cloud continued to evade them and, try as they might, the young men were unable to catch a glimpse of the ground and had only a vague idea of where they actually were. Mindful of the dwindling fuel supply and the value of his aircraft and its crew, Dunn reluctantly gave the night up as a bad job. Judging they were over the North Sea, Dunn gave orders to jettison the bomb load and gradually lost height to search for the English coast. Once found in the early dawn light, a course was set for home, finally landing safely at 04.37 hours: more than seven and a half nerve-shredding hours for nothing.

Rear gunner George Dove's experience of the night was both similar and very different, amply demonstrating the vagaries of the Command's war at this stage. Taking off in the gathering dusk from 10 Squadron's base at RAF Leeming, the Whitley completed its usual circuit of the airfield watched by many friends, colleagues and locals, before swinging east and out over the North Sea towards Hamburg. The fine summer's evening soon faded and was lost in unexpectedly dense cloud. The crew pressed on, flying deep into enemy-held territory and towards the estimated location of the target area. Once again, there was no lucky break in the cloud and the crew decided to turn around and seek an alternative target nearer the coast. Back over Holland, the cloud suddenly dispersed to reveal an airfield dead ahead, fully lit up, with the runway, hangars and buildings all with lights ablaze; to cap it all, several aircraft with navigation lights on were visible doing circuits and bumps. The navigator quickly identified it as Schiphol, a very suitable alternative target. The pilot quickly decided that fortune would favour the brave and switched on his own navigation lights, came down low and joined the circuit. As Dove later recalled:

Picture, if you will, a Whitley on circuit with assorted Luftwaffe aircraft over a German airfield. We must have arrived towards the end of the night's exercise because one by one the aircraft landed until the only aircraft in the circuit was us! The runway controller was flashing us a persistent green to come in – we were astonished at our good fortune. The skipper had by now decided on a course of action. He called us on the intercom, 'I am now going to do a long downwind leg, then come back over the hangars low and fast. Navigator drop the bombs on the hangars and rear gunner spray the airfield as we pass.' By chance our bomb load was all delayed reaction, perfect for the situation. We raced back over the airfield as fast as the Whitley could go, dropped the bombs and as the airfield came into view, I pressed the trigger of the four gun turret and kept it pressed until we reached the other side. As we sped out to sea, I gave a running commentary on what was happening; all the lights went out at once, bursts of flak, searchlights and red flares – all too late – we were well on our way home.

The crew had witnessed actual damage, and headed back elated by their good fortune and success. The contrast with Dunn's crew is stark.

It might well have been the height of summer but Wednesday 24 July did not much look or feel like it. An impenetrable blanket of dark, heavy cloud poured rain all over the country, severely curtailing offensive operations. Ten Blenheims from 2 Group gallantly tried but all but once gave up in the face of the bleak conditions. The lone Blenheim that did press on through the clag located St Aubin airfield, near Dieppe, released its bombs to no visible effect and returned home safely. The night force fared little better. A baker's dozen of Hampdens ploughed through the murk towards Wenzendorf and Wismar; regular targets the aircraft factories might have been but none of the crews could find them this night. Indeed, they could not find any target to bomb at all and were more than thankful simply to make it back home safely. Fourteen Whitleys attempted to carry out their orders to attack the major naval surface assets *Tirpitz* and *Bismarck*, together with the gigantic pre-war liners *Bremen* and *Europa*, potential troop carriers for invasion. Larry Donnelly, a Wireless Operator/Air Gunner (WopAg), was on board one of 10 Squadron's aircraft:

As we flew across the North Sea the weather worsened and we were in cloud all the time, picking up ice. We pressed on hoping the weather would improve, but we were out of luck and we were still in cloud when we reached our ETA at the target. We stooged around hoping to find a gap through which to descend and bomb but we were unable to do so. We presumed we must have been in the vicinity of the target because of the flak bursts in the cloud around us, an alarming spectacle. After some considerable time we gave it up as a bad job and set course for home, still in the murk which persisted all the way until we reached base where we landed safely.

Only a couple of the 10 and 58 Squadron aircraft released their bombs over enemy territory and it was hard to be more precise than that. Even the press reports and official Air Ministry communique found it difficult to wring much joy from the night's efforts. 'RAF defy storms; heavy rain and thunderstorms and severe icing conditions hampered our bombing operations last night. In spite of this, the docks in Emden, Wilhelmshaven and Hamburg and aircraft factories at Wismar and Wenzendorf and the seaplane bases at Borkum and Texel were attacked. All returned safely.'

As one group of weary crews were returning, another, only a little less weary, were up and around preparing for another busy day ahead. At readiness before dawn, WopAg Roger Peacock at RAF Wyton had plenty of time to watch the sky clear and enjoy lounging around in the increasingly warm sunshine outside the crew room. Shortly after lunch, a little later than expected, the call came ordering his crew to mount an attack upon Glisy airfield near Amiens, which, in turn, was busy preparing its crews to do likewise on Britain. No. 2 Group had sent out four Blenheims on a meteorological reconnaissance flight earlier in the day and informed the crews that they should expect ten-tenths cloud over Northern France. Somewhere over the coast near Tangmere, Peacock all but jumped out of his skin as he heard a sudden and deafening bang and became enveloped in dense smoke. Nothing felt amiss with the aircraft and as the smoke began to clear, a detailed check revealed that a small explosive charge fitted to destroy the Identification, Friend or Foe (IFF) device in case of emergency had prematurely self-detonated. The panic over, the crew set about their routines as the aircraft plunged into the expected cloud. Losing altitude, the Blenheim steaked over the green French countryside at about 500ft, just below the cloud base, ready to climb back into its reassuring protection, if necessary. Locating the airfield, the Blenheim was in and out, scattering its bombs in a single pass, before the gunners were able to loose off more than a couple of poorly aimed shots. Swinging round to the west and crossing the coast near Dieppe, the Blenheim flew back into strong sunshine, the blinding sunlight reflecting off the deep blue sea. In front of it on the horizon, several indistinct tiny black specks came into sight – aircraft. The specks grew in size with each passing, agonising second and sharpened into six twin-engine aircraft and finally into six heavily armed and hostile Me 110s. As Peacock readied his guns, the pilot pushed the nose down, turned slightly away and hurtled at full throttle across the Channel, a mere 50ft above its shimmering water. In spite of fervent prayers to the contrary, the Me 110s had spotted the lone bomber and came in to attack in line astern, taking turns to blast away at the jinking Blenheim before breaking away and re-joining the queue. Peacock fired off burst after burst in reply but, out-gunned and out-ranged, he achieved little but force the Germans to take a little more care. After ten minutes of desperate combat, the Blenheim was remarkably intact and still in the air, resolutely holding course for home. With the English coast now in sight, the Germans suddenly broke off the engagement, re-formed and continued on their way. Now regretting the demise of their IFF equipment, the crew crossed the coast near Southampton, skirting the balloon barrage, alone in the sky right back to their airfield in Huntingdonshire.

Not long after landing, the three young men were apologetically notified that they would be required for operations again that night and should report for briefing at 22.00 hours. It really was going to be a very long day. The target, they discovered, was another, more distant airfield: Jever, not far from Wilhelmshaven. Take-off was to be a bare fifty minutes later. The skipper, Sgt P.H. Steele, had some trouble in getting the engines to fire up and run smoothly and for a minute or two there was a glimmer of hope that the sortie might have to be aborted. However, within a couple of minutes all was well and the Blenheim was climbing steadily into the vast sky, heading east, over Orford Ness and the North Sea, the darkness of the cloudy night broken only by a few searchlights and flak some way ahead over the enemy coast. Eventually, as the target area approached, the familiar scene came into view – violent explosions, waving searchlights, flak bursts and tracer vividly lighting up the sky. There was little alternative but to fly directly into it all, hold everything steady for the final bombing run and head out through the other side.

The welcome words 'bombs gone' had barely been uttered when Steele added a laconic codicil 'port engine gone'. Almost without delay, he added, 'Now the other engine's had it,' and 'Prepare to bail out.' So rapidly could a situation change; flying steadily, an efficient and formidable fighting unit one moment, scrambling for the hatch to escape from a useless machine the next. Peacock was the last man out as the bomber fell into a gentle and rather graceful spin, trailing orange flames as it fell through the air. Falling out head first, Peacock saw his aircraft explode on impact before landing heavily but safely only a few yards from his pilot and not much further from the blazing Blenheim, which was still spitting out bullets and lumps of metal as it burned. Before they could gather their wits, the dazed pair was approached by a group of armed civilians led by a Luftwaffe officer waving his pistol to complete the abrupt end to their operational career. Theirs was one of three Blenheims lost on 25/26 July and the only one from which the crew lived to tell the tale. The crews of Plt Off C. Robson of 15 Squadron and Plt Off R.E. Short of 101 Squadron were lost in full.

Three other 15 Squadron crews were also on operations, leaving Wyton at the unusually late time of 23.20. Flying towards the Dutch coast through dense cloud that bubbled up to 15,000ft, Sqn Ldr Webster was unable to locate his position accurately. Working on ETA and in an area with slightly thinner cloud, he dropped to 9,000ft and released a series of flares but unfortunately these failed to illuminate the ground beneath to any useful extent. Suddenly three lights became visible and, a mile further on, another two. Puzzled, he had no idea what they were but, as he later reported, 'While debating whether or not it would be ethical to bomb the lights, they were extinguished and numerous flaming onions drifted up on the port bow about 4,000ft below us. If they were meant to be fired at our aircraft, they were hopelessly inaccurate.' Webster turned towards the flak but it too ceased before he could establish its location accurately. Thwarted a second time, the frustrated Webster stooged about hoping something would turn up, but with his fuel supply dwindling, he decided to return home, landing as the first glimmer of dawn began to brighten the sky.

It was a particularly big night for Bomber Command with 166 aircraft out on operations. Once again, the major target was oil, working on the simple dictum that what food is to a soldier, oil is to a machine. Plt Off Andy Dunn's Whitley was one of those attacking the enormous refinery at Bottrop. Coming over the target a little after midnight, there was nothing sleepy about his reception. Flak liberally peppered the sky and blindingly bright searchlights pierced the darkness, swinging to and fro in search of their prey. Dunn decided to confuse the sweating gunners below by coming in at 5,000ft, well below the usual altitude. He was able to make a clear run-in to the target but the glare meant that his crew was unable to see the results of their efforts. Flt Lt D.D. Pryde, also of 77 Squadron, met with a similarly hostile reception and just after completing his run, the bomber shuddered from a near miss that set one engine ablaze. The crew managed to extinguish the fire before it spread and limped westwards, gradually but steadily losing height, eventually making an emergency landing at Bircham Newton. It was a terrible case of déjà vu for Pryde as this was the second time he had lost an engine over the target in less than a week; on that occasion, the target was Bremen and the emergency landing was at the fighter airfield at Duxford.

The Hampdens of 44 Squadron were also on oil targets that night, heading for the Castrop Rauxel refinery. Sgt T. Henderson was there to add his 500lb bombs to the destruction below. He reported, 'A recce was made of the target area; 2 big fires were seen burning and between them were smaller fires. The whole of the middle of the target area was ablaze. The smoke coming from the conflagration was black with an intense core of flames. The attack was definitely successful.' Sqn Ldr J. Macintyre, who was to lose his life just three nights later when his Hampden collided with a balloon cable over Hamburg, reported repeated hits across the refinery buildings, clearly viewed through gaps in the smoke and haze. Fg Off Eno of 78 Squadron was over the target at 01.05 and noted two storage tanks burning fiercely with large plumes of smoke towering up to 8,500ft. By this time, though the searchlights were still working well as a cohesive unit, the flak batteries appeared to have been reduced to firing only sporadic bursts, enabling the bombers to concentrate fully on the target. The collective picture gleaned from the probing questioning of the intelligence officers a few hours later was very much a corroborated and positive one; significant damage had been done to the targets.

Several Hampdens were again despatched to attack the Dortmund–Ems canal with M mines and of these one, from 83 Squadron, piloted by Plt Off W.O.D. Tweddell DFC, failed to return. A similar loss befell 50 Squadron based at RAF Lindholme. Plt Off W.A.C. Mulloy, another experienced campaigner with a DFC to his credit, had been detailed to join the Castrop Rauxel attack. At 02.15 a message came in from the aircraft reporting that the port engine had packed up over Cuxhaven and that the stricken bomber was following the coast to Calais to reduce the sea crossing. Something must have changed to give the crew hope that they would be able to make it home more directly after all, as the Hampden swung north early. Their recalculation proved fatal as the plane made it as far as the beach at Happisburgh in Norfolk, where it crashed, presumably attempting to make a forced landing, with the loss of all on board. One can only imagine the relief and elation of the tired and anxious young men on board on seeing the English coast appear beneath them, having nervously watched the dials and gauges, listening to the note of the straining single engine, constantly assessing and reassessing the chances of making it home safely. The grim task of recovering the bodies fell to the men of the Cromer lifeboat.

The Wellingtons too were out in force, bound in the main for industrial and transport targets across the Ruhr and northern Germany. No. 37 Squadron was assigned the Messerschmitt factory at Kassel, which was turning out Me 110s, and the regular railway yards at Hamm. Another major rail centre at Cologne was an alternative target and any self-illuminating target in the Ruhr was given last resort status. Weather conditions were indifferent at best and many crews struggled in vain to locate the targets assigned to them. Only two crews, captained by Flt Lt Mitchell and Fg Off Ritchie, succeeded in carrying out high-level attacks upon the aircraft factory, with their bombs at best falling in the target area. Fg Off Warner managed to pick out an airfield 10–15 miles south-east of Kassel and released a stick of bombs across the flarepath, much to the discomfiture of the clearly visible aircraft undertaking the usual circuits and bumps of night time training. Strong moonlight made an appreciable difference over Hamm and several bomb bursts were observed in and around the rail yards. However, the squadron record candidly reveals another, 'aircraft, being unable to identify the exact target, dropped bombs at a point where a stick from a previous aircraft was seen to fall'. Two aircraft were unable to locate any target at all and returned with bomb load intact. Unusually that night, all the Wellingtons were given four large bundles of propaganda leaflets to scatter across enemy territory and those at least, however doubtful their value, were dutifully ejected from the aircraft as ordered. Although 37 Squadron suffered no losses, others were not so fortunate; 75 Squadron lost one near Amsterdam on route home from Kassel, 99 Squadron lost another over Germany in addition to one that crashed into trees as it made its final approach to its airfield. Bomber Command had made a major effort on Thursday 25 July, making more sorties and sustaining greater casualties than its co-defenders in Fighter Command. The Command had hit back, it believed, hard and its efforts prompted its commander Air Marshal Sir Charles Portal to issue a statement to its Groups, 'Please convey to all in Nos 3, 4 and 5 Groups, my heartiest congratulations. Despite adverse weather conditions, they have done a wonderful week's work, culminating in last night's successes.'

It was inevitable that there would be a slackening of the pace after such a busy few days as Bomber Command simply lacked the resources, human and material, to sustain such a high rate of operations. On 26 July, 3 Group was rested, while in 4 Group only nine aircraft from 102 Squadron were deployed. After the usual preparation and briefings, the bombers began to take off about 20.30 and the crews soon found themselves battling the all too familiar rotten weather, with dense cloud and squally showers in evidence all the way to Mannheim and Hamm. Only a third of the aircraft managed to locate any target at all. One Whitley, N1377, under the command of Plt Off R.F. Beauclair sustained serious damage over the target and was forced to crash land about 15 miles south-west of Rotterdam; unusually all the crew survived. A few Hampdens from 5 Group were also over enemy territory, mounting attacks on oil installations at St Nazaire and Nantes as part of the campaign to restrict its supply to the Luftwaffe and Wehrmacht. By contrast, the sky over France was crystal clear and the targets were bathed in bright moonlight, making the task for the Hampden crews far more straightforward. Better still, the targets were all but undefended, enabling the crews to go about their work almost as if on exercise. Accurate bombing was reported and the targets were well ablaze as the crews turned for home.

No. 4 Group was stood down the following night but 3 and 5 Groups maintained the pressure on the oil industry, attacking installations in Hamburg, Bremen and Wilhelmshaven. Yet again, the weather was most unhelpful and many of the crews resorted to bombing what were euphemistically labelled 'targets of opportunity'. At least there were no losses, although seven men lost their lives and five more were injured at RAF Bircham Newton when a 150 Squadron Battle exploded while being bombed up. The explosion was seen and felt for several miles around the local countryside.

No. 2 Group's Blenheims had been busy on both days, seeking to disrupt the build-up of land and naval forces, this time along the Dutch coast and in Wilhelmshaven. Once again, the weather proved unhelpful, one day having too much cloud and rain for the crews to be able to locate the targets and the other too little cloud to offer any semblance of protection from flak or fighters. Flying such operations was notoriously difficult and by turn exhilarating and terrifying. Ted Sismore was a Blenheim pilot:

The great thing about low flying was that it was always the aim to be as low as you could because it protected you … It was exciting to be down among the trees but the pilot had to be looking ahead to see what he had to do next. Over Holland and the north German plain you could get very low indeed.

Further inland, with the hills, not quite so low. You did see everything that was going on. We were navigating then with a map. Church steeples were great navigational aids at low level. If you had a map with churches on the easiest way to navigate was by the steeples. You could also see people, you could see cars, trucks, horses and carts. In hilly country we literally flew past someone's front door and as we flew past I looked across over the wingtip as a man opened the door. I was looking him straight in the eye at about 40ft. On one occasion in the flat country of northern Germany, we were flying very low across some open fields with very few trees and there was a farmer with his horse and cart coming towards us. We went down deliberately low; I doubt if 10 or 20ft would be an exaggeration. As we got close the horse reared up and threw the man off the cart before we went over. We were that close to people. Low flying in itself was not dangerous. We were flying in a Blenheim, cruising at 180 mph. That's slow – you've got time to see the trees, even high tension cables. I've known people clip the target by being a few feet too low but that was unusual. Occasionally, some people came back with a piece of tree. Now, night low level was different. That really was dangerous if you got too low and some people did. We had one night when we were attacking shipping in the Channel at full moon. One Blenheim came back and landed and asked us to come and look at it. 'What happened?' we said. 'Well, I saw a ship so I bombed it and hit it,' he said. 'I pulled up over the mast and I dropped down over the other side. There was another ship there I had not seen so I went through his mast.' When we got out to the aeroplane we found that the propeller had not hit the mast but the engine had collected a piece of wood that was burning gently against the cylinders.

We did hit the sea one night in a Blenheim, off the entrance to the Kiel Canal. It was a misty, frosty night. We were looking for a ship that was reputedly in the canal and as we hurried away from this very flat country, we hit the water and bounced off. It transpired later we'd lost one propeller blade and we'd bent back the other five. We came back with the aeroplane vibrating badly and we set off to fly down the Frisian Islands, really expecting that we would have to make a landing or a ditching. The guns were too active so we said we'd risk the North Sea. We set off for home. I had plotted a position in the middle of the sea and said, 'If we get past there, we'll ditch and the Air-Sea Rescue will pick us up in the morning.' But we came all the way back. We got back to the airfield but because we were making such a strange noise they turned all the lights out. It took us some time to persuade them to put the lights on. Eventually we got them and landed back at base successfully.

The Blenheims were back in the thick of it on Sunday 28 July, for once a proper summer's day, complete with lovely sunshine pouring from a blue sky. That should have been enough to cancel ops and give the crews a welcome day off but, to the surprise of the men of 82 Squadron, they were slated to mount an attack upon Leeuwarden airfield that afternoon. The only consolation was that they were given strict orders to return if there was insufficient cloud cover over enemy territory and from what they could see, that seemed more than a fair bet. Seven aircraft left Watton in blazing sunshine and headed out over the North Sea, for once appearing dark blue and sparkling brightly. There was no doubt about it; not a cloud in sight and with relief and a clear conscience, six of the pilots, sweating in their cockpits, turned around and headed for home. The seventh, however, decided to give it a go. Wg Cdr Lart was an experienced pilot and nobody's fool and his decision was a calculated one; nobody would be expecting a lone raider on a day like this. He would be in and out in a flash. Lart and his crew easily located the airfield and made a single, low, high-speed pass, releasing his bombs right across the busy airfield. Ominously, they counted a dozen Me 109s parked near the hangars and rightly guessed that they would be scrambled in pursuit. Although Lart did not spare his engines and extracted every last mile per hour he could, it was not very long before the rear gunner reported several tiny black dots on the horizon, closing fast. Gradually the tiny dots grew and, as expected, took on the menacing form of four Me 109s. The attacks began over Den Helder, forcing Lart to make ever wilder evasive manoeuvres, while the gunners blazed away in an attempt to keep their assailants at bay or at least put them off their stroke. In spite of this, the Blenheim was hit time and time again. It was not all one-way traffic as one of the fighters was seen to break off abruptly and head earthwards to an uncertain end. By now Lart could see ahead of him the cloud that the met officer had prophesised back at Watton and, realising it offered them their only chance of survival, he headed directly for it, engines screaming. Still under attack and taking hits, the Blenheim made it and was soon swallowed up by the marvellously comforting watery mass. Crossing over the east coast, Lart remained uncertain as to exactly what damage the aircraft had sustained in the prolonged combat. Alerting the airfield, Lart lined up for his landing and gingerly lowered it through the air. No sooner had the wheels kissed the ground than the undercarriage collapsed, leaving the Blenheim to toboggan across the airfield until it came to a grinding halt. Miraculously, the crew's good fortune held and the men scrambled out of the wreckage, very shaken and bruised but otherwise unhurt.

A half dozen more Blenheims from 110 Squadron were on operations that night, intent upon causing further disruptions to the German-occupied French airfields. Four out of six claimed successful attacks. Four Fairey Battles from 142 Squadron, having been withdrawn from offensive daylight operations, were pressed back into service by night to add to the effort to dislocate the German air assault on Britain. Their target was the airfield at Evere but only one returned to RAF Binbrook to report a successful attack. Two more were lost: L5584 piloted by Plt Off M.J.A. Kirdy was lost without trace, while the crew of L5502 under the command of Flt Lt R.H. Edwards was taken prisoner. For Robert Howard Edwards, who rejoiced in the nickname 'Pissy', it was the beginning of a courageous but ultimately fatal period as an unwilling captive. In early March 1941, he was part of a group being transferred from Barth to Fort 15 Thorn by train. As night fell, the alert guards went through the carriages with rifles and bayonets at the ready to demand the prisoners' boots, locking the doors securely behind them. Nevertheless, Edwards, along with Flt Lt R.A.G. 'Nellie' Ellen and Lt J.F.H. Surtees of the Rifle Brigade, managed to break out unseen and hurl themselves out of the moving train. Edwards went first and cracked his head hard on the opposite rail, knocking himself out cold. When he came to about an hour later, it became clear to him, even in his befuddled state, that there was no way he could continue his escape. He staggered to his feet and set off across the deserted countryside in search of help. At the point of collapse, he spotted a house and knocked at the door. He was lucky in his choice for he was taken inside and had his wounds dressed before the police came to take him away. Neither of his companions made it home either, though Ellen managed to avoid recapture for nine days, during which time he had covered more than 200km on foot in a second pair of boots.

Edwards was not daunted by his experience and in May was involved in another calculatedly risky escape attempt. His plan was, like many good ones, simple; to walk out of the front gates with five other prisoners claiming that they had been ordered to report to the Kommandantur. With all the preparations completed, on Wednesday 28 May the six men marched to the main gate where Capt. Earle Edwards of the Royal West Kents explained the situation in perfect German to the guards on duty. So persuasive was he and so disinterestedly nonchalant were the others that the ruse worked and they were let through. Splitting into smaller groups, the men made their way through the German camp and then out altogether into the countryside beyond. Edward, in the company of two others, marched steadily south throughout the evening and night before taking shelter in a remote barn as day broke. Unluckily, their entry must have been noticed, for a short while later a number of armed policemen surrounded the barn and called for them to come out. There was little that could be done so they did what they were told with as much good grace as they could muster. Transferred to another camp near Poznan, Edwards remained a difficult prisoner and determined to escape. On 26 September 1942, he was shot dead during another attempt.

The bombers of 3 and 4 Groups were out that night, ranging over the German heartland to continue the degradation of the German capacity to wage war. No. 78 Squadron, to name but one, sent out fourteen Whitleys to attack the Dornier factory at Wismar, which turned out Do 17s, then deployed over Britain on a daily basis. The crews reported that enemy aircraft were dropping flares high in the sky in an attempt to illuminate the bombers on the run-up to the target. Fg Off Eno failed to locate the factory in spite of spending a good deal of time searching but came across an airfield, perhaps Travemunde, shortly after 01.00 hours and immediately altered course to begin his bombing run. Passing over the airfield at 10,000ft the lone Whitley ran into extensive and accurate flak, supported by a number of searchlights. Nevertheless, Eno held his course and bombs were observed to burst across the airfield, flarepath and hangars, lights from which were clearly visible. It crossed the airmen's minds that it might be a decoy, so neat did it appear, and Eno turned the lumbering bomber around to take another look in spite of the defensive fire. An unidentified twin-engine aircraft was spotted clearly coming in low to land in spite of the attack and this put paid to any doubts so Eno lost no time swinging the Whitley away and into the safety of the darkness, settling down for the long journey home. They were not out of danger yet and at 04.15 as they crossed the enemy coast in a brightening sky, the vigilant rear gunner reported five single-engine fighters, silhouetted against the dawn, flying towards them in formation on an early patrol. Set against the darker sky of the west, the fighters did not spot the bomber and continued on their flight, unaware of the opportunity they had missed. Eno and his crew were more than grateful that they had and made it back safely.

Danger and injury could come in many different and unexpected forms. Plt Off Andy Dunn was in 77 Squadron's N1390 that night, also bound for Wismar. He and his crew also had experienced difficulty in locating the Dornier factory, though they were confident they were in the close vicinity. Dunn ordered his wireless operator Sgt Bain to make his way along the fuselage to the flare chute and release a number of flares. The light from the first of these revealed they were indeed in the right place and Dunn immediately began his bombing run, with the target now positively identified. At this critical point one of the flares that Bain had just released exploded prematurely, temporarily blinding him and wounding him in the leg. The bombs were dropped as planned but it took several anxious minutes to establish what had happened and assess what damage had been caused to the bomber so far from home. Bain was made as comfortable as possible but still had to endure another four hours in the air before the Whitley made it back to Driffield, where he was immediately taken by ambulance for treatment.

The Wellingtons were hitting the oil targets again and 37 Squadron's efforts, in common with most other squadrons, were divided between the refineries in Hamburg, Kamen and Mors. The crews encountered what the squadron log recorded as 'extremely bad weather conditions, with heavy cloud and severe icing'. A combination of ten-tenths cloud and general murk made it virtually impossible to locate the targets. One aircraft, that of Sgt Greenslade, succeeded in attacking the primary target, managing to identify the synthetic oil plant at Kamen by means of the shape of the forests in the local area. The attack was made from 8,000ft and the bomb bursts were observed around the buildings and several explosions of considerable force followed. Plt Off Fletcher returned home with his load intact but seven other crews managed to locate an alternative or last resort target. Plt Off Watt, for example, carried out a high-level attack upon an airfield about 25 miles north-east of Hamm. The airfield was operating normally at the time and was fully illuminated. Indeed, the stick of bombs, which fell across the flarepath, certainly gave the unsuspecting pilot of an aircraft seen coming into land an almighty shock, if nothing else. Two more crews, captained by Fg Off Warner and Flt Lt Mitchell, carried out attacks on Oldenburgh airfield, and Fg Off Griffin another north-west of Bad Zwischenarn. However, the results were uncertain and, perhaps, the experiences of Fg Off Lemon sum up the frustrations of the Wellington crews that night. Unable to locate the oil plant at Mors in spite of several circuits of the area, he, 'carried out a high level attack from 7,000ft on what appeared to be a factory on the banks of the Rhine, about 10 miles north of Mors'. Scant reward for prolonged exposure to the lethal concoction of flak, fighters, ice and storms.

Indeed, summer it may have been but the weather continued to be contrary and severely hampered the Command's operations, particularly at night. Monday 29 July was a case in point. The morning was a glorious one, warm with sparkling blue sky, ideal for a family picnic. It also meant that there would be another sortie for the hard-pressed Blenheim crews, tasked to keep up the pressure on the invasion ports and coastal airfields; once again, it promised to be too pleasant a day to give the crews any realistic chance of survival in the clear, enemy-controlled sky. No. 2 Group gave orders for a total of fourteen Blenheims to take part in operations and at Watton the well-oiled wheels were set in motion to prepare the light bombers for action. No. 82 Squadron had fared no better or worse than other Blenheim squadrons, losing four aircraft since the battle began on 10 July. An official report prepared by a psychiatrist found their morale particularly high, even in the face of such hazardous operations, and the prospect of being expected to continue to carry them out indefinitely and, quite possibly, ad finem.

The sky remained stubbornly clear and blue but the crews nonetheless made their preparations and climbed aboard their bombed-up Blenheims, took off and headed east over enemy territory in penny packets. Eight of the crews looked around at the vast, clear heavens and, with a mixture of profound relief and frustration, turned around but the remainder decided that having got this far unhindered, they would press on. Flt Lt Bill Keighley was among this number, flying as one of a pair of 82 Squadron aircraft set to attack Hamburg docks. As the pair made their final approach, the pair split up, with Keighley opting to go in second. He watched with a fixed fascination as the flak exploded all around the leading aircraft, which held rock steady until its bombs had been released and then sheered off sharply as several Me 109s appeared on the scene. He rapidly came to the conclusion that Hamburg was a very unhealthy place to spend a sunny afternoon and turned away towards the alternative target, Leeuwarden airfield just across the border in Holland. They swung away unseen and located the airfield without difficulty, making just a single pass at only 2,000ft before heading for the coast, low and fast. It looked as if Keighley's considered gamble had paid off until his gunner, Sgt K.D. MacPherson, suddenly reported a pair of Me 109s closing rapidly. Keighley scanned the sky ahead in search of cover and with relief noticed the first signs of the cloud promised by the met men at Watton. He turned towards it, pushing the Mercury 15 engines to their limit in order to win the race, the outcome of which would mean safety or destruction. The seconds crawled by as MacPherson kept up a running commentary on the pursuit, his agonised voice calling out, 'I'm hit! I cannot see!' before falling silent as heavy 20mm cannon fire ripped through the fuselage. Out-ranged, he had not been able to fire a shot. Essentially defenceless, Keighley pushed the nose down even further, jinking and weaving just above the waves in an attempt to thwart repeated attacks; he barely had time to notice that he was bleeding, hit by several splinters as the Blenheim was shredded around him. The beautiful cloud seemed to be as far away as ever but climbing towards it as late as possible the vulnerable Blenheim eventually won the race and hurtled into it. Keighley and his observer, Sgt J.W.H. Parsons, rejoiced in the protective invisibility it offered and, taking brief stock of the situation, dared to hope that they might make it across the North Sea after all. To their horror, within seconds they burst out the other side and back into a clear sky. However, it had been enough and there was no sign of their assailants. Their relief was destined to be all too brief as almost immediately the port propeller detached itself and spun earthwards. Keighley knew at once that the battered Blenheim would have only a few minutes flying time left at best and turned back towards the enemy coast, preferring to crash land on the nearby island of Texel than the chilly and equally hostile waters of the North Sea. As the outline of Texel took shape on the horizon, Parsons threw out all his charts and radio frequency lists before helping his pilot to find a suitable place to attempt a landing. They decided on a flat cornfield and with Parsons taking up his crash position, Keighley brought the wallowing aircraft down for a very creditable emergency landing. The pair scrambled out of the wreckage and after ascertaining the fate of MacPherson, still in his turret, and destroying anything of value they could, sat down to await the arrival of the Germans. When they did arrive, among them was Lt Bosch of Stab.11/JG27, one of the pilots responsible for bringing the Blenheim down. Following treatment for their injuries, Keighley and Parsons were transported to Spangenberg to begin five long years of captivity, more than enough time to mull over their courageous decision to press on to complete their ninth operation.

The conditions that Keighley had prayed for that afternoon played havoc with the operations scheduled for that night. Three Battles from 150 Squadron were dispatched to attack Waalhaven airfield but gave up in the face of the dreadful conditions. Fewer than half the twenty-six Wellingtons were able to locate and attack the various oil targets assigned to them and only just over half the sixteen Whitley crews claimed to have made successful attacks on the rail centres of Hamm and Reisholtz. The Hampden crews fared the best with fifteen out of twenty-two crews claiming successful attacks upon Frankfurt and, once again, the Dortmund–Ems canal. A dozen more were engaged in mining operations.

For Stan Harrison of 61 Squadron, this spot of gardening was his second operation, the first having been to the Ruhr a few days earlier. That afternoon he and his crew carried out the routine night flying test before the briefing, where they discovered they were to drop the highly effective 1,500lb mine in the approaches to the Atlantic port of Brest, already a busy naval base for its new owners. The Hampden would also carry the usual pair of 250lb HE bombs to deal with any targets of opportunity that might come up. After a meal, the crew donned their bulky flying gear and, in the lengthening shadows, made their way to dispersal to chat to the ground crew and deal with any last-minute matters. Shortly after take-off, navigator Sgt John Cooper called out the course for the Lizard in Cornwall and, cruising at 2,000ft, the coast flashed by as the bomber headed south-west. By the time it reached the target area, it was reassuringly dark and with all on board keeping a wary eye out for night fighters and flak ships, Harrison gently brought the aircraft down to 1,000ft. Cooper took a bearing from the lighthouse on the Isle de Ouessant visible to the starboard and gave his pilot the final course adjustments. The Hampden then entered its most vulnerable phase, flying straight and level at a steady 120mph in order to drop its mine. Although it was not always the case, everything went without a hitch and it was only a couple of hours before the four young men were climbing stiffly down from their aircraft back at Hemswell, buoyed by their safe return and the satisfaction of a job well done.

The contrary nature of a British summer reasserted itself overnight and day dawned over England dull and cloudy, with steady drizzle and spells of prolonged rain thrown in for good measure. For the Blenheim crews it was now a case of too much of a good thing. Nevertheless, two dozen crews were ordered to attack the airfields along their usual beat, with an aircraft target in Paderborn and the oil plant at Gelsenkirchen thrown in for good measure. Conditions were as poor as expected and hard evidence of the effectiveness of the attacks was impossible to obtain. There was, however, certainty about the loss of R3764 of 15 Squadron, which came down in the Scheldt on its return from Paderborn, leaving the pilot, Fg Off P.F. Eames, the only survivor.

If anything, the weather deteriorated as the day went on and, as the front was moving slowly westwards across Europe, it was decided early on that 4 Group would be stood down and that 3 Group would mount only limited harassing raids upon oil refineries at Hamburg and Mannheim, along with the marshalling yards at Monchengladbach. Half a dozen of the fourteen Wellingtons deployed came from 38 Squadron based at Marham. The heavily laden bombers laboured into the leaden sky shortly after 20.45 hours and were soon lost from the sight of the well-wishers below. It was unbroken cloud and driving rain all the way and with the cloud rising up to 20,000ft, there was no escape from the murk. Upon ETA at Hamburg, there was absolutely nothing to be seen and Germany's second city might have been anywhere. Three crews bowed to the inevitable and returned home with their bombs still on board and the other three released their bombs in the general area that the sporadic flak seemed to be coming from. There was no question of doing any more and at least the Germans below knew that the enemy had been overhead. The last of the crews returned a little after 02.30 hours, thankful to have located their airfield.

The weather front had cleared west by morning, leaving clear skies for the final day of July. Indeed, rather too clear for the twenty-eight Blenheim crews who sweltered in the strong sunlight pouring into the cockpits and turrets en route to the usual airfields and several industrial targets in northern Germany. Only eleven saw their missions through to the end, with one from 114 Squadron bound for Aalborg coming off second best in an encounter over Ijmuiden with a fighter of Feldwebel Helmut Karstadt of 11/JG54; unusually, all the crew survived to become prisoners.

A further six Blenheims were in action that night, attacking the busy airfield at Le Bourget and the same number of obsolescent Battles were committed to bombing the invasion ports. Airborne interceptions at night were considerably more miss than hit in 1940, with skill and luck playing an equal part in any encounter. In the case of Fg Off B.E. Moss's 12 Squadron Battle that night, the luck was all bad. Heading home to RAF Binbrook, his aircraft was located, misidentified and attacked by a Blenheim night fighter from 29 Squadron. Worse still, the attack was successful and the unsuspecting crew plunged into the sea off Skegness. Unusually, all three bodies were recovered and buried with full military honours in St Mary's Church, Binbrook, their unnecessary loss felt keenly by all at the station.

No. 3 Group decided to field a larger force of thirty, with eighteen of the Hampdens assigned German targets and the remainder to gardening runs, notionally the safer of the options. However, the capricious gods of war resolved to switch the odds with all the aircraft returning largely unscathed from Germany but two failing to return from the mining sorties. Hampden P4383 left RAF Lindholme at 21.13 to drop its single mine in the Baltic and succeeded in doing so, as at 04.10 hours a signal was picked up reporting it was approaching the English coast. For reasons unknown it did not reach it and no trace of the aircraft or crew was found until some six weeks later when the body of the pilot Plt Off B.S. Bell washed ashore on the Dutch coast. The loss of 44 Squadron's L4085 provides another poignant reminder of the dangers of flying at night in 1940. Like Plt Off Bell, Sgt E.D. Farmer and his crew had successfully dropped their mine and turned to cross the North Sea back to Waddington in Lincolnshire. For some reason the crew became disorientated and lost their way, crossing not only the North Sea but the whole of southern England too. As it became light, the weary and stressed young men realised their error and swung the Hampden round to the east. By 06.30 hours the fuel situation was critical and Farmer had no choice but to ditch in Cardigan Bay. The Aberystwyth lifeboat was launched fifty-six minutes later and recovered one body while another vessel, the *Emerald Star*, also rushed to the scene and picked up two men, the observer Sgt R.D. Hobbs and WopAg Sgt D. Seager, both wounded, and the body of the final member of the crew. In happier times, each of the three stories would have made headline news but at a time when horror and loss were everyday occurrences, of necessity they passed largely unnoticed amid the unavoidable flotsam of war.

As Reichsmarschall Goering chaired a meeting of his commanders at the Hague on 1 August 1940, which led to the Adlerangriff directive to step up the Luftwaffe's assault upon the defences of the south-eastern counties of England and London, Bomber Command went about its business as usual, attempting to hamper the enemy's effective use of the Channel airfields and ports and the supply chain upon which the invasion depended. Once again, 2 Group gave orders for a dozen Blenheims to carry our daylight attacks upon a number of coastal airfields and once again the bright and sunny conditions undermined the operation, with seven of the crews following orders to return in order to protect the precious aircraft and crew. Two pressed on to attack the airfield at Leeuwarden but were unable to give any firm evidence of the results. Another, which carried out a low-level attack upon Haamstede airfield, had a clear view of its bomb load bursting on and around a hangar and the destruction was supplemented by the gunners strafing several aircraft and vehicles dotted around the airfield. A fourth attacked a flak ship west of Den Helde without visible result. The fifth was engaged and shot down by Me 109s with the loss of all on board; it was 114 Squadron's second loss in as many days.

Conditions for the night bomber boys were better than they had been for the best part of a week. While 5 Group was stood down, a total of forty-three Wellingtons and Whitleys were on operations. In the clearer conditions nine of the 58 and 102 Squadron Whitleys were able to locate and bomb the oil plants at Hamburg and Reisholtz, causing some significant fires to break out; the remaining six at least managed to locate other industrial targets in the Ruhr area. The twenty-eight Wellingtons fared similarly, with just under half claiming to have hit oil or rail targets at Gelsenkirchen, Hamburg, Hamm and Kamen. Indeed, the crews reported the last of these especially hard hit, having watched some spectacular explosions and large fires emerging, a positive outcome visible for many miles on the long journey home. The remainder all located alternative targets and, since the force returned without loss and scattered thousands of propaganda leaflets to boot, Bomber Command regarded its night's work as being successful and effective. It was a result that was shared with royalty as HRH the Duke of Kent, himself a pilot, had spent the day at RAF Mildenhall and had followed the progress of 149 Squadron's raid on Kamen throughout.

As the young men of 2 Group awoke and saw the patchy cloud outside, they knew they would be on operations and were able to make an educated guess as to where and when. The Germans could too. Around 6 per cent of the 300 plus sorties against the airfields and ports undertaken by the Blenheim crews in the past month had resulted in a lost aircraft. Nevertheless, AVM J.M. Robb knew under the circumstances that no let-up was possible. No fewer than thirty-six Blenheims were tasked to attack the airfields, now more than ever a vital component in the enemy's invasion strategy. Ranging far and wide, two-thirds of the crews were successful in carrying out harassing attacks, in spite of the increasingly formidable defences brought in to counter them. As Plt Off Roberts of 15 Squadron made his bombing run in a shallow dive over Knocke airfield, he came under intense fire from no fewer than eight anti-aircraft guns, which he noted with satisfaction fell silent as the bombs fell around them. His colleague, Plt Off Dench, had a similar reception over Flushing and to make matters worse was then attacked by two roving Me 109s, which caused some damage and only gave up the chase several miles out to sea, with the hard-pressed Dench jinking left and right only feet above the waves of the North Sea.

The attacks that day also provided a very dangerous and steep learning curve for Sgt George Parr, an inexperienced observer with 18 Squadron on only his second operation. Bound for Wenzendorf airfield, south east of Hamburg, he prepared his route entirely over the sea, intending to follow the coast around until the Elbe estuary before turning inland and following the river to the target area. It seemed a great plan on paper but overlooked the fact that it would involve passing through an area heavily patrolled by fighters and defended by numerous flak units. All went well and as the pilot, Fg Off J.A. Douch, popped in and out of the convenient and predicted cloud cover, Parr was able to note several coastal features to confirm his position. Priding himself on his plan, he was as dismayed as Douch and WopAg Sgt R.J. Bassett when the cloud cover abruptly vanished, leaving the bomber in a clear blue sky, as conspicuous as an ink blot on a new sheet of paper, rapidly approaching the defences of Germany's second city. A hurried discussion concluded that they would obey orders, turn around and seek an alternative target, Leeuwarden airfield. Parr's confidence evaporated as quickly as the cloud as he worked rapidly to pinpoint his exact position and plot a new course, very much aware that his aircraft was very exposed, over enemy territory and travelling at almost 3 miles per minute. To his relief, the German seaplane base on Heligoland soon came into sight 2,000ft below and Parr was soon busy photographing it with his hand-held Leica issued to crews for just this sort of opportunity. Cruising around like this was highly dangerous but the crew's luck held and not a shot was fired. Buoyed by their success and the reappearance of the patchy cloud, the Blenheim then set course for Leeuwarden and found it without difficulty. The fledgling crew, keen to do a good job, then circled the busy airfield at about 1,000ft in an effort to locate the most useful target for their bombs at the same time as waving back to the local population clearly visible below. By the time they had selected the target and carefully off-loaded the bombs, which were fused with ten-second delays, a trio of Me 109s was seen in the process of taking off. Belatedly realising the danger, Douch lost height and headed flat out for the sea. In textbook fashion Bassett dutifully reported the progress of the fighters and sought permission to open fire as required. Inexperienced or not, his fire almost immediately destroyed the aircraft of Hauptmann von Ankum-Frank, commander of 5/JG27, and made the other two pilots hesitate and drop back. Douch made the most of this and bolted towards the nearest cloud, emerging from it into an empty sky. The three young men returned safely in jubilant mood but with a growing realisation that they had been both foolish and lucky in equal measure.

Intelligence officers received detailed reports of attacks on several airfields, with hits on hangars, buildings and parked aircraft in spite of heavy opposition. Nevertheless, only one Blenheim was lost, that of Sgt J. Davies of 18 Squadron, although another from 110 crashed on its return to Wattisham on account of battle damage. It had been one of 2 Group's most successful days of the battle so far.

The pressure was maintained that night with more than sixty bombers operational over Germany, although conditions were by then far from ideal. The majority of the twenty-two Wellingtons succeeded in locating their primary targets, the oil plants at Hamburg and the rail yards at Hamm. Large explosions and extensive fires were noted by all crews, as was also the case at the alternative target, the docks at Emden. The Hampden force was divided between the oil plants at Emmerich and Hanover and mining duties in the Lubeck and Helsinger areas. Stan Harrison was one of the pilots gardening. As everything had gone without a hitch on his previous gardening sortie, he and his crew embarked upon this one with confidence. However, just eighty minutes into his outbound flight, the port 1,000hp Bristol Pegasus engine began to overheat and run rough. Harrison weighed up the situation and decided that, so early in the sortie, discretion was the better part of valour and returned early to Hemswell without further incident. The problem was traced to a set of faulty plugs. They at least fared better than an 83 Squadron crew, which also returned early with mechanical problems and crashed 3 miles short of Scampton, killing two of the four men on board.

The Whitleys were also on oil targets. Larry Donnelly was a WopAg in a 10 Squadron Whitley on the Salzbergen raid that night. The new long-range W/T Direction Finding System he was using came in very handy as its fixes enabled his navigator to keep more or less on track, despite flying blind through cloud for three hours. For once, the forecast proved accurate and the sky cleared to reveal the fires, bomb bursts, flak and searchlights in the target area ahead. As the ponderous bomber began its long and painfully slow run-up, Donnelly made his way down the fuselage to the flare chute and got ready to drop the dazzling flares as and when instructed to do so. The Whitley droned on straight and level for what seemed an eternity as the flak thundered around the sky; immediately upon release of the bombs, Donnelly hurled a flare out to act as a marker for any later aircraft before heading back to his wireless equipment. Once more his fixes enabled the navigator to keep on track for home through the murk; it came as no surprise when Donnelly received a signal diverting the aircraft to Driffield, where conditions were deemed marginally better.

With the Battle gaining momentum and ferocity, there was to be no let up for either Fighter or Bomber Command. Plt Off Arthur Hughes, recently awarded a DFC for his sterling work with 18 Squadron, confided in his diary upon his return from a hectic raid upon a Dutch airfield on 2 August, 'The future stretches ahead in a dreary succession of nerve-wracking sorties from which there is no release save death or maiming.' While not everyone took such a grim view of things, protected to some extent by the twin shields of youth and squadron camaraderie, life for the 2 Group crews was often highly dangerous and brutally brief. At least Hughes was not required for operations the following day but a half a dozen crews from each of 107, 114 and 139 Squadrons were, the airfields being their targets once again. Although conditions over England were perfect with low cloud and good breaks, once out to sea the sky cleared and eleven crews decided to call it a day. The others accepted the increased risk and pressed on. At Schiphol, hits were observed on the hangars and at Abbeville, the home base of some of Germany's best-known fighter pilots, the Blenheims streaked across the airfield at hangar top height with machine guns blazing, shooting up, among other things, a small convoy of troops. It was a similar story at Haamstede, where the hangars were damaged. The roving Blenheims also made attacks upon a train making its way along the coast between Dunkirk and Gravelines, a troop concentration and collection of about twenty barges, probably being made ready for the invasion, at Bourburg. While the damage caused in each case was not severe, these daily raids did cause dislocation and disruption to the enemy and their very persistence rammed home the point that the next stage of the war would not be straightforward. This came at a price, and on this day it was paid by three men of 139 Squadron.

As 2 Group's crews were landing, the other Groups were busy making preparations for that night's attacks, which were focused upon the enemy's oil supply and naval assets. Nine of the eleven Whitleys from 77 and 78 Squadrons made it to the oil refineries at Monheim and Dusseldorf. Fg Off D.S. Robinson of 78 Squadron flew over the target at a steady 11,000ft, from where he could see the fires already burning amid the buildings. Although he reported a large number of active searchlights, he considered the flak unusually light. Nevertheless, there was enough to cause significant damage to his aircraft and it did not quite make it home, forced to land near Pickering, fortunately without serious injury to the crew.

A large force of twenty-eight Wellingtons was set for the oil refineries at Gelsenkirchen, Homburg and Bottrop. However, preparations at RAF Feltwell were interrupted by an accident that brought home to everybody concerned the potentially lethal work being carried out on a daily, routine basis. At 18.15 hours an armourer made an error while fitting a fuse wire to a No. 35 fuse in one of the photographic flashes on board Wellington L7781. With a blinding flash, it went off, setting fire to the aircraft in the process. All but ready for the operation, it had already been loaded with 600 gallons of fuel and five 500lb bombs, not to mention thousands of rounds of ammunition. The fire crews acted immediately but were unable to contain the flames. Four of the five bombs exploded with devastating effect, causing significant damage to two more Wellingtons in the vicinity. A third, a full 120 yards away, was hit by red-hot splinters and burning wreckage, which set the tail ablaze. Unaware that this Wellington had not yet been bombed up, the fire crews set about tackling the blaze and managed to prevent it from being entirely burnt out. Surprisingly, no serious injuries were recorded but everyone at the station had been able to experience for themselves the raw power and destructive effects of the ordnance they handled and deployed so regularly. In times of peace in the twenty-first century, the debris-strewn airfield would have been closed, evacuated and a major inquiry begun, but in the summer of 1940 the reaction was rather different; Nos 37 and 75 Squadrons went on operations as planned. The Ruhr was once again protected by its semi-permanent industrial smog, not to mention copious amounts of flak and intense searchlight activity, which combined to make precise identification of the target all but impossible. The nine crews did what they could and released their bombs into the target area from 10–11,000ft, igniting a number of fires. Others sought out the alternative targets, including Cologne where a particularly large explosion was observed, and at Schiphol airfield where conditions were good enough to enable the crews to pick out individual aircraft on the ground. However, on the other side of the sea, the cloud base over East Anglia had dropped to less than 300ft, forcing the signal to be sent diverting the weary crews to other airfields. Finding and landing at an unfamiliar airfield was not as easy a task as it sounds in the darkness of the early hours after the strain of a long operational flight. Fg Off Price of 37 Squadron, for example, was diverted to RAF Benson in Oxfordshire and came to grief when his Wellington collided with a badly positioned crane at the end of the flarepath that tore off the port mainplane. The poor conditions may also have contributed to the loss of a 75 Squadron aircraft that ploughed into a low ridge at 04.20 hours at Barton Mills in Suffolk, killing its pilot, Sqn Ldr W.I. Collett, and injuring the other men on board.

A dozen Hampdens were sent on mining operations off the Danish coast and to attack the seaplane bases at Hornum and Westerland. Several more were assigned the task of bombing the old viaduct over the Dortmund–Ems canal, now recognised as a key waterway in the build-up for the invasion. Once again, the combination of low cloud, haze and the robust defences effectively neutered the attack. There was, however, no lack of determination to succeed on the part of the crews. Sqn Ldr Kydd of 61 Squadron, for example, spent fifty minutes cruising over the target area, making five separate passes at just 200ft when he thought conditions had improved a little; he was still unable to pick out the viaduct, a tiny target in the best of conditions. The remainder of the Hampden force attacked the powerful *Gneisenau* berthed in Kiel and expected to play a major role in the forthcoming invasion.

At Scampton, commencing at 20.40 hours, 49 Squadron's Hampdens took off at five-minute intervals and began their individual journeys to the Baltic port. The crews encountered the same problems with poor visibility and strong opposition. Sgt Hills, a seasoned campaigner who had already earned a DFM, decided his only recourse was to make a low pass over the harbour and hope to pick out the enormous warship; he succeeded and released his bombs but, in the difficult circumstances, could not observe their effects. Plt Off Pinchbeck and Sgt Roberts did likewise and, ploughing through the light flak, saw their bombs explode upon the wharves and dockyard buildings. Sgt Shelton attacked a large warship that he identified as the *Scharnhorst* but again saw his bombs burst nearby on the quayside where, at least, fires were seen to break out. Plt Off Fox failed to positively identify anything over Kiel, even after spending a considerable time over the target trying to do so. He eventually turned away and attacked his last resort, Nordholz airfield. Upon his return he, like several others, was diverted to Harlaxton, where conditions were better; nevertheless, he crashed on landing, writing off the aircraft but, fortunately, not the crew. Sgt J. Unsworth had a similar experience, spending so much time over Germany that he ran out of fuel and had to ditch 10 miles short of Skegness. The four men were picked up quickly, little worse for their unpleasant experience. He later told the press:

We had been attacking Kiel and had spent some 90 minutes over our target, flying most of the time through a very hot barrage. The shells were bursting right above us and showered the aircraft like golden rain. After hitting our objective with our bombs, we started home but, unfortunately, we ran into thick fog, so we climbed above the clouds. Just after dawn broke we came below the clouds again to find we were still over the sea. The petrol was almost exhausted and one engine petered out and then the other and there was nothing else for it but to alight on the water. We glided from about 3,500ft but with visibility patchy and extending sometimes to only about 50 yards, we realised we were likely to spend some time in the dinghy. When we were about 100ft up I saw a naval trawler and I came down about a mile from her. As we passed her we tried to indicate by pointing seawards that we were coming down and needed help. At first the crew thought we were giving a low flying exhibition and they were taken aback when we hit the water. Coming down was rather like hitting a concrete pavement and the impact knocked both engines off the machine. The aircraft went under the water but came up again within a second or two with the cockpit half full. The crew had been standing by and in a few moments, they had launched the dinghy and got on board it. I jumped into the sea and then, pushing the dinghy away from the aircraft, which threatened to sink at any moment, I swam behind it for a short distance and then the other fellows hauled me in. In a few minutes the trawler's lifeboat was heading towards us and soon we were on board the ship. The crew loaned us an assortment of clothes while ours were drying out against the funnel and I got the skipper's socks! Later we steamed over an enemy magnetic minefield. A Naval patrol vessel hailed our skipper and asked him if he realised he had been right over top of it. 'Of course I do but it doesn't bother us,' replied the skipper nonchalantly through his megaphone. We arrived back at base still wearing our motley selection of borrowed garments, part RAF, part naval, part civilian.

For all the positive tone of the published account, it is clear that Unsworth and his crew had been remarkably fortunate and their experience was the exception rather than the norm.

It had been a busy night and, like most others, was described to the public in a clipped Air Ministry communique via the BBC or newspapers. Whilst positive, such releases were transparent and reasonably accurate and were either reported in full or formed the basis of an account; *The Northern Echo*, based in Darlington, Co. Durham, told its readers:

> Some of the most important sources of Germany's synthetic oil supply were attacked on Saturday night by RAF Bomber Command. At Monheim part of the works was set on fire by previous raiders served to guide further raiders to the target. Over Bottrop other crews saw their bombs hit the oil plant. Since the first attack on German oil supplies, the Germans have been forced to strengthen their defences. On this night besides firing at the raiders, many fired at the parachute flares used for illumination. Docks at Kiel were located by other aircraft in spite of poor visibility. Several naval buildings were set on fire by the bombs.

The claims of success were not overly grand but it was heartening to learn that the people of Germany were getting a dose of their own medicine and coming under fire.

By contrast to the efforts of the previous day, Sunday 4 August was as near to a day of rest as Bomber Command had during the Battle. The dull and cloudy conditions prevalent over much of the country was known to extend to much of northern Europe and persuaded AVM Robb to give his hard-pressed 2 Group crews a day off operations. Conditions did not improve significantly as the day wore on and only 4 Group was detailed to carry out attacks over Germany that night. Eleven aircraft, drawn mainly from 58 Squadron, ploughed eastwards from their Yorkshire bases through filthy, murk-laden skies towards the oil refineries at Sterkrade and Emmerich. Bomb loads were dropped, fires raised and vivid explosions observed before the Whitleys turned for home; indeed, the fires were reported as still being visible for 75 miles. One Whitley that failed to locate the refineries attacked an airfield at Krefeld with notable success, its bombs setting on fire several clearly visible hangars and aircraft. Another alert crew spotted an Me 110 creeping into position for an attack just off the Dutch coast but it sheered away as soon as the rear gunner opened fire. All the aircraft returned safely.

The following dawn ushered in a glorious summer's day and it was immediately obvious that 2 Group's cloud-hopping daylight raids would be out of the question, although several aircraft were made ready in case any opportunity arose. As it turned, out a couple of aircraft were put up on the off chance but soon called it a day as the clear sky stretched for miles beyond British shores. There was no reason, however, why the night-time operations should not go ahead and no fewer than eighty-five crews read their names on the ops board that afternoon. The Hampdens continued their association with naval targets, this time primarily the fully-fledged battleships *Bismarck* and *Tirpitz*, which were still being worked upon in Hamburg and Wilhelmshaven, respectively. Unaware of exactly how far from completion and operational use these mammoth vessels were, it was imperative for Bomber Command to cause whatever damage and delay it could. The shipbuilding yards at Bremen were also on the list of targets assigned to the seventeen crews. Fortunately, the coastal locations made the target areas relatively easy to find but amidst the searchlight beams, flak bursts and industrial haze, it was all but impossible to pick out the precise targets; all the crews could do was to release their loads in line with their best estimations. Unsurprisingly, beyond noting the explosions and consequent fires, no definitive analysis of their efforts could be made. One Hampden did not get any further than the North Sea and had only just attained operational height when the intercom packed up. The 20-year-old pilot, Stan Harrison, was faced with an agonising decision. While he was aware that in such circumstances, which were not at all uncommon, he had the authority to abort the sortie and not risk a vulnerable and valuable aircraft and crew, he was also aware that his previous sortie had also been a 'returned early' when his port engine overheated. As a young and inexperienced pilot, he also knew he was still very much under his commander's close scrutiny. He was duty-bound to carry out his orders wherever possible, but was also responsible for the safety of his crew and aircraft. The cramped cockpit of a noisy Hampden bomber flying in darkness towards enemy-held territory at a rate of 3 miles a minute is probably not the best place for calm, rational thought. Harrison made up his mind to put his personal reputation at risk rather than the lives of the men he led and ordered the navigator to give him a course for home. In the event, as the temperamental system remained as dead as a dodo, his decision was never questioned. However, the episode stuck with him for years and vividly demonstrates the severe pressures and strains, beyond those imposed by the enemy, bearing down upon the young men in the course of the execution of their duties.

Another 61 Squadron crew encountered very different pressures that night. One of a dozen Hampdens sent to mine the waters around the Elbe estuary, codenamed Eglantine, Plt Off De Mestre had successfully located his dropping zone and released his mine when a single-engine fighter was spotted closing rapidly. Simultaneously it opened fire and the Hampden shuddered as the heavy-calibre shells found their target. A second or two later, the bomber's machine guns let fly in reply and almost instantly the fighter was seen to pull up sharply and then plunge earthwards out of sight. It was all over in a matter of seconds and later the crew was allowed a 'possible' claim. At that moment the four young men had other things on their mind as they assessed the damage the unexpected and fleeting combat had caused. The bomber appeared to fly well enough but it was impossible to know precisely what had been hit. Once back over the English coast, De Mestre decided that with fuel short after almost eight hours in the air and unquantifiable damage, he would put the aircraft back on terra firma as soon as possible. He forced landed at Boston at 04.45 hours, writing off the Hampden but not the crew.

The Whitley force was split between attacking the oil plant at Sterkrade and the Dornier aircraft factory at Wismar. Larry Donnelly was on board one of the seven 10 Squadron aircraft assigned to the Dornier works.

Given that it had been such a beautiful day, he was surprised to find the conditions over the North Sea relatively poor and deteriorating steadily, so much so that it was hard for the observer Sgt Shaw to keep on track. Carefully skirting the heavily defended port of Kiel, the Whitley chugged along the coast and on to Wismar. There was no mistaking the target area as the searchlights and flak lit up the sky and, more positively, so did the fires raging and spreading on the ground below. As the bomber settled into its long and steady run in, Donnelly made his way to the flare chute where he had gathered a store of small incendiary bombs, his personal contribution to Hitler's demise. Cut off from the rest of the world in the coffin-like fuselage, he could hear and feel the crump of the shells exploding outside, even above the roar of the 1,145hp Merlin X engines. As soon as he felt the main bomb load go, he began to add the incendiaries to mix. Fg Off M.T.P. Henry immediately pushed the aircraft's nose down to gain some speed and set course for home, leaving behind more fires burning than he had found; the aircraft landed safely at Leeming at 04.25. As the weary young men climbed down from the Whitley and stretched their aching limbs, they were astonished to find the high level of flak damage in the main fuselage area, all around Donnelly's temporary position around the flare chute. Suddenly the WopAg felt even weaker at the knees.

Plt Off Gunn of 58 Squadron also had a generous slice of good luck on his return from Sterkrade when he was picked up by a roving Me 110 over the Dutch coast. A deadly game of cat and mouse ensued with the one not being able to break away and the other not being able to get into a favourable position to open fire. The duel lasted for some time and the English coast was in sight before the German pilot gave up the chase, much to the relief of the exhausted Whitley crew.

The Wellingtons formed the largest group operating that night, with thirty-five being assigned a number of separate targets, bombing concentration still being a thing of the future. Twenty-three crews succeeded in locating and attacking their primary or secondary targets, igniting several large fires as the bombs burst in and around the dock area of Hamburg and

Kiel, the oil storage tanks at Nordenham and the oil plant near Hamm. In addition, Cloppenburg and Schiphol airfields and the seaplane base at Borkum came under attack. As so often, the devilish concoction of cloud and active defences made clear assessment of the bombing impossible. The signs from below gave grounds for optimism and what was judged a good night's work was topped off by a clean slate in terms of losses.

The weather front that had caused the problems had covered almost all of Britain by morning, severely curtailing both RAF and Luftwaffe operations. In spite of the low clouds and squally showers, a magnificently British meteorological turnaround from the previous day, 2 Group was determined to mount a series of raids and forty-one Blenheims were put into the air, although all but two failed to locate anything at all and had to put all their effort into finding their way home through the clag. Of the other two, one returned early with a defective engine and the other stumbled across an airfield, identified as Le Bourget, and released its bombs straightaway, though to unknown effect. The atrocious conditions curtailed the night's operations too as 4 Group had to be stood down and 3 Group restricted its effort to a dozen aircraft laying mines, a task that did not require complete visual identification of the target area. One Hampden, piloted by the experienced Sgt R.J. Jennings DFM, failed to return, lost without trace somewhere off the Danish coast. A number of Wellingtons also managed to get into the air, directed towards oil and railway targets across Germany. HRH the Duchess of Gloucester, accompanied by Wing Officer Wynne-Eaton, had watched the preparations for the raid at RAF Feltwell, touring all sections of the station and spending time with a number of flying and ground personnel in both the dining hall and the officers' mess. To complete the red-letter day, a film crew was also on hand to capture both the event and the work of the station. In spite of these welcome distractions, the business of war had to carry on and that evening the locals heard the roar of engines heading east. The weather en route was better than expected but the patchy cloud and persistent ground haze did little to aid target identification, exacerbated as usual by the glare of numerous searchlights and flak bursts. Only a handful of crews managed to attack the primary targets successfully; one was Plt Off Hough from 37 Squadron. Approaching the target at high level, his pass happened to coincide with a gap in the cloud enabling him to not only identify the target but to distinguish it from two nearby adjacent decoy sites. His crew observed the bombs bursting and noted four orange–red and one white explosion and several large fires as a result. Five other crews sought out their secondary targets, the crucial enemy airfields. Plt Off Fletcher dropped his load on a still illuminated Soesterberg airfield and from 9,000ft the bombs were seen to burst across the northern edge of the airfield, although the incendiaries fell neatly across the middle; so complete was the surprise that aircraft were seen landing at the time. At Texel Sgt Greenslade's bombs fell across the busy airfield and Plt Off Chilton's bombs were seen to explode within the perimeter of Ronninghard airfield but some 200 yards off the illuminated flarepath. The gunners in this instance were more on the ball and put up an intense flak barrage, supported well by searchlights, which made life very uncomfortable for the British crew. Two other 37 Squadron crews failed to locate a suitable target and returned home fully loaded. Sgt Culverwell's crew was the first home at 01.15 hours, after being compelled to return early having had a complete hydraulic failure shortly after crossing the Dutch coast. Unsure as to whether his landing gear would function properly, Culverwell was instructed to jettison his bombs in the North Sea and all preparations were made at Feltwell for an emergency landing. As it turned out, the landing was incident free.

The events of the night of 6/7 August sum up the bomber campaign quite well. In spite of the dogged determination and courage of the crews, only 20 per cent of them succeeded in locating their primary targets; very nearly the same percentage failed to locate any suitable target whatsoever. The remainder attacked their secondary targets or whatever else suitable they could find. Damage and dislocation were being achieved on a nightly basis but exactly how much remained uncertain, despite of the best efforts of the crews to see what was going on below. No. 38 Squadron for this night records, for example, that newly introduced and more powerful photo-flashes, intended to facilitate the gathering of hard evidence, 'have so far been unsuccessful, chiefly owing to the mass of searchlights over the target areas, obscuring the objectives and blinding the bomb aimers'. Clearly, Bomber Command still had a way to go to become the fully effective fighting force it was intended to be. In the meantime, the crews could only continue to do the best they could with what was available to them.

The capricious weather remained the chief hindrance to operational success as the events of Wednesday 7 August amply illustrate. Leaden skies, grey with thick unbroken rain cloud, greeted the crews of 2 Group as they woke up and began the usual round of pre-flight preparations. Almost thirty Blenheims were to be readied for attacks upon the standard mix of airfields and oil plants in northern Europe and Germany. Weather reconnaissance Blenheims were launched in the hope of finding better conditions further east but their search was in vain; nevertheless, the other sorties went ahead as planned and all but two crews were forced to abort on account of the filthy conditions. One crew managed to fly beneath the cloud, at great risk, to locate and attack the airfield at Querqueville and another from 82 Squadron had a particularly successful sortie that went some way to counter the disappointment of the others. Plt Off Donald Wellings, with Sgts D. McFarlane and P. Eames, ploughed on through the murk towards the busy airfield at Haamstede. Their persistence paid off and, by good luck or good management, the airfield came into view on cue, complete with a long row of Me 109s belonging to 4/JG54, positioned as if for inspection. The light bomber went straight into the attack, catching those below on the hop, hurtling down the line of parked fighters, releasing its bombs as it went, destroying one aircraft after another. Within a minute it was all over and the jubilant crew were streaking low for home, before climbing hard for the protection of the cloud.

Severe damage was caused to another airfield, this time on the other side of the North Sea. Stan Harrison and his crew at Hemswell had received orders that they were down to do a spot of 'gardening' in their Hampden that night and they were on their way from the crew room to their aircraft when they were stopped in their tracks by an enormous explosion just 100 yards away. They instinctively flung themselves to the ground, peeping up expecting to see German intruders roaring overhead and tensing themselves for further blasts. When none came, they got to their feet and looked around for clues as to the cause of the leaping flames and billowing, thick black smoke. It turned out that a train of bomb trolleys loaded with mines had been making its way across the airfield when a jolt accidentally detonated one of them, setting off a destructive chain reaction. There was not much left of the tractors, the trolleys, nor the eight armourers hitching a lift on them. The medical orderlies were still searching for and gathering up the remnants of their shattered bodies as a subdued and shocked Harrison and his crew made their way to their bomber a little later. Despite this, all aircraft departed as scheduled and on time.

Several Hampdens were under orders to bomb the *Gneisenau* but, as the 44 Squadron log put it, 'it was not identified' amid the thick, low cloud that smothered the port. Nevertheless, most crews opted to drop their loads in the general area of the docks, working on the assumption that any damage caused to these crucial facilities was a good thing. The even larger *Bismarck* in Hamburg was amongst the primary targets assigned to some Wellington squadrons, alongside the regular transportation targets of Hamm and Soest. The conditions were no better over any of the targets and only seven of the twenty raiders attacked their primary targets, although to what effect was anybody's guess. Six returned with their load intact. Plt Off Clark of 37 Squadron would have been the seventh but he stumbled across an illuminated airfield at Soesterburg and released three bombs from 12,000ft. As the ground lights were switched off by an alert German on duty as the bomber was heard making its run, there was no way of determining what damage was caused as a result. Three aircraft that did complete the primary tasks assigned to them were those detailed to set the forests alight in so called 'Razzle' raids by the use of incendiaries, thereby spreading widespread panic, causing the redeployment of fire-fighting resources and denying the German war economy valuable timber. The sceptical crews reported that fires had indeed been raised but, as 37 Squadron's log said, 'none of these were of a really serious nature.' All in all, it had not been a conspicuously successful night, mitigated somewhat by the welcome absence of British losses.

Although the effectiveness of the operations was reviewed and plans for increasing it were drawn up on an almost daily basis by those in command, there was little time to dwell on anything at all at front-line squadron level. Not long after the early dawn revealed another typical summer's day of patchy cloud, showers and sunny spells, the staff at 2 Group was hard at work putting the finishing touches to their plans to keep the pressure on their increasingly active German opponents. Another squadron, 105, was added to the order of battle on this day. Flying the obsolescent Battles as part of the AASF, it had suffered grievous losses in the Battle of France and had been withdrawn and re-equipped with Blenheim IVs. Now ready to re-join the fray, it was to provide three of the fifteen Blenheims designated to carry out harassing attacks on the airfields. Assigned the regular runs to Haamstede in Holland and Knocke in Belgium, the CO, Wg Cdr John Hawtry, proudly led Fg Off Carter and Sgt Costello-Brown into the East Anglian sky to begin a new chapter in the squadron's history. Unfortunately, it was not the momentous occasion he had hoped for as a large break in the cloud robbed the trio of cover and necessitated an early return to RAF Watton. Indeed, all but two of the other crews followed suit; they pressed on to attack Schiphol and Valkenburg airfields but without any obvious signs of success. One aircraft from 18 Squadron failed to return, with the body of Sgt F.F. Parvin later being washed up on a Dutch beach. Unusually, a half a dozen Blenheims joined their Coastal Command colleagues in carrying out a series of sweeps over the northern sector of the North Sea but nothing of any consequence was sighted.

Throughout the day 3 Group was gearing up for its night operations, making ready twenty-eight Wellingtons and eighteen Hampdens to attack several German targets. The Hampdens were assigned to bomb a fuel depot in Frankfurt and an oil target in Ludwigshafen. As fate would have it, the crews were severely hampered by the fiendish combination of cloud, ground haze and glare, which rendered accurate identification and bombing all but impossible. Though several crews felt they had hit the target, most turned away in search of secondary targets and whatever else they could find. No definite results were recorded by any crew. However, Hampden L4053 from 83 Squadron was lost, landing near Mannheim and leaving the crew injured but alive.

The Wellingtons fared a little better but ten crews, more than a third of those taking part, failed to locate a suitable target and returned with their bomb loads intact. Several more made attacks on the secondary target airfields, though without any visible results. The same situation prevailed over Bremen and Wilhelmshaven docks and only in a handful of cases was anything of substance able to be noted. One crew attempting to attack the *Bismarck* in Hamburg dockyards at least saw a particularly large and vivid explosion occur beneath them. Sgt Ralph Edwards of 115 Squadron was on only his second operation as a second pilot, sitting alongside Sgt Neil Cook, already a veteran of some twenty-five operations. Cook had taken off from RAF Marham in Norfolk, set course and then wandered off down the fuselage leaving Edwards at the controls. Cruising serenely over the North Sea, Edwards maintained a steady 4,000ft and made any minor adjustments given to him by the observer, Sgt Alan Overall. As the Frisian Islands slid by to the starboard on time, Edwards began to pat himself on the back for a job well done. Overall made his way forward again to pass on a new course for Hamburg and shortly thereafter about 40 miles ahead the searchlights and flak bursts and the dull red glow of the fires came into view. Still Edwards confidently held course but began to wonder when Cook would return to the pilot's seat. Within a few minutes he did, gesticulating forwards in an agitated fashion. Initially, Edwards thought he was indicating the target by now coming up fast and complimenting him on his undoubted flying skill but it gradually became clear he was pointing at the altimeter, which still showed a steady 4,000ft, a suicidal height at which to approach the defences of Germany's second city. Cook half dragged him out of the seat and urgently opened up the engines and swung away from the target ahead in a wide, climbing turn. It took a further twenty minutes to drag the heavily laden Wellington to a more respectable 10,000ft before, with fuel running low, it altered course to pass through the defences and over the docks. A short while later, the bomber was flying steadily through the undisturbed vastness of the night sky with a somewhat shaken and chastened Edwards back at the controls. Another pilot thought his bombs had triggered a series of brilliant explosions in a line as they hit an ammunition train near Soest, while three crews over Hamm and Cologne at least had the satisfaction of reporting seeing a string of explosions and fires taking hold and spreading on account of their bombs. Hard evidence of substantial damage there was not, and the only certainty the weary crews could offer their debriefing officers on their return was that thousands of propaganda leaflets had been scattered all over Germany; their effectiveness too was much in doubt. Indeed, as what is now considered the first phase of the Battle drew to a close, all that Bomber Command had boldly and doggedly attempted remained hard to quantify in terms of effects but, as there was no other offensive alternative, the effort had to be made. In the desperate circumstances of the day, anything had to be worth a try.

A 20mm flak unit at Beauvais airfield in the summer of 1940. Such weapons were highly effective against low-level attacks.

The confined space of a Hampden cockpit.

A heavy flak battery in action. The Germans were forced to deploy more and more such units to counter the increasingly frequent and destructive incursions made by Bomber Command.

Hampden P1333 of 49 Squadron at Scampton, summer 1940.

Whitley T4134 of 58 Squadron, lost on a raid on Bremen in the early hours of 11 September 1940. Unusually, Plt Off J.E. Thompson and his crew all survived to become POWs.

The Bristol Blenheim was obsolescent by mid 1940 but played a crucial role in harassing the ports, airfields and coastal shipping by day and night.

This 61 Squadron Hampden was one of three lost on mine-laying sorties on 21 July 1940.

The remains of a 40 Squadron Blenheim lost in an attack on Eelde airfield in the early hours of 26 July 1940. All three men lived to tell the tale.

Chapter 3

Phase Two:
9 August to 23 August

As the Luftwaffe was gearing up in earnest for its all-out assault on Britain, the light bombers of the RAF once again set out to thwart the raiders. No. 2 Group despatched fifteen unescorted and vulnerable Blenheims to attack the airfields of northern France, Holland and Belgium. In the bright and clear conditions all but two followed orders and turned for home whilst still over the sea. Those that pressed on were heading due south where a few scattered clouds afforded at least the illusion of protection from the active and numerous fighters stationed all across the area. One managed to reach the recently established flying boat base at Brest from where the aircraft ranged far out into the Atlantic, tracking, reporting upon and harassing the Merchant Navy ships bringing their vital cargoes to beleaguered Britain. Taking the defences by surprise, the Blenheim dropped its load in a single, long stick that the crew observed falling amongst the dozen or so flying boats at anchor and upon the hangars at the water's edge. Thoroughly satisfied with the results of their handiwork, they swept out to sea and headed for home, low and fast. The other one came in low over the occupied island of Guernsey, bound for its small airfield. The crew saw it was packed with aircraft of all types, including Me 109s and, more menacing, transport aircraft, perhaps as many as fifty aircraft in total. As they approached, the light flak batteries around the airfield opened up, hurling shell after shell at the lone intruder. Unequal battle joined, the Blenheim's gunner let fly in all directions as the aircraft swept low over the packed airfield, scattering bombs in its wake. Within seconds, it was streaking over the sea at full throttle, heading for home. Although little more than a fleabite to the armed leviathan bent on subduing Britain, it at least reminded the supremely confident Germans that they still had a fight on their hands.

That night's operations were on a slightly reduced scale with just thirty-eight aircraft scheduled to attack targets in Germany. Fourteen of 4 Group's Whitleys took off from their Yorkshire airfields and, with an hour's daylight left and the sun setting behind them, headed east towards the aluminium factory in Ludwigshafen. Nine of them succeeded in locating and identifying the target and as they turned for home they left several fires raging. Andy Dunn of B Flight in 77 Squadron was among the crews that did not bomb that night. At some point over Germany – the crew did not know exactly where – the Whitley blundered into heavily defended airspace and the first they knew about it was when several powerful searchlights pierced the darkness and locked on to the lone bomber; the first flak bursts were only seconds behind. For too long for comfort, Dunn hurled the cumbersome aircraft around the sky, trying to break free, blasted and buffeted all the while by the flak, apparently being passed from one battery to another like some unwanted toy at a children's party. The Whitley bore a charmed life as nothing vital was hit as hole after hole was punched through the fuselage by a series of near misses. An eternity later, the bomber flew into a welcome sea of darkness, enabling Dunn and his stunned crew to take stock of the situation. In a damaged aircraft, at some unspecified position over the German heartland and increasingly short of fuel, their lot was not a happy one. However, fortune remained on their side and, as they headed west, they picked up sufficient landmarks to put together a course and made it home and on to the ground without further incident. Whitley KN-U was not a pretty sight the next morning. Of the other 4 Group aircraft not to attack Ludwigshafen, two hit Tirlemont airfield and a third an airfield north of Trier, all without any visible results.

Another aluminium works near Cologne was the primary target for another fourteen bombers, this time the Wellingtons of 3 Group. The half a dozen aircraft from 37 Squadron arrived a little late over the target area and, in spite of some ground haze, had no difficulty in identifying the works in the light of the fires already burning and an adjacent area of woodland picked out by the parachute flares. The attacks were carried out at 8,500–11,000ft and Fg Off Warner claimed direct hits resulting in three separate fires breaking out. Sgt Greenslade observed his load bursting on and around the target, once again igniting fires that were visible for a considerable distance. Plt Off Parsons' crew reported that the flaming framework of the gutted buildings were clearly discernible at the time of the attack. Plt Off Price's load overshot the target and exploded in the woodland area while Fg Off Lemon' failed to locate the target and after an intensive search attacked an unidentified but illuminated airfield from just 3,000ft; several others came under attack, including Venlo, Schiphol, Gilze-Rijen and Eindhoven, where the explosions triggered off a number of impressive fires. The marshalling yards at Hamm and Soest, already regulars on the ops boards, were also targeted, though without any particular effects being observed. The night's work appeared to have been a success and was topped off by the most welcome fact that there were no losses.

The 10th of August had been scheduled by Goring as Adlertag, Eagle Day, the beginning of the all-out assault on Britain. He had, of course, failed to take account of the British weather, which turned out to be very unsummery, with thick, low cloud and heavy rain being prevalent for much of the day. Frustratingly for the Luftwaffe but happily for the RAF, the sky just over the Channel was clear. Indeed, too clear for fourteen of the twenty-two Blenheims, which dutifully turned back as they crossed the enemy coast. One of those who pressed on regardless was Plt Off Murray of 105 Squadron, which had only just become operational. As the Squadron's first two operations had been scrubbed due to lack of cloud cover, Murray, with his observer, Sgt Chadwick, and WopAg, Sgt Cameron, resolved to be the first to chalk up an operational success. Flying at 1,000ft, the Blenheim crossed the Dutch coast and headed for Schiphol to the south of Amsterdam, ready to attack. The Germans appeared to have been caught unawares and the crew was able to drop a pair of 250lb bombs pretty well unmolested. The second run was very different as, fully alerted, the many anti-aircraft guns opened fire, pumping shell after shell into the path of the light bomber. Murray, however, held steady until the dozen 40lb bombs had been released over the airfield and only then did he begin to jink his aircraft out of harm's way. By then it resembled a colander, particularly around the tail unit, which had sustained serious damage. As the young men crossed the coast and sped out over the North Sea, it seemed a very long way back to RAF Watton; in the event, they landed safely but L9339 remained out of service for quite some time to come.

Murray and his crew were far luckier than that of Plt Off N.H.H. Smith of 82 Squadron, also based at Watton. Blenheim R3910 failed to return and the three men probably fell to the guns of Oblt Karl-Heinz Metz of 8/JG2, who claimed a Blenheim at 12.33 hours off Le Havre. Plt Off A.R. Storrow and his Wattisham-based 110 Squadron crew were also lost without trace that morning. It had been a significant price to pay for the attacks on the airfields at Le Bourg, Dinard, Caen, Cherbourg and Flushing, where one crew at least had the satisfaction of watching a Henschel 126 blown out of the sky by the airfield's own defences.

As the Blenheims touched down in the early afternoon, the preparations for that night's attacks were well under way at airfields across the eastern side of the country. At 3 Group, twenty Wellingtons were being made ready to bomb the docks at Hamburg and the large marshalling yards at Soest. Poor visibility hampered proceedings over the large port but several crews who did manage to locate the target area reported seeing their bombs bursting near and around the enormous SS *Bremen* and SS *Europa*, judged to be key naval assets in the forthcoming invasion. Only a couple of crews located Soest and they released their loads without visible results, the rest being reduced to searching for targets of opportunity. No. 38 Squadron's log for the night concludes rather dispiritedly, 'The last half dozen raids have been unsuccessful because of the bad weather encountered,' and added ominously, 'the searchlights and AA seem to have become fiercer.'

No. 5 Group were also operating that night with seventeen Hampdens bound for the docks at Duisburg and the oil plant at Homburg. Once again the poor weather caused problems, forcing several crews to turn to alternatives or targets of opportunity. Only at Krefeld was an outcome clearly discerned. A Hampden stumbled across an airfield that was still fully illuminated and busy with aircraft practising night flying; bombs were quickly released and were seen to land across the airfield, destroying at least one aircraft. Sadly, this was offset by the loss of a 144 Squadron Homburg-bound Hampden over Holland.

No. 4 Group's effort was led by 58 Squadron. The target was the oil refinery at Frankfurt am Main. The night got off to a poor start when Sgt Terraneau was compelled to return early when his W/T operator fell seriously ill while over the North Sea. His unannounced and unexpected return triggered off an Air Raid Warning Red Alert over Lincolnshire. Oblivious to all this, Terraneau landed at RAF Linton at 01.05 hours, having met no more serious opposition than a single searchlight being waved vaguely in his direction over Boston, which he conscientiously noted was poorly blacked out and easily identifiable. A similar fate befell Sgt Archer, an experienced pilot with a number of operations under his belt. Feeling unwell that evening, he had decided that he would be fine and took off as scheduled at 20.00 hours. Once airborne, his stomach decided otherwise and the second pilot, Plt Off Wilding, had to take over and returned to Linton, where a waiting ambulance rushed the unfortunate Archer off to the station sick quarters. Several of the crews that retained their good health were able to observe a number of significant explosions in the target area. It was not all smooth going, however, with WO Sutton, for example, happily following the river to the target from 9,000ft but deciding to drop sharply to 2,000ft in search of greater accuracy. It proved to be an impetuous and almost fatal move as much of the fabric was torn from the upper surface of both main planes, making the laden bomber all but impossible to control. Shrieking through the darkness, a frantic Sutton managed to arrest the headlong descent but by then had lost sight of the target. Not to be beaten, Sutton caught his breath and began to cruise around enemy territory, the crew scanning the ground through the gaps in the cloud for a suitable target. Heading generally east, they spotted a railway line somewhere in the area of Frankfurt and released their bombs towards it from 4,000ft and then continued slowly and gingerly on their way home.

For Plt Off Crooks that was where his problems began. Having bombed shortly before midnight, Crooks set course for home but soon discovered a major electrical fault that rendered all the lights on board and the wireless unserviceable. Running seriously short of fuel, the Whitley arrived unannounced over Hemswell and set about landing straightaway. Unable to judge his height accurately, Crooks landed heavily, causing the undercarriage to collapse and the bomber to grind to a halt across the flarepath amid a storm cloud of sparks and dirt. The emergency crew, caught unawares, hurtled across the airfield towards the bomber to find the shaken and bruised airmen sitting patiently a discreet distance from the shattered aircraft.

Once again day dawned dull and damp but this did not deter the Luftwaffe from mounting the largest raids of the battle so far. Substantial attacks were made on Portland, Dover and several convoys moving temptingly along the east coast towards the Thames estuary. To counter this tidal wave of hostile aircraft, Bomber Command dispatched seventeen Blenheims to cause damage and dislocation to a number of vital enemy airfields. Yet again, the sky over enemy-held territory, just the other side of the Channel, was crystal clear, making it too dangerous to press home the attacks. Seven returned home but the remainder pressed ahead regardless and the conditions at least made locating the airfields and observing the results easier than usual. Hits were claimed on the hangars and aircraft and one Blenheim surprised a pair of destroyers on patrol off the Dutch coast and somewhat audaciously went straight in, achieving near misses but nothing more substantial. One aircraft failed to return, that of the experienced and respected Sqn Ldr J.B. Fyfe DFC of 107 Squadron. An extant claim for a Blenheim over Dinard made by Leutnant Erick Bodendieck of 4/JG53 probably accounts for the loss of the aircraft and all on board.

That night no fewer than seventy Wellingtons, Hampdens and Whitleys took to the darkening sky bound for German war targets. Although the story penned by the Berlin correspondent of a Madrid newspaper that anti-aircraft fire had been heard over the German capital at 03.30 hours received widespread coverage and acclaim in a number of British newspapers, there were no bombers within miles of the city. Instead, a number of aircraft from all Groups were unleashing a new weapon of war upon specially selected targets. A few weeks before in June, the newly created Ministry of Economic Warfare had concluded, following a systematic analysis of the German economy, that certain key areas were especially vulnerable to attack. A predicted poor harvest and an apparent over-dependence upon timber led to calls for heavy incendiary attacks upon the rural economy. The result was known as Razzle. A wad of wet phosphorous gauze placed between two strips of celluloid self-ignited to produce a substantial 8in flame when the chemical dried out in the open air. Stored in airtight tins, with each aircraft being allotted a complement of around fifty in addition to the ordinary bomb load, it was a difficult and time-consuming task, particularly in the dark and cramped conditions of the fuselage, flying over enemy territory at night, to carefully open the tins and pour the soggy incendiary down the flare chute and on to the fields and forests below. The idea had more to recommend it to those behind a desk than those in the air.

Larry Donnelly of 10 Squadron was one of the WopAg guinea pigs that night. Having taken off from Leeming at 21.00 hours, the crew's first port of call was the extensive oil plant at Gelsenkirchen, by now a regular and well-defended target. Bracketed by searchlights and buffeted by several near misses, which caused some damage to the Whitley, the aircraft ploughed on and into the darkness over open countryside. As the sweating Donnelly in full kit beavered away in a confined, dark space, urged on by his impatient crewmates, it became clear that Razzling was not a swift process. Like several other men that night, he heaved a great sigh of relief as the contents of the forty-eighth and final tin slipped down the chute. After conscientiously making a final check with a shaded torch that he had not dropped any inside the aircraft by mistake, Donnelly wearily made his way back to his wireless and settled down for the long haul home. By 05.25 hours the wheels were just kissing the ground when the crew were startled by an urgent shout from George Dove in the rear turret that the fabric on the rear elevators was burning fiercely. Uncertain as to the cause and unwilling to waste precious time finding out, the crew were out of the bomber just as soon as the wheels stopped turning. The ground crews quickly brought the blaze under control and established the cause as several Razzles that had been blown by the slipstream into the elevator hinges, where they had proceeded to dry out and ignite. No fewer than five other aircraft on the squadron had suffered similar potentially lethal mishaps. No. 4 Group was lucky to lose just one Whitley, that of Sgt Kearney of 51 Squadron whose last radio contact after some eight and a half hours in the air was timed at 04.49; all the crew survived to become POWs.

The Wellingtons focused on the oil plants at Wanne-Eickel and Castrop-Rauxel and the railway centres of Hamm and Soest. Twenty of the crews, a far higher percentage than usual, managed to attack their primary targets and a significant number of explosions and fires were noted. The sole loss was P9244 E of 149 Squadron, which crashed into an unlit radio mast at 03.48 hours at Beck Row, only a few miles from its base at Mildenhall, killing all on board. The Hampdens too concentrated upon oil targets at

Wanne-Eickel and in Dortmund, as well as the railway yards at Dusseldorf. The *Daily Express* for 13 August led with the headline 'The Biggest Raids of All', referring to the Luftwaffe attacks upon Britain but, defiantly sub-headlined with 'And WE did this to THEM'. The article read:

> The crew of a RAF bomber which bombed a synthetic oil plant at Dortmund in the Ruhr during Sunday night reported that they saw and HEARD an explosion of exceptional violence. The attack took place in darkness and cloud but soon after midnight an early raider saw four of his bombs fall on the oil plant to be followed by a big flash. An hour later a plane took up the attack. After a salvo of its heavy bombs had struck the plant, there was a violent explosion and even though they were flying at several thousand feet, the crew could hear it above the roar of the engines. That was the high spot of a series of raids which cost us three planes.

One of them was over that city.

Just so that nothing could be left out from Bomber Command's efforts that night, several Hampdens, mainly from 44 Squadron, were sent to mine the waters around Hornum and Sylt, code-named 'forget-me-nots', and off Kiel. Yet more bombers were in action, delivering propaganda leaflets over French towns. Fighter Command lost twenty-five aircraft that day, one of its worst days of the Battle, but its losses in terms of aircrew was comparable to that of Bomber Command, for which it was, sadly, all too standard.

Monday 12 August was destined to be a glorious summer's day from the outset. So much so that offensive operations for 2 Group were all but cancelled; only a single 82 Squadron Blenheim was despatched on a double mission, one photo-reconnaissance and the other an attack upon the oil plant at Kamen. In the former, the Blenheim was successful, in the latter it was not, releasing its bomb load over De Kooy airfield as an alternative target. In spite of all of the military logic, the contrast with the large-scale attacks mounted by the Luftwaffe could not have been more pronounced. That night, however, though conditions were not expected to be better than poor over Germany, the situation was quite different with seventy-nine bombers heading east to attack a number of targets. No. 3 Group sent twenty-eight Wellingtons to attempt to stem the flow of aircraft to the Luftwaffe squadrons by attacking the aircraft factories at Gotha and Diepholz. Nine of the crews located the targets and reported a number of explosions and serious fires blazing in the vicinity but the other crews had to resort to alternative targets, including the docks in Amsterdam and the airfields at Kassel and Schiphol and the seaplane base at Borkum. Five Blenheims from 2 Group, which was beginning to operate more frequently at night, also kept up the pressure on the airfields, putting in attacks at Caen, Dinard, Querqueville and Maupertus. No. 15 Squadron was one of those squadrons warned it was likely to be involved in more nocturnal attacks. It quickly discovered that darkness did not provide absolute protection; Plt Off F.G.H. Dench and Sgts A.N. Gray and E.E. Scrase lost their lives when their Blenheim came down near Fermanville, about 9 miles east of Cherbourg. No. 4 Group mounted an attack upon the large aluminium factory at Herringen but the god of weather was set against them that night. Of the fifteen Whitleys over Germany, only one claimed to have located and attacked the target, but then without visible result. Most were in the same boat as 77 Squadron's new B Flight commander, Sqn Ldr G.T. 'Bull' Jarman, so named because of his strict enforcement of discipline and regulations. Having scoured much of the western part of the Reich for a break in the ten-tenths cloud without success, it was a frustrated Jarman who turned for home still fully loaded but light on fuel. A couple of crews were slightly more fortunate and off-loaded their bombs over industrial targets in Dusseldorf and Dortmund but exactly what they were, where they were and what effect their efforts had remained a mystery.

It was, however, to be 5 Group's night, though its success did not come without a hefty price tag. Two out of ten Hampdens from 61 Squadron were lost, for example, on a mine-laying sortie off Salzbergen, while several others attacked an oil refinery nearby. Two more were lost on the raid that was to bring Bomber Command its first Victoria Cross of the war and prove to be

'The Glorious 12th' for one man, Flt Lt R.A.B. Learoyd. The target was the old aqueduct where the Dortmund–Ems canal passed over the river Ems, about 6 miles north of Münster. The 168-mile long canal linked the industrial Ruhr to the port of Emden, giving vital access from the Rhine to the North Sea, as well as extending its reach via the interlinking Mitteland Canal. The target, which had been attacked before, was a difficult and heavily defended one and required a low-level precision pass to drop a 1,000lb delayed-action mine into the canal as it passed over the river. Each mine had a delay of ten minutes and the first of five was scheduled to be dropped at 23.15 hours, with the others following at two-minute intervals. This left the fifth and final aircraft a safety margin of just 120 seconds – and that in the face of a thoroughly alerted and potent defensive force.

Although there had been some recent practice on low-level mine laying, the crews of 49 and 83 Squadrons only found out where they were going that night at the briefing, which began at 19.30 hours. Six of the Scampton-based crews were to make diversionary raids before making a number of passes of the target area at just 200ft to draw enemy fire and add to the general confusion. In the meantime, Flt Lt James Pitcairn-Hill would lead Australians Fg Off Ellis Ross and Flt Lt Allen Mulligan, followed by Plt Off H.V. Matthews and Flt Lt Roderick Learoyd into the attack. Immediately after briefing, the crews were taken out to dispersal and by 20.50 hours all the Hampdens were airborne and heading east into the darkening sky. Not long after take-off, Learoyd's gunner, LAC Rich, drew his attention to the long, bright flames streaking out of a leaky exhaust manifold. Although this presented a real danger to the bomber flying at night and would have certainly constituted a valid reason to abort the sortie, Learoyd decided to press on and had no cause to regret his decision as by 23.03 he was circling the target at 4,000ft, waiting for zero hour in serene tranquillity and apparent isolation.

Bang on time the darkness was rent by a series of blinding flashes and dazzling beams of light. As Pitcairn-Hill made his run, hurtling across the countryside at just 150ft, he was met by a wall of flak and tracer and pretty well blinded by the series of searchlights that quickly picked him up and illuminated him for all to see and shoot at. In spite of taking several hits, which caused him significant damage and wounded two of the four men on board, the large mine was released as planned but, at 23.16, one minute late. As Pitcairn–Hill hauled his battered aircraft higher into the sky and out of the target area, the second Hampden was already lined up for its final approach. It never completed it, exploding in a giant fireball short of the aqueduct as the flak hit home. Undeterred, Mulligan positioned his aircraft and prepared to face the massed defences, now alert to the line of attack. The Hampden shuddered and staggered in the air as the flak smashed into the aircraft, mortally wounding it and half of its crew. Struggling to keep the wallowing bomber in the air, Mulligan released his mine and turned away; he almost made it to the Dutch border before having to crash land, with himself and his navigator Sgt W.G.W. Younger the only ones to scramble out of the wreckage. Next to run the gauntlet was Plt Off Matthews, an experienced pre-war pilot. He and his crew received the same vicious treatment and it was no surprise when one of the engines was hit. Managing to keep the bomber more or less under control, the mine was released at 23.22 and, using every bit of his skill to keep the bomber in the air, Matthews turned west, mindful of the hostile territory and inhospitable sea between him and home. After several gruelling hours, he made it.

The last man in was 27-year-old 'Babe' Learoyd. Well aware of what was ahead of him, he knew he would, at best, be able to get through by the skin of his teeth and, at worst, meet oblivion. Banking around from the east, Learoyd lost height and levelled out at a bare 100ft, lined the Hampden up on the canal ahead and began his run. Almost at once he came under heavy and sustained fire. As he said in a later wartime account, 'As we ran up the canal, the searchlights were switched on and I had to fly blind on the navigator's instruments. The light AA flak was intense and we had two hits, one on the starboard wingtip and one through the starboard flap. They put the hydraulics gear out of action.' Further hits followed before at 23.35 the mine was released, slap bang into the middle of the canal, clearly observed by the under-gunner Sgt Rich, who was blazing away for all he was worth at the lights and flak positions flashing close beneath him. Learoyd held the Hampden low before climbing up into the dark sky and setting course for home. There was little opportunity for prolonged jubilation or relaxation as the four airmen knew that the damage done to the hydraulic system meant that there would be serious problems on landing, even if they got that far. Learoyd decided to wait for daylight and to burn off as much fuel as possible before attempting to land at Scampton. For almost two nerve-shredding hours, Learoyd coolly circled the airfield before, finally, at 04.53, after more than eight hours in the air, much of it in a damaged aircraft, he brought the Hampden down for what turned out to be a textbook wheels-down landing. Photo-reconnaissance later that day confirmed that Learoyd's mine had blown a large hole in the north-east corner of the aqueduct and had succeeded in draining the canal. It would remain out of action for almost a fortnight, a crucial blow to the movement of men and materials in the build-up to Sea Lion. Harris, AOC 5 Group, who had already approved the award of a DFC to Learoyd, at once upgraded this to a recommendation for the Victoria Cross, which was subsequently approved. Learoyd was enjoying a drink in the mess at Mildenhall a while later when he received a message that he was wanted on the telephone. He picked it up to be told it was Air Vice-Marshal Harris on the line and that he had been awarded the Victoria Cross for his exemplary courage, determination and skill on the Dortmund–Ems raid. It was thoroughly justified.

Tuesday 13 August was due to be Goring's much-vaunted Adlertag – Eagle Day – when the massed ranks of the Luftwaffe would begin their all-out assault upon Fighter Command in preparation for Operation Sea Lion. As it turned out, a potent mix of indecision, unhelpful weather conditions and poor communications conspired to make it go off at half-cock initially but by mid-afternoon a series of heavy and punishing raids were being mounted against numerous airfields across southern Britain. It was not, however, intended to be all one-way traffic. Operational Instruction No. 38 issued by Bomber Command on 3 July was still very much in force:

'The enemy are using airfields and landing grounds in France, Belgium and Holland … The intention is to destroy as many aircraft as possible on the ground, thus forcing the enemy to withdraw. Airfields are to be attacked by sections escorted by fighters or sections of individual aircraft using cloud cover when definite information is received from fighter reconnaissance.' Of course, there never were any fighters available, but there never was any shortage of verified targets for the hard-pressed and exhausted crews. A report had come in that a number of Ju 88 bombers and a large fleet of Ju 52 transport aircraft had been gathered on the large grass airfield at Hamstede, near Aalborg in north-east Denmark, some 450 miles distant. Although towards the limit of the Blenheim's operational range, such was the importance of the target that it was decided that 82 Squadron would mount an attack. Briefing was at 05.30 hours and none of the young airmen was left in any doubt of the magnitude and perilous nature of the task assigned to them. Each Blenheim would carry four 250lb HE bombs and eight 25lb splinter bombs to cause maximum damage to parked German aircraft. Although the dozen Blenheims would attack as a unit in two flights, each aircraft was to make its way back as best it could on account of the critical fuel situation.

Take-off was for 08.30 and one by one the Blenheims took to the sky, broke through the thin layer of cloud and into the azure sunlit world above. Forming up around Wg Cdr Edward de V. Lart DSO, they held course across the North Sea. Two hours later as they approached the Danish coast, the crews watched with trepidation as the cloud cover beneath them at first began to break up and then fade away entirely. It was going to be rough but just how rough was still not clear. At this point Sgt Norman Baron, flying in the second section, made a difficult decision, in full cognisance of its implications, concerned about his higher than expected fuel consumption and reasoning there was no point in throwing away the lives of three trained airmen, he turned around and headed for home. At the subsequent court martial, his decision was upheld and he went on to win a DFM before being killed in May 1941.

The rest pushed on, their presence and course noted by a German observation post on the coast at Sondervig. As bad luck would have it, nine Me 109s had just landed at Aalborg, having made the short hop from Norway. They and the aircraft from II/JG27 were immediately scrambled to intercept the light bomber force, which was holding its north-easterly course at 180mph and 8,000ft. The first of the 109s were picked up by the crews while they were still 20 miles short of the target. The gunners made their final preparations but, as more and more fighters hove into view, hurtling through the cloudless sky towards them, they knew it would be a hopeless and one-sided fight. It was. Within the next frenzied ten minutes, the lethal combination of flak and fighters blasted all eleven Blenheims from the sky, leaving twenty of the thirty-three British airmen dead and most of the others shocked and wounded. Plt Off Douglas Parfit's aircraft took a number of hits and he had no choice but to jettison his bombs over farmland in order to keep airborne; seconds later another hit severed the tail unit, the wreckage falling dead weight to the ground. Flt Lt Tom Sym's Z-Zebra was turned on its back by the blast of a near miss and set alight, trailing smoke and flames as it too headed earthwards. At least he and his navigator, Sgt Wright, managed to get out and landed in shallow water off the island of Egholm, from where they were rescued by a group of Danish men watching the slaughter overhead. Sgt Donald Blair's aircraft quickly lost an engine and in another attack his gunner, Sgt Greenwood, passed out after three bullets slammed into his leg. The observer, Sgt Bill McGrath, lifted him out of the way and blasted away at anything that came into range of the .303s. With the aircraft now fully ablaze, Blair aimed to ditch the aircraft in the shallow waters north of Egholm but just before reaching the surface, the port fuel tank exploded, tearing the bomber apart. Incredibly, all three men survived the blast and were pulled ashore by a father and son who waded out to the wreckage.

Plt Off Hale managed to jink his way through to the airfield before being hit and plunging vertically on to it, exploding in an enormous petrol- and explosives-fuelled fireball. B Flight commander Sqn Ldr 'Rusty' Wardell's Blenheim had already sustained serious damage from both flak and fighters before being hit again on his final approach run to the target. Just after he had released his bombs, a shell exploded directly beneath the cockpit, blowing the Blenheim upside down and causing it to break up. Wardell, though burned, was thrown clear and managed to deploy his parachute to land safely near Vadum; his crewmates were not so fortunate.

The six leading Blenheims from A Flight had so far fared rather better, having bombed the airfield without loss. It did not stay that way for long. Plt Off B.N.J. 'Bingy' Newland's aircraft had taken hits from flak over the airfield and was gradually dropping back, losing height and speed, when a new wave of fighters bored in. His Blenheim fought back but staggered in the air as canon shells and bullets ripped into it. With a bullet lodged deep in his left shoulder, he gave Sgts Ankers and Turner the order to bail out but received no reply. Painfully releasing his straps and opening the hatch above his head, Newland was immediately sucked out of the doomed aircraft and with his good arm reached across to pull his parachute ring. At the same time, Flt Lt Ellen's bomber was also raked from end to end, killing his gunner, Sgt Davies. Ellen lost no time in ordering observer John Dance to bail out via the nose hatch as he reached up for the one above his head. It would not shift, probably twisted by a fragment strike. Losing height rapidly and spiralling out of control, Ellen heaved his way to the nose hatch and forced his body through the gap, pulling his ripcord almost immediately. He landed in a marsh seconds later to be joined by Sgt John Bristow, the sole survivor from Sqn Ldr N. Jones' Blenheim. Bristow had been engaging the German fighters when the fuselage disintegrated around him and caught alight. As he struggled his way to the rear hatch he noticed Jones slumped motionless over the controls. His flying boot caught on the twisted metal around the hatch as he jumped and for a heart-stopping moment he found himself suspended head first from a blazing, earthbound aircraft. He kicked out frantically and broke free, leaving his boot to share the fiery fate of the bomber. Ellen and Bristow were met by a farm labourer, who borrowed some bicycles and led them to a house nearby. Given the massive search already under way and the danger to the civilians helping them, the pair decided that the only viable course of action was to give themselves up.

By now there were only three Blenheims left in the air, fighting their way towards the North Sea. The contest was an uneven one and the outcome never really in doubt. First Plt Off Wigley, then Wg Cdr de V. Lart were blasted from the sky, leaving no survivors. Only Sgt J. Oates and his crew Plt Off R. Miden and Sgt T. Graham were left, well out to sea, streaking for home but still under attack. Suddenly, the Me 109s broke off and turned east, content to leave the damaged aircraft to its watery grave. The crew's joy was short lived as a rapid appraisal of the situation revealed the fuel gauges reading prematurely empty, probably as a result of battle damage. Not relishing a close encounter with the sea, Oates reluctantly turned the bomber around and headed for the Danish coast on the horizon. Once back in range, the Blenheim came under heavy fire from the still alert flak batteries, which did little to help Oates as he tried to make a forced landing. The 26-year-old pilot was found by two local men amid the scattered wreckage with a broken back and head injuries; Miden was also seriously injured but Graham was virtually unscathed and had the presence of mind to burn anything of value before the German soldiers arrived on the scene. All the wounded were taken to Christ's Hospital in Aalborg, where they were treated well before being taken on a further hour and a half to a POW hospital in Schleswig-Holstein. One, Sgt Bill McGrath, in spite of losing an eye, later escaped from a camp near Rouen on 21 November 1941, eventually crossing the Pyrenees on 29 December. Arriving back in Britain on 4 March 1942 and awarded a Military Medal for his escape, McGrath was able to give the first detailed account of the disaster that had unfolded in the bright summer sun over Aalborg.

What must have happened was all too apparent to those left at RAF Watton. Plt Off Frank Metcalfe, with his crew George Martin and Sid Merritt, happened to arrive there from their Operational Training Unit (OTU) on that day. They were greeted by the adjutant, who explained that the mess was empty as the whole squadron was out on a show but would be back for late lunch. The nervous new 82 Squadron members were told to make themselves at home and that he would return later to introduce them to the others on their return. It was a long afternoon and as the hours slipped by and enquiries about stragglers making it to other airfields drew blank after blank, the dreadful truth began to emerge. It was not the introduction to an operational unit that Metcalfe and his crew had hoped for. It had been known from the start that this raid and many of those carried out on the airfields by 2 Group were especially hazardous but the risks were not taken without justification or good reason. Two days later, on 15 August, in spite of the brave efforts of 82 Squadron, around fifty Ju 88s of KG30 launched a major assault upon targets in north-east England. Many had taken off from Aalborg.

Even as these unfortunate events were unfolding over Aalborg, thousands of other men and women were hard at work planning and preparing for the night's operations, in which more than 100 aircraft would be involved. No. 5 Group's efforts focused upon the German aircraft industry with attacks being mounted against the large Junkers factories at Dessau and Bernberg. Although high cloud nullified the effects of the bright moonlight, the target area was still well illuminated by parachute flares, which allowed accurate identification and observation. Numerous hits were noted and one bomber was reported as sweeping across the factories at less than 1,000ft to release its load. The airfield adjacent to the Bernberg plant was also said to have been hard hit. The flak defences were, however, especially active and Hampden P2077 of 44 Squadron sustained a number of hits, sealing its fate. Plt Off H.P. Clarke and his crew bailed out safely near Alkmaar in Holland when the Hampden finally gave up its unequal struggle with the laws of physics.

No. 3 Group joined in the attack on the aviation industry with thirty-four Wellingtons attacking the aluminium works at Lunen and Gravenbroich and a component factory in Frankfurt; the old favourites of Hamm and Soest were also on the list. No. 37 Squadron's night was fairly typical. Crossing the coast outbound at Orford Ness, the crews found much of their route obscured by a layer of cloud, which, fortunately, began to break up over northern Germany, allowing bright moonlight to flood the ground below and enabling the crews to identify the targets clearly, even from 10,000ft or more. Plt Off Parsons claimed that his bombs straddled the target causing a large explosion, immediately followed by several blue–green fires that were still visible for some time on the way home. Plt Off Price also claimed direct hits, though his load appeared to ignite only a single but sizeable conflagration. Plt Off Hough stated that his bombs resulted in three separate but sustained fires. However, Fg Off Ritchie and Plt Off Chilton unluckily arrived at the wrong time, just as a sheet of cloud slid over the target area; having orbited for some time searching for a break in the cloud, the pair gave up and located and attacked alternative targets in Cologne and Flushing airfield, respectively. Of the trio ordered to attack Frankfurt, none was able to pick out the target on account of cloud cover. Flt Lt Mitchell headed off to the Ruhr area, where he knew he had a good chance of locating something suitable; his report states he came across a blast furnace 'somewhere east of Cologne. A high-level attack was carried out through a gap in the cloud but the bursts were not observed. A good run-up was made on the target so it is probable that the bombs fell near or on the target.' Sgt Greenslade had slightly more substance behind his claims for his bombs were actually seen to burst amid existing fires burning in the Ruhr; as to exactly what was burning, he had no idea. Only Plt Off Lemon, an experienced operational pilot, failed to identify any worthwhile target, in spite of an intensive search and, consequently, returned with his bomb load intact.

The Whitleys of 4 Group were allotted targets much further south, the Fiat aero engine plant at Turin and the Caproni aircraft factory in Milan, the first time Italian targets had been attacked since the fall of France. As both were at the limit of a heavily laden Whitley's endurance, 10 and 51 Squadrons, which formed the bulk of the thirty-odd strong force, flew south to airfield at Abingdon and Harwell in Oxfordshire that afternoon. Refuelled and with any niggles sorted out, the Whitleys took off around 20.00 hours for the long flight over occupied France and the Alps, which towered up almost as high as the bombers themselves. Flt Lt Bradley of

51 Squadron was forced to return early as his aircraft was hit by flak over Dunkirk, while Fg Off Henry of 10 Squadron got as far as the Alps, having the lights of Geneva in sight, before an engine failure forced him to turn around and embark upon a long, slow and tense flight home. Conditions over Italy were generally favourable and the crews were able to locate the massive Fiat factory with relative ease, especially as one of the parachute flares lodged itself on the factory's roof. Indeed, later press reports made much of the bright moonlight reflecting off the extensive glass roofs and the far from perfect Italian blackout. The ground defences too were comparatively weak and ineffectual and this happy combination of factors enabled the crews to bomb with greater precision and effect than usual. Nevertheless, there was still a long flight home over now fully alert enemy territory.

Plt Off Pip Parsons of 10 Squadron had completed his attack over Turin when he came under attack from an Italian night fighter. It did its job well, its bullets reducing one engine to a heap of useless metal and causing significant damage to the starboard aileron. Fortunately, the fighter lost contact in the darkness but the outlook for Parsons and his crew was bleak. The bomber managed to pick its way over and through the Alps, but slowly but surely lost height on its long journey across France. Anxiously listening to the sound of the remaining engine, ticking off the miles and peering into the darkness for any sight of hostile aircraft, their hopes constantly rising and falling, the young airmen could hardly believe their eyes when the English Channel came into sight not so very far beneath them. With the south coast now clearly in sight in the early morning light and the sea beneath them, the Whitley finally reached the point of no return and, reluctantly, Parsons gave the order to take up ditching positions. Parsons just about managed to keep the aircraft stable but, without warning, the damaged aileron broke off and the bomber immediately plunged nose first into the sea. It was 05.40 hours and they were only a mile short of Hythe. Parsons and Campion, the second pilot, did not make it out but the other three men did, their plight noticed by two local fishermen and a young physical training instructor, Peggy Prince. The fishermen launched their boat at once and succeeded in picking up Sgt Chamberlain, the observer, and the gunner Sgt Sharpe. Miss Prince, meanwhile, still clad in her pyjamas, hurried to her canoe and paddled out to pick up the WopAg, Sgt Jimmy Marshall, who had drifted some way from the others. She managed, with some difficulty and no little risk to herself, to haul him on board and return to the shore. For this courageous and selfless act, she was awarded the British Empire Medal. It had been a particularly busy twenty-four hours for Bomber Command, framed by the disaster at Aalborg and the unusually high 95 per cent rate of successful attacks.

That was yesterday and today was another day in what was becoming a long and increasingly costly war. Although mindful of the possibility of another Aalborg calamity, 2 Group did not have the luxury of being able to suspend and review its operations, especially not in the face of the unprecedented and sustained assault upon Britain. Therefore, two dozen Blenheims were tasked to carry out a series of daylight attacks upon a number of airfields, oil depots and aircraft factories across northern Europe. Unfortunately, the conditions were once more against them and only a handful of attacks were pressed home, though at St Omer airfield a number of direct hits upon hangars were observed and they were left well alight. Undeterred, another thirteen Blenheims were sent out to harass the airfields that night, even though conditions were once again marginal. Four aircraft from 15 Squadron, for example, were detailed to attack an airfield near Forêt de Guînes. The crews flew through the inky blackness and ten-tenths cloud, dropping to less than 100ft over the target area to clear it. They released their bombs but the results achieved, if any, were too quickly enveloped by the gloom to be observed. By 00.55 hours they were back at Wyton, climbing down stiffly from their cramped positions on to the grass beneath. The crews from their sister squadrons at Wyton were not so fortunate. Two of them failed to return from their operation to Chartres, though, unusually, all six men survived the experience and two, Sgts Easton and Watson, evaded capture, the latter being the first home on 4 December and awarded a Military Medal.

Sgt K. Newton, one of the pilots, later recalled what had happened that night. Suspecting that his fuel system had been fatally damaged by flak over the Channel Islands on his return flight, Newton reckoned that there was no way his Blenheim would make it back and gave orders to prepare for ditching. The sea was calm but still very hard and after skimming the surface, the aircraft bounced in bone-breaking fashion before coming to a halt, settling rapidly nose first. With water pouring in through the smashed front end, the three men with several broken and dislocated limbs between them, climbed painfully out and managed to inflate the dinghy. They could see a light nearby and presumed it was a lighthouse and as it grew lighter they could see they were less than a mile from the French coast. With no viable alternative, they began to paddle towards the shore where they could see a group of German soldiers already waiting for them. Upon landing, they were bundled into a truck and taken to hospital in Cherbourg for treatment and later fed into the POW system.

An unusual feature of the night was the concentration of Wellingtons, Whitleys and Hampdens on several oil storage depots at Blaye and Pauillac near Bordeaux, only recently occupied and now working at full capacity for the Germans. The attack turned out to be palpably effective. No. 38 Squadron's Wellingtons left Marham at 20.30 hours and shortly after midnight arrived over the target area in a clear sky; identification was easy on account of the bright moonlight and distinctive river and coastal features. The squadron log records, 'The oil refineries and oil storage tanks were repeatedly hit and large explosions followed by clouds of thick black smoke belched forth from the target. It is considered that the target was totally destroyed. Enemy action was nil, although some heavy flak was fired in the Nantes area.' No. 49 Squadron's Hampden crews reported a similar story, describing the scene as, 'the entire target area ablaze and streams of burning oil seen flowing from south to north'. The return journey was not, however, so easy as the crews ran into thick cloud once back in British airspace. For most crews it was an unwelcome complication to a long flight and for two it proved to be a fatal one. Plt Off S.P. Swenson was carefully making his way up the country towards Dishforth at just 1,500ft when his 51 Squadron Whitley collided with barrage balloon cables near Langley in Buckinghamshire. There were no survivors. It was much the same with a 77 Squadron Whitley making its way back to Driffield from St Nazaire as it flew into the balloon barrage near Eastleigh in Hampshire.

Nine Whitleys from 102 Squadron made the long trek over the Alps to Turin, the Caproni factory being the aiming point. Once again, opposition was practically non-existent and a pilot was quoted in the press as saying on his return, 'I got the target with my first bomb and then planted the rest on in one stick. Fires and explosions were added to those already in progress.' Another commented, 'We came down to 4,500ft and cracked the Caproni works good and hard. We could watch our bombs burst and knew they were on target.' Certainly, damage was done to the factory and surrounding area, much to the consternation of the local population, which began to fear repeated attacks. They were right as four Whitleys from 10 Squadron were over Milan and Turin the next night. On this occasion, the generally sporadic and inaccurate flak did claim a victim, a direct hit setting the bomber ablaze. Although four men survived, the body of Fg Off K.H. Higson was found among the wreckage. The Italian authorities buried him with full military honours and permitted his colleagues to attend the funeral, a much-appreciated gesture.

Thursday 15 August was a beautiful summer's day, with hardly a cloud in the sky. So beautiful, in fact, that 2 Group's operations were greatly curtailed, with just a lone Blenheim succeeding in carrying out an attack upon De Kooy airfield. Conditions were, conversely, perfect for the well-escorted Luftwaffe bombers, which mounted major attacks across the country throughout the day. One of these had a particular effect upon Bomber Command. The most easterly of Bomber Command's northern airfields, RAF Driffield, had been opened on 30 July 1936 and four years later was home to 77 and 102 Squadrons. A little after 13.00 hours the radar station at Staxton Wold near Scarborough, a little to the north of Driffield, picked up a significant hostile force coming in from the North Sea. A dozen

Spitfires from 616 Squadron at RAF Leconfield were scrambled, along with a further six Hurricanes from 73 Squadron, which by chance were already airborne, to intercept the raiders. They were rapidly guided towards the fifty-plus formation of Ju 88s and in the ensuing battle nine of the bombers were brought down. However, the majority ploughed on through the thin defensive screen and a substantial force split off towards Driffield.

Dan La Plain, an air mechanic attached to 102 Squadron, had just finished his lunch and was making his way back to continue working on the starboard engine of Whitley DY-E when his ears picked up the sound of an unfamiliar engine approaching. He looked around the familiar and peaceful scene and casually walked on until his eyes picked up thirty or so twin-engine aircraft heading low and fast directly towards the airfield. Although taken aback, he reacted at once and sprinted for all he was worth to the nearest shelter; as the first explosions shook the ground, the air raid siren began its mournful wail. Plt Off Jim Verran was enjoying a little after lunch nap in the mess, still feeling the effects of the previous night's long flight to Milan, when he was abruptly awoken by the siren. Drowsily dismissing it as a mere drill, he snuggled back into his armchair until a few seconds later a 500kg bomb exploded with ear-splitting force a matter of yards away. It was the first of many as the Ju 88s roared overhead with virtual impunity, rapidly reducing a well-organised and fully functional airfield into a blazing and chaotic scene of devastation.

A German newspaper reporter was in one of the Ju 88s and gave his readers a colourful and vivid – if not wholly accurate – account of the attack:

At last, the target – Driffield! Those fighters were beginning to get damned uncomfortable. This is it. I would not give tuppence for the lives of those down there. Let's get rid of the bombs. Down they go – the bomber is put into a dive. The speed increases, the wind roars and howls. The hangars rise up to meet us, they are still standing but not for long. The flak guns are shooting out of everywhere but it cannot help them. A shudder – the bombs are gone! Their steel bodies whizz into the depths. Down there all hell is let loose, steel crashes into steel and stone, bomb after bomb explodes, tears and destroys whatever it hits. The walls and roofs of the hangars fly up like tin sheets and fly through the air. Aircraft on the ground are turned into sieves by the shrapnel. Barracks collapse in dust, huge smoke and dust clouds grow like mushrooms out of the ground. Here and there flames shoot up and there are explosions; fields and hangars are raked over and over and still the bombers behind us are dropping their loads. The flak has been extinguished, their stations turned into craters. Thick smoke fills the air and fire shines through the grey, now gradually disappearing from our view.

As the dazed airmen and women emerged from their shelters a few minutes later, they found a scene barely recognisable. Four of the five brick-built C Type hangars had been laid waste, as had a good proportion of the station's other buildings. Ten Whitleys were destroyed and several others left in differing states of disrepair. Fifteen people had been killed, including a WAAF attached to the station headquarters and a civilian attached to the station; scores of others were wounded. The gory discoveries went on for some time. Richard Pinkham had just made it in time from the officers' mess to the shelter and emerged to find the rescue operation under way. Passing another shelter with its entrance blocked by debris, he volunteered to be lowered into the emergency escape hatch to see what conditions inside were like. Struggling to make his way through the dusty gloom, he found the shelter empty until he came across the body of a young airman slumped against a wall, his bloody head squashed flat. To his surprise, he felt absolutely nothing, reasoning that the airman could not either. The damage to the station was severe and forced its immediate closure; it would not open again until January 1941 when, temporarily, it was transferred to 13 Group, Fighter Command. What was left of 77 Squadron was transferred to RAF Linton and 102 to RAF Leeming.

At the other stations that night, it was business as usual. No. 2 Group, more available than usual because of its quiet day and steadily increasing commitment to operations at night, put up eighteen Blenheims to attack enemy airfields. No. 15 Squadron, for example, found itself over the Forêt de Guînes for a second night, though on this occasion not without loss; Sgt Garvey and his crew were lost without trace, perhaps in the Channel. Fires were also started at Leeuwarden and Chartres airfields. Attacks were also made upon the new gun emplacements at Cap Gris Nez housing the long-range canons intended to support the invasion fleet. Nos 3 and 5 Groups had a wide range of German targets, focusing upon aircraft and oil production and the rail network. No. 61 Squadron dispatched its Hampdens to attack target A28, an oil plant at Benrath in Dusseldorf. The weather conditions were good and navigation proved easier than usual in the sharp moonlight. Indeed, the only thing to hamper the squadron's attack was the smoke from the burning tanks set alight by earlier aircraft. The anti-aircraft defences were officially deemed feeble but they were potent enough to compound Sgt Wathey's port engine trouble, forcing him to turn around and release his bombs on a target of opportunity, a canal north of Bocholt. Stan Harrison's problems began rather earlier, shortly after crossing the coast at Orford Ness, as the famously trigger-happy gunners of the Royal Navy opened fire on his Hampden, fortunately with little physical effect. Later, on his final run in, the Hampden was suddenly bathed in the dazzling glare of a searchlight. Three more soon locked on, illuminating the bomber to all and sundry for miles around and drawing what flak there was like a magnet. The bomber was blown about like a leaf in the wind by several near misses and remained gripped by the beam in spite of Harrison's violent manoeuvres. Just as suddenly as the ordeal began, it was over and the crew, badly shaken in more ways than one, were plunged back into the soothing embrace of the darkness. As matters became more settled the target came into view, partially hidden by the dazzling glare of searchlights and intense fires. Although the actual refinery could not be identified with any degree of certainty, their bombs were seen to land slap bang in the middle of the concentration of fires. Harrison immediately put the bomber's nose down to pick up speed and made a steep 90 degree turn to get out of range as quickly as possible. The return journey was completely without incident and as dawn broke, now back on terra firma, the weary crew gathered to inspect the damage sustained over Dusseldorf. Somewhat to their embarrassment and certainly to their astonishment, neither they nor the ground crew who had listened to their tale could find anything more than a couple of minor fragment holes.

No. 37 Squadron was amongst the 3 Group contingent to attack the large and crucial railway junctions at Hamm. For once, the sky over this oft-attacked target was almost cloudless, enabling the crews to see far better than usual in the moonlight. Coming in between 8,500 and 10,000ft, the Wellington crews were confident that their loads had fallen in the target area and were unanimous that large fires, visible for many miles, had taken a good hold. It was a similar story over Soest. Indeed, such were the conditions that it was decided to give three crews under training some operational experience by mounting an attack upon Eindhoven airfield. Sgt Elstub claimed his bomb load had landed amid the hangars and beside what he rather ambitiously decided was the watch office. Plt Off Clarke located the airfield but his load was released too early in error and fell in open country well short of the target. Still, he had fared better than Fg Off Mobley, who failed to locate the target at all, though the squadron log did note that he had become unwell during the flight. Clearly, bombing by night was not an easy task.

The squadron log also made much of the dangerous presence of the barrage balloons to be found over many of the targets. Far more effective and deadly than their innocuous and bulbous appearance suggested, they posed a significant threat to the bombers approaching at their normal operational heights at this stage of the war. A tale told by an unnamed 23-year-old pilot gained widespread coverage in the press and amply exposed the dangers they posed:

On this night our target was a synthetic oil plant at a place called Gelsenkirchen. It was a dark night and we had come down to about 6,000ft to find the target. We dropped our flares, located and bombed the works, then we climbed and went back to see what results we'd had. My second pilot was flying the plane. I'd been down in the bomb aimer's position. Suddenly, I saw a long dark shape silhouetted against some clouds, the searchlights played across them, I saw three more about 100 yards away. By now, I'd gone from the bomb aimer's position and was standing behind the second pilot. I gave instructions to the gunners to open fire at the balloons and we started to turn away to starboard to get away from them. Immediately afterward the second pilot threw the aircraft into a very steep right-handed turn for he had seen another balloon coming straight up in front of him. It had loomed out of the darkness dead ahead and our wing tip just caught the fabric. If the pilot had not yanked the aircraft over quickly, we should have flown right into it, the envelope would have wrapped itself around the 'plane and that would have been the end of the trip. But all that happened was that the aircraft bucked a bit; then there was a terrific explosion which we could hear above the roar of the engines and I imagine the Germans were minus one balloon. When we'd climbed higher we found we'd been flying along a row of balloons, right in the thick of them. It was pretty amazing we hadn't hit a few more for when we'd been bombing we must have been among the cables.

As Fighter Command's epic battle with the Luftwaffe intensified by day, so did Bomber Command's efforts by night. On Friday 16 August it put 150 aircraft into the night sky, one of its highest totals for the entire Battle. The blazing sunshine that prevailed for most of the day put paid to the offensive activities of 2 Group's unescorted Blenheims but by night it was a different story. At Mildenhall, the ground crews toiled in the hot sun to make ready the Wellington 1Cs of 149 Squadron for that night's attack upon the aircraft storage depot near Wismar, another attempt to reduce the flow of aircraft to the Luftwaffe's front-line units. For Maurice Fisher it was a red-letter but nerve-wracking day. Having joined the squadron on 8 August, the young navigator was preparing to face his first operational flight. Reassuringly, his pilot was to be Sqn Ldr E.H.T. Twaites AFC, an old hand who had done it all before. As the shadows lengthened across the airfield, the six men, fully briefed and all kitted out, clambered clumsily aboard the bomber and began their final checks, familiar routine soothing their jangling nerves. At 21.23 OJ-A took its turn on the runway and slowly but steadily climbed eastwards into the darkening sky. Fisher worked methodically and accurately, fully absorbed in his work in spite of the novelty of his situation. Pretty much on time the target hove into view, the fires already acting as a beacon for the later crews. Thwaites brought the Wellington into position and carried out a textbook approach in unusually clear conditions. Suddenly the air of calm efficiency and purpose was shattered as the bomber took a direct hit from flak and immediately burst into flames. Only half of the six-man crew would survive the next few frantic seconds. Fisher was amongst them, his first not quite complete operation being his last. His younger brother George, himself a navigator in 1945, was at home three days later when the telegram arrived bringing the news that Maurice was missing. Confirmation that he was alive came from an unusual source on 30 August when his name was amongst those broadcast by William Joyce, Lord Haw-Haw. The attack itself was hailed a success as several crews reported large fires engulfing the various hangars and buildings on the site.

Other Wellingtons made attacks upon the massive Krupps works in Essen, an aircraft factory in Frankfurt and the usual railway targets in Hamm and Soest. One of these crews, from 38 Squadron, good humouredly unnamed in the squadron narrative, had an unusual return flight. Heading for RAF Marham in Norfolk, the Wellington was over the Atlantic before the crew realised something was amiss. Swiftly making an about turn, the bomber made landfall near Plymouth and, with the fuel gauges showing alarmingly low levels, the need to find an airfield was becoming acute. Mile after mile went by until eventually one was found; to their amazement, the disorientated but relieved crew discovered they had landed at Abingdon in Oxfordshire. Not all mishaps turned out so well, even when close to home. The 144 Squadron Hampden of Sqn Ldr P.H. Rebbeck had completed its sortie to Merseburg and returned to Hemswell where it crashed, killing all on board. The squadron lost another aircraft that night, though two men did survive to become POWs. No. 5 Group lost a third; Sgt M.G.P. Stetton's 49 Squadron Hampden came down near Breda in Holland, having attacked the well-defended oil plant at Leuna. Conditions had not been as clear there as elsewhere and even their CO, Wg Cdr Reid, had been unable to locate the target and had been forced to jettison his load in open country 6 miles south of Blankenburg.

No. 4 Group's targets had also been distant ones, a power station at Bohlen, an aero-engine factory at Augsburg and the Zeiss optical works at Jena, a place 10 Squadron's CO, Wg Cdr Bill Staton, stated at the meeting 'has never heard the sound of gunfire since the Napoleonic war', before urging his crews to, 'make sure it hears it tonight'. The trip to Jena would take nine hours, most of the route over enemy territory and fraught with all sorts of dangers. Plt Off V.F.B. Pike of 58 Squadron got no further than Norwich when the city's over-eager gunners caused enough damage to force him to abort the sortie. Fg Off G.W. Prior and his 10 Squadron crew noticed with apprehension the sinister shape of a Me 110 taking off from an airfield near Wismar, thankful that they would be long gone before it climbed to their height but concerned for their friends following on. Just before beginning his bombing run over Jena, Flt Lt Raphael's Whitley did come under fire from a roving Me 110 but, fortunately, rear gunner L.A.C. Cowie, still awaiting promotion to sergeant as air crew, quickly spotted it and squeezed off three accurate bursts from his quadruple Brownings, driving it spinning downwards, apparently out of control; he was credited with a 'possible'. There was no such escape, however, for Fg Off Max Nixon and his crew, who would not see England again for five long years. Having made it to Jena without a hitch, they were on their run in at 6,000ft when their aircraft was brilliantly illuminated and held by a single searchlight beam. Nixon hauled the bomber into a steep turn and soon broke free of the beam. Undaunted, Nixon went around again and made a second run at 10,000ft, successfully releasing his load before the port engine suddenly packed up amid a shower of sparks and fingers of flame. It was clearly going to be a long flight home to Leeming, anxiously counting off the miles. Ploughing into a strong headwind, the bomber began to lose height, even after everything not bolted down had been unceremoniously ejected by the desperate crew. It did not matter in any case as the lumbering bomber proved easy meat for the flak units in Holland, further hits sealing its fate. RAF Leeming received a signal from the stricken aircraft at 03.24 hours and minutes later Nixon pulled off a superb forced landing west of Breda from which all of the crew walked away largely unscathed. Indeed, they reacted swiftly enough to evade capture and it was reported that a German radio broadcast offered a substantial reward for their capture or information leading to it. The almost inevitable happened and the men were hunted down in a major search operation and sent into captivity. The raid itself was judged to have been effective and, if nothing else, showed that nowhere in the Third Reich was immune from the attentions of Bomber Command.

Much of Britain was spared such attentions from the Luftwaffe during the daylight hours of Saturday 17 August; even it needed some respite before renewing the onslaught upon the industrial towns of the Midlands that night. No. 2 Group also operated on a much reduced level, the clear and bright conditions restricting their effort to just three Blenheim sorties to Fecamp and Dieppe airfields. Come the hours of darkness, it was a much different story as on airfield after airfield the air reverberated with the throaty growl of hundreds of aero engines. Once again, 2 Group, after their enforced idleness during the day and as part of a general shift in deployment, put up thirty-six Blenheims. Their objective was to cause destruction and dislocation to no less than twenty-one enemy-held airfields, their attritional approach producing an appreciable detrimental effect upon the Luftwaffe's operational effectiveness. One unnerved German pilot later recalled, 'At St Omer those fellows [the Blenheim crews] came over our aerodrome every night. I'll never forget those bombs. None of us was wounded but they did hit a lot of aircraft. Every night they were there. Every morning the ground had to be levelled again.' At RAF Honington there were cheers at the 13.00 hours briefing as the target for the night was revealed:

G225 – Berlin. Later in the afternoon, however, some senior figure must have had second thoughts about such a portentous move and the target was switched to Gottingen. As ever, the marshalling yards at Schwerte, Soest, Hamm and Osnabrück were chalked on 3 Group's boards; with 75 per cent of Germany's coal, 85 per cent of its coke and 70 per cent of its iron and steel production passing through these yards on their way out of the industrial powerhouse Ruhr Valley, it was hardly surprising. Conditions that night were far from ideal with large patches of cloud augmenting the omnipresent layer of industrial haze and smog over the target area. None of 37 Squadron's aircraft was able to locate the yards at Schwerte but two managed to move on to Hamm to release their 250lb bombs from just 5,000ft, though without visible results. Plt Off Dingle did see his load of incendiaries burst on the south-eastern edge of the yard and ignite a number of brightly burning fires. One of the bombers assigned to Soest managed to locate it, Sgt Elstub attacking from 11,000ft and claiming most precisely to have started sixteen small fires and explosions in the yards. The other crews realised they had overflown not only the target in the ten-tenths cloud but the entire Ruhr Valley. Gamely, Plt Off Clarke turned around and spent a good while stooging around in search of a target; when a major road appeared beneath them, he decided that was the best he was going to get and plastered it.

Of the three remaining aircraft despatched by 37 Squadron, only one managed to locate the oil plant at Zeitz. After a long search Plt Off Price and his crew picked out, through a rare gap in the clouds, some fires burning around a group of industrial buildings. Dropping quickly to 6,500ft, the bombs were released but the cloud spread across the gap before any results could be observed. Plt Off Hough was one of the pair who had given up the sortie as a bad job and turned for home, bomb load intact. Fifty miles off Great Yarmouth, the Wellington was flying in a peaceful, clear moonlit sky when an Me 110 suddenly attacked from the port quarter, closing rapidly and blazing away with its heavy 20mm cannon and machine guns. The shells and bullets passed harmlessly scant feet beneath the main plane; the German rear gunner also opened fire as the Zerstorer flashed beneath and astern of the Wellington, again to no effect. Sgt McDermid, in the rear turret, returned fire at 200 yards but could not keep his opponent in his sights. Plt Off Hough banked to port and dived but the Me 110 managed to maintain contact and came in again for a second attack from the port quarter. McDermid was better positioned this time and let fly with long bursts from 150 yards resulting in sparks and smoke pouring out of one engine. The aircraft broke off, diving sharply and trailing smoke and increasing amounts of flame; still heading earthwards as it dropped out of view, the jubilant crew claimed it as destroyed.

The Hampdens too were operating over the Ruhr with the Krupps works in Essen as their primary target; eleven of the twenty aircraft made claims for a successful attack. A further five laid mines in the Elbe estuary and several more made their way to industrial targets in Dortmund, Dusseldorf and Emmerich, though in poor conditions. It is significant that local records note that an attack was carried out on Brunswick, a decent-sized town that was not on the Command's target list for the night.

The next day, Sunday 18 August, was not a traditional day of rest. The daylight battle for the airfields reached a new level of intensity with the Luftwaffe losing some sixty aircraft and Fighter Command some thirty-five in the sunlit sky over southern England. Once again, the clear sky put paid to the Blenheim's offensive but by evening cloud had crept across the country and over the Continent. Only the Whitleys of 4 Group were able to operate and then only in challenging conditions. With briefing at 13.00, the four crews from 77 Squadron departed from their enforced new home at Linton-on-Ouse at 14.00 for Abingdon, where their fuel tanks were topped up for the long flight over the Alps to the Fiat factory near Turin and the Caproni aircraft plant near Milan. The thick cloud en route provided welcome protection from enemy fighters but it rapidly dispersed as the majestic snow-covered peaks of the Alps came into sight. The laden Whitleys could only clear the jagged peaks by 1,000ft or so and it was with a sense of apprehension and awe that the crews gazed ahead at the mountain barrier and the plain beyond. The strong moonlight and a poor blackout made identification of the targets comparatively easy and the lack of effective defences was another bonus, as there was precious little prospect of a battle-damaged bomber making it home from there. Fires were left burning and were visible for some time to the crews as they turned for home, now able to clear the Alps more easily. To cap it all, the welcoming cloud was still waiting for them as they headed up through France and across the Channel.

Ten Whitleys from each of 10 and 58 Squadrons were detailed to bomb the aluminium works at Rheinfelden. Take off from Leeming was later than usual at 23.00 hours in the hope of conditions improving over Germany. At least as far as the young airmen in the Whitleys were concerned, they need not have bothered to wait. Their turbulent passage through the dense cloud was punctuated by brilliant flashes of lightning amid a sea of electrical storms. Even so, more than half the crews claimed to have attacked the target successfully, though the results were hard to discern, while others sought out targets of opportunity, such as the airfields at Freiburg and Hashemite and a chemical plant at Waldshut. In some cases, the tenacious crews were cruising over enemy territory at just 1,500ft to get beneath the cloud base and identify a target, pushing the prudent limit of endurance to the utmost. It had been broad daylight for several hours by the time the last of the bombers touched down at Leeming at 08.00 hours, after a gruelling nine hours airborne. The uncertain outcomes were scant reward for the crews' determined efforts to press home their attacks.

There was still sufficient cloud that morning to encourage those at 2 Group to mount long-range attacks upon a number of oil and aircraft targets in northern and central Germany. Once airborne and over Europe, however, the cloud began to fragment, leaving the Blenheims horribly and unacceptably exposed. As instructed, most broke off the sortie but one made a determined and daring attack on a flak battery near Amsterdam, while another offloaded its ordnance over the airfield at Flushing. The vulnerability of the Blenheims was reaffirmed by the loss of one from 114 Squadron, brought down over the sea at 08.05 by Unteroffizer Woick of 8/JG54.

Attacks upon airfields were very much two-way traffic and once again, although not a German priority, Bomber Command's airfields came under heavy attack. At RAF Honington, it had been a normal, busy day with the thousand and one tasks necessary to mount an operation being carried out. Confirmation that the airfield would be providing Wellingtons for that night's operations had been received at 12.37 hours. Seventeen minutes later an air raid warning yellow came through, but nothing came of it and business continued without interruption. Then at 16.15 hours the sound of aircraft engines began to carry on the breeze but on an airfield, nobody took the slightest notice until the first explosions rocked the station. There was only one assailant but its bombs were well placed and caused widespread devastation. Many buildings received blast damage, shattered brickwork, glass, tiles and wood strewn over a large area by high explosive bombs; fortunately, most of the incendiaries fell on open ground and harmlessly burnt themselves out. Eight airmen lost their lives and a further sixteen sustained injuries. Seven minutes too late the station received its second yellow warning of the day. Work to make good the damage began at once and the race to become operational was being won by 18.30 when a second raider was seen sneaking in. There was sufficient time for a warning to be sounded and with everybody under cover only one man was wounded in the attack. However, a hangar was all but destroyed and part of a barrack block was flattened. In spite of a noisy reception laid on by the AA defences, the lone raider flew on unscathed. Clearance and repair work resumed and at 20.52 hours the first of the Wellington crews took to the sky, somewhat shocked by the grim events of the day but heartened by the dislocation and damage wrought by just two aircraft; with 120 Bomber Command aircraft operating that night and on many other nights, the conclusion to be drawn was obvious to all. At Honington the day was not yet done; at 21.57, with the repair work still very much work in progress, the airfield once again resounded to the blast of an unseen delayed action bomb. Although the concussion was felt throughout the station, there were no casualties and further damage was slight.

That night 2 Group made its largest nocturnal effort to date, launching three dozen aircraft to harass no fewer than twenty-one airfields. Conditions were far from perfect and the attacks often not without complication or danger. Fg Off Harris, with Sgts Box and Cartwright, left 15 Squadron's base at Wyton for the high-class resort of Deauville on the Normandy coast. In spite of an intensive search, the three men could not locate the airfield but, rather than return empty handed, as it were, they widened their scope in the hope of locating a suitable alternative. Their persistence was finally rewarded when they came across Lisieux. Almost immediately, the light bomber came under intense fire and as it made its approach at just 5,000ft, the crew could not fail to see the almost continuous lines of 'flaming onions' arcing lazily up towards them before whizzing past at lightning speed. Shortly after releasing their load, several searchlights swung into action, one picking out the lone intruder in its dazzling beam. Harris immediately throttled right back and banked away, breaking free of the beam and leaving the flak far behind. There was no time for congratulations as an aircraft loomed out of the darkness and attempted to get into position to launch an attack. A deadly game of cat and mouse ensued, with neither side able to gain the decisive advantage until contact was lost in the darkness. After that, the most pressing challenge for Harris and his crew was to identify their position and set course for home while there was fuel enough to get there. It was 01.00 hours before the Blenheim finally touched down after their supposed milk run. Two of 101 Squadron's Blenheims were not so fortunate, though the pilot and observer in one were picked up after ditching off Lowestoft a little after midnight.

Plt Off de Mestre of 61 Squadron was pilot of one of the Hampdens detailed to bomb the oil depots and refineries at Ambes, near Bordeaux. Having spent too long searching for the target, its fuel ran out as it crossed the coast near Lyme Regis. De Mestre executed a textbook forced landing without his crew sustaining serious injury. The attack itself was deemed a particular success, with all but one crew claiming to have bombed the target and reporting a massive conflagration, with fingers of flame stretching up half a mile into the sky. No. 4 Group lost a single Whitley from 51 Squadron that had been part of a small force attacking a power station at Schornewitz near Dessau. Fg Off P.G. Brodie had sent a signal stating his attack had been successful but that his aircraft had been hit by flak. At 01.42 hours, a further distress signal was received; the durable Whitley managed to stay in the air for a further hour, clawing its way home, before plunging into the Ijsselmeer.

The forty-eight Wellingtons formed the largest contingent of the attacking force that night, dividing their efforts between the marshalling yards at Hamm, Soest and Osnabrück, oil targets at Hanover, Salzbergen and Ostermoor and the docks at Kiel and Wilhelmshaven, both key locations for the Kriegsmarine and the preparation for Sea Lion. The bombers making their way to the Baltic ports encountered dense cloud en route but found the target area comparatively clear, with large holes in the cloud helpfully admitting the powerful moonlight. The aiming point in Kiel was the *Gneisenau* and once again strenuous efforts were made to secure hits. Fg Off Lemon of 37 Squadron brought his Hampden down to just 4,000ft, ploughing through a storm of mixed flak to gain a clear view of the warship, using his first pass as a dummy run. He then came around a second time but was so blinded by the searchlight glare that the crew could not discern any ground detail, making it impossible to put in an accurate attack; later, the crew identified and bombed Schleswig Jagel airfield as an alternative. Plt Off Parsons came in higher at 10,000ft but had to break off his run when he came under particularly heavy fire, near misses buffeting the aircraft and peppering it with splinters; he too attacked an alternative target, an oil depot at Brunsbüttel, though without visible effect. Sgts Greenslade and Culverwell pressed home their attacks but saw their bombs fall wide of the mark, landing among the labyrinth of dockyard buildings. A colourful account of the attack was published in the Swedish newspaper *Ny Dag* (New Day) and reproduced by the British press. A Swedish sailor was on a tramp steamer in the port and described how:

Hell broke loose 200 yards from our boat. Most of us were asleep and were awakened by a noise as if the world was breaking in two. It was caused by all the guns around the aircraft factory near the harbour firing at once. A large bomber appeared between the clouds and dropped a flare, bathing the area in light. Then came the dive. It began with the worst engine noise I have ever heard and the aircraft dropped like a stone … and let fall some bombs. We heard the cries of the AA men as they were swept off the roof. The English appeared not to be satisfied. They withdrew to the clouds and then let fall another flare. The racing of the engines was heard again. The AA guns were firing for all they were worth but nothing touched the diving aircraft. Now came the direct hit and a whole range of buildings flamed up and of the factory buildings there was only a steel skeleton left.

Though hardly a definitive and analytical account, it was all grist to the mill and offered apparent confirmation of the veracity of the crews' accounts and the effectiveness of the Command's offensive.

The crews fared less well over the inland targets, finding them smothered by a nigh on impenetrable blanket of cloud. Once again a number of crews circled the area for some time in the hope of finding a break or came down as low as 4,000ft, often under direct fire, in generally unsuccessful endeavours to get at the targets below them. Although some fires were observed, nobody held out much hope for a significant return on the effort expended. The crews were very much at the mercy of the climatic conditions they encountered and would remain so for many bitter months to come. Indeed, the conditions for the next twenty-four hours were so bad, summer or not, that Bomber Command had little choice but to call off operations, apart from a trio of Blenheims sent to reconnoitre and harass Ostend and Schiphol airfields; one of these was unable to locate its target, confirming further efforts to be a dangerous waste of time.

Matters were not much better on Wednesday 21 August when only a half a dozen of the twenty Blenheims despatched succeeded in carrying attacks against coastal airfields, including that on the home territory of Jersey. Conditions remained poor throughout the day, prompting 2 Group to call off its night operations. Nos 3 and 4 Groups had already come to the same conclusion and stood their squadrons down. Only the pugnacious Harris at 5 Group decided there was still a chance of a successful attack; many of his crews might not have agreed. Nos 61 and 144 Squadrons took off from Hemswell and were immediately enveloped in layer upon layer of leaden, grey cloud. The Hampdens ploughed on through heavy rain and almost continuous electrical storms, with icing providing a rapid and deadly complication. Their target was M42, the code name for the vital ship-lifting equipment on the Mitterland Canal. The only sign that they had arrived in the target area was the sudden appearance of searchlights and heavy flak bursts, accompanied by lighter batteries. The defences, though active, were equally hampered by the filthy conditions and the attack was effectively reduced to the status of a game of blind man's buff. Only two crews claimed to have actually located the target and only one of them, Sqn Ldr Kydd of 61 Squadron, was confident enough to put in a claim that his bombs had landed in the trough of the canal adjacent to the target. A handful of crews from other squadrons made claims for near misses, but all displayed more hope than certainty. A further dozen Hampdens bombed the oil plant at Magdeburg and secondary targets such as the marshalling yards at Osnabrück and the seaplane base at Texel. Nevertheless, thirteen aircraft, just under a third of the total, failed to locate any worthwhile target and one, that of the experienced Plt Off A. Robson DFC, failed to return to Hemswell; no trace of the aircraft has been found.

The grim summer weather showed no sign of abating and continued to play havoc with operations. No. 2 Group, however, felt compelled to mount its usual raids on the coastal airfields and added the newly installed gun battery at Cap Gris Nez, which was able to offer heavy-duty support to an invasion fleet. Of the thirteen that took off, only two managed to locate their target, one the airfield at Merville and the other the battery, which was also photographed. With the Luftwaffe's attacks across Britain continuing to intensify, there could be no let-up in the pressure applied to the airfields and, as a result, thirty-three Blenheims were sent that night to harass and disrupt the work of no fewer than eighteen of them. In only a handful of cases could the results be seen but in one widely reported case, there was no missing them. At Abbeville one Blenheim managed to ignite a fire estimated at 300 yards in length before heading for home. A couple of minutes later when some 14 miles distant, it was discovered that only the incendiary bombs had been dropped on account of an electrical malfunction and so the pilot made a snap decision to add his high explosive load to the strip of flame still clearly visible. With a bit of joggling and bumping, the bombs cleared the aircraft and exploded with satisfying accuracy amid the flames, leaving an elated crew to make its way home. Only one crew failed to follow suit, a 218 Squadron Blenheim from Oakington that crashed a few miles south of Calais on its way back from Bruges, leaving a sole survivor.

A 115 Squadron Wellington was the only other aircraft lost that night. The attack on the marshalling yards at Mannheim was the sixth for second pilot Sgt Ralph Edwards and his last before becoming a fully-fledged captain. After the usual full briefing, promising a clear sky and good visibility, the sceptical crew loaded their flying kit on to the 3-ton lorry, jumped on board and were driven out to B-Beer. Soon after 23.00 hours the heavily laden bomber hurtled down the runway and clawed its way into the darkness and set course eastwards, crossing the coast at Orford Ness. The flight over the North Sea and Low Countries passed uneventfully, the aircraft bathed after all in bright moonlight. They were guided towards the target area by the already probing searchlights and the lethal pyrotechnic display of flak. Proceeding steadily towards and through the maelstrom, the Wellington was rocked by a series of near misses but emerged out the other side apparently more or less unscathed. Their main job done, Sgts Cook and Edwards swapped places and it was the second pilot who brought the bomber back over the English coast, bathed this time in the nascent light of a new day. Suddenly, there was an urgent shout over the intercom from the navigator Sgt Alan Overall, who was standing in the astrodome. Thick black smoke was pouring from both engines. Within seconds first one, then the other, spluttered then packed up, leaving the bomber eerily quiet. Edwards hastily moved over as Cook hurriedly appeared at the controls and gave orders for the front gunner to abandon his vulnerable position. Edwards was on the way back from informing the gunner when he looked out of the window to see fields and some very solid looking trees in far greater detail than he had expected. With no power to manoeuvre, the Wellington smashed into a line of trees alongside the Saxthorpe–Hayden road near Corpusty in Norfolk at 05.15, severely injuring all on board. Front gunner Sgt Watts later died of his injuries while Edwards remained in hospital well into the New Year, only returning to Marham in May 1941.

The Hampdens were also out that night, with two dozen assigned to attack industrial targets in Frankfurt and another dozen on gardening duties in the Lorient area. No. 61 Squadron's Stan Harrison had little trouble on the outbound flight and was one of only four to locate and attack the target. The return journey was not quite so smooth. The flat Lincolnshire countryside was partially hidden beneath patches of dense fog and in spite of receiving a green from the controller, at 400ft Harrison could barely pick out the glow of the flarepath. Weary after the stresses of an operational flight, neither he nor his crew much fancied a diversion to another airfield and Harrison decided to go around again. It made no appreciable difference and it was still impossible to judge the height accurately as the pilot gingerly lowered the Hampden through the damp fog. All of a sudden the ground came into sharp focus and rushed up to greet the speeding bomber, the two almost immediately meeting with a bone-jarring bump; bouncing into the air again, Harrison quickly regained control and guided it on to the ground more smoothly, much to his and his crew's relief. Most of the crews engaged alternative targets in the Ruhr area and the mine layers completed their tasks. One could scarcely credit it when a surfaced U-boat was picked out in the moonlight gliding through calm waters about 5 miles off Lorient. The Hampden was armed with

250lb bombs as well as a mine for just such targets of opportunity and banking steeply it bored in to attack. One bomb was seen to explode barely 10 yards astern, blasting an enormous mass of water high into the air. The outcome remained inconclusive as the crew lost sight of the U-boat which, at the very least, had received an unexpected and nasty shock.

No. 38 Squadron had been operating over a number of German targets – Mannheim, Koblenz, Soest and Hamm – meeting with only partial success. Four aircraft returned with their bomb loads intact although others pressed on to release their bombs but without identifiable results beyond the outbreak of fires; one crew, however, claimed direct hits upon the tracks at Soest. The following day's lunchtime BBC news bulletin reported the night's raids in a heartening but accurate manner, noting that conditions had hampered the attacks and giving assessment of the damage caused. It had been another night of mixed results for the Command and the complexity and difficulty of attacking pinpoint targets by night was becoming increasingly apparent with every one throwing up its challenges to be met and overcome by each individual crew working in isolation. Only the danger itself, which was ever present from take-off to landing, remained a constant.

As the sun began its daily traverse of the sky, the ground crews of 2 Group were already beavering away to get their Blenheims ready for their daylight strikes. Some twenty were scheduled to keep up the pressure on the coastal airfields, with a couple of oil targets thrown in for good measure. It was not to be a successful day as only seven managed to carry out their attacks, with one returning early on account of engine trouble and a dozen judging the conditions too unsuitable to carry on. Flying singly or with just two or three others in broad daylight was acknowledged to be exceptionally dangerous and standing orders gave considerable latitude to the crews to act as they saw fit. There was also no right or wrong method of attack and in the absence of firm operational directives, the crews tended to experiment and then pool their experiences. In 101 Squadron, for example, there were those who espoused a high-level method, making their way to and attacking from heights of up to 20,000ft, while others were equally passionate exponents of the low-level method, often flying as low as 50ft on route, with some climbing to 500ft immediately before the attack. Nevertheless, many were not too disappointed when 2 Group began to switch more of their effort to night raids, reckoning the hours of darkness to be less dangerous than those by day and, possibly, in good conditions, no less accurate and effective, particularly as fewer sorties would be aborted. At least, the joke went, they would keep the Germans awake. Either way, 2 Group was now regularly operating twenty-four hours a day and as the first batch of Blenheims was touching down, preparations for the night operations were well under way, making it an especially punishing schedule for the ground crews.

On this day, a grand total of thirty-five were assigned to fifteen airfields across northern France, Belgium and Holland. For one gunner stationed at RAF Wattisham, it was to be his first night of operations. Mike Henry had joined 110 Squadron – led by Wg Cdr Sinclair who, the following year, would be awarded the George Cross for his courageous efforts to rescue the crew of a blazing Blenheim – only a few days before and now found himself settling into his dark and cramped turret, wondering what the night would bring. Soon he was bouncing across the slightly uneven grass runway, gathering pace before that slight pressure on the stomach confirmed he was airborne and leaving the dimly lit airfield and safety behind. With Fg Off Sandy Powell at the controls, the aircraft crossed the Suffolk coast north of Harwich before turning south over the North Sea, bound for the French coast and the airfield at St Omer 35 miles inland. From his lofty perch, Henry, although supposed to be scanning the inky darkness for roving night fighters, could not resist watching the flak, tracer and searchlights probing the darkness for the aircraft already over the enemy coast. He had plenty of time to watch the show as Powell coolly circled the airfield for some time until the airfield below had been positively identified. Only then were the bombs released and the crew looked on with satisfaction as they burst across the target area. The Blenheim turned north and barely an hour later was trundling safely over Wattisham's grass.

Most crews claimed to have made successful attacks and a number of fires and explosions were noted and corroborated by other crews. It was a similar story with the ten Wellington crews attacking the oil plant at Sterkrade and the railway yards at Mannheim. Nothing concrete could be claimed but it seemed clear that damage had been caused in the vicinity. The 5 Group crews did not expect to see any spectacular results from their night's work, making the largest mining effort of the year with some forty crews all targeting the Brittany area, more than three-quarters successfully. Sqn Ldr Hyde of 44 Squadron, having released his mine, came across a sizeable merchant ship near Brest and made a pass over it at 600ft, dropping a pair of 250lb bombs as he went; one exploded close to the vessel but without visible effect. Plt Off Price DFC from the same squadron released his bombs over the airfield at Dinard and reported the destruction of a building on the eastern edge of the airfield. A couple of smaller naval vessels and barges were also attacked as targets of opportunity. With well over eighty aircraft operating that night, there was but one lost. A 144 Squadron Hampden crashed on landing at RAF Boscombe Down, fortunately without loss to the crew. Such nights were becoming increasingly rare and it was clear that matters were unlikely to improve. Bomber Command was in for the long haul.

Chapter 4

Phase Three:
24 August to 6 September

Saturday 24 August 1940 was one of those rare, pivotal days that change the course of history. By day the Luftwaffe took full advantage of the clear, sunny conditions that prevailed over southern Britain to renew and redouble its heavy and destructive assault upon the airfields of Fighter Command. By night, and in all likelihood by error, the Luftwaffe dropped its first bombs on London, the heart of Empire. Churchill's response was as immediate as it was calculated. Bomber Command would bomb Berlin, thereby initiating a war of urban attrition that would, in time, lead to the devastation of almost every city and town of any note in Germany and the loss of hundreds of thousands of lives.

As around forty Ju 88s and Do 17s, escorted by seventy Me 109s, carried out the first attack of the day on the RAF's most vulnerable airfield, Manston, the young men of 2 Group were again preparing for battle. A mere nine Blenheim crews were to make their way, unescorted, through the crowded and overwhelmingly hostile sky to harass selected coastal airfields. Four of the crews judged the sky too clear over France to continue, but the remainder, further east, found enough cloud cover to press on with their attacks upon Schiphol, Schellingwoude, Hingene and the harbour at Zeebrugge. The hard-pressed crews were unable to observe definite results but had, at least, caused some disruption to the vast war machine on the other side of the Channel.

The scale of the night's raids was a little more even, though still tipped in the Luftwaffe's favour. As part of the intense drive for effectiveness and efficiency, twenty-five Blenheims took off around dusk bound once again for the airfields. At Bourges the 250lb bombs were clearly seen to burst on and around the hangars, while fires were noted as breaking out at Lisieux, Brest, Lannion, Dinard and Rennes; for the others attacked, no specific claims of damage were made. This was also the case at the massive gun emplacements nearing completion at Cap Gris Nez and the harbour at Zeebrugge, where there had been a significant increase in the number of small ships and barges moored there. As on the previous night, AVM Harris at 5 Group opted to keep up the pressure upon the enemy's maritime transport. A little less glamorous and with results even harder to quantify, Harris remained a firm believer in the efficacy of mining throughout the war, ordering thousands of gardening sorties along the entire length of enemy-held coastline. On this occasion, the focus was on the waters off St Nazaire and La Pallice. As was usually the case, the bombers were also armed with 250lb bombs and the airfields at Vannes, Rennes, Dinard and Coetquidan, the oil storage tanks in St Nazaire and shipping in Brest harbour all received unwelcome calls from the gardeners.

At 3 Group the Wellingtons were assigned targets in western Germany, intended to keep the pressure on the enemy's oil supply, railway and transportation systems. Unfortunately, the heavy cloud conditions prevalent in northern Britain for most of the day had now slipped steadily east where it mingled with the semi-permanent industrial haze to shield the designated targets. Only seven of the forty crews succeeded in locating and identifying their primary target, the rest turning to secondary or targets of opportunity, primarily railway yards, airfields or large industrial premises. Plt Off Alec Cranswick, later Sqn Ldr DSO, DFC, one of the most respected Pathfinder captains with more than 100 operations to his credit, was a newly fledged first pilot in a 214 Squadron Wellington detailed to attack the power station at Knapsack, near Cologne. In spite of repeated circuits over the city, he could not find a break in the cloud and finally decided enough was enough and headed towards his alternative target, Schiphol airfield, which he located without difficulty. Dropping down to just a couple of thousand feet, Cranswick carefully lined up the Wellington with the runway and flew its length, giving his navigator Sgt Harry Brown down in the bomb aimer's position a perfect opportunity. He made the most of it and the bombs were seen to burst on the runway and those on board were near enough to feel the blast. Jubilant, the crew raced for home across the North Sea, confident they had hit the airfield hard.

The Whitleys of 4 Group fared much better, with two-thirds of the twenty-nine aircraft launching attacks on their primary objective, notably the large Messerschmitt factory at Augsburg, where direct hits were claimed and sizeable fires were reported as blazing a little to the north of the target, remaining visible to the crews for some time as they began the long journey home. Plt Off C.J.D. Montagu DFC did not make it, crashing with the loss of all on board south west of Haarlem around 03.00 hours. The other 77 Squadron crews returned to find that Driffield had been attacked again and had sustained further serious damage, which resulted in its closure for repair and the transfer of 77 and 102 Squadrons to Linton and Leeming, respectively.

An impressive 100 per cent success rate was claimed for the attacks upon the Daimler-Benz complex in Stuttgart. In a raid that began at about 23.00 hours, lasted until after midnight and was met with considerable ferocity by the robust defences, a good number of fires were seen breaking out and taking hold right across the target area. The satisfied crews would, however, have been astounded to read the city's official report of the raid; just four people lost their lives and a further five sustained serious injury, the city's first casualties of the war. These were sustained as the bombs fell on the residential suburbs, well away from the massive factory complex where production continued without interruption.

A further ten crews were allotted the long haul attack upon the Marelli magneto works in Sesto San Giovanni in Milan. Once again, the North Yorkshire-based Whitleys had to call in to RAF Abingdon to refuel before taking off on a lovely summer's evening at 20.00 hours. Four aircraft were forced to return early at different points because of mechanical problems but the others pressed on, heading south and eastwards across France. Flying conditions remained excellent and the still snow-capped Alpine peaks not far below the laden bombers gleamed in the moonlight. Aided by the bright lights of neutral Geneva, the crews had no trouble in locating Milan and, facing only moderate opposition, several of the crews made more than one run to ensure that their bomb loads fell accurately. One crew could not identify the Marelli works with certainty and turned instead to the easily identifiable Savoia aircraft factory at the southern end of Lake Maggiore instead. Secondary explosions and fires were observed at both sites and the crews turned for long-distant home buoyed by the thought that they had done a good night's work.

Sunday 25 August dawned bright and clear, the sun's early morning rays streaming over the still smouldering rubble across several areas of London. Other cities and towns across the length and breadth of Great Britain had already been on the receiving end of the Luftwaffe's bombs but for the residents of the heart of the capital, this was a novel and distressing experience. Although the actual damage and casualties were very light, there was an immediate call for an appropriate response and that was the bombing of Berlin. Churchill thought so too. Writing in 1942, Leonard Cheshire, later Gp Capt Lord Cheshire VC OM DSO DFC, recalled the day:

> Berlin in the air. Only rumours at the moment but these sort of rumours usually turn out to be true. Taffy running round in a state of wild excitement: says that that is all he asks for, one trip to Berlin. Well, everybody is the same; after all, Berlin is the reason for most of us joining Bomber Command.

Whilst thorough preparations were being made on airfields across the country, 2 Group continued its campaign to undermine and disrupt the Luftwaffe's daylight assault upon the United Kingdom. Nos 114 and 119 Squadrons put up eighteen Blenheims to carry out spoiling attacks upon the coastal airfields but in the face of clear skies, eleven followed orders to turn for home. The remainder, judging local conditions to be more favourable, pressed home their attacks on airfields including De Kooy, Evere, Wünsdorf and Bergen. A low-level attack was carried out at Texel, where direct hits were claimed on several hangars and buildings, and at the seaplane base of De Mook, where hits were observed on the slipway and waterside hangars. Operating that night, 2 Group maintained the pressure, with a further dozen sorties added to its tally. Focusing upon the French airfields, the crews reckoned they had had a successful night but any damage caused had come at a price; 40 squadron lost two crews without trace.

According to an unnamed pilot, 'when at the briefing before we started the Intelligence Officer mentioned Berlin, everybody was pleased,' but the euphoria did not last long as 'the weather was bad right from the start; as soon as we gained any height at all we ran into heavy cloud and during the journey we caught sight of only three small gaps in the cloud.' It quickly became apparent to all concerned that this was going to be neither an easy nor a successful night; so much so that of the twenty-two Whitleys tasked to attack the vast and crucial Siemens works, only two claimed to have located and bombed it, without visible result, while another released its load over a concentration of searchlights and flak batteries over the western part of the city. Plt Off Clements of 58 Squadron, which had taken part in earlier propaganda leaflet raids over Berlin, gave it up as a bad job and headed a long way north in search of a suitable target, eventually finding the port of Bremen. Greeted by numerous searchlights and flak bursts, Clements came down to just 200ft and released his bombs as the bomber roared over a large factory. Not content with this, he made an even lower pass to enable his front and rear gunner to let rip at the defences, causing several guns and lights to stop abruptly. Flt Sgt Clayton of 44 Squadron was another who failed to locate his target in Berlin but released his load of four 500lb bombs straight on to a series of large buildings at Johannistal, with clearly observed devastating effect.

Others were a little more fortunate. Stan Harrison of 61 Squadron had made good time to the Reich capital thanks to a strong tailwind and a direct route plotted by his navigator, Ted Gray. Picking up a little desultory flak as the Hampden skirted Hanover and Osnabrück, the crew watched with dismay as the cloud continued to thicken to the point where it merged to form an impenetrable screen. The best the young men could do was to head towards the dull flashes that lit up the cloud below them and to drop their high explosive where the concentration seemed most dense. His squadron log noted the target as H324 Tempelhof airfield but added, 'the weather conditions made the attack almost fruitless – a layer of cloud from 1,000 to 5/6,000ft with rare breaks.' Some, including Wilf Burnett of 49 Squadron, brought his Hampden right down in an attempt to get beneath the cloud barrier, only to come under heavy fire for his troubles. Hearing a loud, distracting banging noise, he ordered his rear gunner to close the door in the middle of the aircraft, only to be told in an exasperated fashion that the door was not making the banging sound; the flak was – and it was very close!

The unnamed pilot was one of the few who did locate one of the few gaps in the cloud:

Suddenly, we saw a small gap beginning to open in the clouds three or four miles away and we made for it. First of all, we thought we could see a main road junction. Then the hole in the clouds widened still more and we saw that we were right. Next, we caught sight of the reflection of the moon on a lake and these two points gave us our position. Working down the lake we got on to our target. More flak and searchlights than ever started and we could not keep a steady enough course to bomb the first time. So we did a preliminary canter and two or three minutes later we came back. We didn't dare to go very far away because, having had a bit of luck in finding the place, we were afraid of losing it once more in the clouds. We went just far enough to shake off the guns and searchlights and then came back over the target. By this time the friendly gap had opened up just a bit more. Having dropped our bombs we turned away, dodging violently because the guns were getting warm again. We could see a large red fire burning and then the clouds finally closed over the scene.

For many crews that night the return journey was one of nightmarish tension as the brisk tailwind that had hastened the crews towards Berlin now dangerously slowed their laborious progress home. For the Hampdens, already towards the limit of their endurance in decent conditions, the outlook was particularly bleak. Plt Off Stan Harrison, for one, was eternally grateful for the direct route there and back selected and adhered to by his skilful navigator, eventually landing back at Hemswell after more than eight and a half hours in the air. Others were not so fortunate and 49 Squadron lost one Hampden, 50 another two and 83 no fewer than three. Plt Off G.A.C. Potts of 50 Squadron drifted off course to the north and finally ran out of fuel within sight of Scarborough at 07.50 hours. Easing the Hampden down, he pulled off the perfect landing, which left the aircraft intact and bobbing gently on the calm sea. The uninjured crew had little difficulty in clambering out and jumping into their dinghy to await rescue by a rapidly closing trawler that had tracked the bomber's final moments. So steady did the Hampden look that ropes were attached and an attempt was made to tow the bomber ashore, getting to within 200 yards of the broad beach before giving up the unequal battle and slowly letting the aircraft settle beneath the waves.

Plt Off R.H. Bunker DFC had drifted even further north and was using the very last of his fuel heading towards RAF Usworth in Co. Durham. He did not quite make it, crashing heavily at Boldon on the outskirts of Sunderland at 06.15, badly injuring himself and his WopAg, Sgt G. Thomas. Fg Off N.H. Svendson, a New Zealander from Pukekohe who had joined the RNZAF in 1936 and had been awarded an immediate DFC for his skill and determination in bringing home his aircraft and wounded crew from a mine-laying trip, was at the controls of 83 Squadron's OL-Y and, like many others, had reached Berlin, only to find it smothered by cloud. Acting upon orders, he turned towards his alternative target, the airfield on the island of Texel. Even after some searching, that too eluded him and with his fuel gauges reading very low, he called for a course home. He had left it too late and, after a few minutes, first one engine and then the other began to cough, splutter, then die, leaving him in charge of a very heavy and unwieldy glider. Eventually at 1,500ft, the crew spotted two ships on the horizon and Svendson gingerly steered towards them. One of the ships turned out to be a destroyer escorting a Trinity House boat laying buoys; deciding to be safe rather than sorry, the destroyer opened fire but, fortunately, with more enthusiasm than accuracy. The Hampden touched down on the water not too far from the destroyer, leaving the barely wet crew to spend less than ten minutes in a dinghy before being picked up, offered apologies and treated to naval hospitality. To cap it all, upon arrival at Harwich that evening, Svendson was taken to the officers' mess where, with the help of a couple of whiskys, he gave a first-hand account of the first raid on Berlin to an enthralled group of senior naval officers. Plt Off Tony Mills of 83 Squadron had also taken off from Scampton just before 21.00 hours that night for Berlin. He too had found the night frightening and frustrating in equal measure before watching his fuel gauges fall faster than the number of miles home. His Hampden came down some 30 miles off Grimsby and it was seven long hours before a vessel spotted their fragile dinghy bobbing in the wide expanse of the North Sea.

Guy Gibson, later of Dambusters immortality, was then a young flying officer with a DFC to his name and offered his verdict on the attack, 'The raid was in fact lousy. There was thick cloud over the target itself and I don't suppose more than ten bombs actually landed in Berlin.' He was not far wrong. The only damage caused within the city boundaries was to a wooden summer house in the suburb of Rosenthal; two people suffered slight wounds. The majority of bombs fell in open country to the south of the city. Nevertheless, the raid was astonishingly successful on both sides of the Channel, though in very different ways. At home the sense of grim delight at hitting back at Berlin was all pervasive among the civilian population and RAF personnel. The Mass Observation Survey recorded from Cardiff, 'The bombing of military objectives in the suburbs of Berlin has met with unanimous approval and indeed there is widespread criticism that our planes should bring back their bombs if unable to locate a definite target.' And from Manchester: 'Much interest is aroused by our raids over Berlin and there is a feeling that we should have no scruples about bombing civilians there.' The week's official summary concluded that morale was at a high level and that there, 'was an increased confidence in our ability to secure ultimate victory. The offensive and defensive exploits of the RAF are almost entirely responsible for the present outlook and in particular, the bombing of Berlin has caused great satisfaction.' Twenty-one-year-old New Zealander James Bracegirdle sent a letter to the *Auckland Star* in which he wrote, 'We went over Berlin and, boy, am I proud! This was the first time Berlin had been raided and, though the RAF has been over since, I am able to say that I went on the first raid,' and when the target had been announced he went on, 'we could quite easily have sold our seats to any of the boys who were not flying. One chap asked me to give him the trip. But I believe it is unlucky to change jobs, so held my own seat. We had a good trip there and back and although it was cloudy, we were able to see our eggs go off.' Such a powerful boost to morale at such an otherwise dark moment was priceless. On the other side, the raid's impact was equally electrifying. The long-serving CBS correspondent William Shirer noted the material damage as far as he could ascertain was negligible but the effect upon morale was 'tremendous' and his diary for 26 August records, 'The Berliners are stunned. They did not think it could ever happen. When this war began, Goring assured them it wouldn't and they believed him. Their disillusionment today, therefore, is all the greater. You have to see their faces to measure it.' The three-hour raid had gouged a deep scar across the minds of the people of Berlin and leaflets dropped alongside the high explosive for once deepened it further, declaring pugnaciously, 'the war which Hitler has started will go on as long as Hitler.' Shirer wryly added, 'This was good propaganda but the thud of exploding bombs was better … It was an early sign to those in the regime that the war might be longer and more bitter than many had expected.' The Luftwaffe assault upon Britain far outweighed that on Bomber Command upon Germany and would do for some time to come but this was a key moment in a gradually shifting balance of power.

Once again, the weather remained capricious; as bad and difficult as it had been over Berlin the night before for Bomber Command, a fact openly acknowledged in the morning's press, for the Luftwaffe the morning over southern England dawned bright with a few patches of fluffy white cloud; too few once again for the daylight Blenheims to be able to operate with any modicum of success and safety. All but two of the sixteen returned early in accordance with standing orders. All but one of the eighteen sent out that night, on the other hand, carried out successful attacks on no fewer than fourteen separate Dutch, Belgian and French airfields. Fires were ignited on several and a particularly large explosion was noted at Texel. The long-range Whitleys of 77 and 10 Squadrons were again tasked to attack the Marelli magneto works in Milan and the massive Fiat complex in Turin. Having made the short flight from Yorkshire to Oxfordshire that afternoon, the Whitleys were refuelled and ready for take-off from Harwell by 20.00 hours. However, engine trouble prevented three from taking off, leaving just eleven to make the long flight across occupied Europe and the lofty Alpine peaks, themselves significant threats to the laden bombers. Five Whitleys attacked each of the targets after a trouble-free flight and at Milan the crews reported an enormous column of dense black smoke billowing some 6,000ft into the dark sky. The eleventh crashed with the loss of all on board some 30 miles north west of Milan and it remains uncertain whether this occurred before or after making the attack. Although encountering unusually high levels of activity in the early morning over the Channel, all the other aircraft returned more or less unscathed.

A thirty-two-strong force of Hampdens was despatched to bomb the oil plant at Leuna and the airfield and gas works at nearby Leipzig. Seven aircraft managed to complete their primary task and for one of them in particular it proved a hair-raising experience. Plt Off Paaps of 61 Squadron found the target area hidden beneath an impenetrable layer of cloud and haze and drifted into the Leipzig defensive area, which opened up at him as if his was the only aircraft in the entire sky. Paaps immediately rammed the Hampden's nose down and headed earthwards, pulling out at just 1,200ft and roaring over the city with guns blazing. Finding the AA fire still rather hot, he dropped to just 400ft and weaved his way out of the city limits. Within minutes, by a happy combination of skill and good fortune, the giant oil plant loomed out of the darkness dead ahead, the tallest chimneys seemingly level with the bomber. Instinctively he pulled the nose up and, levelling out once more at 1,200ft, swung back over the plant, dropping his bomb load as he went. The crew were low enough to hear and feel the explosions left in their wake. Paaps steadily climbed back to a more usual height and had an uneventful flight back to Hemswell. There was to be no such return for his fellow squadron member, Plt Off P.D. Tunstall, whose aircraft had also met the poor conditions over the target, searched a little too long and ran out of fuel on the return leg. Opting to land his undamaged aircraft rather than bail out at 07.20 hours, Tunstall located a wide, flat area of scrub beach on the Island of Vlieland and made a perfect wheels-down landing. The four-man crew immediately attempted to set fire to the aircraft and smash the instruments with the escape axe but were captured within minutes, leaving an intact bomber to be recovered and flown to Germany for evaluation and performance trials.

The dispirited crew was taken off to the Dulag Luft at Oberusel near Frankfurt on 29 August for processing. Sgt Michael Joseph Joyce from Co. Mayo, a cousin of the infamous William Joyce, Lord Haw-Haw, eventually managed to wangle a job on the permanent staff there as a carpenter. In the summer of 1942, following an illness, he was transferred to a farm, from which he escaped, eventually crossing occupied Europe with the Comet line and arriving in Britain via Spain and Gibraltar in November. Promoted to Flt Lt, he was awarded a Military Medal for his courageous odyssey. However, at the end of the war a number of German security personnel were brought to Britain for questioning, amongst them Sonderführer Heinrich Eberhardt from the Dulag Luft and Major Richard Kommerich from the Gestapo in Luxembourg. Eberhardt had worked as a stool pigeon amongst new Allied prisoners in various locations and in September 1942 came across Joyce in a hospital near Munich. Finding him receptive to his proposals, Eberhardt took Joyce to Luxembourg to meet Kammerich, who was trying to break the escape lines working in the area. Joyce was dropped off near the abbey at Orval where it was known the monks were sheltering and passing on Allied airmen. Wandering in apparently by chance and using his own identity, Joyce was taken in and made contact with the resistance on 28 September. Moving down the line, he left a long trail behind him. When this came to light in July 1945, Joyce was interviewed by Sqn Ldr W.P. Thomas and Flt Lt G.E.T. Nichols and, under questioning, admitted his original version of events was somewhat selective. With section 161 of the Air Force Act providing that nobody could be court-martialled for an offence committed more than three years prior to the trial, Joyce was in the clear. However, his Military Medal was withdrawn and full notification published on 4 June 1946, and he was forced to resign his commission. By contrast, his pilot, Peter Tunstall, became a serial escaper and inveterate troublemaker, eventually ending up in Colditz in March 1942 where he continued to be a thorn in the Germans' sides and endured several spells in solitary confinement. His constant baiting of the guards was not his only contribution to the war effort as whilst in Colditz he devised a method of conveying messages to MI9, the Military Intelligence Directorate, written on tracing paper and concealed inside letters and photographs sent legitimately to relatives in Britain.

The largest individual force was that comprising forty-nine Wellingtons from 3 Group sent to attack several industrial and transportation targets.

It is both interesting and revealing to note how these fared; only nineteen claimed to have bombed their primary targets, nine their designated alternative targets, twelve targets of opportunity, eight located no target at all and returned fully loaded and one, from 38 Squadron, jettisoned its load on account of heavy icing. The others in 38 Squadron were over Frankfurt and encountered seven-tenths cloud, exacerbated by a significant ground-industrial haze. Crews reported seeing four large fires and a number of smaller ones and claimed hits upon a bridge and inland dock area. No. 37 Squadron crews were also hindered by cloud and haze, commenting in the log, 'Targets were identified in all cases by map reading. This was difficult, however, in view of the lack of a moon and the haze. Cloud conditions over the Ruhr rendered identification extremely difficult. Some crews were, however, fortunate in finding gaps through which the targets were seen.' Even on these occasions matters were far from plain sailing. Fg Off Price was at 10,000ft over Frankfurt and on his final run up towards the identified target when the sharp-eyed front gunner suddenly opened fire at what he perceived to be a fighter boring in to the attack. The couple of seconds it took to discover it was a false alarm distracted the bomb aimer, who released the load fractionally late, resulting in an overshoot, 'but it was thought that some may have hit a portion of it', added the log rather wishfully. The difficulties in carrying out accurate bombing caused by the weather were compounded by accurate and intense flak, supported by very active searchlights and balloons, floating menacingly at heights of up to 10,000ft. As if this was not enough, there was also the potentially lethal risk of mechanical failure or battle damage. Plt Off Clark, inevitably styled Nobby, lost a propeller complete with reduction gear over the North Sea. Clark, a pre-war regular flight sergeant fitter, would have been aware that this had resulted from the seizing of the engine due to lack of oil, possibly a result of flak damage. 'Plt Off Clark showed great skill and coolness in bringing his aircraft back to base on one engine, which involved a one engine flight of 1 hour 55 minutes,' the log noted. However, it did not add that the flight and landing were made with a full bomb load as the crew had been unable to locate their target. Not all battle-damaged aircraft fared so well. Sgt Abbott's 50 Squadron Hampden had been hit by flak over Leipzig and managed to make it back as far as Hemswell, where it crashed on landing. This was the squadron's third loss in two nights, though on this occasion, the crew emerged from the wreckage unscathed.

With the dawning of a new day the Blenheims tried again but with no greater success. Of the thirteen aircraft committed, all but one turned around in the face of an uninterrupted clear sky. Plt Off Prosser of 105 Squadron was the odd man out. His target was Alkmaar airfield on the narrow peninsula west of the Zuiderzee. However, as he and his B flight crew approached, the decision was made to call it a day as there was no vestige of cloud cover. They did spot several ships tight in to the coast on the Zuiderzee side of the peninsula and, aware of the importance of all enemy shipping at the time, decided to attack. Armed with just a pair of 250lb and a dozen 40lb bombs, Prosser chose his target carefully, selecting a large 5,000-ton freighter, sitting at anchor with its hatches open. A number of barges moored nearby became the targets for the smaller ordnance and from their 1,000ft high vantage point, they also noticed a small convoy of camouflaged lorries making its way along the coast road and turned to make a low-level pass, strafing the lorries from end to end. Deciding discretion was the better part of valour, especially given the proximity of several enemy airfields, Prosser broke away over the strip of land and out to sea. Although the damage caused remained a matter of conjecture, it was just the kind of intrusive spoiling attack 2 Group was after.

Although the night Blenheim squadrons did not operate, there was to be no break for the main force. Half a dozen Whitleys from 58 Squadron found themselves following the now familiar route to Abingdon and from there across France and over the Alps to attack the enormous Fiat complex in Turin and the magneto factory at San Sesto Giovani. However, familiarity did not lessen the dangers and the crews had to endure some terrifying periods over the mountains as thick ice formed on the already heavily laden bombers, threatening to drag them from the sky and on to the unforgiving, snowy peaks not far below. However, the danger was dispelled by the warmer air and the crews went on to encounter far less danger over the targets themselves, for the defences appeared lighter and even less well coordinated than usual. No results were observed at the Marelli factory, though two crews were buoyed by the sight of fires breaking out in the easily discernible Fiat works as the incendiaries did their work. Satisfied by what they had achieved, the crews turned for what was a very long but uneventful flight home across more than 500 miles of enemy territory. Nos 51 and 78 Squadrons launched attacks upon another long-penetration target, the aircraft plant at Augsburg, and the marshalling yards in Mannheim, respectively. Again, the results could not be verified beyond signs of fires at Augsburg.

No. 3 Group's Hampdens were split between minelaying sorties off Lorient and various oil targets. The 'gardeners' dropped their mines without significant interference from the shore flak batteries and added a couple of targets of opportunity, notably an E-boat off the Isle d'Eu and a Do 17, which was last seen at low altitude with flames streaming from its starboard engine. Sqn Ldr Bridman DFC of 83 Squadron was happy to support the claim for a 'probable'. Fg Off Guy Gibson DFC from the same squadron was equally confident about the E-boat, having observed two 250lb bombs land within 20 yards and having raked it from end to end with machine gun fire. Several fires were the only discernible results of the attacks on the oil targets. No. 61 Squadron's Stan Harrison did not get that far, and indeed never left the ground. Settling into his familiar routine around 23.00 hours, the Hampden had almost reached take-off speed when there was an enormous bang that shook the whole aircraft and everyone in it; the starboard engine had exploded and packed up at a critical moment. Controlling and stopping a speeding fully bombed up and fuelled aircraft already part of the way down a runway at night is no easy business. Acutely aware of the end of the runway and the rapidly approaching, yet invisible, boundary fence, Harrison stood on the brakes, willed the bomber to slow down and attempted a gentle turn. Just as it looked as if they might get away with it, the starboard wheel collided with an unseen bomb shelter covered by several feet of grassed earth. Unable to run over the top of it, the over-stressed undercarriage collapsed, hurling the fuselage on to the grass, scattering great clods of earth as the increased friction dragged it to a halt. The stunned crew, mindful of the danger of fire, lost no time in clambering out and putting some distance between them and the wreckage. Upon regrouping, the horrific realisation gripped them that the gunner, Archie Sinclair, was trapped in the lower turret as the suddenness of the disaster had afforded him no opportunity to extricate himself from his cramped and vulnerable position. The rescue trucks were soon on the scene and hacked their way to him, pulling him out only a little worse for wear. It had been a very close shave and, as they sipped a mug of scalding hot, strong, sweet tea (laced liberally with rum) in the ops room and went over what had just happened and what might so easily have happened, the reaction kicked in, leaving the young men shaken and thankful in equal measure.

The Wellingtons were similarly divided between a munitions factory in Cologne and the docks in Kiel, where the *Gneisenau* was the principal target. An unnamed pilot gave a widely publicised account of his night's work. Having approached at 13,000ft from the east of the target without difficulty:

One searchlight picked us up and then suddenly we seemed to be in the centre of the biggest collection of AA bursts and searchlights I have ever seen. They all came on at once – just as though someone had pushed over a switch. We flew on, taking every evasive action … We had it all worked out before we took off and I was manoeuvring trying to get to the target in between us and the moon, though unfortunately the moon was only just coming up and wasn't very bright. From my height I could definitely make out the shape of the mole. There was no mistaking it. I decided to take a chance and dived down to 800ft. I was trying to keep the target just underneath the nose of the aircraft all of the time. We got up a dickens of a speed. I estimate we had about 350mph on the clock. When we got down to about 8,000ft they had about 15 searchlights on us. The heavy flak had been coming up all the time and now the light flak started. It just came straight up at us; I have never seen so much before. I thought we couldn't go back, having gone so far, so we just carried on. The lower we went the more intense the flak became. Now and then I was able to catch a glimpse of the mole in front of us. It was impossible to say for certain whether there was a ship there or not. I saw a long dark shape to the west of it which certainly looked like a ship. We carried on diving. I gave the order to release the bombs at 800ft. Then straightaway we shot down to 100ft over the mole and just above the water. There seemed to be more searchlights than ever. At times I was blinded. It was impossible to see the results of the bombing.

Suddenly in front of me I saw lots of trees coming up straight ahead. I pulled the aircraft up and flew over the top. The trouble was we did not dare to go up too high because as soon as we did, every gun in the place started opening up. I tried to get up to 300ft but all the guns seemed to be banging away at us. We went down low again and flew over the town at about 100ft. The front and rear gunners were blazing away at the points of fire on the ground. They used up 3,000 rounds between them. I just hoped to get out of it but I must say that I never really expected that we would. We went south, zigzagging all the time. We got about 15 miles away and then, although we were being shot at, we were able to gain height. As we went up, we still had to take violent evasive action all the time but, finally, we got away.

Such a stirring story certainly made good copy but it is significant that the pilot did not play down the strength of the enemy's defences nor their effectiveness, and did not make any great claims for accuracy or damage caused. In fact, none of the crews over Kiel that night claimed to have located the *Gneisenau*, let alone hit it. Indeed, for some, the cloudy conditions were bad enough to warrant switching to a secondary target and for one of these the decision was to have far-reaching and long-term consequences. Flt Lt Paul Vaillant of 149 (East India) Squadron could not distinguish a suitable target over the port and swung his Wellington west to try his luck over Wilhelmshaven. Over the Elbe, however, his aircraft was picked up by searchlights and, brightly illuminated, pounded by flak from all directions. Although Vaillant managed to break free of the beams by taking violent evasive action, the damage had already been done; his port fuel tank had been riddled by the flying steel of several near misses, leaving the crew with no option but to bail out. All six men cleared the bomber safely around 02.00 hours but by mid-morning were all securely in German custody, where they remained for the next five, long years. Other crews attacked an airfield at Husam and a transformer station at Kelsterbach, near Frankfort, where a stick of bombs released from just 2,000ft was observed to hit the target squarely, with devastating consequences. It was heartening for the crews to hear their colleagues bring back such definite reports of success as they were very aware that they were all too rare.

The sun shone on 28 August and it was clear from the outset that conditions were wholly unsuitable for daylight operations. It was no great surprise when the only two Blenheims sent out to attack French airfields returned early. They were, however, busy that night when fifteen mounted intruder raids upon a string of airfields across northern France and Holland, though to little visible effect. Although a number of targets were attacked that night, notably the Junkers aircraft factory at Dessau and another airframe factory in Leipzig, Bomber Command's main thrust was directed towards Berlin. When the target was announced in closed briefings across the country, there was a buzz of excitement and no little satisfaction, as such attacks were still a novel experience and the appeal of hitting a militarily worthwhile target in the Reich capital, given the raids on Britain, was very strong. At RAF Marham the Wellingtons of 38 Squadron were ready and waiting by early evening and as the clear summer's day faded into darkness, the keyed up crews gratefully clambered on board to make their final checks and preparations. Heading out over a calm North Sea, the Dutch coast was visible at a distance of 10 miles and the navigators had little difficulty in map reading their way across Europe towards the German capital. For some it was a far quieter trip than they had expected. R.J.P. Warren was the navigator/bomb aimer on Wellington V-Victor of 38 Squadron, B Flight, captained by Flt Lt Hubbard:

We had a perfectly routine trip and arrived over the target soon after midnight. I was amazed to see that the street lights, although very dim, were on and the city's roads were easily identifiable. Part of my target, a power station, was already burning but I hope that my contribution added to the damage. The last bombs of the stick seemed to shatter a large glasshouse, which I assumed was part of a market garden nursery. The return trip was uneventful and we landed back at Marham at 05.15.

His squadron colleague, Plt Off Boggis, had Tempelhof airfield as his aiming point and he could see fires burning there already as he made his approach. His load fell on the eastern edge of the airfield and across a nearby railway yard. Upon his return his comment was, 'AA fire appeared to be less than expected and nothing like the barrage which is known to be put up over London. Some enemy aircraft activity was seen but no attacks were made on our machines.' Plt Off Andrew Jackson, later Sqn Ldr DFC, also based at Marham, indeed had a more dangerous time getting there. Whilst climbing gently over the North Sea 'without warning we were under attack from AA fire coming from our own ships below, presumably protecting a convoy. Having escaped serious damage, we continued our long flight to the German capital. Searchlights and heavy flak were encountered on our flight back but over the target, very little opposition – not what we had expected. We had a clear view of the city of Berlin, the marshalling yards were identified and attacked.'

Another anonymous pilot later broadcast an account of his attack, noting similar experiences of early defensive fire but calm over the target:

Several times the aircraft was shaken and I could see bursts of fire immediately underneath us and about 50 yards off the port wing, dead on our height. As we approached Berlin, there seemed to be a semi-circle of heavy guns to the west of the city firing outwards. Once we had passed through these there was very little opposition. As we approached, we had seen for some time a large fire burning on the eastern outskirts of Berlin, so we went to have a look at it. We knew that somebody else from the squadron – loaded with incendiary bombs – had gone in earlier to try to set our target on fire to help the rest of us who were following to find it. We flew right across the centre of Berlin. If we had been bombing indiscriminatingly we could have put our bombs down there but our instructions were to bomb the target and the target only. We were warned about that in no uncertain way. As we got nearer to this fire, I could make out the girders of a huge, gutted building, which was blazing fiercely. We circled around above it, then when we had satisfied ourselves that this was the target, I decided to go in and attack. We flew away a bit to the east, turned around and made a dive attack. Running up to the target we met with no anti-aircraft fire at all, so that we were able to carry out a careful attack. It was just like a bit of practice bombing – left, left, right, right, left and so on. They opened up on us as when we dropped our bombs so we got out as quickly as we could but as soon as we got a little distance away we turned around to see if we could observe any results. There were four fires burning beside the big red one which we had seen earlier. They were intensely white and they formed a long line across the target. Going back was much the same as it was on the inward journey.

There was no official recognition of the damage caused but the official casualty count was given as ten dead and twenty-nine wounded. Goebbels, who had ordered that there be no more than a cursory and derisory mention of the first attack on Berlin in the press, now gave full rein to his journalists, emphasising the base nature of the raid; 'Cowardly British attack' and such like was the headline in many German newspapers, followed by long tirades against the airmen who waged war on innocent women and children by night. A CBS reporter in Berlin, William Shirer, wrote in his diary:

I think the populace of Berlin was more affected by the fact that British planes had been able to penetrate to the centre of Berlin without trouble than they are by the first casualties. For the first time, the war has been brought home to them. If the British keep this up, it will have a tremendous effect upon the morale of the people here.

As ever, there was a price to pay but on this occasion, on balance, it was arguably a good deal; only a single bomber failed to return. Flt Lt Jamie Pitcairn-Hill DSO DFC (his DSO had been awarded only recently for his part in the Dortmund–Ems canal raid on 12/13 August), whom Guy Gibson described as 'always doing things wrong but always getting his bombs on target', had taken off from Scampton at 21.10 hours and successfully bombed his target in Berlin. The journey was a long one for a Hampden and Pitcairn-Hill's eyes flicked constantly from the fuel gauge to the horizon as the bomber crawled across the never-ending North Sea below. Still about thirty minutes from the Lincolnshire coast, as the gauges read zero, he noticed a trawler ahead, turned towards it and pulled off a perfect ditching alongside. The uninjured airmen were taken on board within minutes. The time was 06.20 hours; the Hampden had been airborne for well over nine hours.

It was not, however, the Command's only loss that night. Sgt Norman Bott of 102 Squadron was temporarily attached to 19 OTU and had taken off from RAF Leeming to carry out a routine cross-country training flight to the Isle of Man. For some reason, the Whitley ploughed into a hillside at Silsden, near Keighley, killing four of the five men on board. A report filed by Private Jack Welsh of 2 platoon, 33rd West Riding battalion, Home Guard, on duty at his Silsden reservoir post, explains what happened:

A plane passed over flying in a westerly direction at approximately 23.07 hours, flew back again, circled a few times and crashed about 500 yards away. We immediately ran towards the plane, which was burning furiously, and we were about 50 yards away when there were two explosions which I thought were exploding petrol tanks. Private Dobson and myself were first on the scene and managed to get through the petrol blazing on the ground, to one flyer near the trailing edge of the starboard wing and the rear gun turret which had apparently broken off on impact. I sent Private Fort back to the reservoir to telephone Major Driver. Ammunition was continually exploding but the flyer was too heavy for us to carry and we could not drag him away because of possible internal injuries. He was badly burned about the face and hands but nothing could be done except try to clean the cuts with a field dressing. He appeared to be conscious but we were unable to get any intelligible replies as to whether there were any more still in the plane or whether they were carrying any bombs. He spoke vaguely about Dishforth, Driffield and Leeming, which I subsequently found out were in the same group of Bomber Command. This was the first intimation we had that this was a British plane.

B section's bravery in tackling the hazardous situation – before the men knew if it was a German or British plane – is commendable and certainly saved the life of the rear gunner, Sgt Len Smalley. He recovered fully to resume his eventful flying career, being wounded again in 1941 before being shot down and taken prisoner later in the same year. The loss of Whitley DY-C brought home to everyone the dangers of flying by night in 1940, with or without the additional dangers of enemy action.

With dawn came the routine preparations for 2 Group's daylight attacks. A twenty-strong force was made ready to attack a number of airfields along the Channel coast and further inland as far as western Germany; given the showery nature of the day, there were reasonable prospects of the raids going ahead. Indeed, seven crews did successfully harass the airfields at De Kooy and Alkmaar in the teeth of fierce flak opposition, now in place to counter these frequent incursions. One Blenheim suffered serious damage and others slighter, but all made it home safely. Several other switched targets. Plt Off Prosser, a 105 Squadron stalwart, was bound for Rotenburg airfield deep in Germany but as he was approaching Den Helder, he sighted a large convoy of eleven mixed merchant ships close in to the shore and decided to strike at once this wonderful target of opportunity. Manoeuvring into position for a single pass, he released his 250lb and 40lb bombs as he roared over. In the hectic moments that followed, the results of his attack went unnoticed, although the crew was confident their flight path was directly over many of the ships. Within seconds, the Blenheim was over the harbour and under fire, weaving and jinking until safely out of range. Upon landing, the crew also reported to the intelligence officer the ominous presence of three large ocean-going ships in the outer dock basin and a number of other merchant vessels at anchor in the inner one.

Plt Off Pitcairn, also of 105, was en route to the Soltau area of Germany when he too came across a small convoy off the Dutch coast. Singling out a large merchant ship, he released a single 250lb bomb and was disappointed to observe it explode impressively but ineffectually about 30 yards from the vessel. Pressing on, he came across another convoy a few miles north of the Frisian Islands, this time comprising fourteen trawler-sized ships. This time, he released his remaining 250lb bomb and his dozen 40lb bombs, small but powerful enough to cause significant damage to an unarmoured ship. As he turned for home, one of the trawlers was seen to slew around off course, belching thick black smoke high into the sky. The three men headed back to Watton thoroughly buoyed up by their morning's work.

That night a further eighteen Blenheims were again tasked to harass the enemy's airfields. As was generally the case, few results were observed, though large fires were reported to be burning at le Treport and Dinard. One aircraft from 107 Squadron failed to return to Wattisham, being blasted from the sky by flak at 04.30 hours, a little to the north of De Kooy airfield, with the loss of all on board. The deeper penetrations into Germany were largely thwarted by poor weather conditions and thick ground haze, particularly over the heavy industrial areas. No. 4 Group, represented by a dozen Whitleys from 51 and 78 Squadrons, was to focus its efforts upon a synthetic oil plant near Cologne and the oil storage facilities at Ludwigshafen. Only one aircraft from each squadron claimed to have located and bombed the primary target, although neither was able to assess any damage caused. Several other crews managed to locate unspecified industrial targets in Bonn and Reischoltz but the rest simply brought their bombs back home, weary and frustrated by the whole affair. The Wellingtons were also after the oil supply with attacks on the Bottrop plant and storage facilities in St Nazaire, now fully repaired after being blown up by the Kent Fortress Royal Engineers in a secret XD operation in early June to deny the enemy oil depots. No. 37 Squadron crews took part in both attacks and reported a group of vivid white explosions and subsequent fires at the German site. There, several bombers were overhead simultaneously, an unusual event in 1940, and several crews commented that the flak and searchlight defences appeared confused, ill-coordinated and unable to put up effective resistance. As was expected at this stage, the defences at St Nazaire were light and did little to bother the Wellingtons.

The Lincolnshire-based Hampdens also targeted oil, this time the oft-visited Gelsenkirchen complex. Despite the poor conditions, a good percentage of the twenty crews reckoned they had successfully located and attacked the target. Several other crews headed for equally familiar targets in the Ruhr or 'Happy Valley'. No. 61 Squadron's Stan Harrison left Hemswell at 23.00 hours and followed the well-trodden aerial highway, crossing the coast at Orford Ness, out over the North Sea, into enemy territory near the Schelde estuary before swinging down towards the Ruhr. Weaving vigorously and constantly losing and gaining altitude in an attempt to confuse the numerous flak and searchlight crews below, the crew grumbled once more that they had come all this way to see damn all but cloud and murk. The ten or so seconds flown straight and level on the final approach seemed an eternity as the shells burst all around, hurling red hot, jagged shell splinters far through the air. Once the bombs had been released, Harrison pushed the stick forward to pick up speed before heading westwards into calmer and more tranquil night air. The German border came and went, Rotterdam passed silently beneath the starboard wing and what little moonlight there was reflected brightly off a mill pond like North Sea; the contrast with the scene only an hour earlier was stark. A mere four hours and forty minutes after take-off, the Hampden touched down to make a smooth landing. One Hampden failed to return, that of Plt Off Hymes of 44 Squadron, though he and two others survived to become prisoners.

Friday 30 August was destined to be a very long and busy day. Making good use of the decent daytime weather, well over 500 Luftwaffe aircraft roamed the sky over southern England, wave after wave. The fierce skirmishes with Fighter Command were watched by hundreds of thousands of citizens, willing the dashing pilots on, the visible front-line defenders of the beleaguered island; The Few brought down twenty-four raiders but at an unsustainable cost of twenty fighters. Throughout the day, Bomber Command's Blenheims remained on the ground, victims of the same fair weather. As night fell, however, removed from public gaze, the 2 Group airfields resounded to the roar of the Bristol Mercury engines as eighteen fully bombed up Blenheims took up their positions for take-off. Most were bound for Emden, where shipping was being gathered and readied for the invasion, but three were sent to attack the new and enormous cross-Channel gun emplacements at Cap Gris Nez. This attack was felt to have gone well and the crews were delighted by the lack of effective opposition, leaving them undisturbed to bomb accurately before scuttling back across the Channel to safety. The Emden raid was a very different affair, with the port well defended by flak, searchlights and a belt of airfields in northern Holland and the Frisian Islands. At a time when individual crews were still responsible for their route, most chose to fly south before swinging north to approach the port from the landward side, hoping to avoid over-flying the airfields and gaining an element of surprise. In the event eight Blenheims attacked the primary target, though without being able to provide confirmation of whatever damage was caused; the remainder bombed the airfields at De Kooy and Papenburg. The price paid was high. Plt Off W.R. Evans of 40 Squadron crashed on take-off, the aircraft instantly becoming the crew's funeral pyre, the leaping flames visible to all the men and women at RAF Wyton. Sgt L.A. Williams, the pilot of 18 Squadron's L9378, had made it back from Emden as far as the Norfolk coast before his bomber, perhaps battle damaged, ploughed into the ground near Weasenham in poor visibility. There were no survivors. A similar fate befell Plt Off J.S.F.P. Price of 110 Squadron when his aircraft crashed a few miles north of Ipswich at 02.20 hours, though on this occasion, the WopAg, Sgt Macdonald, lived to tell the tale.

The twenty-five Hampdens operating that night kept the pressure on Germany's oil supply with attacks upon plants at Magdeburg and, again, Gelsenkirchen, as well as transportation targets, including the Dortmund–Ems canal. A 50 Squadron Hampden captained by Plt Off K.R.K. Smettem was shot down east of Arnhem at 00.32 hours by Oblt Werner Streib with the loss of all on board. Just fifty-eight minutes earlier he had accounted for the demise of a 214 Squadron Wellington over Emmerich, again with the loss of all on board. Fg Off L.M. Craigie-Halkett and his crew had taken part in the main attack of the night on Berlin, a target that in the eyes of the beleaguered British people had assumed, as Churchill had hoped, an importance beyond its direct and military value. Such was the thirst for information about these attacks that the Air Ministry took the unusual step of authorising a journalist to fly on the raid in a 38 Squadron Wellington. The twenty-nine-strong force focused their efforts upon the enormous Siemens factory and the Henschel aircraft works and a little over half reported that they had definitely identified and bombed the target area. Others picked out a power station at Klingenberg and railway yards, leaving a number of fires burning fiercely. No. 4 Group added a further dozen to the total; the stories of two crews typify the resolute determination shown by the airmen to carry out their orders to the best of their ability, accepting high levels of risk to do so. Plt Off Crooks arrived over the blacked out city and began his search for Tempelhof airfield. Scanning what ground detail was visible, the 58 Squadron Whitley criss-crossed the capital until the crew spotted something that looked promising. Fixing their gaze on that area, Crooks circled around and released a flare, which did indeed reveal the airfield below. Approaching at 8,000ft to keep above the bulk of the light flak, Crooks ordered a part-load release and their fall was noted to be to the west of the target. Not satisfied, Crooks swung around again to make a second pass, his bombs this time falling across the airfield and buildings and igniting several fires. Once again, Crooks orbited the target to check his position before embarking upon a third pass, his bombs again detonating on the airfield. Whilst the city's defences were not what they would become in 1943, the sky over Berlin was still not a healthy place to be, especially for such a long period over essentially the same area.

Fellow 58 Squadron pilot Plt Off N.O. Clements, who just a few days before had swept over Bremen docks under heavy fire at just 100ft to carry out his attack and engage the searchlight and flak batteries with the Whitley's machine guns, found himself over the city and literally in the dark. Unable to identify anything of interest, Clements ordered a series of flares to be released as he cruised over the unusually quiet capital. When all these had been exhausted without effect, reluctantly he turned for home. Passing over Nordhorn, his crew spotted a large factory complex and they decided to attack that in preference to taking the bombs back, in the full knowledge that doing so would use up more of their dwindling fuel supply. Mentally plotting the distance to fuel consumption graph, Clements eked out the fuel as best he could, gently easing the bomber out over occupied Europe and the North Sea until, with the coast of Yorkshire visible on the horizon in the pale glow of dawn, the engines began to cough and splutter. Coaxing the bomber as far as he could, he gave the order to bail out while there was still height to do so and the aircraft was still under control. Clements knew as he gave the order that he would not have the time to get out and instead attempted to ditch the bomber; it was around 05.00 hours and he had been in the pilot's seat for nine and a quarter hours. While he and three of his crew did survive, the experienced Sgt M. Hill was caught by an off-shore breeze and drifted further out to sea, his body being lost. Such was the slender line dividing life from death.

The final day of the month dawned bright and clear, the sun blazing from blue sky from the off. It was clear that 2 Group would be stymied during the day and switched its effort to the hours of darkness, with twenty Blenheims making attacks upon Cap Gris Nez, the shipping in Emden harbour and the regular airfields. Although 4 Group sent nine Whitleys to attack the oil plants at Wesseling near Cologne and a petro-chemical plant at Leverkusen, the Command's main thrust was again made towards Berlin. No. 61 Squadron's log pretty well sums up the night, 'Weather conditions were bad. Ten-tenths cloud to 2,000ft made it impossible for the pilots to pinpoint with accuracy. Those who bombed the target found breaks in the cloud but only made approximate positions over the cloud.' There was little chance for the Hampden crews to locate their primary targets, Tempelhof airfield and the BMW aero engine plant, though several did have more success over the oil refinery at Magdeburg. The Wellingtons too, although including the regular targets of Hamm and Soest, also focused on Berlin, this time the Henschel aircraft plant. No. 38 Squadron navigator/bomb aimer R.J.P. Warren recalled:

There was ten-tenths cloud over that part of Germany so, because we were not allowed to bomb unseen, we started to bring the bombs back home. Unfortunately, having spent some time searching for the target, we were running a little low on fuel so the skipper decided to drop the bombs in the North Sea. We were well north of where we should have been, a fact I blamed on the Germans moving a radio beacon which I had used as a navigation aid. As we approached the coast, I was able to identify a flashing beacon as one near Scarborough. A quick change of course got us back to Marham just in time.

What turned out to be Warren's thirty-second and final operation with Bomber Command had lasted nine hours and ten minutes but had achieved very little more than irritating the population of Berlin. Plt Off D. Romans DFC and his 44 Squadron crew were not quite so fortunate. Their Hampden had taken off from Waddington at 20.05 hours and at 05.35 hours finally ran out of fuel, tantalisingly close to the beach at

Cromer. Pulling off what was termed 'a perfect pancake landing', the four men took to their dinghy and rowed the 400 yards to the shore, wringing wet but otherwise none the worse for wear.

The Air Ministry communique noted the raid had taken Berliners by surprise on account of the thick rain cloud prevalent over the city. Drawing on the reports of the Berlin correspondent of the Swiss *Basler Nachrichten*, it stated that a large aero engine factory in the north-east of the city had come under attack soon after 23.20 hours, as had a power plant in the western part of the city. Fires had broken out in both areas. Whilst CBS correspondent William Shirer was adamant that the damage caused was slight, he was clear that the raids were having a major effect upon the population. Goebbels too confided in his diary, 'All Berlin up in arms,' and, 'incredible anger towards the British'. Although he found the AA barrage 'a wonderful spectacle' and was delighted that 'Berlin too is in the midst of the war and that's a good thing,' ordinary Germans were not so sure. Having taken personal control of the defence of the Reich on 9 August, Goring's bombastic proclamation that no British plane would ever fly over the Reich and 'if any does, you can call me Meier', was now being seen for what it really was: the air raid warning was widely, if discreetly, referred to as 'Meier's hunting horn', a reference to the corpulent commander's favourite pastime. For many citizens, outraged by the impudence of the RAF and confident in the might of German arms, it was easy to dismiss as a grandiose fantasy the message printed on the leaflets that also rained down on Berlin; it read, 'Do you finally understand? Have you forgotten about our air force flying around over Germany and doing whatever it wants, which in July dropped 37,000 bombs on military targets in the Ruhr region and Rhineland alone? We are the ones who will decide when and how this war will end.' For a few, however, Bomber Command was doing just enough to make them wonder.

On the first anniversary of the Germans' attack upon Poland, they were doing their damnedest to do the same to Britain. Although the statistics would show that the Luftwaffe committed slightly fewer aircraft to the battle on 1 September, nobody at Biggin Hill, Eastchurch, Detling and other towns from Kent to the Tyne would have noticed the difference. The patchy cloud over the eastern counties of England at least gave 2 Group some grounds for optimism. Eighteen Blenheims were made ready to carry out the by now routine attacks upon the airfields and invasion-related targets. No. 105 Squadron, for example, launched four aircraft, each to separate targets: the Dortmund–Ems canal, an oil storage site in Hamburg and aircraft parks at Diepholz and Paderborn. All four were in enemy air space when the clear and cloudless sky in front of them put paid to their sorties. Plt Off Prosser, who had been bound for the canal, was already well over the Zuiderzee so he decided to seek out an airfield. Suddenly, the Blenheim was rocked by a series of near misses as an unseen heavy flak unit opened up 14,000ft below. The gunners did a good job, one burst smashed in the perspex nose section, seriously wounding the observer, Sgt H.H. Duncan, in the shoulder. Prosser reacted immediately and pushed the aircraft's nose down to gain speed, a 300mph gale howling through the aircraft. Setting course westwards, Prosser raced for home, intent upon getting treatment for Duncan, who was bleeding profusely. Although still alive on landing, he died shortly thereafter, the squadron's first casualty since converting from Battles to Blenheims in June. Only three of the eighteen completed their missions successfully.

Once again, the focus switched to the night's activities with a total of seventy-one aircraft bombed up and ready to go. The Blenheims were on the order of battle bound for Germany. Sgt Jim Moore was a gunner with 18 Squadron based at West Raynham. Having made his operational debut on a raid on the airfield at De Kooy on 16 August, this was to be his first visit to a German target. At the briefing the met officer had assured the assembled crews that the sky would be clear en route and over the target, ideal conditions for bombing in 1940. Moore, together with his pilot, Sgt Roger Speedy, and observer, Sgt Bob Watson, finished off the preparations and they were airborne as planned at 21.30 hours. Climbing to around 12,000ft over the sea, the three men were dismayed to find themselves flying over a solid layer of cloud that completely shielded the

Bomber Command expended much effort in their attempts to disrupt vital canal traffic in northern Germany.

The wreckage of 311 Squadron's Wellington L7788 shot down on a raid on Berlin on 23/24 September. The six-man Czech crew survived to become POWs.

Into the Night Sky. A Wellington crew climbs on board to face an uncertain future in hostile skies.

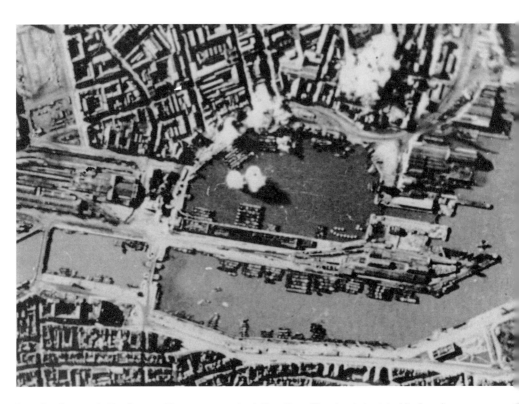

Invasion barges in Boulogne. There was no doubting the offensive intent behind such an enormous build-up of shipping.

214 Squadron Wellington takes off.

44 Squadron crew poses in front of a Hampden at twilight.

The boot on the other foot. Bomb damage at RAF Driffield following the attack on
15 September 1940.

A write-off at Driffield on 15 September 1940.

ground below. The odd burst of flak in the distance and the dull glare of searchlights playing on the cloud gave the only clues that the light bomber had crossed into enemy airspace. Droning eastwards, the view from the cockpit remained unchanged and with little prospect of any improvement, Weston, uncertain as to where they were, handed Speedy a general course for home, remaining vigilant for any break that might enable them to make an attack. Finally, in the region of Schiphol airfield, a searchlight battery came into sight and Speedy at once seized the opportunity and released his bombs in a single stick. Within seconds the cloud blanket was back in place and the onus fell back on Moore to pick up a radio fix to locate their position. After an anxious few minutes, he picked up RAF Bircham Newton, enabling him to fix a course. No sooner had he done so before a signal came through redirecting them to Honington on account of poor weather. So much for the assurances they had been given about clear conditions. However frustrating, after five hours in the air, it was a good call. No. 40 Squadron's Plt Off R.V. Whitehead crashed while attempting to land at West Raynham and 18 Squadron's Flt Lt Howden did likewise at Great Massingham a few miles away; in both cases the crews were lucky to escape without serious injury. This was not the case, however, with Plt Off R.N. Peel of 75 Squadron attempting to land at East Wretham, also in Norfolk, on his return from Hanover. Losing sight of the flarepath in the misty half-light of dawn at 04.38 hours, he ploughed into a line of trees on his approach; a fire broke out as the crew scrambled out of the wreckage, swiftly followed by an impressive explosion as the last of the fuel went up.

Although Bomber Command attacked numerous targets throughout Germany, from Emden to Munich, few fared any better than Moore's crew. No. 37 Squadron sent five Wellingtons to an oil storage facility in Hanover, a pair to an aircraft factory near Leipzig, another pair to a power station at Kassel and three more to harass airfields. Only four of these succeeded in identifying their primary targets beneath the dense, unexpected cloud. As the squadron log noted pithily, 'Cloud conditions made identification extremely difficult. Under such conditions crews are largely dependent upon flak and searchlights to identify the locality of their targets.' The lack of success was, once again, not due to a lack of effort. Plt Off Chilton failed to locate the power station at Kassel but did locate and made runs over three airfields, heavy defensive fire preventing him from making an accurate attack on each occasion. Undaunted, Chilton pressed on and managed to carry out an attack to his satisfaction over a fourth airfield, although the results were impossible to observe in the prevailing conditions. Flt Lt Lemon, an experienced campaigner, met with ten-tenths cloud over Leipzig and set about circling at decreasing heights in search of the cloud base; some 8,000ft lower at just 3,000ft, the Wellington popped out into clear air and immediately came under intense fire. Half blinded by the searchlights at such close quarters and buffeted by a series of near misses, Lemon was forced to withdraw without bombing; he had spent more than half an hour over the target area. Sqn Ldr Collard spent double that time over Hanover, tantalised by intermittent and fleeting gaps in the cloud. His efforts proved equally futile and rather than release his load indiscriminately, he began the long journey home, fully loaded in spite of fuel being at a premium. Sqn Ldr Golding's persistence did pay off and he did put in an attack upon the oil plant from 7,000ft, resulting in near misses, scant reward for the crew's determined efforts under fire. When it became known that his incendiaries had failed to drop for some reason, Golding embarked upon a search for a suitable target, eventually finding an airfield 35 miles north-west of Hanover; only then did he turn for home. Plt Off Burberry was also heading home from Hanover and a routine fix was received from his Wellington at 02.50 hours, placing it 50 miles from the English coast. It was the last Feltwell heard of it as it crashed into the North Sea shortly afterwards, killing all but the pilot, who endured two days at sea before a keen-eyed lookout on HMS *Niger* sighted his dinghy. In his official report, Burberry courageously admitted that he may have fallen asleep but, having also noted that there had been problems with the altimeter, that was judged to be the more likely cause of the tragic loss.

The Whitleys of 4 Group ranged the furthest afield, with 51 and 78 Squadrons dividing their efforts between the marshalling yards at BMW works in Munich, the Fiat works in Turin and the Marelli magneto factory in San Giovani, near Milan. Being such a distant target, Munich was caught largely unawares and the crews were astonished to find it only partly blacked out. Fg Off L.H. Eno was one of the first to arrive at 00.40 hours and enjoyed an interference-free run over the works at 9,000ft; his rear gunner reported several bombs bursting amid the factory buildings. Sgt G. Samson followed a little later, drawn by the fires burning below. He reported his first stick as falling into the heart of the works and his second into the workshops a little to the north. By the time he was leaving, the defences were at full throttle and flak bursts and searchlights were scything through the sky. All the Whitleys returned safely, with one crew dropping low enough over France to machine-gun an airfield where the German crews were busily and unsuspectingly practising night flying.

The mist and fog that had caused such difficulties for the returning crews dispersed quickly in the face of the warming rays of the summer sun to set up a gloriously fine day. As Fighter Command and the Luftwaffe joined battle once more, Bomber Command could do little but prepare and wait for darkness. The Command mustered eighty-four bombers, a reasonably high percentage of the total available and serviceable, but still far fewer than its German counterpart. The light Blenheims were assigned a range of targets across north-western Germany, with the airfields set as worthwhile alternatives. As ever, the success rate varied in the face of enemy opposition and the sheer difficulty of flying long distances in the dark. Plt Off Goudge of 15 Squadron, for example, was unable to identify any distinguishable landmarks or features on the ground on account of a thick haze. The sky around him remained eerily silent and empty, providing him with no means of accurately fixing his position. Lost and alone over hostile territory was a frustrating and frightening situation to be in. Eventually, Goudge bowed to the inevitable and set course westwards. Passing over Holland, some lights became visible on the ground and, keeping his eyes glued to them, he swung around and reduced his height to get a better look. The three men on board decided it was a flarepath, possibly one near Eindhoven that lay on their projected route home. In any event, it seemed to be a worthwhile and legitimate target in enemy territory, so the crew carried out an attack, dropping their load of high explosives and incendiaries in one go. The bomber circled for several minutes to ascertain the results and the young men were gratified to see the explosions amid the lights, which went out to be replaced by small fires that continued to burn for some time, well beyond that of their own incendiaries. It was the best that could be done for the night and Goudge turned for home, landing safely at Wyton. The sole Blenheim lost that night was also based there; the body of 40 Squadron Plt Flt Sgt R.B. Broadhurst was washed ashore on the Dutch coast some time later, those of the other two men were never recovered.

No. 5 Group's Hampdens maintained the pressure on several of their oft-visited targets, the Dortmund–Ems canal, the Bosch factory in Stuttgart and oil facilities in Ludwigshafen and Mannheim. Flying in good conditions, the crews could see the ground features at the latter targets and it was reported in the 61 Squadron log that Flt Sgt Saunders was in a buoyant and patriotic mood for he, 'dropped his bombs on the target to the accompaniment of "God save the King" which he heard on his TR9'. There was to be nothing light-hearted about the flight of Hampden P4370 of 144 Squadron, which like 61, was based at Hemswell in Lincolnshire. Plt Off R.S.A. Churchill and his crew were on their return from Ludwigshafen when at about 00.45 hours their aircraft came under brief but devastating attack over Holland. The night fighter, flown by Feldwebel Paul Gilder of 3/NJG1, opened fire at close range, the canon shells shredding the rear section of the fuselage and killing the gunner and WopAg, Sgts Walter and Edmeads. A little further forward, Churchill and navigator Plt Off I.C. Kirk, were unscathed but immediately headed for the hatch and a long spell behind barbed wire at Barth and Spangenburg, respectively. The Hampdens also carried out the first of many attacks upon a new target, the U-boat base being established at Lorient. Although the vast U-boat pen complex was at this stage no more than a wishful doodle on a naval architect's sketchpad, intelligence reports suggested that a half a dozen of the submarines had been transferred to the former French base to threaten Britain's Atlantic supply lines. Scampton-based 49 Squadron, which provided part of the thirty-nine-strong force, already knew the area well from its recent mining operations and had little difficulty in locating the port and, in the absence of serious opposition, was able to carry out an accurate attack. Several claims were made for bomb loads falling in the dock area and fires taking hold and remaining visible to the Hampdens for many miles as they headed home.

The Wellingtons of 3 Group began a sporadic series of attacks upon the vast wooded areas of Germany where, amongst other things, it was thought that the Germans had established enormous military storage facilities. At best, it was like looking for a needle in a haystack, even with the use of specially developed incendiaries. Half a dozen crews each from 77 and 58 Squadrons were 4 Group's contribution to the night's effort. Although one of 77 Squadron's aircraft failed to make the start line, the others pressed on eastwards towards the oil plant in Frankfurt and, unusually and in the teeth of significant opposition, all the crews claimed to have made successful attacks in good conditions and returned safely. No. 58 Squadron had a little further to go to their target, a key power station in the great port of Genoa. Being at the limit of a fully loaded Whitley's endurance, the crews stopped off at RAF Honington to refuel before setting course across occupied France. Although one remained grounded there with mechanical failure, the others succeed in attacking the port or, in two cases, alternatives in the vicinity. The margins for error in navigation, adverse weather conditions and time spent searching for the target, were very slight if they were to make it back to Britain and the dangers of encountering an early morning fighter patrol over northern France were more than an outside chance. For two of the crews that night, the journey was just a handful of miles too long. Flt Sgt D.H.A. Moore had taken off shortly before 20.00 hours and almost ten hours later was still in the air – just. The Whitley had drifted slightly off course and a thin strip of coast that appeared on the horizon was Essex. For a while it looked as if the bomber would make it but first one engine then the other began to splutter with fuel starvation and Moore had to give his crew the order to take up ditching positions. Having carried out a beautiful landing, the men were relieved to be able to scramble out and get into the dinghy but dismayed to find the current swiftly propelling them on a course parallel to the coast, drifting northwards. By the time HMS *Pintail* found them, they were off Aldeburgh in Suffolk still heading northwards, ironically back towards their home base in North Yorkshire. Sqn Ldr Bartlett and his crew were still over enemy territory when Moore's Whitley had finally given up the ghost. Not too long later, they were in a similar position. The Kent coast was clearly in sight, bathed in the morning sunlight, when the engines fell silent and Bartlett told his weary crew to prepare for ditching; he gently eased the bomber down into the water just off Margate at 06.20 hours and after a few minutes of paddling, the soggy but uninjured airmen stepped safely on to terra firma.

While the Whitleys were still finishing off the night's battle, the new day's was well under way. On the first anniversary of Britain's declaration of war, there was little time for contemplation as the Luftwaffe made the most of the fine weather, which put paid to 2 Group's daylight sorties. In fact, some Blenheims did take off in daylight intending to be over their targets at very last light. No. 15 Squadron was amongst these, tasked to harass the coastal airfields. Fg Off Morris was over the former British Great War airfield at St Omer shortly before 22.00 hours and reported several hits upon buildings that were well ablaze as he headed for home. Plt Off Gilmore also reported the fires, one now especially large, as he watched his load fall on the north-east side of the airfield adjoining a wood. Plt Off D.E.C. Myland, already awarded the DFC, completed his attack but probably took several hits, causing his aircraft to crash near Kettering at 00.25 hours with the loss of all on board. An 18 Squadron Blenheim was lost attempting to land at Great Massingham at 01.00 hours, after attacking a target in northern Germany; two of the three men on board lost their lives.

No. 3 Group once again despatched a number of Wellingtons to raise fires in the wooded areas of the Hartz mountains and Gruneval forest near Berlin, although more usual names such as Hamm, Soest and Swerte were also on the target lists. Ground crews had been busy throughout the day at RAF Marham, home to 38 Squadron, to prepare a dozen Wellingtons for the night's attacks. As it turned out, only eleven made it into the air as Plt Off Sargent misjudged his aircraft's size and had a run-in with a fence while taxying out for take-off. In good, clear weather, the sturdy, twin-engined bombers droned eastwards singly towards their targets and, for once, had no difficulty in locating them. As the official log recorded, 'In all cases many fires were started and very many white and red explosions were seen and much damage is believed to have been done.' Although hardly conclusive evidence-based statements of fact, there was still little reason to doubt the veracity of the reports given independently by the crews, especially when the heavily censored and controlled Nazi press appeared to bear out such reports, the *Nachtausgabe* led with the headline 'New Acts of the Air Pirates' and the *Borren Zeitung* reported, 'Last night Churchill continued a series of his criminal blows against the German civilian population. Frankly, Churchill belongs to the category of criminals who in their stupid brutality are untreatable.' These righteous protests were written in response to the previous night's raid upon Berlin. The targets were gas works and power stations and there were reports of large fires and explosions being caused, especially after direct hits upon a gas works were clearly observed. Perhaps another less publicised explanation for Goebbels' outrage was the fact that not a single intruder was brought down anywhere over the Reich, in spite of the impressive barrages. Indeed, all but one made it back safely; Flt Lt D.G. Tomlinson had lifted his Whitley off Leeming's runway at 20.26 hours and carried out his attack successfully but at 06.45 it was still clawing its way through the air. Only a handful of miles from base, fuel starvation finally silenced the Merlin X engines, leaving Tomlinson no alternative but to make a forced landing in the flat, open fields around Northallerton. Coming in slowly, the pilot eased the bomber to the ground with remarkably little damage to the machine and the men in it. Within the hour, the young men were back in the familiar surroundings of Leeming, albeit minus their aircraft.

Though the airfields of Yorkshire were not set for a sunny, fine day, those further south were and once again the Luftwaffe made full use of it with more than 650 aircraft sweeping over the country. As the day drew to a close, unusually, Bomber Command mounted almost a rerun of the previous night's attacks. Eighteen Blenheims headed for the coastal airfields and claims were made for numerous buildings being bombed or burned out. No. 101 Squadron, which had been operating at night for only three weeks, sent its Blenheims a little further afield, to the great marshalling yards in Hamm. Visibility was poor, a problem compounded by a persistent ground haze and vigorous use of searchlights, and none of the crews were able to locate the yards, even though they were 4 miles long and not far short of a mile wide. Nevertheless, the determined crews did manage to seek out suitable alternatives, a ship that was carelessly showing lights off the Dutch coast, the airfield at Berck-sur-Mer and another unidentified one. The light bombers did not get through the night unscathed. Plt Off F.J. Otterway of 107 Squadron had attacked the airfield at Mardiek and at 03.00 hours was carefully but routinely lining up R3824 to land back at Wattisham. Within seconds of the Blenheim's wheels touching the ground, it smashed into an unseen parked aircraft, killing two of the three men on board.

Two dozen Hampdens were sent in clear conditions to the oil plant at Stettin on the Baltic coast, a location that led to all but four of the crews identifying the primary target. The journey back, however, was especially difficult for one crew. Fg Off Lewis Hodges, an old hand, was well aware that Stettin was stretching the Hampden's range a bit and as soon as he ran into large banks of cloud on the way home, his eyes immediately turned to the fuel gauges and he told his navigator to get a fix on their exact position, knowing he had little margin for error. The radio chose that moment to go U/S so Hodges had little option but to plough on with engines set for economical cruising, relying on compass bearings and dead reckoning calculations by Sgt S.J. Hitchings. All on board were oblivious to the fact that the wind direction had changed and that a strong northerly wind was both slowing their progress and steadily pushing them south of track. As darkness was little by little replaced by daylight, the cloud began to break up and Hodges was able to make out a rugged coastline – Cornwall, a very long way from their base at Scampton. With the time at 06.15 hours and the fuel situation critical, Hodges' spirits soared as he saw an airfield come into view. Straightaway, he headed towards it, lowering his undercarriage in preparation for an immediate landing as he went. Suddenly, all hell broke loose as the airfield's defences sprang to life, light flak hurtling towards them. Hodges was forced to turn away and as he did so one engine coughed and died, either on account of flak damage or lack of fuel. Realising the game was well and truly up, he immediately gave the order to bail out while there was still just about enough height to do so. Hitchings and gunner Sgt Turnbull reacted at once but Sgt Wyatt for some reason did not hear the order. Having held the bomber steady, Hodges knew his only chance was to make a forced landing and, unaware that Wyatt was still on board, headed towards a patch of open ground. As soon as it ground to a halt, more or less in one piece, Hodges scrambled out of the mangled bomber and, taking stock of the situation, decided it did not look much like the Cornwall he knew. Suspecting that he had somehow strayed even further off course into enemy territory, he set about trying to set fire to the aircraft, fortunately without much success. To his amazement he saw Wyatt emerge from the wreckage. Together they managed to destroy the wireless, some charts and anything else they thought might be of use to the enemy. They were soon joined by a farmer, who addressed them in French and gave their location as St Brieuc in Brittany. The pair set off at once in order to put some distance between themselves and the crash site and hid in a wood where they decided to walk by day and rest by night, trusting they would get support from locals in isolated houses. This simple and audacious plan worked far better than they dared hope and having acquired some civilian clothes, they crossed the demarcation line into Vichy France at Chauvigny on 26 September. They were put in contact with an Englishwoman who generously gave them a full set of smart clothes, shoes, food and money before sending them by train to Luchon via Toulouse, with the intention of crossing the Pyrenees into Spain, a far more difficult proposition than it initially sounded. The pair was arrested by two suspicious gendarmes, ending up in the medieval Fort St Jean in Marseilles, the older of the two fortresses that dominate the harbour of the Vieux-Port, on 18 October. After a couple of abortive attempts to make use of the lax Vichy supervision to make good their escape by sea, Hodges reverted to attempting to cross the mountains, which he eventually did at Easter 1941. Following an unpleasant interlude at the detention camp of Miranda del Ebro, he finally reached Gibraltar in June, before returning to Britain to resume a career that saw him rise to the rank of Air Chief Marshal. Sgt Wyatt, who had escaped from Fort St Jean on Boxing Day, beat him home by nearly two months.

The Wellington crews, thirty-two of them, were again on 'Razzle' fire-raising sorties. Strips of wet phosphorous sandwiched between thin pieces of celluloid and covered in gauze were packed in water, 500 to a tin and sealed with foil. Over the target forest, the lids were removed and the contents emptied down the flare chute, a delicate task to complete without spilling the contents in a dark and confined space in flight. As the Razzles floated down they began to dry out and once fully dry would spontaneously combust and burn with a powerful 8in flame, setting alight anything it was in contact with. Smaller versions were known as Deckers. The novel but effective weapons were not popular with the crews as it was not unknown for these tiny incendiaries to be dropped or blow back unseen into the dark fuselage or lodge on the tail plane, then dry out and ignite. The *Neue Frankfurter Zeitung*, outraged, carried a story relating how the curious and innocent-looking strips had been found, picked up and put into their pockets by locals, with very unpleasant results.

No. 37 Squadron launched ten Wellingtons on Razzles, most to the Black Forest near Kaiserslautern and a pair to the Thuringian Forest in the Hartz mountains. Using flares to enable them to see the ground below, all the crews successfully located these vast swathes of forest and scattered their incendiary loads widely. As the squadron log baldly put it, 'Fires were started, some of which appear to have set light to the forests. No great forest fires, however, were observed by any of the crews,' who were in most cases a little bemused by the whole process. Sqn Ldr Collard was probably more impressed by the sight of an aircraft coming in to land at a well-illuminated airfield. Dropping sharply to just 800ft, Collard homed in, ordering his gunners to blast the original aircraft and another that had come into view and strafe the airfield as a whole. Although no particular results were observed, the rear gunner alone had fired well over 1,000 rounds before the Wellington turned for home. Fg Off Baird-Smith also put in an attack upon Duren airfield from 7,000ft and observed his bombs falling across the site, the last one triggering a spectacular explosion, which in turn triggered several more. For good measure, he made another pass at 3,000ft to enable his gunners to add to the confusion and destruction below.

Although 78 Squadron sent half a dozen Whitleys to the oil plant at Magdeburg, it was the six from 51 Squadron that made greater headlines by attacking Berlin. Although the raid on the Charlottenburg power station and railway targets across the city was not especially damaging or effective, it kept up the pressure on the Nazi regime, which could not conceal the casualties – ten people were killed, for example, when bombs fell on the Gorlitzer station – nor the fact that the RAF was able to range over the Reich more or less at will. Goebbels noted in his diary that Hitler, who did not take to the shelters during such raids, 'is really charged up' and that there was much discussion of reprisal raids on London, adding, 'At the moment the Führer is still holding back. How much longer?' The public answer came in the huge rally at the Sportspalast on 4 September where Hitler vowed to erase the cities of Britain and put the British night-time pirates out of business once and for all. Goaded beyond tolerance by the persistent attacks upon Berlin and with the credibility and prestige of the whole regime on the line for the first time in the war, Hitler was forced to respond and take on a war of attrition in which he assured his nationwide audience 'The hour will come that one of us will crack and it will not be

National Socialist Germany!' Hitler had in fact already given the orders to switch the weight of the Luftwaffe's attack away from the airfields and military targets to London, thereby changing the entire course of the battle. Confident that the invasion was just days away, Hitler's decision, driven as it was by political rather than military necessity, was by no means a rash one.

Such high-flown considerations were far from the minds of the young men who were struggling to carry out their orders over the city that night; they were simply doing their best to destroy legitimate targets allocated by people who did think about such things. For one crew the night was to become a very personal battle of life and death. Fg Off J.M. Taylor's Whitley had sustained flak damage over the city and was forced to ditch just off the Dutch coast in the early hours of the morning. Although four of the men managed to scramble out and into the dinghy, Sgt M.H. Jones was still inside when the Whitley lurched suddenly and slid beneath the waves. The next few hours were spent bobbing uncomfortably across the North Sea and it was more with relief than anything else when an He 59 seaplane spotted them and picked them up. By 09.30 hours the group was back on dry land and beginning what turned out to be four dreary years behind the wire.

The Indian summer continued and on 5 September the Luftwaffe again carried out more than 400 sorties over southern England. Bomber Command's response that night was a full 80 per cent smaller. The Blenheims were assigned to French coastal targets and in good conditions achieved a higher than usual success rate. Plt Off St John of 15 Squadron was one of those who could not claim hits with certainty; he had passed over Boulogne harbour several times under fire until he had finally identified his target, the small but potent E-boats known to be based there and set to play an important role in the invasion. St John made his run at 10,000ft amid the dazzling glare of several searchlights and bursting flak, somewhere, at least, over the target area.

The Whitleys of 4 Group again divided their effort between two long-distance targets, Regensberg in south-eastern Germany and the Fiat works in Turin. Five of the nine 58 Squadron crews put in claims for successful attacks on the oil plant in Regensberg, coming down to heights of between 1,000 and 4,500ft and making several runs in order to improve accuracy; the crews reported leaving a wall of flames leaping hundreds of feet into the sky. The other four all located and attacked secondary targets. As an innovation, all the aircraft carried a supply of Razzles, which were dropped over wooded areas on route home. No. 77 Squadron put up a half a dozen aircraft for the now well-trodden but dangerous path through the Alps. For Plt Off Richard Pinkham, the flight was far shorter than expected as one of his Whitley's engines began to overheat while off the Thames estuary, causing him to throttle back and rely on the other, an uncomfortable position to be in in a fully-loaded aircraft. Having received permission to jettison his load in a designated area, he put down at Wattisham without mishap, his night's work over. Plt Off Andy Dunn was back in action after a week off. N1365 had an uneventful flight south and the experienced crew were almost able to enjoy their panoramic, moonlit view of the snowy Alps before descending to 8,500ft for the run-up to the target. The defences were once again fairly desultory and ineffective, allowing all the crews to locate and attack the massive works. Dunn's crew had just watched their bombs fall in the target area when there was 'a colossal explosion' that lit up the darkness for miles around and forced a column of debris and dense smoke well over a mile into the sky. Turning for home with a comparatively rare feeling of satisfaction for a job well done, the crew set about the long and hazardous flight back, eventually touching down at Linton-on-Ouse at 05.00 hours after more than nine gruelling and nerve sapping hours in the air, most over enemy territory. The weary crew were delighted when the others independently confirmed their observations. Then on Sunday morning, they also had the pleasure of reading about their exploits in the morning papers. The official Air Ministry communique read:

The Fiat works in Turin was lit by parachute flares. The first bombs hit what is thought to be a power station and a huge fire was started. The Fiat aircraft factory was also heavily bombed. The work's buildings were hit and enveloped in the yellow flash of a huge explosion. When more raiders returned 20 minutes later, a fierce fire was raging and only the walls of one building were left standing. There was heavy anti-aircraft fire but little searchlight activity was encountered.

The Hampdens fared badly on this occasion, even though their targets were well-known, oil plants and depots in Stettin and Hamburg, both usually identifiable on the Baltic coast. Several more attacked the Dortmund–Ems canal and a single aircraft was sent to take on the mighty *Gneisenau*, though foul weather meant that it did not come under the slightest military threat. The raids went more or less to plan with a mixture of primary and secondary attacks being carried out, raising some significant fires. What was unusual was the loss rate, a total of six Hampdens being lost, RAF Hemswell being the hardest hit with four failing to return. Plt Off J.E. Newton-Clare and his 144 Squadron crew were lost without trace. His colleague, Sqn Ldr G.F. Lerwill, did return from Hamburg to become the sole survivor when his damaged Hampden overshot on its first attempt and then stalled and crashed on its second; amidst the wreckage was the body of Sgt W.I. Mackay, who had been awarded a DFM at the end of July. Two of 61's Hampdens almost made it back to Hemswell. Operating at the limits of endurance in battle conditions, Flt Lt D.J. How would have been acutely aware of the need to conserve fuel from the outset. Nevertheless, the last drops were consumed as the bomber crossed the English coast, compelling him to make a forced landing near Stradsett in Norfolk, saving his own life and those of two of his crew; Sgt C.J. Knight, though alive when pulled from the wreckage, later succumbed to his injuries. Plt Off Earl was forced to do likewise near Burton in Lincolnshire when one of his engines began to play up; initially intending to make use of the flat, open countryside to attempt a normal landing, the undercarriage jammed part of the way down and resolutely resisted all attempts to shift it. Having no choice in the matter, Earl guided the earthbound bomber down as best he could, hoping the undercarriage would not cause the aircraft to cartwheel; in the event, it simply collapsed and all four men were able to walk away from the mangled aircraft more or less unscathed. Two other crews might well have wished for a dry landing. No. 49 Squadron's EA-L came down in the English Channel just off Calais, somewhat off track on its return from Stettin; all on board survived to become prisoners. For most airmen ditching was a once in a lifetime ordeal but for Plt Off D. Romans DFC it was different. In the early daylight hours of Friday 6 September, Romans' Hampden ran out of fuel, tantalisingly within sight of Lowestoft. Just the previous Sunday, at almost the same time, Romans had played out the same perilous scene off the coast of Cromer. His luck held once again and he and his crew were soon picked up by a naval patrol vessel. It says much for the spirit of the day that Romans – and WopAg Sgt Logan, who had been with him on the previous ditching – were flying on operations at all so soon after what would have been seen in the twenty-first century as a traumatic event that warranted prolonged counselling and psychiatric therapy. It says yet more as both resumed their flying duties within days, still taking the fight to the enemy in defence of their country.

A similarly determined and pugnacious spirit was to be found in Flt Lt Harold Burton, who became the first RAF officer to escape successfully from a POW camp during the war. Burton lifted his 149 Wellington into the darkening sky over Mildenhall at 20.30 hours to carry out a Razzle raid on the Black Forest. Having done so without difficulty, the bomber came under brief but accurate anti-aircraft fire. Several near misses rocked the aircraft but the Wellington ploughed on its way much as it had done before and the crews' heart rates fell back to normal. About ten minutes later, however, the temperature gauge for the port engine began to show an alarming increase and within minutes the powerplant had seized solid. Burton, acutely aware that he was still a long way from home, gave orders for all movable equipment to be jettisoned and the crew set to the task with a will. The flight had become a nerve-jangling contest between the remaining engine and the force of gravity, distance travelled against height lost. Slowly but remorselessly gravity won and Burton eventually was forced to give the order to abandon the aircraft while there was still sufficient altitude to do so safely. The last to leave the moribund bomber, Burton landed unhurt in a bog and quickly buried his parachute in the convenient sludge. For two days and nights he alternately hid and walked before his luck ran out as he emerged from a dyke straight into the path of a startled but armed German soldier. He was taken to Fort St Mahon, a few miles south of Berck, before being transferred to Stalag Luft I at Barth on 16 September as a member of a sixty-strong group of prisoners. He quickly became involved in a series of escape attempts and it was as a result of one that in May 1941 he found himself kicking his heels in a solitary confinement cell in a wooden building within the camp. The window of his cell was barred, fixed by screws to the outside of the wall but, not daunted, Burton discovered he could just reach them and painstakingly began to loosen them with his eating knife. The delicate task took him several nights but, on the night of 27 May, he undid the screws, silently removed the bars, climbed out of the window and dropped into the compound, which was covered by three searchlights, patrolled by armed guards and enclosed by a high double barbed wire fence. Burton bided his time and then, knowing that the guard's beat took him past them every three minutes, headed for the double gates. Having scraped a shallow trench under the gates, he squeezed beneath them and ran through the darkness towards a second barbed wire fence some 50 yards away. Timing his effort precisely, he scaled the fence and dropped to the other side as a free man. He made his way to a local train line and followed it in the direction of Stralsund, hiding and sleeping during the day and walking by night. By the 30th, and growing weaker by the day, he arrived at Sassnitz, where he knew a closely guarded ferry left for neutral Sweden each day. Scouting around, he discovered some trucks that were bound for Sweden and wedged himself into an uncomfortable position on the axle of one of them, praying that he would not have to be there long. Shortly afterwards, Burton heard the trucks nearby being searched but his precarious hiding place remained undiscovered and he was overjoyed to find that they were being loaded immediately. He spent the four-hour crossing lying flat under the truck before climbing back on to his cramped perch prior to disembarkation. Once safely ashore, Burton dropped to the ground and headed towards a police station to give himself up. On 19 July 1941 he was awarded the DSO and resumed his flying career, eventually rising to the rank of Air Chief Marshal. The dogged and determined exploits of men such as Burton and the less well known men including Romans and Logan bear eloquent testimony to the calibre and courage of the men who flew the bombers in the summer of 1940.

The run of good, late summer weather continued with a clear sky once again putting paid to the Blenheim daylight counter-attacks but enabling the Luftwaffe to mount more than 700 sorties. Bomber Command's reply was on a smaller scale than on recent nights but did include the high-value target of Berlin. No. 10 Squadron was the sole operational unit in 4 Group and then only with five aircraft on the ops board. The crews mounted their airborne steeds as usual around 20.30 and headed up into the darkening eastern sky, settling in for the long haul to the Reich capital. Over the city the best part of five hours later, the crews began their search for the Salzhot oil depot, which they all claimed was well ablaze by the time they left; one crew was able to pick out a railway junction and marshalling yard in the Spandau area of the city and upon their return to Leeming informed the intelligence officer that their bomb load had hit it square on. Fg Off R.H. Thomas and his four-man crew did not make it back for the debriefing. A signal from the aircraft, placing it not far from the English coast, was received at 04.00 hours but it certainly did not cross it and, in spite of an extensive search, was lost without trace.

No. 3 Group's Wellingtons were once again 'on the Razzle' over the Black Forest but a number were allocated a power station in west Berlin, adding to the nocturnal consternation and confusion in the city. The 38 Squadron log records that cloud and haze over the city prevented accurate observation of the results of their efforts but added somewhat doubtfully, 'but it is thought by some that extensive damage was done'.

The log was on far more secure ground with its entry upon Brussels, where conditions were far better. Two crews, searching for a suitable target, having failed to find one over Berlin, managed to identify a busy railway yard on the outskirts of the Belgian capital. The small patches of cloud proved no hindrance and in the absence of opposition and mindful of the Allied civilians beneath them, the crews took their time to carry out an accurate attack. The bombs were seen to fall on target and the explosions that followed ignited a number of fires.

No. 5 Group's Hampdens fared badly over the Ruhr, where adverse weather conditions and the omnipresent industrial haze resulted in only three aircraft making any sort of attack on the primary target, an oil plant in Dortmund. One of them was flown by Stan Harrison of 61 Squadron, back on operations after a rare week off. He and his crew had easily slipped back into the tried and tested routine with all on board alert to the dangers facing them. The starry sky gradually became dotted with cloud and then was blotted out the further east the bomber flew. The clearest indication that the target area had been reached was the flak, flashes and explosions cleaving through the darkness and murk. Navigator 'Jimmie' James decided to drop his load into the largest concentration of light beneath the cloud, making the best of a bad job. Pushing the nose down a little to gain speed, Harrison headed for home, arriving back at Hemswell after just shy of five hours in the air. The same scene was being played out at several stations across eastern England but at RAF Waddington with a novel and most unwelcome twist. Fg Off Beauchamp of 49 Squadron was on his final approach at 03.25 hours after attacking the marshalling yards at Emmerich when he came under fire from an enemy intruder. Fortunately, no damage was done beyond scaring the living daylights out of a weary crew and the enemy aircraft roared away after just a single pass. The incident was, however, a salutary and widely publicised reminder of the need to remain vigilant at all times, even when 'back home'. One 44 Squadron aircraft did not make it back home following its attack upon Krefeld, an alternative target. Hit by flak over the target, the starboard engine all but exploded, causing the bomber to lurch and begin a spiralling dive. Plt Off Vollmer was still in the process of clipping on his parachute when an explosion blew him out of the aircraft and sent him hurtling earthbound through the darkness. Desperately attempting to hook his parachute on and breaking two of his fingers in the process, he succeeded in securing one clip and immediately pulled the cord, thereby saving his life. Following a dizzying and uncomfortable descent, he landed safely and became, like his crew mate Plt Off S.R. Taunton, a prisoner of war; the other two members of the crew lost their lives.

Attacks from the Blenheim crews, who often acted as intruders, upon the coastal airfields and gun batteries at Cap Griz Nez completed the Command's strategic and anti-invasion effort for the night. As crews flopped thankfully upon their beds in the early hours of the morning, none would have had any inkling of the momentous events that would unfold within the next twenty-four hours. Saturday 7 September would irrevocably change Britain's perception and conduct of the war and provided a pivotal moment that crystallised and defined an entire nation's spirit both then and for generations to come.

Chapter 5

Phase Four:
7 September to 31 October

Nobody had ever seen anything like it. Street after street of the East End
of London was burning. Thick black smoke billowed high into the bright
summer sky, a malevolent marker of misery, visible for miles around. It was
the Armageddon long prophesised, long feared and long awaited. Wave
after wave of bombers, clearly visible to those far below, flew over London,
the capital of Great Britain and the heart of the mighty, worldwide Empire,
unleashing destruction, devastation and death on an unprecedented scale.
Darkness offered no respite or protection and by dawn on 8 September, a
Sunday, 448 men, women and children lay still amid the smouldering ruins;
a further 1,337 were counted as seriously wounded and many hundreds
more injured. Terrible as this was, far worse was expected to come with
the dawn for, at 20.07 hours the previous evening, a signal had been issued
by GHQ Home Forces to Eastern and Southern Commands, just a single
word – Cromwell – bringing them to readiness in the face of imminent

invasion. It was the blackest day of many black days in the war so far. The situation could not have been graver. General Brooke, Commander in Chief (C-in-C), Home Forces, had much to think about as he walked through London's streets that night, 'I had not even got a hat on and there was an inferno of a bomb raid,' he wrote in his diary, 'a continual roar of falling bombs and AA fire and through the middle of it that unpleasant, vicious hum of AA slinters as they came raining down … Went to the office in the morning where I found further indications of impending invasion. Everything pointing to Kent and East Anglia as the two main threatened points.'

Just under twenty-four hours earlier, Goring's personal train, codenamed Asia, which required two of Germany's heaviest locomotives to pull it, had brought him to the Pas de Calais. Standing on Cap Blanc Nez within sight of the Kent coast, surrounded by his sizeable and sycophantic entourage, Goring, who, as he proudly announced to the German people, had personally assumed command of the attack, waited in eager anticipation for his aerial armada to fly overhead, bound for London, codenamed Loge. A low rumble became audible, gradually swelling into an ear-splitting roar as 2 miles above, formation after formation of heavily laden bombers and their nimble fighter escorts passed overhead, seemingly invincible and unstoppable and certainly unmolested and unhindered by any significant opposition. The outcome seemed inevitable and beyond doubt.

It was almost one-way traffic as the Command's daylight response to this gargantuan onslaught had been just a half a dozen light Blenheims, given the task of disrupting the enemy's airfields. The clear, sunny skies brought an early conclusion to their sorties. As night fell and the Luftwaffe returned to stoke up the fires still raging in London, Bomber Command put up well over 100 aircraft in an attempt to thwart the invasion. All over eastern England, the airfields hummed with a vibrancy born of long anticipated and dire emergency. The diary of RAF Honington records, '18.45 hours – we were warned to take certain anti-invasion precautions as an attempted invasion was believed imminent. Aircraft were bombed up, loaded with ammunition and fuelled, and crews stood by. Parachute guards, gun crews and all defence personnel were on the alert.' The aircraft that had been held at readiness for the past few weeks in case of invasion were to be put to the test.

The Channel ports were the obvious targets. Photographic reconnaissance had provided plenty of evidence of an ominous build-up of invasion barges and shipping and of the heavy defences put into place to protect them. On 2 September, for example, Bomber Command Intelligence Report 904 reviewed the situation and included much evidence along the lines of:

Photographs taken on 1 Sep. show in southern four miles of South Beveland Canal 160 barges, 20 proceeding South, none moving North. Until 26 Jul. there had been no barges and no traffic in the canal and barge traffic considered abnormal.

Report 908 the next day:

Photographs taken 2 Sept. show: off Calais, 35 small motor boats in line astern setting course northwest from the neighbourhood Calais harbour. West of Dunkirk eight E-boats in line astern proceeding west reported by visual reconnaissance four miles from shore. Increase of 50 barges Ostend since 31 Aug. Increase of one hundred and forty barges at Temeuzen since 16 August. No concentration of barges at north end of Beveland Canal, slight increase since Sept. 1 at south end where total is now approaching two hundred.

Report 920 for 7 September made widespread comment on that day's photographs including:

Ostend: increase of 100 barges making total of 300. 30 vessels 40ft in length possibly tugs or motor boats for towing which are also new arrivals. Naval unit 280ft long possibly coastal defence ship Peder Skram. Bruges-Ostend Canal: six tows comprising 33 barges moving towards Ostend.

Dunkirk: In harbour increase of 45 barges total 75. No change in the barges in the waterways in the town. 32 barges anchored offshore. Calais: In the harbour are 86 barges, 13 smaller vessels probably for towing and 35 small craft 45ft long. Lying off are 17 barges and 30 small vessels probably for towing.

The detail in report after report went on and on and there could be little doubt as to the aim of this monumental effort.

Sgt Mike Henry, a gunner in a 110 Squadron Blenheim and a Londoner by birth, was one of the many men who recalled that night gazing in awe at 'an ominous glow on the western horizon' en route to attack the docks at Dunkirk. The thought of his family and friends in the midst of such an inferno did much to generate a grim determination to fight back against such aggression. Coming in to attack at around 6–8,000ft, the Blenheims were perfect targets for flak of all calibres, supported by dazzling searchlights probing the darkness, seeking and ready to grip their prey for the benefit of the gunners nearby. Fg Off Hugh Lynch-Blosse was on his first operation, though his target was further along the coast at Boulogne. As he approached the dock area somewhat higher at around 12,000ft, he:

> … suddenly saw red and white tracer curving upwards towards the aircraft. It seemed slightly ridiculous that such a firework display of lights could be lethal if any struck us. Then I saw black shapes all around us. For a fleeting moment I thought they were balloons, part of the barrage, and I panicked momentarily at the thought of flying into the cables. Then I realized it was flak bursting.

Steadying his mind and resisting the natural urge to turn away, he held the Blenheim as steady as he could to give his observer, Sgt Richmond, as good a platform to take aim as possible. After what seemed like an age, Richmond released their load and plotted the bursts:

… which, he said, were in the dock area, then I dived away to get the hell out of the flak. In a minute or two, all was peaceful and we were on our way back to Wattisham … When we got back there was a noisy party in full swing in the mess.

Not everyone reacted to these vitally important sorties in the same way as the pressure mounted. No. 15 Squadron's log tersely noted that it had despatched three aircraft to Dunkirk but to little apparent effect, although Flt Lt Mahler had carried out a diving attack to deliver his bombs to the dock area and ignited a number of fires. It continued '[they] were unable to identify any barges owing to the glare of numerous searchlights. It seems that bomb aimers are unable to get accurate results owing to slackness on the part of the pilots. Sgt Garrioch was unable to locate the target owing to the haze.' The Hampdens of 61 Squadron fared little better a few miles along the coast at Ostend. Its log noted, 'All dropped their bombs on or near the target areas allotted to them. Owing to thick haze, it was impossible for them to distinguish any shipping or assess the damage that may have been caused to them. Bombs which fell among the harbour buildings were seen to start fires.' Seven Whitleys from 51 and 78 Squadrons, unaccustomed to such short-range targets, fared even less well; being unable to locate the target area with any degree of accuracy amidst the haze and glare from the searchlights and flak and mindful of the friendly and only recently occupied people below, many crews opted to return with their bomb loads intact.

The strength of the defences caught some by surprise, although some of the older hands were able to make good use of their experience. Plt Off Sam Hall, a New Zealand newcomer to 9 Squadron, was sent to attack the docks at Calais and later recalled the calculated shrewdness of his pre-war regular pilot, Bertie Bernard:

We went to Calais for the barges and I got down into the bomb aimer's spot, issuing instructions to the pilot who took no notice at all and veered away to starboard. I said, 'There's the target, away to the left, can't you see it?' Bertie who usually stuttered said very firmly, 'Are you flying this aircraft or am I?' He waited until another Wimpy was coned by searchlights, then turned in and followed my directions while the enemy was otherwise engaged.

While experience could and did play a part in increasing the chances of survival, when it came to the war in the air it was not the only nor the dominant factor. The only aircraft lost that night belonged to 51 Squadron, a Whitley flown by Sqn Ldr J.B. Tait, later of 617 Squadron fame and a Group Captain, who would be awarded a DSO and three bars and a DFC and bar. On this night, one of his engines simply packed up just before the enemy coast. Tait managed to keep the Whitley in the air long enough to make landfall in Suffolk but around 01.00 had to force land in fields near RAF Bircham Newton, fortunately without serious injury to those on board.

Whatever the actual outcome of anti-invasion raids, which became known as the Battle of the Barges, they certainly looked impressive and were heart-warmingly visible from the southern shores of England. Whitelaw Reid, Yale graduate, journalist and scion of the Reid publishing family, whose flagship newspaper was the *New York Herald Tribune*, donned a bullet-proof vest and tin hat and boarded a small armed trawler on an anti-invasion patrol. It went a little way out of Dover harbour and bobbed about in the Channel, faithfully covering its beat, the very front of the anti-invasion front line, diligently looking for and ardently hoping not to find enemy shipping. As he had hoped, the trawler provided him with a ring-side seat, 'I remember the far coast being quite a sight [he wrote] it was like the 4th July, all kinds of fireworks on the far side. And the reflection of it came across a very still Channel in the water right up to the edge of the boat I was on.' A sign of last ditch desperation they might have been but, aside from the actual damage caused, the raids served to remind the massed German troops sheltering far beneath the bombers that Britain had not yet thrown in the towel and that there would be some serious fighting to do if they were to cross the Channel successfully and set out on the march for London.

As dawn spread across the sky the following morning and the news of the onslaught upon London began to filter out, all serviceable aircraft were ready and waiting, fully bombed up at any number of stations across the country. Those lucky enough to be away on leave were urgently recalled to join those waiting nervously for the order to send them into battle, while hundreds of men and women bustled about making final preparations that would enable them to do so. The outline of the Command's response to the direct threat of invasion had been drawn up some four months earlier in May 1940 when such an outlandish eventuality began to appear a little less absurd. The Banquet Plan aimed to maximise the Command's strength by drawing in and deploying all the aircraft at its disposal, including training aircraft such as the Oxford and Anson and even outdated models such as the Audax and Hart, to be manned by the more senior pupils still under training. By early September a total of 500 aircraft and crews had been scraped together to support the frontline squadrons and were ready for deployment. No. 49 Squadron's log records these desperate but bold measures. At 21.50 hours on the evening of 7 September a signal was received from 5 Group stating that Invasion Alert No.1 was to be effective from 00.01 hours on 8 September. All aircraft not specifically detailed for existing operations within the next twelve hours were to be bombed up and remain on standby, with crews confined to the station. 5 Group also undertook to provide detailed information on the aircraft likely to be deployed at Scampton as part of the Banquet Plan. Finally, all personnel, ground crew and anti-aircraft defence were to be kept on alert and be ready for immediate action throughout the day and night. In the meantime, every effort was to be made to take advantage of the prevailing conditions to carry out spoiling bomber attacks on the barge and shipping concentrations.

For the first time in quite a while the patchy cloud cover, combined with the absolute necessity to press home an attack, converged to allow a total of thirty-four Blenheims to carry out a series of offensive and reconnaissance sorties over the Channel ports, especially Boulogne and Dunkirk. Little could be observed with any degree of certainty but the target areas were considered by the crews to have been hit as hard as the light bombers could hit. This did come at a cost; a pair of 82 Squadron aircraft was lost without trace.

As darkness fell, 130 bombers, all loaded to capacity, climbed into the late evening sky and headed south, flying against the even larger Luftwaffe force making its nefarious way north. Once again, a twenty-five-strong contingent of Blenheims led the way, bound for Ostend and Boulogne. The fortunes of 101 Squadron are typical. The ten light bombers on their way to the French port soon ran into poor weather conditions, sufficiently severe to compel half of the force to abandon the search for the target and return to West Raynham without releasing its bombs. Three did manage to release their loads over the harbour but with little idea as to their effect. The final pair failed to return, with no sign of Sgt C.W. Cooke's aircraft and that of Flt Lt E.J. Palmer being forced into the sea; the body of the observer Sgt J. McKee was washed ashore some days later and was buried in his home town of South Shields. The loss of this crew had a heavy impact as Palmer was a well-known figure in the squadron, having served with it since May 1937. A further four Blenheims were lost, bringing the loss rate to a shocking 25 per cent of those committed.

The thirty-strong Wellington force was divided between the Channel ports and the harbour at Emden, which, though further away, was still a naval hub packed with shipping assembled for the invasion. They too encountered rain bucketing down, dense low-level cloud and severe electrical storms, accompanied by the very real and lethal risk of icing. Twenty-year-old Plt Off Alec Cranswick was one of the young pilots struggling through the murk. Passing over Boulogne, or at least where he thought Boulogne was, at 10,000ft proved to be a pointless exercise and so he pushed the nose down and dropped to 7,000ft to begin a square search of the area. Confirmation of their location came from an unwelcome source as an intense barrage of light flak engulfed the Wellington, blasting them from left and right. Undeterred, Cranswick turned a deaf ear on the suggestions of his crew mates to call it a day and, coming around again, was rewarded by a glimpse of the barges, which he promptly bombed with his mixed load of 250lb and 500lb bombs; beyond satisfying explosions, the results remained as obscure as much of the harbour. Another Wellington of 149 Squadron, piloted by Sqn Ldr L.V. Andrews, was not so fortunate, as the weather not only put paid to the operation but also cost several crews their lives. Andrews left Mildenhall at 00.14 hours bound for Boulogne, barely 100 miles away. The Wellington soon plunged into a major electrical storm and was tossed about in the turbulent conditions. Heavy ice rapidly began to form on the aircraft's surfaces, forcing the bomber to lose height in spite of the use of increased power from the engines and, to make matters worse, the storm rendered the compass and several other delicate instruments U/S. Within a few minutes of turning back on a course that the crew hoped would bring them back over Britain, the over-taxed port engine burst into flames, soon followed by the starboard. The crew was at least buoyed up by the sight of searchlights probing the sky ahead of them and assumed they were part of their homeland's coastal defences. They waited as long as they dared in the now silent aircraft as it glided towards the lights so as to make sure they were over land before bailing out. Sadly, the young men got it wrong and they were still several miles out to sea when they abandoned the doomed aircraft. Only the second pilot, still gaining operational experience, lived to tell the tale. Supported by his Mae West, Plt Off C.W. Parish alternately rested and swam towards some searchlights visible on the horizon. In spite of severe cramp, sickness and exhaustion, and still in full flying kit, he doggedly closed in on the lights that, as it turned out, were some 7 or 8 miles away. In the watery light of dawn, he eventually staggered ashore near Clacton in Essex. He was back on the squadron's order of battle within a fortnight, eventually completing fifty-three operations before his luck ran out and he lost his life on his fifty-fourth mission. Plt Off J.L. Leeds and his crew left Mildenhall forty-five minutes before Andrews and were not heard of again, making it a bad night for 149 Squadron.

Several Whitleys headed for Ostend, where the results were little different. Of the eleven bombers sent by 10, 58 and 77 Squadrons, all but one failed to locate the harbour in the rotten conditions. The dispirited crews, mindful of the compelling urgency of the situation, did their best and flew over the general area repeatedly in the hope of catching a glimpse of the invasion fleet laid out below. Richard Pinkham of 77 Squadron was flying as second pilot to gain experience, staring through the cockpit windows at the vicious storm and the St Elmo's fire – static electricity – playing around the propeller and wing tips, when a deafening crack and blinding flash engulfed the aircraft. Momentarily stunned by the lightning strike, he thought his final moment had come but the engines continued to roar and the bomber held steady. A quick check upon both aircraft and crew revealed that no damage had been caused and, after a pause to gather their thoughts, they continued their search, finally releasing their load over the estimated position of the harbour. It was a long six hours or so of nervous strain and danger for little reward, as Plt Off J.C. Cairns found out. At 04.53 as he came in to land at RAF Leeming, Whitley P5094 suffered a hydraulic failure, giving the pilot no chance to do anything about it but to wait and pray. In the ensuing crash, during which the aircraft careered across the A1 and into a field beyond, Cairns was trapped in the wreckage and suffered a broken leg. As flames began to lick greedily around the wing surfaces, Sgt R.E. Nicholson, the WopAg, returned to the bomber and managed to haul his pilot unceremoniously through the top hatch and to safety. Nicholson received no recognition for his courageous action beyond a gruff 'well done' from his CO, Wg Cdr Bufton. Barely three weeks later, the sergeant was shot down on a raid upon Berlin, to spend the rest of the war as a prisoner.

Bomber Command had not lost sight of its aim of taking the war to the German heartland in direct support of the anti-invasion agenda. The Whitleys were also in action over the docks of Bremen. Here, although the conditions were far from ideal, there was not the added complication of a friendly populace around the target area and eleven of the fifteen aircraft released their loads. Flt Sgt D.H.A. Moore, who had ditched a week earlier on his way back from Genoa, was back in action, flying over the target at 9,000ft and dropping his load in two sticks at 22.25 hours. The general conflagration ignited was visible some 40 miles away. The Hampdens of 5 Group, the largest individual force of the night at just shy of fifty bombers, were sent to attack the Blohm and Voss shipyards in Hamburg, stretching for some distance along the Elbe. Conditions were poor there too but the majority of crews pressed home their attacks aided by the river and, ironically, the flak and searchlight defences that illuminated the area. A number of fires were started and it was recorded that the yards did suffer damage in the raid. Only one Hampden was lost, a 50 Squadron aircraft, under the command of Sqn Ldr F.A. Willan. Unusually, a signal was picked up at RAF Scampton at 23.59 and passed on to the home station at Lindholme, stating that the crew was about to bail out; later reports confirmed the crew were POWs. It had been a busy twenty-four hours for the Command acting in the face of invasion. The losses had been significant – ten aircraft destroyed and thirty-four trained airmen killed or captured; Fighter Command's losses amounted to four aircraft in the same period.

The long night passed without any sign of the anticipated invasion, though for most, including General Alan Brooke, C-in-C Home Forces, it was taken as read that there would be one. The alert remained in force but the crews were given marginally more room for manoeuvre. At RAF Marham at 09.00 hours the crews of 38 Squadron were given the news from 3 Group HQ that, 'The invasion is still imminent, although the standby has been lifted to 5 hours' notice.' It was largely academic anyway as an hour and a half later orders came through about a raid on Berlin that night, supported by others on Emden, Brussels, Krefeld and Hamm. At 105 Squadron at Watton the Blenheims were made ready, although the crews were given permission to be off station that evening after 18.00 hours but only within a 5-mile radius. Nevertheless, that morning they were detailed to provide more than half of a seven-strong force tasked to carry out a reconnaissance of the Channel ports and that afternoon the crews set off into a rapidly clearing sky. With the enemy coast approaching and the sky as clear as glass, the crews decided to call it a day and turned for home. Sgt D.D.R. Hodson left it too late and was last seen being hounded by a pair of Me 109s a few miles south of Den Helder; it was the crew's first and last operational sortie. Flt Lt Swain had Lady Luck on his side as his crew successfully fended off no fewer than three separate attacks by fighters before returning to base. Although the reconnaissance was a complete failure, that evening twenty-one Blenheims put in attacks upon the port of Ostend, long known to be packed with barges and naval craft. In fact, on this very day a Bomber Command intelligence report noted, 'All barges in the Low Countries and France, especially Rhine barges of 500t or more have been seized by the Germans. It is reported that the shipyards are deployed altering the bows of these barges so that tanks and guns can be easily disembarked.' This did not leave much to the imagination and, taken as a whole, the intelligence was more than persuasive; there would be an invasion very soon.

Somewhat courageously Bomber Command also stuck to the long game, pounding away at directly related targets further afield. Eighteen Hampdens, for example, made their way to Hamburg, which turned out to be well protected by cloud, making observation all but impossible. Three more did some gardening off the mouth of the Gironde, which runs down to Bordeaux. It was to be Observer Sgt Eric Woods' first operational sortie. After the completion of a flight test earlier in the day, Woods was surprised at how smoothly everything went at 106 Squadron, based at RAF Finningley. The crews set off in daylight, although it was dusk by the time the three Hampdens flew over the south coast at Chesil Bank and headed out to sea. This was the point at which the crews could split up to make their way independently to the target area and very soon each aircraft was alone in the sky. The much-vaunted enemy coastal defences on this occasion turned out to be a handful of searchlights moving erratically across the sky a few miles away. Peace and tranquillity were restored and the Hampden was undisturbed throughout its route, descent and run-in; with the captain's words 'OK, the bastard's away' booming through the intercom, the Hampden was put into a steep turning climb and all hell broke loose. Several searchlights suddenly burst into life, scanning at low level, probing the darkness for the minelayer they knew was nearby. They were accompanied by flak of all calibres hurling up all manner of multi-coloured tracer shells and larger explosions that scattered red-hot shards of metal in all directions. By misfortune, they had stumbled across a heavily armed flak ship, cunningly stationed on a known flight path to pick off the unsuspecting crews. Within seconds it was all over and the dark sky seemed as vast and empty as ever. The inbound flight then became as tranquil as the outbound but in time each man on board could see a dull red-orange glow in the sky away to the east and was well aware of its cause and significance.

Three crews operating that night did not manage to cross the coast again. The Fairey Battles had endured a torrid time in France in May 1940 and, although often flown with reckless and selfless courage in the face of heavy losses, it was obvious to one and all that the single engine light bomber was outdated and little more than an airborne death trap. Nevertheless, such was the perilous situation that they had to be brought back into the line for these Channel attacks. No. 103 Squadron, based at RAF Newton, was one such unit pressed into service; Sgt Drinkwater and his composite crew, which included Sub Lieutenant (Sub Lt) De Sanoval-Servier RN, was lost without trace during an attack on Calais. A Blenheim of 101 Squadron was also lost. Plt Off N. Bicknell was en route home after attacking Antwerp when the port engine packed up and, although everything was done to keep the bomber in the air, it gradually succumbed to the pull of gravity, leaving the pilot no option but to attempt a ditching in the open sea. With impeccable and almost theatrical good timing, a British trawler hove in to view and at once Bicknell used his remaining height to steer towards it. Having made sure the crew had seen the Blenheim, Bicknell gingerly lowered the aircraft on to the waves as close to the trawler as he could and once down lost no time in getting out. Bicknell and his observer, Sgt W.B. Gingell, clambered out but it soon became apparent that the WopAg was unable to follow them. Both men immediately hauled themselves back on board to do what they could but were forced to get out a second time as the Blenheim began to slip beneath the surface. Both men were soon picked up and on 29 September

Bicknell and Gingell were awarded the DFC and DFM respectively for their courageous, if ultimately futile, actions.

The other aircraft lost that night also came down in the sea, this time some 120 miles east of the Firth of Forth. The Whitley crews of 51 Squadron received Operational Order 163 at noon to mount attacks upon the docks at Wilhelmshaven, Bremen and the petrol storage facility in Emden. Operational Order 164 followed a few minutes later to mount an attack upon Berlin Tempelhof. Once again, Dishforth hummed with activity throughout the afternoon and by 19.45 Plt Off A.W. Millson was lined up ready for take-off. The outbound journey was largely uneventful and passing over the target at 00.30 hours at a rather low 3,500ft, the two 500lb and five 250lb bombs and assorted incendiaries fell earthwards and added to the already substantial fires raging below, the tops of which stretched more than 300ft into the air and were clearly visible for miles around. Just then it all changed; a close burst of flak rocked the aircraft and punched several large holes through the main surfaces, fracturing the main fuel lines and setting one engine alight. Millson steadied the bomber and gained a measure of control but he knew his efforts could do little more than postpone the inevitable. As it turned out, the sturdy Whitley endured far longer than the young crew had dared to hope, dragging itself slowly westwards through the cool air and, in the end, it was lack of fuel that brought about P5021's demise, compelling Millson to ditch in the North Sea at 07.15 after a mammoth eleven and a half hours in flight but still more than 100 miles from the English coast. Millson and three others managed to extricate themselves and clamber on board the dinghy but Sgt W.G. McAllistair drowned. It was several hours before a Coastal Command aircraft on patrol spotted the dinghy and alerted the Royal Navy to rescue the men, who were awarded fourteen days' leave to recuperate.

There was no such respite for Plt Off C.S. Robson of 78 Squadron. Taking off from Dishforth about a half an hour after Millson, Robson was bound for the docks at Bremen. Once over the city, the aircraft ran into heavy flak, which was working effectively with a battery of powerful searchlights. Pushing through this hostile reception, Robson judged his attack a success as there were a number of large fires blazing in the dock area, a view supported by Sqn Ldr R.K. Wildey who also reported three dummy decoy airfields between 3 and 6 miles south-west of the city and another a few miles east of Emden. It is uncertain if the bomber sustained any damage during its rough passage over the target at 10,000ft but just a few minutes later one engine packed up, leaving the crew to face a long and anxious flight home. Having clawed its way to RAF Linton, a few miles south of Dishforth, Robson brought it in for what turned out to be a very rough landing that wrote off the aircraft but, fortunately, not the crew. Five nights later, Robson and his crew were lost without trace on a raid to the oil storage tanks at Vlissingen.

As the ground crews were picking through the wreckage of Robson's aircraft to salvage what they could, elsewhere the RAF was gearing itself up for the onslaught of a new day. As it happened, low cloud and rain hampered the Luftwaffe's effort and the slow start gave the hard-pressed defenders a welcome opportunity to draw breath. The leaden sky, by contrast, offered the eight Blenheims sent out on sweeps along the coast a modicum of operational safety, though the conditions did little to help the effectiveness of their reconnaissance. Nevertheless, thirty new ships were photographed in Boulogne, as were a dozen larger ships heading to the port, another dozen off Ostend, fourteen large ships off Flushing and around 140 barges in Calais. There was no surprise in Bomber Command's choice of targets once night fell.

The Fairey Battles of 103 and 150 Squadrons were out once again with six releasing their maximum load of six 250lb bombs on to Boulogne harbour. A stronger force of thirty-three Blenheims were sent to Flushing and Ostend as well as to the gun emplacements at Cap Gris Nez. One Blenheim pilot, Fg Off R.S. Gilmoir, described the hellish scene along the Channel:

The whole of 'Blackpool Front' as we call the invasion coastline stretching west from Dunkirk was now in clear view … Calais docks were on fire.

So was the waterfront at Boulogne and glares extended for miles. The whole French coast seemed to be a barrier of flame, broken only by intense white flashes of exploding bombs and vari-coloured incendiary tracers soaring and circling skywards.

The Hampdens joined in too with 49 Squadron, for example, bombing Ostend, timing their attack for the early dark period to afford the crews some protection for the roving fighters known to operate in the area by day. A layer of patchy but substantial and troublesome cloud lay at 2,500ft above the port and did its best to thwart the crews. Plt Off Stewart of 61 Squadron, frustrated at not being able to execute his important mission properly, threw caution to the wind and guided the aircraft down, gathering speed through the cloud, before bursting through and levelling out at just 120ft above the water. Immediately drawing heavy fire, Stewart and his crew worked quickly to identify their exact location, before manoeuvring into position to release their load. As the squadron log later noted, he was rewarded by having, 'the satisfaction of seeing not only barges but also his bursts among them as well as the shower of debris that followed, with fires breaking out from the incendiaries and some explosions amongst the fires'. Stewart and his crew made it back home without further ado but the Lindholme-based 50 Squadron Hampden of Flt Lt R.J. Reed did not, having been brought down into the sea by the harbour flak with the loss of all on board, a fate shared by Flt Lt D.J. Rogers and his 44 Squadron crew while attacking Calais.

The Wellingtons too were busy over the Channel ports and Belgium. These crews, who took off a little after the Hampdens, encountered more cloud while crossing the southern North Sea and by the time they reached the Belgian coast, the patches had amalgamated to form an uninterrupted blanket. To make matters worse, passage through the cloud led to severe icing and Plt Off Lax of 37 Squadron, on his way to Brussels, was very lucky to survive when his bomber was rapidly encased in a thick layer of ice. There was little Lax could do and the bomber plunged some 6,000ft before warmer air broke up the ice and enabled the desperate pilot to regain control. Unsurprisingly shaken and uncertain as to what damage the Wellington had sustained, Lax remained at low altitude and turned for home, jettisoning his bombs safely in the sea. The dangerous conditions also had an impact upon the other crews and only one managed to locate and attack the designated target. Sgt Palmer-Sambourne was another pilot who took a calculated risk to drop below the cloud base and put in a low-level attack. Screaming across Ostend's heavily defended dock area at 600ft in a Wellington by night was hardly recommended practice, nor for the faint-hearted, but it did enable the crew to release the bombs on target, although with their night vision ruined by the blinding glare of the searchlights, fires and explosions, they were unable to say with any degree of certainty whether the bombs had hit the docks or barges. It was nonetheless a bold effort typical of many made that late summer.

The Whitleys of 4 Group were sent to keep the pressure on the German homeland, mounting attacks upon Bremen and Berlin. The raid on the port was to prove costly with two of the ten bombers involved being shot down by flak, unusually without resulting in a single fatality. One of these airmen was 26-year-old Glaswegian Sgt James Deans, whose outstanding work as a Man of Confidence (from the German Vertrauensmann), mostly in Stalag Luft IV, throughout the rest of the war brought him the respect of his captors and fellow captives alike and recognition in the form of a MBE at the war's end. It almost proved to be the final raid of Plt Off Andy Dunn's brief but intense flying career. Flying 77 Squadron's O-Orange, his crew was one of the few to locate the dockyard through the cloud. In order to keep it in sight and to mislead the alert defences, he elected to carry out a shallow diving attack, releasing his first stick of bombs at 6,000ft before continuing to release his second at 3,500ft. The crew clearly saw the explosions their ordnance had caused together with several new fires igniting. However, all was not to remain well. As Dunn gunned his engines and began to turn away, there was a deafening roar accompanied by the unmistakeable odour of smoke and cordite spreading throughout the aircraft as a near miss smashed the front of the Whitley, leaving Sgt Saville shaken and deafened but largely unhurt in the front turret. With a 150mph wind whistling through the bomber, it was an unpleasant, long and bitterly cold flight back to Linton.

It was, however, the efforts of the half a dozen or so Whitleys that mounted the arduous attack upon distant Berlin that grabbed the headlines. For a second consecutive night the air raid sirens wailed their dismal howl across the Reich capital and this time the bombers inflicted appreciable damage that could not be glossed over or played down by the authorities. Instead, Goebbels launched a major offensive of his own, loudly proclaiming his righteous outrage. The American correspondent in Berlin William Shirer noted:

> The German papers are beside themselves. The Borsen Zeitung calls our pilot visitors of last evening 'barbarians' and has bannerlines 'Crimes of British on Berlin'. The unfortunate death of nine children at an asylum in Bethel led to the headlines 'Murder is no longer war, Herr Winston Churchill' and trenchant calls for revenge.

Shirer also noted that Berlin society was being forced to modify its normal rhythms to ameliorate the effects of such raids – theatre performances were brought forward to 18.00 hours and schools remained closed until midday if there had been an alert after midnight. More to the point, Shirer could now see and report actual bomb and incendiary damage across the city and close to, if not actually upon as claimed by the Air Ministry in London, the major city centre Potsdamer railway station. He also thought it worth mentioning that bombs had indeed fallen in the government area around the Reichstag and Brandenburg Gate, and even Goebbels' own garden.

The official German news agency was also unusually communicative, stating:

> The British bombed non-military objectives in Berlin again on Tuesday night. Aided by clear moonlight, they dropped a great number of bombs

on the centre of the city and the western residential area – in fact they just missed the United States embassy. Fires and explosions damaged offices, hotels, public and private buildings. Roof fires were quickly extinguished but a number of works of art and quantities of fine furniture were damaged. The walls of some buildings were seriously damaged. Blast caved in the sides of several houses and as others were threatening to collapse, whole blocks in the centre of the city had to be evacuated. This new attack on Berlin reveals a definite plan to terrorize the civil population. The assassin Churchill has given the order to the RAF to avoid all targets of military importance and to destroy as many monuments as possible. There can only be one answer to these cowardly crimes – the answer of the German Air Force.

Hyperbole aside, such reports, confirmed by photographic evidence and the cross-referenced testimony of neutral observers, furnished concrete proof of at least some success on the part of Bomber Command and delighted the people of beleaguered Britain. Newspapers across the land trumpeted the success and called for more of the same; the *Daily Mail*, for example, demanded 'the most devastating offensive that has yet been seen' to be launched across Germany. Significantly, in Berlin a voluntary scheme to evacuate vulnerable people to the Protectorates of Bohemia and Moravia was set up, though Shirer noted that some Germans were moving to Berlin from more western areas 'to get some sleep, since in western Germany they are visited by the RAF nearly every night'. While clearly not on the scale of the Luftwaffe's new and sustained assault on London, Bomber Command's response was proving to be more than a mere nuisance and inconvenience; it was proof to the world that the heart of Nazi Germany was not beyond the reach of a determined enemy who showed no sign of throwing in the towel. Perhaps most significant of all, four Whitleys from each of 51 and 78 Squadrons were back over the city the following night.

The official German communique asserted that the attacks were centred upon the working-class residential districts as well as famous national memorials, while adding that a single incendiary bomb had fallen upon a small factory and that it was immediately dealt with. The British Air Ministry version was a little different, stating that the attack was centred upon Potsdam and Anhalter stations and Tempelhof aerodrome. *The Northern Echo* was not alone in declaring with relish, 'Already the Germans are beginning to squeal now that they are getting a taste of their own medicine.' Conscious of the more extravagant claims being made by the British and given some credence around the world, Goebbels released an official statement that, since 10 May, the actual number of deaths caused by bombing throughout Germany was just 617 – comparable, he added, to that of a single day in London and around Britain.

Certainly, on Wednesday 11 September the Luftwaffe did its best to inflict such casualties, with a single raid of 250 aircraft crossing the Kent coast at 15.30 hours, bound for the capital. Further raids came in throughout the evening and night, spreading over the Midlands and north-west and resulting in significant, if patchy, damage. Once again, the clear sky made it too dangerous for the Blenheims to conduct daylight operations, although three did mount an armed reconnaissance of the Channel coast and attacked a small convoy, though without definite results. They were far more active once the sun had set, as three dozen and a further half dozen Battles once again set course for Calais, Boulogne, Flushing and Ostend. Mike Henry, a gunner with 110 Squadron, recalled, 'the awe-inspiring sight that met our eyes that night, a plethora of searchlights and bright flaming onions rising up in bright strings'. He added:

The Channel ports were amongst the most heavily defended targets I can remember. Hitler's intention of preserving his invasion fleet was clear and his minions ferociously threw up everything but the kitchen sink. What made matters worse was the altitude at which we had been briefed to attack i.e. between 6,000 and 8,000ft. At this height, light flak was at its deadliest. It came up like an inverted monsoon of vivid colour; from all directions it poured to culminate at the apex of a cone of searchlights. They were at the time some of the most terrifying experiences of my life. 'How can any aircraft can survive in that lot,' I thought as we made our bombing run, 'is a miracle.' But, as we found out, the age of miracles was not past and we came through unscathed. Many, of course, didn't and were seen to plummet, flaming pyres earthwards.

No. 15 Squadron provided eleven aircraft to attack the shipping in Ostend but few could make concrete statements about their effectiveness, although Wg Cdr Cox did report that his load ignited 'four large fires, still visible 20 miles out to sea'. However, the squadron log noted tersely that amid the glare, ground haze and heavy defences, 'results on average were poor', before adding, 'pilots on return showed a lack of respect for the flare path. It appears that these pilots have been brought up in an exceedingly bad way as regards night flying in general and require further tuition. Damage on the whole (after a concentration of attacks) was a series of large and small fires on the Avant Port.' The exhausted young men who risked their lives over and over and had been trained to operate in daylight would not have been happy to read such a dismissive summary of their efforts, however realistic and accurate.

No. 38 Squadron's Wellingtons were also over Ostend that night. Although still on invasion alert during the day, 'the squadron was allowed to go to King's Lynn to see the news reel taken at Marham of flying crews, provided they attended first house and came away directly after the film. The squadron bus took 32. There were no defaulters.' A couple of hours later, RAF Marham resounded to the throaty roar of powerful engines as one after the other, the Wellingtons taxied into position and hurtled across the ground and eased up into the darkening sky. By the time these medium bombers arrived over the Belgian port the cloud had increased to such an extent that it made it 'very difficult to report results but a red glow showed fires spread along the water like petrol and then a big explosion, then several smaller ones'. Several aircraft reported being shadowed by an enemy fighter but no reports of attacks were logged, suggesting the other aircraft were British aircraft making their way to and from the narrow Channel target area. No.38 Squadron's contribution to the anti-invasion onslaught was not without cost. HD-R, flown by Fg Off R.G. Allen, was hit by flak over the target and came down almost immediately, crashing near to Ostend's railway station and killing all six men on board.

The remainder of the Command's substantial effort was directed towards German targets, either communication, such as Hamm, Mannheim and Cologne or naval, such as Bremen, Hamburg and Wilhelmshaven; several Hampdens also laid mines off Verdonne and the Elbe estuary. Experienced campaigner Larry Donnelly was on board a 10 Squadron Hampden that left Leeming at 19.35 hours bound for Bremen:

> As we approached Bremen at 9,000ft we could see the defences already in action, searchlights probing the darkness while the coloured balls of light flak hosed upwards and the heavy stuff exploded in dull red blossoms. As we got closer there were fires burning in the target area. There was no need for flares so I stayed up front to watch the proceedings. We ran through the usual gauntlet of flak on our first run and dropped our first stick. Our new skipper had decided we could carry out three runs – I think he was trying to impress. Beginner's luck must have been with him because we got through without a scratch. George Dove called from the tail turret that we had stoked up the fires and indeed when we were about 60 miles from the target we could still see them.

The Whitley kissed the soil of Yorkshire gently at 02.35. The other six aircraft made it back more or less unscathed too, though one was a man down. When Flt Lt D.G. Tomlinson carried out his routine roll call over the intercom after the attack, the rear gunner failed to reply. Fearing the worst, Sgt Walters, the observer, was sent back to investigate. To his amazement, the rear turret had been turned to the beam position with the doors open and there was no sign of the occupant. For whatever reason, he had abandoned ship and was later reported as a POW. The crews of two 44 Squadron Hampdens were not as fortunate, being shot down and killed in an attempt to cripple the huge liners *Bremen* and *Europa* at anchor in Bremerhaven. The four-hour-long raid on Hamburg was reported as being especially successful by the jubilant crews, who claimed direct hits, large explosions and extensive fires creeping across the docks and the Blohm and Voss shipyards, together with the north-western areas of the city. As the last crews departed in the early hours of the morning, the fires were still clearly visible more than 40 miles away.

The following day, Thursday 12 September, turned out to be a typically British summer's day, with heavy rain showers punctuated by the odd sunny spell. It was a curiously quiet day in the air, with far fewer massed Luftwaffe raids, though smaller-scale incursions ranged far and wide, from Tunbridge Wells to Harrogate, Wales to East Anglia and, of course, around London. Bomber Command's response was even more muted on account of the rotten weather all across the Continent. Most Groups took the opportunity to rest their crews and catch up on vital maintenance, but 3 Group decided to press on regardless, sending a sizeable force of Wellingtons to strike railway targets in Germany. The conditions facing the crews were dreadful with dense storm clouds making accurate navigation and precision bombing a forlorn hope.

New Zealander Plt Off Sam Hall was the observer in Fg Off Bertie Barnard's 9 Squadron crew based at RAF Honington, bound for Hamm. He later recalled:

Conditions were cloudy and at ETA there was little to be seen below which was recognizable. Bertie was repeating 'Can you see the target?' and I was replying with a laconic 'no' until he finally burst out, 'For Christ's sake, bomb something! I want to get home for breakfast!' In the end I persuaded myself that a concentration of lights could be the marshalling yards but the evidence was meagre – a first practical lesson in realizing that better methods and equipment would be needed before an accurate bombing campaign could be mounted.

He was not alone in having difficulties that night.

No. 37 Squadron's target list looked impressive on paper: marshalling yards at Schwerte, Krefeld and Hamm, with the massive Krupps works in Essen and the barge concentration at Emden added on for good measure. The crews did not have especially high expectations for, as they made their way to the waiting aircraft, they could see that the unbroken, leaden grey clouds were barely a couple of thousand feet above their heads. By the time the Wellingtons crossed the Norfolk coast, the mass of cloud reared up in excess of 13,000ft. Fg Off Baird-Smith climbed to well over this height in his heavily laden bomber in an unsuccessful endeavour to get beyond the thick, ice-bearing cloud; on ETA for Krefeld, he eased down many thousands of feet in an attempt to get below the cloud but, with the altimeter giving readings too low for comfort, gave up having seen nothing at all except the damned cloud. In the end, one of the crew glimpsed what he identified as a railway line and the bombs were dumped in its general direction. Plt Off Clark was in a similar position over Hamm and eventually let loose three bombs upon an active AA position and stooged around, often coming under fire, dropping his bombs in pairs upon such AA and searchlight positions he could find scattered across the Ruhr. Benny Goodman, still learning his trade as second pilot to Clark, years later recalled the problems the crews faced in such conditions:

They were all legitimate targets but we often couldn't find them. Everywhere was blacked out and you couldn't see the details on the ground. You could see the coast when you crossed it and the navigator could then work out a wind. This then had to carry you through hundreds of miles of enemy territory before you got to your target and then back again. Of course, the wind would change, it would drop or it would veer and so you could be miles and miles out. Even if you dropped a flare to see where you were, you would very often see open fields underneath. It was very difficult to find targets unless the Germans started to fire at you and then you could turn towards where the firing was coming from and know you would be over a town or city which you might or might not be able to identify.

This was pretty much what happened to Sgt Elstrub, who on ETA over Hamm eased down through the crowds, breaking out at beneath 3,000ft. Discovering nothing but inky blackness beneath him, he ordered a flare to be released. It revealed nothing more than open fields. After repeating this procedure several times with similar results, Elstrub set course for home, remaining at a dangerously low 2,500ft in the hope of locating a worthwhile target. After a while, a long line of lights came into view and he turned towards them. Deciding from the pattern of the lights that they were likely to be those in a marshalling yard, tentatively identified as Esterich, he made an attack that resulted in an electric blue flash of several seconds' duration amid the explosions. Plt Off Dingle was more fortunate, locating the yards at Schwerte after a brief and daring search at a mere 1,000ft and setting off a number of fires, including a large one that was still burning fiercely as the crew turned for home. The two crews sent to Emden benefited from slightly better conditions and the town's coastal location, and managed to locate and clearly identify the target. The results of Plt Off Parson's attack was not observed amid the heavy defensive fire but the crew of Sqn Ldr Golding's Wellington clearly saw explosions amid the massed barges. These young men and many like them would have been heartened if they had been able to read a signal sent to Berlin by Naval HQ Group West on this day, 'Interruptions caused by the enemy's air force, long range artillery and light naval forces have, for the first time, assumed major significance. The harbours at Ostend, Dunkirk, Calais and Boulogne cannot be used as night anchorages for shipping because of the danger of English bombing and shelling. Owing to these difficulties, further delays are expected in the assembly of the invasion fleet.' In spite of all the problems and difficulties, the strenuous efforts of Bomber Command were making a significant contribution to the defence of the United Kingdom. As far as the crews involved that night were concerned, they had done all that they had been able to do and were grateful that there had been no losses.

Friday the 13th is not a good day for those of a superstitious bent but it dawned sunny, if pregnant with the expectation of the onslaught to come. Once again, the Luftwaffe struck far and wide but still focused upon London, where bombs and incendiaries fell on Buckingham Palace, Downing Street and the House of Lords. The scale, however, remained surprisingly small, even once darkness had fallen. Although the fair weather all but put paid to the Command's daylight response to the invasion threat, it did assist the efforts by night when its entire focus was on the Channel ports, with ninety bombers in the air. Wilf Burnett, a Hampden pilot with 49 Squadron, recalled the briefing in which he was told:

> … that it appeared invasion was imminent and that we should be prepared for it. I remember the silence that followed. We left the room and I don't think anybody spoke but we were all the more determined to make certain that we did everything possible to deter the Germans from launching their invasion. I remember one operation in particular against the invasion barges. We had part moonlight which was very helpful because navigation in those days depended entirely upon visual identification. We flew to the north of our target so that we could get a clear outline of the coast. We followed the coast down towards our target, letting down to about 4,000ft so that we could get a better view of what was below and to increase the accuracy of our bombing. At that height, light anti-aircraft fire was pretty heavy and fairly accurate so we did not hang around after dropping our bombs.

His fellow squadron pilot, Plt Off Parker, reported his attack upon Ostend rather more succinctly: 'Barge concentrations successfully bombed and at least 20 fires started.'

Stan Harrison had good cause to remember 13 September 1940 as it was his 21st birthday. He had had several days off and, although he had flown test flights in preparation on the 10th and 12th, his name had not appeared on the ops board. By the early afternoon when nothing had been heard, hopes were rising that he and his crew might not be needed for a third time and that his special occasion might be celebrated in appropriate style. However, at 14.00 hours when the list of crews operating that night went up, there, inevitably, was his name; any celebration would have to wait. Having been briefed that there was a good deal of flak, searchlight and balloon units now in the Boulogne area, there was an additional warning to keep well clear of urban areas over England as anti-aircraft gunners were likely to let fly at any and all aircraft overhead. Thus, doubly heartened, Harrison and his crew boarded the fully bombed up Hampden and took off for the birthday flight. Crossing the coast at Aldeburgh, he flew in a wide arc over the southern part of the North Sea, eventually passing in mid Channel between Dover and Calais to approach his target from the north. His caution and carefully considered plans came to nought as gunners on both sides of the Channel opened up, though to little actual effect. Closing in to the enemy coast off Cap Gris Nez at 6,000ft, the Hampden was met with a veritable flak storm, lighting up the sky and doing little for the crew's already strained nerves. There was no problem in locating the target in the moonlight and soon four 500lb bombs were on their way to the packed harbour area. Immediately, Harrison swung away to the north and back out over the Channel, leaving the flak and fires far behind. One consolation for the crew, more used to distant German targets, was the short duration of the operation, a mere three and a half hours. An early finish it might have been but it was still far too late for Stan Hrrison to celebrate his birthday. In any case, the squadron would not have been in the mood because, as the log put it, 'Flt Lt How, one of the most experienced pilots, failed to return – an aircraft was seen to go down in flames from a low altitude and fell into the outer harbour.' There were no survivors. This was also the case with the loss of a 15 Squadron Blenheim that had left RAF Wyton on a similar mission. The Grim Reaper continued to take his steady toll.

The first day of the weekend was one of heavy rain, low cloud and thundery showers and the sky remained fairly quiet over southern England until late afternoon when several raids were launched against London, continuing well into the night. The poor weather during the day was enough to encourage 2 Group's Blenheims to keep up the pressure on the invasion ports. Eight crews from 105 Squadron were briefed and made their way in mid-morning to their laden aircraft, which stood ready under the leaden sky. Taking off from Watton, the crews headed south-east towards the Dunkirk–Flushing coastline but as they crossed the southern North Sea, they were dismayed to find the cloud breaking up and clearing rapidly to create a beautiful blue sky and leave them horribly exposed. In accordance with standing orders, seven crews, all making their way to their targets independently, turned around and by 11.15 only Plt Off Murray was still bound for the enemy coast. He crossed it over the island of Schouwen and quickly located Haamstede airfield, dropping his bombs across the southern part of it from 3,200ft before banking away and streaking for home at top speed.

That night, Bomber Command divided its efforts fairly equally between the invasion ports and rail communication targets across Germany. In both instances, the capriciousness of the weather conspired against them. Over the North Sea, the crews found themselves confronted with dense ice-bearing cloud, spawning several major electrical storms. In spite of this, the crews pressed on to carry out attacks all along the Channel coast. Sixteen of the eighteen Blenheims despatched, for example, succeeded in locating and bombing the barges at Ostend, Calais and Dunkirk and the cross-Channel gun emplacements at Cap Gris Nez. Further west, a dozen outdated Battles from the newly operational Polish 300 Squadron put in strong attacks at Boulogne and caused considerable dislocation and destruction. No. 38 Squadron's Wellingtons, operating the furthest north, bombed the barges and harbour at Zutphen and Ijmuiden, where bursts were clearly observed on the docks. These ignited several fires, visible some 10 miles away, and within 50 yards of several 1,000–2,000 ton merchant vessels. Sqn Ldr Gardner of 44 Squadron reported six of his eight 250lb bombs exploding amidst the barges moored in Calais harbour. He and Plt Off Perkins also observed an enormous explosion after bombs had been dropped on the eastern side of No. 6 dock, while Sgt Kneil claimed a direct hit on a 5,000-ton merchant ship in the harbour; dense clouds of smoke were seen billowing from it.

Sqn Ldr Tom Sawyer had more reason than most to remember this particular night. Having been posted to 10 Squadron as a Flight Commander on 12 September, this was to be his first operational flight and, squadron leader or not, he was to fly as second pilot to a young sergeant in order to gain experience. Sawyer decided he wanted to have a good view of the proceedings and took on the role of bomb aimer. Lying in the prone position in the nose, Sawyer first picked out the searchlights, flak and fires at Antwerp, his target, in the distance and then watched them become larger and clearer as the Whitley approached. He later wrote:

> We were to drop two sticks of bombs in two runs over the target from 8,000ft, the aiming point being the centre of the dock area. There was much searchlight activity with several aircraft obviously in the vicinity and on our run in a great increase in the amount of light flak tracer which seemed to be sprayed all over the area almost indiscriminately and in all directions in prodigious quantities. Multi-coloured strings of orange, red and even green were hosed upwards, sometimes with a short 'S' bend in them as the gunners swung their barrels around. White and yellow blobs of fairy lights creeping almost lazily at first, then with gradually increasing velocity to zip past the wings at terrific speed and some a little too close for complacency … The whole panorama criss-crossed in an untidy melee yet somehow almost beautiful, as I pored over the sights giving the pilots the directions. Left, left, steady – right a bit, steady etc.

He recalled 'a feeling strangely exultant welling up inside' of him as the whole colourful panorama opened up beneath him. He could not pick out the effects of his bombs amid the flashes below but busied himself preparing for their second run:

Just like a Brock's Benefit Night I called to the crew as I steered our pilot onto our second run. I pressed the bomb tit for the second time and this time I got them. Peering anxiously downwards and slightly backwards, I saw four lovely flashes appear in a line right across the docks. A bull's eye. Three flashes from the basin where the barges were berthed and one on the dockside itself.

Sawyer asked the pilot to do another circuit of the dock area so that he could observe the situation as a whole for a later report and then the Whitley V turned for home, the crew and Sawyer in particular cock-a-hoop at a job well done.

Larry Donnelly, a far younger but more experienced hand in 10 Squadron, manning the four Browning machine guns in the rear turret over Antwerp that night, recalled:

The weather was anything but good and we had to weave through numerous electrical storms but, fortunately, it improved as we neared the target area and saw the searchlights and flak. Our new bomb aimer took us in for two runs at 12,000ft and after the second I saw a big explosion in the dock area, followed by fires. We lost no time in getting away from the defences and setting a course for base. We got a bit of a jolt when I spotted a Bf 110 night fighter flying above us. I kept him in my sights but, thankfully, he flew off without spotting us.

By 01.50 hours, it was all over and the crews were climbing stiffly from the now silent bomber, their feet now firmly back on Yorkshire soil.

However, Sqn Ldr K.F. Ferguson's crew was about to experience something even more hair-raising. Their 10 Squadron Whitley had taken off from Leeming at much the same time as the others, at 19.38 hours, and set course for Antwerp. While out over the North Sea, the starboard engine gave up the ghost and, though Ferguson immediately turned for home, it became clear that the aircraft would have to ditch. Their plight had not gone unnoticed and another 10 Squadron crew made an accurate report of their position. Rear gunner Sgt Mark Niman stated that, at about 21.00 hours, 'The skipper carried out a remarkably fine ditching and the dinghy was launched successfully. However, in my haste to leave the rear turret, I went head first into the huge metal tail wheel spar which I had to climb over to reach the rear hatch, which raised an egg shaped bump which I didn't feel until hours later.' Some 20 miles off Spurn Head:

> We all got into the dinghy and cast off from the rapidly sinking aircraft, which took only a couple of minutes to disappear beneath the waves. The dinghy bounced around in the very rough North Sea for the next few hours before we were sighted and picked up by the crew of a Royal Navy minesweeper Kurd, a 200ton vessel which had just laid a minefield that we were shocked to learn that we had just alighted into! We also learned later that they had been very reluctant to pick us up until it had firmly been established we were British. We remained their passengers for the next two days while they completed their task, then they returned to Grimsby where they took us on one hell of a pub-crawl before we were taken back to Leeming.

There was to be no such good fortune and happy ending for the 78 Squadron crew of Fg Off C.S. Robson, lost without trace while attacking the oil storage facility at Vlissingen.

A strong force of around fifty Wellingtons took their anti-invasion fight further afield, attacking rail centres in Germany. No. 37 Squadron was heavily involved in attacking both Channel ports and German targets, where conditions were far from ideal. Two crews, for example, failed to locate their primary target, the marshalling yards at Soest, or their secondary target, the marshalling yards at Schwerte. Fg Off Dingle was not one to give up easily and, flying at low level beneath the thick slab of cloud, searched for some time for a suitable target. Eventually, identifying a railway line, he decided to make the best of a bad job and, climbing a little, dropped his load on to the line. Plt Off Clark, faced with the same problem and displaying the same tenacity of purpose, was also stooging around German airspace at 1,000ft, scanning the darkened landscape beneath for anything worth bombing. Benny Goodman, flying as second pilot to Clark whilst gaining operational experience, later explained:

> If you couldn't find either of those [primary or secondary targets], you would go for something called a SEMO or MOPA. SEMO were Self Evident Military Objectives and MOPA were Military Objectives Previously Attacked. We were SEMO or MOPAing and we came upon a railway line with a train puffing along it. We decided this was a jolly good military objective, a goods train and flew over the top of it dropping bombs, which exploded. We were at about 2,000ft and we turned away at the end of the bombing run. The train stopped and, suddenly, to our astonishment, there was the most enormous explosion in the middle of the train. It was clearly an ammunition train; it blew up and went off in all directions. Of course, we scuttled out of the way.

While not quite always being the attack intended, Bomber Command was maintaining a presence far and wide over Germany and keeping up the pressure, however light, upon the railway system at a time when it was needed to run at peak efficiency.

Sunday 15 September was far from a day of rest and contemplation. The relatively low-key attacks made by the Luftwaffe on the previous couple of days were replaced by several mass attacks throughout the day and night, the climax of the Battle of Britain. During these frantic skirmishes in a clear blue sky, the Luftwaffe lost a total of fifty-six aircraft, more than double those lost by the RAF; the morale of the young German pilots and crews, already sorely tried, never fully recovered. With no more information than was available to the general public via the wireless news broadcasts and newspapers, their counterparts in Bomber Command simply went about their business as usual.

The spectacular summer's day that did so much to aid the German assault, once again thwarted the efforts of 2 Group, restricting the Command's effort to the hours of darkness. It was a substantial effort too, with more than 150 aircraft allocated to anti-invasion targets across Germany and along the Channel coast. Frustratingly, conditions over the Reich were nowhere near as helpful and the crews struggled to locate their primary targets. Nos 77 and 58 Squadrons, for example, sent five aircraft to attack industrial targets in Berlin but all were compelled to head for alternative targets. The rest of 58 Squadron found things little better over Hamburg, where Sgt Crossland failed to identify his target, even after making several passes at just 3,000ft over the heavily defended port. After some time, he located Cuxhaven in driving rain and came under sustained fire, which destroyed the front turret and holed much of the cockpit area, though without causing casualties. Crossland held steady and after releasing his bombs, he turned for home, eventually landing at Linton at 03.20 hours, after an arduous and freezing seven hours in the air. The Hampdens were allotted communications targets in Germany and 61 Squadron's Stan Harrison had been assigned the Dortmund–Ems canal near Münster, north of the Ruhr valley. Harrison had little difficulty in finding the general area and even snatched not one but two tantalising glimpses of the crucial inland waterway viaduct. Having cruised around in the hope of a third and longer sighting in vain, he decided to follow the line of the canal north. Dropping down to around 4,000ft, it was just about possible to keep the canal in view and, after fifteen minutes, the town of Rheine came into sight, complete with road and rail bridges across the canal. Doubtful of locating a better target, the four 500lb bombs were rapidly despatched earthwards through a gap in the clouds, which closed up before any results could be observed, beyond a dull flash of red. Totally undisturbed and in splendid isolation, the Hampden turned around and set course for home.

Conditions were better over the Channel ports, although this proved to be a double-edged sword, enabling the alert gunners to unleash fearsome and accurate defensive fire. It was enough to force Plt Off Andy Dunn, who had come under heavy fire at 6,000ft while bombing the barges at Ostend, to push the nose of his unwieldy Whitley down and keep it down, levelling out at just 100ft to steak across the harbour with Sgts Savill and Riley in the front and rear turrets respectively, blazing away at the barges and making the most of this hair-raising and unorthodox opportunity. Well over fifty Blenheims and Battles, supported by a handful of heavier Wellingtons and Hampdens, put in attacks on all the usual ports but it was over Antwerp that the most extraordinary events took place that night.

For all those working at RAF Scampton, it had been a particularly busy day. No. 83 Squadron alone was scheduled to provide fifteen of the twenty-four Hampdens for the attack on the Belgian port. Eight of the squadron's aircraft carried out the attack successfully and three more bombed the secondary targets at Flushing and Dunkirk. Guy Gibson, later to command 617 Squadron, was one of the pilots over Antwerp that night and was in no doubt of the vital nature of such sorties. He later wrote:

These raids on the invasion ports were organised to destroy as many barges as possible. On that night [15th] we made our biggest raid on Antwerp. It was the night of the full moon; many barges were sunk, many blew up, destroying others around them. They were full of stuff and we could see, there and then, there was no doubt about it, the Germans were ready. Flying low around those docks that night, we could easily see the tanks on board, the tarpaulins over the sinister objects on the docks. 'Der Tag' was drawing near for the Hun.

As he came back he:

… flew for a while alongside an aeroplane which was on fire. It was a nasty sight because I could see it was one of our own. As flames and sparks came out like the wrong end of a rocket hanging in the air, I saw one chap bail out and land in the river and I remember hoping that he could swim. When I got back, I asked young Connor, a Canadian boy, what sort of trip he had had. He did not say much except that he had caught fire over the target and had got hell from the light flak.

It was a piece of masterful understatement.

Hampden P1335 was the last to get airborne from Scampton at 22.28 and was due to be the last over Antwerp. Plt Off Arthur Connor was a pre-war regular from Toronto. The WopAg on board was a short, slightly built 18-year-old from Glasgow, Sgt John Hannah. The Hampden passed over Skegness pier and set course south-east, climbing to 5,000ft and, after an uneventful, if tense, flight reached enemy territory south of the island of Flushing before heading towards Antwerp. Bathed in bright moonlight, the crew had no difficulty in picking out the massed barges and Connor throttled back and began to lose height as he approached the target. Then a shell burst directly beneath the starboard wing, blasting the bomber violently to port and ruining the bombing run. Connor turned around to make a second run and this time it seemed as if every searchlight and flak cannon was aiming at this tail-end intruder. The Hampden ploughed ahead steadily more or less unscathed until the moment the bomb doors were closing; the entire aircraft was then suddenly rocked violently by an enormous explosion. A shell had scored a direct hit on the partially closed bomb doors and ignited a fierce fire, fanned by the air streaming into the fuselage. Connor immediately asked for an assessment of the damage, though he could already see the flames reflected in his windscreen and feel the heat rising from behind. Hannah reported the aircraft was on fire and described it as 'bad but not too bad'. Still preoccupied with getting the battered bomber back under control and trying to evade the incessant flak still hosing up at them, Connor gave the order to bail out, just about possible from a height of 1,800ft. The navigator, Hayhurst, and gunner, James, did so but Hannah decided to tackle the flames, first with his gloved hands and then with his wireless log book. Realising the situation required far more, Hannah made his way through the flames, yanked open the fire door, buckled with the heat, pulled himself through and grasped the main extinguishers. When these ran out, half blinded by the flames, amid stifling heat and in constant danger of becoming trapped in the wreckage or falling through the gaping holes in the fuselage, he continued to beat the flames with his hands, feet and log book. After about ten minutes of Herculean effort, Hannah managed to put the last flames out. Plugging himself back into the intercom, which, miraculously, still functioned, he reported calmly, 'The fire is out, sir.' Collecting whatever maps he could find, Hannah made his way forward and, as Connor later said, 'his face was badly burnt, his flying suit scorched all over and altogether he looked a sorry sight.' While Connor flew the battle-scarred and charred Hampden in the direction of Scampton, Hannah stood behind him helping him to spot landmarks and navigate as best they could. They landed at Scampton at 03.05 hours.

Hannah later wrote to his mother, 'Dear Mum, at last I have managed to get a rest. As you can see from the address, I am "in dock". I suppose you have had some official news that has got you all worried. Still, I am OK and would have written sooner but I only managed to get my eyes open this morning ... My pilot is getting the DFC so I expect that I will be getting something too.' That something was the Victoria Cross. When AVM Harris, AOC 5 Group, learned of the flight, he drafted a highly persuasive recommendation for the Victoria Cross, noting Hannah had every opportunity to save himself but chose to save the life of his pilot and the aircraft in the most exacting of circumstances. He concluded, 'This is one of the clearest examples of most conspicuous bravery and extreme devotion to duty in the presence of the enemy under the most harassing conditions that I have come across.' On 10 October at Buckingham Palace, he and Connor received their awards from King George VI. Sadly, on the night of 3/4 November, just twenty-four days after the investiture, Connor failed to return from an attack on Kiel, his thirteenth operational sortie. His body was discovered the next day in an otherwise empty dinghy in the North Sea, not far off Spurn Head. Hannah's health never fully recovered from the ordeal and as a result of respiratory problems, he was invalided out of the RAF in December 1942 and died of tuberculosis on 7 June 1947, still only 25 years of age.

In the typical manner of a British summer when the contrast between one day and another can be stark, 16 September dawned dull, wet and very cloudy. Nevertheless, it was estimated that more than 350 German aircraft broke into British airspace during the hours of daylight and the same number the following night, causing particularly heavy damage to Liverpool and London. Ten Blenheims made good use of the prevailing conditions to carry out further harassing attacks upon the ports of Calais, Ostend, Zeebrugge and Dunkirk, as well as the airfield at Haamstede. That, as it turned out, was Bomber Command's entire contribution to the defence of the country as, most unusually, it was judged that the adverse weather conditions precluded the execution of an accurate attack and, as a result, all operations were called off. As far as the crews were concerned, the respite was welcome but, inevitably, short-lived as the following day saw the Command's largest effort since the beginning of the war.

By sunrise, the heavy cloud cover was beginning to break up to make a day of sunshine and showers. Fifteen Blenheims of 2 Group took off mid-morning to make the most of these conditions, which were ideal for intruder sorties. Unfortunately, on the near Continent, the sky was far clearer and several of the crews again turned around. No. 105 Squadron's day was typical; half a dozen Blenheims set out and three turned back. The remainder pressed on to attack an airfield on the outskirts of the Hague and two convoys, one off Zeebrugge which consisted of five small merchant ships and the other about 6 miles north of the Hook of Holland. No hits were observed, though it was felt that some very near misses might have caused some damage.

By night, it was a very different story with a whopping 194 aircraft on operations and, importantly, a much higher than usual figure of 187, or 96 per cent, reported bombing a target. Roughly two-thirds returned to the Channel ports and forty-six Blenheims hit Boulogne and Dunkirk without loss, though Plt Off Megginson of 15 Squadron was forced to make a 'pancake landing' on his return to RAF Wyton, when his port engine gave up the ghost and he was unable to lower the undercarriage. The Germans were well aware of what had become an established routine and prepared a warm reception for the crews. No. 78 Squadron's experiences were typical of many over Ostend that night. Still able to make their own arrangements, the crews were over the port between midnight and four in the morning, though all met considerable opposition from flak and searchlights. Sqn Ldr Wildey was one of the early arrivals but was forced to abort his first run flying at 4,000ft when he and his crew were illuminated and blinded by several searchlights. Swinging around again, he climbed to 9,000ft and released his load in a single stick. Then, determined to do his bit to help others, Wildey brought the Whitley around a third time, this time at 3,500ft to enable his gunners to engage the searchlights, of which two were claimed as being shot out. Even so, that left a good number still active and Sgt Samson estimated no less than fifteen were operational in the harbour area. Sgt A.S. Ennis was one of the last over the target at 03.46 hours but he too came under heavy fire as he attacked from just 2,000ft, at least in part from a couple of flak ships off Nieuport that had been brought in to bolster the defences. His wireless operator, Sgt A.R. Edgar, had a narrow escape when shrapnel burst through the fuselage just inches from his position; one piece tore into his thumb but a larger and more deadly chunk ricocheted off his parachute buckle. The rear gunner reported their bombs as exploding on the edge of a wooded area, adjacent to a railway line emerging from the docks.

Danger came in many forms but some were avoidable and of the crews' own making. No. 150 Squadron had only recently converted from Battles when Sgt Edwin Wheeler remembered:

We were briefed to fly in Wellington L7859, take off at 22.40 hours to attack the invasion barge concentrations at Ostend. After the discomfort of flying in Battles, the Wimpy was luxury indeed. I had a reasonable seat and warmth to operate TR1154/55 radio receiver/transmitter. The security of having two pilots and armament front and rear and armour plate behind my seat gave me much more confidence than I had felt before. Ginger had the luxury of a seat and a table to consult his maps and his log was at last glycol free! We reached the target and sighted rows of barges but Rocky must have had a lapse of memory as he put the Wimpey into a dive – must have thought he was still flying Fairey Battles! The reaction from the crew was immediate. 'What the bloody hell!' was yelled from each crew position. It is a wonder the wings were not torn off, such was the angle of the dive. However, we survived and there were fewer barges when we left.

Sgt Joe Taylor recalled a close shave of a different kind over the same target. His 61 Squadron crew:

... had bombed the barges at Ostend and [was] heading out from the coast, feeling rather pleased with our efforts. The barges were so thickly concentrated that it was well-nigh impossible to miss. Suddenly, to our starboard, there was a flash as a cigarette lighter sprang into flame and illuminated the helmeted head and face of a German Bf 110 pilot as he carelessly lit a cigarette. Up to this time, we hadn't seen him, although he was flying a parallel course not more than 50ft away. More importantly, he had not, it would appear, seen us. I called the skipper and shouted 'throttle back'. The skipper and the rest of us held our breath while he eased the throttles back to allow the speed to decay and the 110 to draw ahead. We all breathed a sigh of relief and were somewhat shaken to see how easily we could have been stalked to death by him.

For others, one of the greatest dangers was a lack of experience, a valuable commodity that can only be gained over time and that was not always available to the young crews. Twenty-five-year-old Hedley Hazelden later summed up his feelings, 'After leaving on my first trip and getting involved with the enemy guns, I thought it would be curtains for me and was rather surprised when I got back. By later experience, it was not a tough op, but to me as a beginner, it was.' Hazelden was acting as a navigator to Sgt Jimmy Kneil in a 44 Squadron Hampden bound for Antwerp:

Navigation was all dead reckoning. We had a magnetic compass but no radio compass and none of the radio aids which became commonplace later on. I did all the navigating, then when we got to the target, I moved round to the bomb-sight, advised the skipper how to steer onto it and, eventually, released the bombs. Navigation was very much what we called 'eye-balling', being able to see where you were going. Clear, moonlit nights were our busy times. If you couldn't see, you probably could navigate into the target area by using compass and calculations for dead reckoning. But if the target was covered by cloud, you wouldn't know where you were dropping your bombs.

On this occasion, his first operation, 'There was a lot of gun-fire which I'd never seen before and I made an error while going across the North Sea by laying off the wind the wrong way. I fortunately realised the mistake after about a half an hour and was able to correct it, so we did make the target, but we must have done rather an odd track across the North Sea.' When he finally got there, Kneil approached the target at about 8,000ft and succeeded in both identifying and attacking the crowded docks beneath, much to Hazelden's relief. 'I was delighted when we got back,' he concluded. 'Coming under fire for the first time, you had a feeling that anyone on the ground who pointed a gun at you could not miss. In fact, of course, he could and most of the time, he did. There's an awful lot of sky and we later realised it took a bit of doing to direct a gun to hit a moving target.' He was right but it did happen and it happened that night to Hampden P2121 from his own squadron. Sgt T.V. Henderson, together with all his crew, died when flak brought down his aircraft over Antwerp.

Many aircraft that night were assigned targets in Germany. In 9 Squadron Tiny Cooling had the unusual experience of starting the same operation twice. Bound for the vast marshalling yards at Hamm, several times larger than those at Clapham Junction, Cooling took off from Honington at exactly 19.30 hours and reached the coast at Orford Ness only to find that:

… there was something seriously wrong with the aircraft, although we could not tell what. We could not get above what felt like 85 knots, although we couldn't tell that either because the airspeed indicator was u/s. So, I turned around and came back with a full load of fuel and bombs. We came in grossly overweight and the airspeed indicator showing as zero and the crew showing every sign of confidence in me, such as tightly clenched arse cheeks and badly bitten lips. Anyhow, we got down somehow by the seat of my pants, transferred to the standby aircraft and took off again. We had a pretty fair trip, crystal clear skies and bombed Hamm as ordered. I was back at 20.10 the first time and 02.30 the second time.

He later discovered that one of the ground crew had smeared Kilfrost de-icing paste over the pitot head in the leading edge of the starboard wing by mistake. As it worked on air pressure, this had rendered the instruments unserviceable. With greater experience, he concluded, 'When I think back on it, I feel I was a bloody fool. Anybody in their right senses would have jettisoned the bombs over the sea and flown around for a couple of hours. But to come in with the bloody bombs on board! It never crossed my mind to dump them!'

Sqn Ldr Tom Sawyer was also over Germany in one of the Whitleys trying to damage the *Bismarck,* which photographic reconnaissance had revealed as being in Hamburg's main dry dock. One aircraft was forced to return early after just a few minutes in the air when the tail turret hydraulics were found to be inoperable but the others headed through the clear night, easily locating the mouth of the Elbe and following it to the city. Trundling along at barely 130mph through the heavy defensive fire and piercing searchlights, to Sawyer, again on bombing duties, it once again seemed to take for ever to get over the target. When the bomber finally did, to his frustration, he could not make out any ground detail on account of a heavy haze, augmented by an effective smokescreen. Under orders to release the bombs only if the target could be positively identified, Sawyer ordered the pilot to carry on across the target and search for an alternative. This turned out to be an airfield at Shillinghorn, conveniently in operation and fully lit up. The *Bismarck* remained unscathed. It had been a very busy and relatively successful night for the Command, marred only by the loss of the 44 Squadron Hampden. The next twenty-four hours would be very different.

Once again, the sunshine and showers over Britain enabled the Luftwaffe to forge ahead with their campaign; more than 800 aircraft were estimated to have entered British airspace during the day, with several hundred more following on throughout the night. The single Blenheim sent on a reconnaissance flight to Ostend was aborted owing to a lack of cloud cover on the other side of the Channel, putting a premature end to the Command's paltry effort for the day. Later, however, a force only slightly smaller than the previous night's, assembled and set out for the Channel ports and Germany once again. The Blenheims and Battles headed for the former, and in 105 Squadron's case it was Ostend. Five aircraft, led by Wg Cdr Coggle, left Watton in the early evening, aiming to be over the port just after nightfall. Meeting strong opposition from the flak, the crews pressed home their attacks successfully. Sgt Costello-Bowen had a heart-stopping moment when, boring in at a little over 1,000ft, his Blenheim was blown upside down and earthwards by the force of his own bombs exploding. Shocked but acting on instinct, he managed to regain control, flipped the bomber over and roared out of the target area at rooftop height, arriving back at Watton by 21.40 hours, well before closing time and with a great story to tell. Another aircraft from 105 did not fare so well, being lost without trace; pilot Sgt Bowles was a long-standing member of the unit but his gunner Sgt Lockerby had only just joined.

At 101 Squadron, a new procedure was attempted. A dozen Blenheims were bombed up and ready for an early take-off from West Raynham. At 19.30 hours the crews climbed on board and set course for Dunkirk, the barge concentrations being easily spotted and bombed. By 23.00 hours all the aircraft were safely back on the ground. The armourers and ground crews were on hand at once and had the aircraft back in the sky within the hour. Once again, the conditions were clear and the target was hit again. The last weary crew landed safely at 03.40 hours. The following morning, messages of praise and congratulations for the efforts of all concerned flooded in. The AOC 2 Group, AVM J.M. Robb sent his congratulations to, 'the CO and crews of 101 Squadron for their efforts last night and to the ground personnel who effected the rapid turn-around'. The icing on the cake was provided by Air Marshal Sir Charles Portal, AOC Bomber Command who signalled, 'To OC West Raynham. I have noticed with much pleasure the extreme keenness and efficiency behind your recent night operation, which reflect great credit on all concerned with flying, arming and maintenance.'

Pressure was being kept up on all forms of enemy-controlled shipping. A strong force of Hampdens attacked Le Havre, while another eight mined the waters off the Elbe estuary. Flt Lt Ogilve was over Le Havre and had the satisfaction of watching two of his 250lb bombs explode on an oil tanker but his elation was short-lived as it replied with accurate AA fire, punching several holes in his starboard main plane. Guy Gibson observed the death of his good friend Sqn Ldr Jamie Pitcairn-Hill DSO, DFC, one of the last 83 Squadron pre-war regulars. He wrote, 'I saw him flying straight and level over one of the basins, taking his time about his run, making sure that all his bombs went into the right spot. Then he blew up – and Pitcairn-Hill had gone to join his forefathers.' It was a journey shared by 106 Squadron's Plt Off E.T. Wakins on mining duties, the first operational loss sustained by the squadron since becoming operational earlier in the month. The danger did not end at the target, for many of 61 Squadron's aircraft were delayed in landing or forced to land elsewhere as enemy aircraft were all over the Lincolnshire area.

Other crews were busy over German targets too. No. 58 Squadron sent several aircraft over Hamm once again. Sgt Boothby reported carrying out his run from south to north, dropping his load in two sticks that were observed to land on target, triggering a series of blue and green explosions visible to crews for miles around. He also reported seeing an aircraft in flames over the target at 22.26 hours; this was almost certainly the Whitley of his fellow squadron member Sgt A.A.E. Crossland, which finally came to earth in Holland with the loss of all on board.

Conditions over the rail targets were not so good. Plt Off Dunn of 77 Squadron, flying Whitley O-Orange, had great difficulty in locating the marshalling yards at Soest through some stubborn, patchy low cloud and haze. Eventually, a fair-sized factory did come into view from 2,000ft so Dunn ordered his crew to keep an eye on it as he lined up for an attack. The factory remained in sight just long enough but the cloud swept over preventing any assessment of the effects, beyond a dull red glow, scant reward for what turned out to be almost eight and a half gruelling hours in the air. Sqn Ldr Sawyer was in the same area and his Whitley also cruised around for some time, intermittently releasing flares in the hope of illuminating some ground detail. The crew's actions provoked a response from the ground defences and Sawyer decided to aim at a flak and searchlight concentration and dropped his load in one stick. On its way home, the bomber flew into some towering banks of cumulonimbus, which it proved impossible to climb over and it was bounced about alarmingly, causing the pilot to become completely disorientated. Officially only a second pilot but a more experienced one, Sawyer tactfully asked the young sergeant pilot whether he would like a break, a suggestion that was taken up with alacrity. Sawyer took over the controls and brought the Whitley back to Leeming without further ado.

Elsewhere people were struggling too. Several Wellingtons had been assigned to the railway yards at Erhang. Sgt Palmer-Sambourne of 37 Squadron described the cloud cover as a full ten-tenths and was forced gradually to lose height in a delicate search for the cloud base. Breaking more or less clear at 3,000ft, the target hove into view, eerily quiet as there was no opposition of any sort. Several large explosions were clearly seen amongst the rails, igniting four large fires, one of which was described as having a slightly greenish hue. The situation was not as quiet over the Belgian capital, where Sgt Culverwell spent an unpleasant period under fire searching for the marshalling yards through patchy cloud and a substantial ground haze. Eventually giving it up as a bad job, he set course for Dunkirk as an alternative target but came across Zeebrugge first and decided the town's docks were just as valid a target and let his bombs go, though without observed results. While it was felt that much had been achieved in terms of disrupting the obvious preparations for invasion, it had come at grievous cost. The night of 18/19 September turned out to be the Command's most costly of the war so far. Nine aircraft had been lost, only two fewer than Fighter Command during the daylight onslaught; the difference was that it resulted in the deaths of forty-one trained airmen as, unusually, there were no survivors from any of the aircraft lost.

Equally unusually, there was some opportunity for the aircrew to draw breath after such a bruising night. The bad weather encountered on route home worsened the next day, providing a cloudy and wet day over most of the country that restricted flying activity. Of the dozen 2 Group Blenheims sent out, only one made it to the enemy coast, attacking Dunkirk and bringing back clear photographs of the crowded dock area, revealing both the scale of the preparations and damage caused by the repeated raids. By night only 4 and 5 Groups deemed the conditions suitable for operations, although their Luftwaffe counterparts did mount raids, principally upon London. No. 4 Group's contribution amounted to eight aircraft from 78 Squadron attacking the marshalling yards at Mannheim; three turned to alternative targets but five managed to press home their attacks although without accurate observation of the results. Several Hampdens in 5 Group laid mines off the mouth of the Gironde, while others harassed Flushing and Ostend. A few more headed towards the Dortmund–Ems canal with similar nondescript results. The only positive thing that could be said was that there were no losses.

Unaware that Hitler the previous evening had ordered the invasion fleet to be dispersed, 'so that the loss of shipping space caused by enemy air attack may be reduced to a minimum', Bomber Command was determined to keep up the pressure on the Channel ports and transport network in Germany.

Attacks began at dawn on 20 September when three Battles raided the cross-Channel guns at Cap Gris Nez. The Blenheim force was essentially called off because of adverse weather conditions, although half a dozen did mount a reconnaissance patrol over the North Sea, encountering nothing of consequence. By night, however, there was a steady flow of aircraft heading south and east; the bulk of the 170-strong force was again hurled against the heavily defended Channel ports but a number of Hampdens and Whitleys penetrated the Reich, heading for the Dortmund–Ems canal and the railway junctions at Osnabrück, Mannheim and Krefeld. No. 10 Squadron's fleet of ten Whitleys was the largest sent to a single target, Hamm, the sixtieth time since the outbreak of war just over a year earlier. Sgt Larry Donnelly was on board T4143 as it left Leeming at 21.25 hours. A frequent visitor to the target, he rated it as 'a hot one' and had a healthy respect for its defences, which had developed the technique of putting up barrages at different heights and mixing them up in order to disturb the intruders at whatever altitude they came overhead. In decent conditions and relatively good visibility, the crews had little difficulty in locating the target area but had to stooge around just beyond the defensive zone for some time to pinpoint the actual aiming point. Making the final approach, the flak came uncomfortably close, buffeting the bomber and peppering it with red-hot shards of metal. Donnelly, who had been in the fuselage by the flare chute during the bombing run, had just returned to his wireless position when he observed drops of blood appearing on his log book. Only then did he notice the sharp pain in the fleshy part of his thumb. He quickly but gingerly removed his gloves, his white, silk inner one now being worryingly crimson, to reveal a small but deep hole caused by a sliver of metal that was still protruding from his hand. Fortunately, it came out easily after a gentle tug and, after wrapping his handkerchief around the wound, he put his gloves back on and resumed his duties as normal, grateful that the fragment had not found anything more vital. Setting foot on firm ground at 04.30 hours, he did not bother to tell anyone about his narrow escape. More than half the squadron's aircraft had sustained significant flak damage over their targets.

Guy Gibson had an even luckier escape over Antwerp, later writing:

Once again, I had the pleasure of hearing that crump, crump, crump just behind my tail plane as our bombs went off. Then, that illuminating flash which lit up the ground all around as some ammunition barge exploded. But this time, something had happened. There was a rending crack and a noise like a crack of thunder. At first, I did not know what had happened and was rather frightened that Houghton in front had been killed. Then, as one does on these occasions, I suddenly realised that something was wrong with the aeroplane; she was flying in a queer way. There was no rudder bar. Then Houghton told me what was wrong. He had to crawl up to do so as the intercom had gone. A shell had entered by my feet, had got to the toe strap on my rudder bar and then had hit its pivotal point and knocked it spinning forward on to Houghton's head where it had laid him out. Quite an unlucky shot.

The squadron log also recorded the incident and noted Gibson's skill in getting the Hampden back to Scampton in just about one piece, a small detail he omitted to mention, preferring to end on a more humorous and self-effacing note. Upon his return, Flt Sgt Longford inspected the damage:

"Cor, sir," he said, "that's blooming providence, that's what I call it, blooming providence. It missed your foot by half an inch." I did not know quite what to say but Houghton replied succinctly, "No it wasn't, Flight, it was just a question of having short legs."

The other ports were attacked with equal determination. Over Flushing, 37 Squadron's Plt Off Nobby Clark, for example, delivered three separate attacks from 8,000ft, 7,000ft and 6,000ft. The effect on the inner harbour went unseen owing to the bright glare of the flames leaping from the burning petrol storage tanks in the area. The second and third were made on the Walcheren Canal and were also without observed effect, despite the cloud encountered on route clearing. Sqn Ldr Golding plumped for a silent, gliding approach, descending from 10,000ft to just 1,000ft before releasing his bomb load in a single stick in a line from the west to the Inner Harbour. His crew at least had the satisfaction of seeing four large fires break out behind them. Fg Off Baird-Smith split the difference, coming in at 5,500ft, while Sgt Gillanders on arrival noticed the blazing petrol installations and made for them at 9,500ft. Dropping part of his load on to the blaze, the fire swelled and boiled up further, practically doubling in size; his second stick was dropped on to a quayside with far less spectacular results. The crews arriving individually at various times and on separate headings all reported vigorous opposition from both heavy and light flak, supported by a ring of very lively searchlights. Nor did the dangers end there. Plt Off Lax was about 20 miles from the Dutch coast when a single engine aircraft, identified as a Me 109, was spotted stalking the Wellington. The rear gunner immediately opened fire, though at extreme range. The enemy aircraft closed to 300 yards and let fly. The rear gunner returned fire and, although some hits were taken on both sides, the result was inconclusive and within seconds the night sky was as peaceful as ever, leaving the gunners nervously scanning the darkness for an assailant who did not return.

There was an equally vicious reception for the crews over Calais. Some thirteen Wellingtons of 38 Squadron left Marham to attack the port, where they encountered patchy cloud and intense defensive fire that did not waver in intensity throughout the raid. Many bursts were observed on the quayside and docks and numerous fires were started, one especially large and developing rapidly. The flak, however, was equally accurate and deadly and three of the bombers sustained significant battle damage. Plt Off Lane had to make a wheels-up landing after the Wellington's hydraulics were put out of action, a dangerous operation at the best of times and even more so in the dark. The pressure really was on the young pilot due to the immobility of Sgt Lawton, the observer, who had been wounded by shrapnel in the thigh and would not have been able to escape in case of fire breaking out. As it turned out, Lane made a textbook forced landing and Lawton was soon extricated by the emergency crews and rushed for treatment.

Even the supposed mining 'milk-runs' were not without lethal danger. Eight Hampdens were mining the Loire estuary off St Nazaire and 61 Squadron's Stan Harrison was one of those delighted to be selected for the task after several forays into Germany. Routed with the enemy-held Channel Islands to port, the Hampdens crossed the Brittany peninsula to La Boule, turned south and began a 'time and distance' run to the drop zone. Focusing on the calculations to ensure the mine was dropped in the correct place, Harrison was flying straight and level at 900ft through the darkness when a blinding searchlight beam locked on to the aircraft, immediately followed by stream after stream of multi-coloured light flak tracer from multiple, quick-firing 20mm cannons. Momentarily stunned by this sudden and unexpected turn of events, Harrison threw the bomber into a steep climbing turn, instinctively pulling away from the storm of fire hurtling towards him. At such a low level, it was vital for the pilot to keep track of where he was in the sky, so he ducked down low in the cockpit and concentrated on the instruments. Within seconds that felt like hours, all was calm and the Hampden was able to proceed serenely through the sky as the flak ship was left behind. The mine was still on board and, after a few minutes for everyone on board to regain their composure, Harrison began another timed run a mile or so further out to sea. Having dropped the mine on target and noted its position, the Hampden turned for home and it was a very relieved and weary quartet that stretched their aching limbs back at Hemswell after some six and a half hours in the air, still pondering what might have been on this 'piece of cake'. Only one crew would not have that opportunity to wonder that morning; all on board 75 Squadron's Wellington T2463 died over Ostend.

By the time it became certain that Plt Off Brown and his crew would not be returning to Mildenhall, the late summer sun was already up and shining, the blue sky picturesquely dotted with puffy, white clouds. Eighteen Blenheims from 2 Group were ready and waiting, the sun drying their dew-dampened surfaces. The three-man crews clambered on board and went through the usual drills and procedures. They were bound for their regular targets stretching along the Channel coast and they knew the German gun crews would be expecting them. Six searched the southern North Sea for shipping on the move but found nothing astir; five returned early on account of a lack of cloud cover but the remaining seven successfully carried out harassing attacks upon the ports. A further ninety-plus aircraft followed up that night. A twenty-six-strong force of Blenheims was out over Dunkirk and Ostend, the resultant fires stoked later by a few Battles, Hampdens and thirty Wellingtons; 4 Group, with a night off German targets, put twenty-two Whitleys over Boulogne. Every one of the crews commented upon the stiff opposition encountered, the sky becoming a positive inferno of flak bursts, criss-crossing streams of light flak and searchlights probing the sky for prey. Years later, Tom Sawyer would still recall this particular 'barge bashing expedition', comparatively short as it was:

With only two or three other aircraft over the same target, we received a very healthy welcome and, for the second time, I heard heavy flak bursting at close quarters. This always sounded as though a giant fist was pounding the outside of the fuselage and you knew then it was getting a little too close for comfort. But we only received a few small shrapnel holes, which did no real damage.

Not all the damage done was in the air. Wg Cdr J.N.H. Whitworth DFC was leading 77 Squadron. In good conditions, he attacked from 8,000ft and could see a large amount of shipping in the harbour and fires taking hold along the dockside and barges moored there. Plt Off Denney also ploughed through the heavy AA fire and, in bright moonlight, saw an estimated twenty-five large barges in the harbour and picked out one 2,000–4,000-ton ship south of the harbour wall. The whole area was well ablaze and being rocked by explosion after explosion as the bombs fell to earth. Sgt A.S. Ennis reported several oil and petrol fires burning, presumably from ruptured storage tanks and so, all in all, with no losses, it had been a most satisfactory night's work. At a time when London and other cities were being pounded nightly, the newspapers made the most of such successes, based upon the Air Ministry communiques. 'Invasion Ports Hammered Night and Day' ran the headline in the *Northern Echo* and the main text noted the daylight raids, 'Then from dusk till dawn waves of bombers continued their raids. Soon a great oil fire was burning on the quayside at Boulogne, heavy black smoke and an angry red glow dwarfing the other numerous fires. Dunkirk had huge fires which could still be seen 50 miles away, with smoke rising up to 5,000ft.' Every newspaper followed suit, trumpeting the Command's success against the invasion threat, which, though waning with each day ticked by on the calendar, was still a very real prospect.

Although the weather put paid to maintaining the pressure during the day, as darkness fell another potent force numbering almost 100 took to the sky and headed south to the Channel ports. None of the ports from Le Havre to Flushing escaped the hail of bombs and incendiaries. Plt Off Gilmore was flying a 15 Squadron Blenheim towards Ostend, easily locating the port which was already under attack. Approaching the defensive screen, he 'made a very shallow diving attack on a point in the outer harbour where the barges were reported. One very large explosion was seen, with debris flying high into the air and a very large cloud of greyish black smoke was seen rising to 6–7,000ft.' Plt Off Woodbridge was in a 61 Squadron Hampden on the same target and reported seeing, 'debris, presumably barge debris, thrown high into the air'. The squadron log summed up the raid, 'The aircraft attacked with commendable likelihood of success and, although they could not see the barges themselves, the outline of the docks was sufficiently clear to permit aiming with precision.' Opposition over the ports was uniformly fierce but these short operations, mostly around three hours in duration, did at least have the benefit of having only a brief period over enemy territory. There was no prospect of such a benefit for the fourteen 4 Group crews as they climbed into their Whitleys bound for Berlin or the aluminium works at Lauta, near Dresden.

For Sqn Ldr Sawyer, this was his first deep penetrative operation and over the target area he faced a difficult problem of his own making. The whole area was obscured by a thick ground haze, forcing him to circle while the crew tried to discern some ground detail or feature in the inky blackness below. All remained quiet and, in desperation, he ordered flares to be dropped and:

> … had opened the sliding window beside me to get a clearer view and was peering hopefully downwards, when I realised the controls were getting a trifle sloppy. Looking down quickly at the instruments, I found that we were in a steep, climbing turn with the airspeed indicator below the 90mph mark while still rapidly unwinding. I just managed to stuff the nose down before a spin developed, straightened up at the same time and all was well. Good old Whitley V, any other plane would have spun long before that.

Now concentrating on flying and leaving the spotting to others, the flares eventually showed up a large lake to the west of Berlin and, after some quick calculations, Sawyer began a timed run to the Siemens works. With only a handful of attackers in the area, the capital's defences remained silent and Sawyer dropped his bombs on ETA, the target remaining unseen throughout. Several hours later, he found the flarepath to Great Massingham almost equally difficult to locate from the air. Normally a Blenheim base and one that received quite a lot of attention from unwelcome intruders, all lighting was kept to a minimum. Having crossed the Suffolk coast on track, Sawyer picked up the airfield's beacon flashing with considerable relief after more than ten hours in the air. However, no matter how hard he and his crew tried, they could not pick up the glim lamps marking the runway. It took Sawyer several attempts to find them, each time returning to the beacon to follow the predetermined course to the airfield, every weary eye on board straining and scanning the ground not far beneath.

Eventually, they came into view and eased the Whitley down, returning home to North Yorkshire the following day.

The flight to Lauta was no shorter but, being a virgin target, the nine crews from 10, 58 and 77 Squadrons hoped it might be only lightly defended. Their hopes were dashed. Larry Donnelly's Whitley left Leeming at 19.10 hours and once out over the North Sea, it became clear that it was not going to be an easy night. The weather conditions deteriorated rapidly and in no time the bomber was pushing its way through dense clouds and electrical storms, making it an uncomfortable flight for all on board. Fortunately, 77 Squadron had arrived over the target a little earlier, making locating it far easier for those following on behind. It was also clear that the area was strongly defended and it was with some trepidation that the crew began its search for the target itself. With flak exploding all around them, the Whitley made two runs at 11,000ft, releasing half a load on each pass. The glow of the fires burning was visible through the cloud. Then it was a quick about turn and back into the rotten weather for a long slog home. If anything, conditions were even worse and, at one point, the bomber was struck by lightning, which burnt off the trailing aerial, destroyed Donnelly's wireless set and contributed to the demise of the engine-driven generator. Fortunately, the weather cleared as they reached the English coast, though they were still diverted to Linton on their return. As the Whitley turned off the flarepath at 05.40 hours after a marathon ten and a half hours in the air, mostly over hostile territory, one of its engines spluttered and died as it ran out of fuel. Later investigation revealed that the other would not have been far behind and confirmed the narrowness of the fine line between making it home and not.

Plt Off Pinkham was flying as second pilot to Plt Off Brownlie in Whitley P4969. Having struggled through the murk, they found Lauta, some 80 miles south-east of Berlin, smothered by cloud but, after circling for a while, located a break in the cloud, which had closed by the time the aircraft had reached it. Frustrated, Brownlie turned for nearby Dresden, where a train steaming into the station was soon spotted and attacked. Hits were observed on the station and on some warehouses along the riverbank, in spite of heavy and accurate defensive fire from the ground. Buoyed by their success, the crew headed home and landed at Massingham, where they passed on the results of their efforts and enjoyed a hearty breakfast before taking off for the short flight back to Linton. The weather was fine and all seemed well with the world until one engine cut out, followed seconds later by the other. A swift check revealed that the bomber had not been refuelled at Massingham and none of the crew had thought to check. Dropping like a stone from just 4,000ft, there was little time to do anything more than look for an open space in the Lincolnshire countryside. Acting on habit, Brownlie lowered the undercarriage, which, landing on broken ground, could have had disastrous effects. As it turned out, the Whitley simply hurtled across the flat landscape, clearing a path through the shrubs and hedges and bouncing over a couple of drainage ditches before coming to a halt, incredibly without significant damage to either the aircraft or the crew. It took a little while longer to reach Linton than expected.

It was clear from the outset that Monday 23 September was going to be a lovely sunny day, ideal conditions for the heavily escorted Luftwaffe bombers but precisely the opposite for the unescorted 2 Group raiders. The half dozen Blenheims launched aborted on account of the crystal-clear conditions. However, Bomber Command was not idle and the ground crews toiled in the sunshine to prepare an unprecedented number of aircraft for operations that night. For the first time, a force of more than 200 bombers would head for enemy territory, two-thirds of them to Berlin, where eighteen railway stations and yards, power stations, gasworks and aircraft component factories were on the target list. The remainder kept up the pressure on Calais and Ostend. It was the first operation for one of these crews and what a baptism of fire it turned out to be. The majority of 38 Squadron's Wellingtons had already left Marham for the German capital when the fresher crew climbed on board their aircraft with a heady mix of excitement and trepidation. Sgt Roy Richards was its gunner and later recalled his eventful initiation to operational life:

Take off was at 22.30 hours and after an uneventful flight we arrived over the target area and carried out our bomb-run. However, our New Zealander observer missed the target with his first stick. After a crew conflab, it was agreed we should go around again and carry out another attack from a shallow dive. I cannot recall at what height we were when we were hit by flak. The observer was badly hit in the groin so he was helped back to the bed in the fuselage and injected with morphine. We set course for home but the WOP then reported his W/T was U/S. However, between them, the captain and the second pilot managed to navigate back across the Channel and from there, map-read us back to Marham. I was flying in the front turret and I was able to guide us to our identification beacon. As we prepared to land, the captain informed us that our hydraulics had been damaged by flak and a belly landing would be necessary. Our W/T managed to work so we were able to inform ground control of our intentions. I left the front turret to take up my landing position and I am glad to say that the skipper carried out a first class wheels-up landing. Fortunately, there was no fire and we were able to get out of the aircraft and into the waiting ambulance without delay. I seem to remember the next morning being told that a 500lb bomb was found hung up in the bomb bay.

The flight had amounted to three and a half hours.

However important the events along the northern coastline of France and Belgium were, the headlines the next morning were all about the heavy and sustained assault upon the German capital. Claiming that it amounted to a heavy bomb falling on the city every four minutes for several hours, the newspapers were full of the explosions and intense fires left blazing at each of the industrial and military targets. Conditions over the target were predicted to be clear and, apart from a slight ground haze, they were, enabling the crews to bomb with comparative accuracy. Flt Lt Eustace DFC of 44 Squadron was positive he had located the Charlottenberg power station and gas works, dropping his four 500lb bombs in a single stick from west to east. Three strikes were observed in the northern area of the target, triggering a very large, vivid, blue explosion. All eight of 37 Squadron's Wellingtons succeeded in locating their target area but were prevented from pinpointing the targets themselves by the haze and glare of the searchlights, not to mention the heavy flak bursts. Nevertheless, the crews all reported widespread fires being ignited by their bombs and a larger than usual weight of incendiaries. Plt Off De Mestre of 61 Squadron brought his Hampden down low through the flak to allow his gunners to direct their fire towards some of the many searchlights probing the night sky; three were claimed as destroyed. His fellow squadron member Stan Harrison also had trouble identifying the target and chose to bomb 'somewhere in Berlin' before turning for home. He quickly noticed all was not well with his Hampden as it seemed sluggish and unresponsive, wallowing around in the air. Initially, he concluded the aircraft had been hit by flak but a quick check revealed nothing amiss. This perilous position did not show any signs of improvement and Harrison, a seasoned campaigner, forced himself to work logically through the options and it was with a mixture of relief, annoyance and embarrassment that he realised it was his fault; as he had tried to close the bomb doors, he had inadvertently lowered the undercarriage, creating a huge amount of unwanted drag. A deft flick of the switch and the error was rectified, leaving the Hampden to fly serenely back to Hemswell, the crew blissfully unaware of the drama in the cockpit. No. 9 Squadron, which was making the largest contribution to the Command's total with thirteen Wellingtons in the air, sent four to attack the barges and nine to Berlin. Plt Off Sam Hall was in the latter group and succinctly described the night as he saw it:

We went to Berlin, September 23rd, with clear skies and good visibility and a particular target, the Siemens-Schukert works. I am reasonably sure that we found it. Bertie did his run, we dropped our bombs and the rear gunner saw them explode. Can't say much more than that. There was plenty of flak but, as with us bombers, there was not much coordination.

The flak was, however, sufficiently coordinated to bring down three of the bombers over the city that night. Guy Gibson recalled the loss of Sqn Ldr Anthony Orlando Bridgman, always known as 'Oscar' and an 83 Squadron stalwart: 'It was one of those trips which were so common in those days. Cloud all the way, flak all the way; no one knowing where Berlin was, our loop bearings continually being jammed by the enemy and general chaos all round ... On the way home there was another headwind of gale strength so we came back at 1,000ft with our radio shot away.' On his arrival in the briefing room, fellow pilot Jackie Withers informed him that his Hampden had returned on one engine after it was damaged by flak and added quietly that 'Oscar's had it'. Opening a bottle of beer, Gibson asked, 'What do you mean?' and was told, 'About a half an hour ago, he sent out a signal, saying that one engine had been put on fire and that he was bailing out. Later, another message that he was trying to get home. Since then, there has been silence.' Gibson concluded the episode, 'We waited all night, we waited until the grey darkness of the early hours became purple, then blue as the sun rose in the east over the Lincoln Wolds and it became daylight. But Oscar never came back. And so, I went to bed. I was the last one left, the last one of the bunch of boys who belonged to 83 Squadron at the beginning of the war to fight until the end of Hitlerism.' Sqn Ldr Bridgman DFC was far luckier than the other three men on board; they were killed as the aircraft crashed near Bethen in Germany but he survived to join a steadily growing band of RAF aircrew at Oflag IXA/H, Spangenberg.

No. 311 Polish Squadron suffered the loss of its first aircraft since becoming operational when Flt Lt K. Trojacek's Wellington force landed at Leidschendam in Holland after suffering engine failure, probably the result of flak damage. All the crew escaped from the wreckage but it was reported that Sgt K. Kunka shot himself with the Very pistol as the Germans closed in to capture him the following day.

There was to be only a single survivor from the crew of Whitley P5046 'O' of 77 Squadron, originally consisting of Plt Off Andy Dunn, gunner Sgt George Riley, WopAg Sgt Dudley Allen, Second Pilot Sgt Derek

Gibbons and Sgt Bernard Savill. Plt Off Andy Dunn had been assigned the aircraft factory at Spandau as the target for his twenty-fourth operational sortie. He had no real problem in locating Berlin and he tried to pick his way through the flak as he made his way over the city to Spandau. Once in the area, he ordered flares to be dropped and gunner Sgt George Riley was able to identify the factory by their light. Dunn pulled his Whitley around in a tight turn and began his bombing run, carefully following the instructions of the equally experienced Sgt Savill in the bomb aimer's position. Riley once again made a report, describing the explosions as the bombs ripped through the buildings and started a large blaze. Unfortunately, this was not the only damage done. Shrapnel from several misses had holed one of the fuel tanks and it rapidly became obvious that with the current rate of leakage the aircraft would not make it home. Cruising as economically as possible while trying to maintain height, Dunn skilfully coaxed the bomber westwards and, with the crew's unanimous support, over the Dutch coast and over the North Sea. They got further than they had initially dared to hope and were beginning to think the unthinkable, that they might make it after all. About 30 miles from the Dutch coast, Sgt Allen sent a signal informing Linton of their parlous situation and current course, speed and position. The minutes ticked by, each mile taking the anxious young men a couple of miles nearer to safety. Eventually, the inevitable happened and, with the Whitley slipping inexorably towards the waves, Dunn ordered his crew to take up their ditching positions and Allen to send out a final position signal. Dunn knew what to expect as this was to be the second ditching of his eventful operational career, which had only begun on 10 May 1940 but, this time, the sea was far rougher than the waters off Hastings pier in the early morning of 20 June on his way back from Wanne-Eickel. The bomber hit the waves hard, bounced like a skimming flat stone, before coming to rest in one piece. Elated to have made it down safely, the five crew members scrambled to get out and clambered into the dinghy without mishap. It was 05.50 hours on the morning of Tuesday 24 September and, according to Sgt Savill, who had been with Dunn at Hastings, they were just 80 miles from the English coast and their exact position known to their would-be rescuers. Things could have been far worse.

In fact, a Coastal Command Hudson was already in the air searching for them. It failed to locate the small dinghy but its relief did so at 10.50 hours and immediately radioed its position as 100 miles east of Hartlepool in Co. Durham. The Hudson circled the dinghy until 12.35 when another took over and the process was repeated again at 14.00 hours. The first message had triggered the immediate despatch of a rescue launch but, as the sea conditions worsened, it was forced to turn for home, having sustained serious damage from the crashing waves. The weather then began to worsen around the dinghy and the wet and drained young men in it began to feel the first pangs of doubt about their rescue. Their spirits took another tumble as the weather closed in, cutting them off from the comforting sight of the circling Hudson. The next few hours saw a succession of Hudsons searching in vain for the dinghy as it drifted at the mercy of the choppy North Sea. Eventually, one picked out the coloured dot in the heaving sea and radioed its new position and heading before dropping a container of rations. It was a skilful effort in the blustery conditions and it landed a mere 10 yards from the weary but excited men, who had to watch helplessly as the heavy sea took it and them in opposite directions. The condition of the men began to worsen as fatigue and exposure began to grind their resistance down and, as darkness fell, they had finished the last of their emergency and carefully eked out hard rations and water. When dawn finally brought an end to a miserable and interminable night, there were only four men left in the dinghy, their comrade having been washed overboard in the night.

At 06.00 four more Hudsons resumed the search, extending the area to account for the expected drift during the night; two destroyers, HMS *Ashanti* and *Bedouin,* were also deployed. By 11.00 a Hudson had located the dinghy and, having notified its position, remained on station until 13.00, by which time the destroyers were just 16 miles away. Once again, the capricious weather closed in, reducing visibility to just 400 yards and at 14.30, with the destroyers now only a handful of miles away, contact was lost. Two Heinkel seaplanes now approached the scene and the Hudson gamely turned towards them to drive them off; its charge was successful but it had, in the meantime, lost sight of the dinghy. The men below could do nothing more than watch the events unfold, wait and hang on. A little while later, a destroyer was spotted in the distance, raising their hopes only to have them dashed as it steamed into a squally shower and vanished from sight, leaving only the near certainty of a second night in the open sea. That night took a deadly toll as daylight revealed only three men in the dinghy, Sgts Riley and Allen and Plt Off Dunn, the latter by now in a bad way and barely alive. Throughout the following day, several Hudsons, Blenheims and Ansons scoured the area without success, fighting several skirmishes with the Luftwaffe which was well aware that some operation or other was under way. As day broke on Friday 27 September, the fourth day of the rescue attempt and with hopes of a successful outcome fading fast, four Ansons and five Hudsons were out again and at 11.15 hours, against the odds, one of the Hudsons caught sight of the dinghy but was unable to keep it in view in the heavy showers. The two destroyers, still on task, and the other aircraft homed in but to no avail. It was not until 14.00 hours that another Hudson caught sight of it and succeeded in dropping marker flares and an emergency ration pack right next to it. Riley, with a great effort, managed to retrieve the pack from the choppy sea but by now his two companions were past caring, lying unconscious in the bottom of the pitching dinghy. Determined not to lose it again, the Hudson circled the dinghy at wave-top height and the crew could clearly see what was happening in it. With mounting horror and an overwhelming sense of powerlessness, at 16.00 hours, they watched one of the previously inert figures stir a little and roll out of the dinghy as it was tossed up on a wave; these were the final moments of Plt Off Dunn's life. Finally, a bare ninety minutes later, HMS *Bedouin* came to a halt nearby, lowered a boat and picked up Riley and Allen. The signal the destroyer sent read, 'One fair, one very ill.' It was an accurate assessment and Sgt Allen slipped away within the hour. Over the course of the four-day ordeal, the dinghy had drifted the best part of 100 miles in rough seas and rotten weather. Nobody could fault the commitment or scale of the rescue operation and, certainly, nobody would have quibbled if Riley wanted no further active part in the war. However, he volunteered to return to operational flying, serving with 106 and later 617 Squadrons, completing forty-nine sorties.

Whilst this tragic drama was being played out in the North Sea, there was no let-up in the air war. The worsening weather conditions, which had hampered the rescue, favoured 2 Group's daylight operations and eighteen were sent out on sea sweeps. Twelve of them from 114 and 139 Squadrons were quickly routed to an area 9 miles off Dover where a number of German R-boats were reported to be engaged in minesweeping. For once, fighter protection was provided and the Blenheim crews had no problem locating the enemy formation, which greeted them with a hail of light flak as they roared in to attack. Five of the R-boats were attacked and two direct hits and several near misses were claimed. Even with the fighter cover, several Blenheims came under attack from Me 109s and Sqn Ldr M.F. Henry of 139 Squadron was shot down almost at once and Flt Lt Turnbull's was hit and badly damaged, though he managed to claw his way back to RAF Manston. Unusually, one under-armed Blenheim managed to strike back; Plt Off Hunt succeeded in bringing down his assailant using its single .303 machine gun in the port wing, a remarkable and confirmed feat.

At night, it was back to Calais, Le Havre and Ostend for the Blenheims. The invasion menace might well have receded a little and continued to do so with the turning of every page on the calendar but there was still a powerful enemy force on Britain's doorstep and it had to be tackled. Twenty-nine out of the thirty-two aircraft sent out put in claims for a successful attack and once again the Channel coastline glowed orangey-red as the fires burned. No. 15 Squadron had provided nine of the light bombers for the raids on Le Havre and, on their return, several reported a new form of attack. Two enemy aircraft of unknown type were spotted approaching from astern and carrying fully illuminated, powerful headlamps. It was presumed these were to help the pilots to pick out the intruders but as far as they were concerned, it rather helpfully alerted them to the presence of their opponents and enabled them to take evasive action. Nevertheless, it is a good example of the innovations and experiments in techniques and tactics deployed in this unprecedented, mass-scale war in the air.

The Wellingtons and Hampdens of 3 and 5 Groups were also over the Channel ports in force, with more than fifty bombers participating in these raids. No. 38 Squadron, for example, divided its twelve-strong contribution between Boulogne and Le Havre, and in both instances the patchy cloud did little to hamper the attack. Crews claimed to have hit the dock warehouses and installations, leaving large and developing fires, often intensely bright and of unusual hues, visible for miles out over the sea. On such nights, few crews had good reason not to complete their sortie, especially as many were now given instructions of the kind given to 49 Squadron; should a crew not locate their primary target, it should attack 'any invasion port between Le Havre and Rotterdam inclusive'.

As the offensive waged by Bomber Command intensified, the Luftwaffe attempted to curb it at source. Several intruders were present over the bomber airfields in Lincolnshire and at Hemswell, and the comparative air of tranquillity that lay across the airfield like a blanket as the men and women on duty quietly waited for the return of their aircraft was torn apart at 02.30 hours by the growing growl of engines of an unfamiliar note. This was followed almost at once by the ear-splitting crack of explosions and the high-pitched whirr of machine guns. The attack was brief, though the aircraft remained in the vicinity for some time to provide a potential threat and increase disruption, the same tactics employed by the RAF over enemy territory; Hemswell was effectively closed for seventy-five minutes. Fortunately, damage and casualties were light. The raid did, however, round off a bad night for the station as a few hours earlier at 23.03 two Hampdens collided on take-off, resulting in the death of one of the pilots, Sgt J.E. Hills.

Nor was this the only fatal accident on home soil. Sgt H. Cornish had just lifted his heavily laden Whitley off the runway at Linton a minute before 21.00 hours when, for some reason, it faltered and plunged to earth just over the airfield boundary fence. Within seconds, the bomb load went off in an enormous fireball. Three men perished within clear sight of all on the airfield gathered to watch the departure; amazingly, two men survived, although both sustained serious injuries. The other six 58 Squadron aircraft carried on regardless of these shocking events to join fourteen more from 10 and 77 Squadrons bound for Finkenheerd power station near Frankfurt am Oder and various rail and industrial targets in Berlin. The weather conditions were poor in both instances but slightly better over the capital as the crews bound for the power station noted as they abandoned their primary target and headed for the alternatives in Berlin. Larry Donnelly was on board a 10 Squadron Whitley that found nothing but an impenetrable shield of cloud when ETA indicated he was over Frankfurt. After cruising around more in hope than anything else, the crew turned for Berlin, where they found the cloud beginning to disperse and enabling them to discern ground detail below. Greeted warmly by flak and searchlights, they knew they were over the great city and began to search for Tempelhof airfield. Unable to locate it and under heavy and almost constant fire, there was relief all around when a railway station came into sight. When the bomb aimer complained that patchy cloud was impeding his view and that another run would be needed, he was firmly advised in the bluntest of terms by all on board via the intercom that it was not. The bombs were duly released and with flak bursting audibly all around, the Whitley turned away to seek refuge in the cloud and darkness beyond the city's defences. The journey back to Leeming was uneventful but long, the wheels eventually kissing the soil of Yorkshire some ten hours and forty minutes after take-off. A day later, the crews were able to read the Air Ministry communique carried by most newspapers. Berlin had been hit for the second consecutive night in a raid that had lasted over two and a half hours; the great Siemens factories had been left ablaze, as had a major power station at Friedrichsfelde; the attack had been pressed home vigorously in spite of heavy opposition and had caused considerable disquiet among Berliners. The *Daily Mail* added a bullish editorial comment, 'Berliners are learning that their city is no more immune than is London from large scale bombing. The one difference is that our airmen select their targets and concentrate on objectives of military value. We hope to see Berlin bombed again – repeatedly.' Bomber Command would oblige in the months and years to come and with increasing accuracy and destructive power.

The next morning, Wednesday 25 September, promised a bright, early autumn day and the sun shone pretty well throughout. German attacks caused considerable damage at Filton, Plymouth and Portland by day and, inevitably, London by night. Bomber Command's response was to keep plugging away at the Channel ports, to disrupt communications in Germany and to maintain the pressure upon the Kriegsmarine and general shipping. A baker's dozen of Blenheims set off early on two separate anti-shipping sweeps, one over the North Sea, the other off the Dutch coast. Nothing was found in either case, though the maintenance of the offensive did come at a price. For reasons unknown, shortly after take-off, a 101 Squadron Blenheim crashed at 05.30 hours, a mile south of Swaffham. It exploded on impact and began to burn fiercely, an instant funeral pyre for the men on board.

The Blenheims were busy again that night and, together with several Battles, once again attacked the Channel ports and carried out several intruder raids and patrols in the Calais and Boulogne areas. They were joined by twenty-seven Wellingtons, although one of these from 99 Squadron did not get very far, crashing soon after take-off. Fortunately, the crew escaped serious injury and were able to extricate themselves from the wreckage and clear the area before the full bomb load went off in spectacular fashion. Tiny Cooling of 9 Squadron was not scheduled to fly that night and was waiting for official confirmation that his first tour of operations was over. He was relaxing in the mess when another pilot, Tommy Purdy, came over and complained that his pilot had reported genuinely sick and that he was having difficulties in finding a replacement. Before he knew it, Cooling had broken his vow never to volunteer and had his offer confirmed by the CO. Purdy was at least, he reasoned, a great chap and experienced pilot and, in this event, his trip to Boulogne was successful and trouble free, apart from the usual heavy opposition over the target. It would not be his last operation; that would not be until 14 July 1943, when he bombed Pomigliano airfield near Naples on his sixty-seventh sortie. A handful of other Wellingtons attacked the usual railway suspects in Germany, Hamm, Mannheim and Schwerte and a few Hampdens and Whitleys were over Berlin for the third night in a row. The inhabitants were awoken by the sound of sirens and sharp cracks of the flak guns opening fire; the dull crump of high explosive bombs bursting quickly followed. One of the most high-profile figures inconvenienced that night was Count Ciano, Mussolini's son-in-law and Foreign Minister. No doubt to Hitler's embarrassment, his visit to Berlin by rail was delayed. He noted, 'Attacks by RAF endanger the zone and the Führer does not want to expose me to the risk of a long stop in the open country. I sleep in Munich and will continue by air.' Although nothing is recorded, the significance of the event cannot have escaped the shrewd Ciano.

Although the threat of immediate invasion was receding as the autumn progressed, there was always the spectre of next spring and with that in mind, whatever could be done at this point could be set against that time, especially in the form of deterrence. As a result, 51 and 78 Squadrons launched attacks on Kiel harbour where three powerful ships of the German navy were at anchor, the *Scharnhorst*, *Lutzow* and *Gneisenau*. The Germans were understandably aware of their importance too and the aircraft met with very heavy defensive fire and, although the conditions were decent, they were unable to identify the ships clearly amid the glare and smoke. Nevertheless, nine aircraft released their loads in the target area and were able to observe fires raging as they turned for home, arriving without loss.

The next day's operations followed a similar pattern, though the weather had returned to the seasonal norm, with cloud and rain spreading over a wide area. Six Blenheims carried out an uneventful patrol over the North Sea and six more from 114 Squadron set off for an armed reconnaissance along the Channel coast. Only one carried out an attack, releasing its load over Calais harbour but, once again, the steady trickle of casualties continued. One was shot down over the sea at 13.46 hours by Feldwebel Schramm of 7/JG53, who misidentified it as a Hampden. The body of Sgt F.A.R. Wheeler, the pilot, was recovered from the sea off Sandown Castle on the Isle of Wight but there was no trace of his two companions. By night, the Blenheims fared much better with five heading to each of Calais, Boulogne and Ostend. The Wellingtons and Whitleys again concentrated on what was for them short incursions into enemy territory; this time thirty-one of them hit Le Havre. In 58 Squadron, the Whitleys made their runs from 7,000 to 9,000ft but Plt Off Clements decided that he could not see well enough and so dropped down to just 800ft before streaking across the harbour from east to west, letting his bombs go as he went. Unscathed by the startled flak gunners beneath him, he headed back out to sea with his rear gunner confirming explosions across the docks and into the adjacent buildings of the town; three large and two small fires sprung up. Plt Off O'Duffy also came in far below the recommended height, his first run at 4,000ft and his second at 2,500ft. His bomb bursts were observed amid the clustered buildings and by the time the raid ended, several parts of the dockyard were well alight, the flames and smoke visible for miles out to sea.

Three Hampdens carried out successful mining sorties off La Pallice but only at a cost. No. 106 Squadron, based at Finningley, lost its second aircraft since becoming operational at the beginning of the month when X2914 crashed at 04.45 hours at West House Farm, Chilton Polden in rural Somerset. Only the pilot, Sgt W. Huggins, made it out of the wreckage alive. Another Hampden crashed that night; Plt Off R.T. Mulligan of 50 Squadron had left Lindholme at 19.23 hours and had no difficulty in carrying out his attack upon the docks at Calais, nor in returning to his airfield around midnight. Unfortunately, a patchy autumn fog had developed, and Mulligan was no doubt keen to avoid being diverted to another station so, in accordance with instructions from those on the ground, he lined his aircraft up to where he thought the runway was. He did not notice until it was too late that he was slightly off line. He and Plt Off G. Kilner required hospital treatment following the crash but the other two members of the crew escaped injury. Sadly, a third Hampden was lost from 61 Squadron on a sortie to attack the Kriegsmarine's surface units. Damaged by flak, Plt Off R.P. Earl, a pre-war regular from Australia, decided to head across the Baltic to neutral Sweden. The bomber made it but all on board were killed when it crashed near Oresund.

Others from 61 Squadron mounted another attack upon the Dortmund–Ems canal. Sgt Stan Harrison was able to identify the target in relatively clear conditions and made his run at 6,000ft, amid copious quantities of light flak whizzing all around; a near miss was observed. It was a few hectic and hair-raising minutes in an otherwise routine flight. There was, however, a certain lack of satisfaction in such a raid. Guy Gibson was in an 83 Squadron Hampden over Kiel late in the night and graphically described the conflicting emotions of fighting the bomber war in 1940, collectively yet in isolation. He wrote:

This time we carried a flare on our 2,000lb bomb so that we could see it go into the sea. It missed by some 200 yards, so the rear gunner said, and we got the hell beaten out of us for the attack. I swore then and there, at that moment that I would never bomb the *Scharnhorst* again. It seemed so foolish to go all the way there all alone. It seemed that we were the only ones fighting the war for England when you sit up there on top of a great cone over a great harbour surrounded by coloured lights and smelling the flak. You feel a long way from home, you feel you want to get back, you feel you never want to go again. And when you do come back, it gets you and you want to go and have another crack. God knows why.

It was just as well for those millions left behind on the ground in hard-pressed Britain that he and others like him did.

Around 850 Luftwaffe aircraft were in action over Britain by day on Friday 27 September and several hundred bombers attacked Liverpool, Edinburgh, Nottingham and, inevitably, London by night, taking the number of intruders to well over the 1,000 mark for the twenty-four-hour period. Bomber Command's response was very much less than 10 per cent of that for the same period. By day, a total of fifteen Blenheims were sent to carry out a reconnaissance over the North Sea and to attack any targets of opportunity. The majority of the unescorted and vulnerable light bombers turned back in the clear conditions, leaving just three to mount attacks on the coastal shipping they came across. No claims for hits were made. That night the bulk of the Command's effort was focused upon the French and Belgian ports, notably those further west at Le Havre and Lorient, with only a handful of Wellingtons being sent further afield to railway targets in Hamm, Mannheim, Cologne and Soest; a distress signal from a 214 Squadron aircraft was picked up at 04.35, shortly before it came down over Belgium, with the loss of three airmen. For the Wellingtons of 38 Squadron, it was one of their last operations before being posted overseas at the end of the month. The crews were very happy with their work over Le Havre and the squadron logs states:

> One captain reported a terrific explosion in the town ten minutes after the bombs had been dropped there. Another aircraft started a chain of fires on the dockside which merged into one large fire. Despite adverse weather conditions, the operation to Le Havre can be judged highly successful. It is reported that the AA fire barrage at Dover is far heavier than any seen on the French coast.

Whether this is a facetious remark or not is moot but the British defences were likely to open fire at any and every aircraft, day or night, just to be on the safe side; statistically, their approach was the correct one.

For the dozen 4 Group Whitley crews, the attack upon Lorient's nascent submarine base, both in terms of the hours spent over enemy territory and its overall duration, was a refreshing change and in stark contrast to their marathon slogs to the German heartland. Larry Donnelly summed it up as, 'I suppose that if any operation could be classified as easy, then this was it.' He took off at 19.45 and headed south over England, flying along a route designated as a safe corridor through the defensive system, before heading out over the Channel and south-west towards Brittany. Following the coast, Lorient was picked out with ease and, given that it had not yet been attacked on the same scale as other French ports, the defences were comparatively light, enabling an accurate attack to be carried out. Several fires were certainly left burning as the crews turned to follow their route in reverse. Sqn Ldr Tom Sawyer also described the attack as successful but had a far more unusual flight home. At a time when he should have been over the spires of Oxford, very much an inland city, he idly glanced out of the cockpit window and with a jolt noticed water gleaming in the faint light through patchy cloud. Looking again, he discerned a jagged coastline and wondered where on earth he might be. An urgent conversation with a bemused navigator revealed that he had no idea either. It took a couple of minutes for the wireless operator to obtain a fix, which placed them over the Gower peninsular in west Wales, a couple of hundred miles and 90 degrees off course. Sawyer turned due east and, mindful of his dwindling fuel reserves, made for an area he knew well, hoping all the while not to come under attack from a rogue raider. A couple of hours later, with a few adjustments here and there, he landed safely at Abingdon near Oxford, making the last leg home the following day. Given that his navigator, Plt Off Beeston, was a Welshman, there was a good deal of ragging but it could have so easily have turned out so very differently and vividly demonstrates the skill and concentration – and a smidgin of luck – required to fly, fight and survive by night in the 1940s.

Plt Off D.D. Snooke of 83 Squadron did not survive the night's attack on Lorient. Although the official records are sketchy, it appears that his Hampden had made it back to Lincolnshire but was unable to find Scampton. After several fruitless square searches and running low on fuel, the decision was taken to bail out and the crew succeeded in doing so.

Snooke, the pilot and last to abandon the aircraft, did not and met with a terrible fate. He made it to the hatch and jumped out but deployed his parachute too soon and it became entangled in the tail plane, dragging him through the air for some time to his death near St Matthias church in Lincoln. The crew of Sgt Turner's 101 Squadron Blenheim fared better on their return to West Raynham. Unable to control the aircraft properly on his final approach, Turner managed to get the bomber down some 350 yards to the right of the landing lights, ploughing spectacularly into two parked aircraft before grinding to a halt. Incredibly, all three men were able to climb out of the mangled wreckage with only minor injuries.

The next day might have heralded the weekend but the relentless activity went on just the same. The weather was by now distinctly autumnal, though occasional bright spells could quickly lift the gloom and give the day a warm, summery feel. Certainly, the cloudy conditions encouraged the crews of the seven Blenheims sent to harass the Channel ports but, fickle as ever, the skies cleared towards the enemy coast and most turned for home. Two pressed on to carry out attacks on the remaining barges in Ostend harbour; no particular results were observed. By night, though, a force of 100 plus headed south and east to attack a range of targets in the less than ideal conditions. Thirty-four of the forty-seven Blenheims sent to the ports managed to complete their attack, although the conditions did not allow for any realistic assessment of the results. The others returned with their loads intact, as did several of the Whitleys, which failed to locate the Fokker factory in Amsterdam. Conditions over mainland Europe were little better and the crews struggled to operate effectively, even in cases where the targets were regular ones. No. 61 Squadron, for example, contributed to the raids on the massive railway yards at Hamm, one of the most frequently attacked targets in the whole of Germany. Plt Off Massey encountered cloud from the moment he crossed the Lincolnshire coast and it never let up; criss-crossing the target area in vain, he could only see cloud and more cloud. Reluctantly, he turned for home, bidding his crew to keep an eye out for any break that might lead to a worthwhile target. The crew remained silent until a strip of railway line appeared far beneath them. It was marginally better than nothing and their bombs were released at a position estimated to be near Ommen in Holland; Massey added in his report that it was the only moment that the ground became visible while over enemy territory. His night was far from over as upon his return to Hemswell, one leg of the undercarriage only partially extended and no amount of wiggling and jiggling could entice it to drop and lock into place. The decision was made to attempt a landing in any case as there was little enthusiasm among the crew for taking to their parachutes. Massey lowered the Hampden down as gently as he could, with all on board in their crash positions, uncertain of what the next few, vital seconds would bring. Favouring the port side, Massey guided the bomber down and ran for much of the runway on a single wheel. It was only as the speed lowered that the starboard wing dropped and grazed the ground, slewing the bomber around. The damage to the airscrew and wing was slight and to the pilot's delight, everyone clambered out unscathed, chattering loudly about their lucky escape to the waiting crash teams, who were in place and fearing the worst.

Most of the Wellingtons attacked the nickel works at Hanau, east of Frankfurt. For one crew it was to be their final sortie of the war. Wellington R3164 B of 149 Squadron, with Plt Off H.R. Peterson at the controls, took off from Mildenhall around 21.00 hours and was soon out over the North Sea. Ploughing through patches of dense cloud, the aircraft began to ice up, compelling Peterson to reduce altitude. Otherwise, the flight was routine enough for rookie second pilot Sgt W.T. Hallam, to get some flying time in. Peterson resumed control as the Dutch coast slid beneath them and took minor evasive measures as the flak and searchlights below opened up. A little over an hour later, the flak and brilliant white beams came on to the horizon as the formidable defences tried to ward off the assault on Frankfurt. In his turn, Peterson tried to avoid the worst of it but had to fly straight and level for the final run-in; within seconds, the bomber was rocked by the blast of a near miss and picked up and held by a roving searchlight. More and more flak came their way and after another near miss, the port engine packed up, making it difficult for the pilot to keep control. At one point, Sgt Hallam had to hold on to the rudder bar with his hands and apply his full body weight, while Peterson pushed as hard as he could with his feet. The flames from the port engine, fanned by the slipstream, began to spread over the wing and it became clear that the end was in sight. The order was given to abandon the aircraft and one by one the crew jumped out, leaving Peterson to hang on grimly, wrestling with the controls. Satisfied that his crew were out, he made a dive for the hatch and fell out into the darkness, though not without wrenching his neck painfully. Peterson, however, was unaware that, for whatever reason, Hallam was still in the Wellington. He had released the front gunner, New Zealander Sgt McKenzie-Laird, from his turret and had helped him to the hatch but was not seen after that. His body was recovered from the wreckage. The remaining aircraft completed the 900-mile round trip safely, although patchy fog over some of the airfields did little to cheer up the weary crews as they groped their way to touching down after six or more hours in the air.

In Monday's newspapers, the crews were able to read an account of their exploits given by an unnamed pilot, possibly from 99 Squadron based at Newmarket:

Going out there was cloud most of the way but 60–70 miles from the target, it broke up, although Frankfurt was covered by cloud. A fire was burning in the factory when we arrived. We went down lower until we could make out two oblong buildings; one was well alight but the other one hadn't caught properly. It was too good a target to miss. I stuck the nose down and went straight for it. The smoke from the fires was curling up 1,000ft above us when we pulled out of our dive. One of our bombs caught the edge of the building and I got the impression that the roof fell in. At any rate, the whole building went up in flames. We came around again and bombed level for the second time. It looked as if the factory block had gone up together, not just one building, but the whole block. When we left, it was just a roaring mass of flames.

The Whitleys had the dubious pleasure of making the long flight to Berlin, concentrating upon the power station at Waldeck and the gas works at Charlottenberg and Neukoln. Of the twenty aircraft assigned, nine made attacks on their primary targets and a further six on alternatives, with the remainder being unable to locate anything worthwhile at all. Plt Off M.L. Steadman of 78 Squadron was searching for Charlottenberg for some time, hoping in vain for a break in the cloud; he and his crew never saw a thing all night. Plt Off J.R. Davy fared slightly better, confirming his position by a chance sighting of the Hollenzollen canal, amid the colourful but lethal flak bursts and the dazzling beams of thirty or more searchlights probing the sky over the Reich capital. Flt Lt Barclay of 51 Squadron must have thought his sortie would never end, not happily at least. For some reason losing his way in the poor conditions, his Whitley managed to fly over England without being aware of it and both pilot and crew were much relieved when land and better still, an airfield came into sight; it was just as well as the aircraft had taken off from Dishforth at 20.30 hours and it was now approaching 07.20 – on paper the bomber had run out of fuel some time ago. The airfield turned out to be near Belfast but the crew could not have cared less; they had landed safely and that was all that mattered. As far as the weather conditions had allowed, the night had gone well for Bomber Command and with the autumn gaining ground and with the cumulative effect of the almost continual attacks on the Channel ports, it looked increasingly certain that the threat of invasion had been averted, at least until the spring.

Bomber Command had no intention of giving the Germans any respite at all and the following morning the Blenheims were ready for action. The fine weather was not helpful and the sorties were abandoned, restricting the anti-invasion work to be done at night. Some twenty-one Blenheims divided their efforts between Calais, Boulogne, Le Touquet,

Flushing and Ostend in continuation of their attempts to cause dislocation and disarray. Another sixty-odd aircraft headed for more strategic targets in Germany itself. Many of the Hampdens went for transportation targets. Stan Harrison of 61 Squadron was amongst them as he made his way back to Hamm. It all seemed rather familiar as he followed his usual route – Orford Ness–Schelde – final run-in from about 10 miles north of the marshalling yards and then the reciprocal flight home. Coming in a little higher than usual at 14,000ft, the crew's tranquillity was thoroughly shattered by prodigious quantities of accurately predicted heavy flak bursting noisily and much too close for comfort. Unable to do much else but grin and bear it on the final approach, Harrison watched with horrified fascination as another Hampden was picked out and held by the searchlights, illuminating it starkly against the night sky. Within scant seconds, it disappeared from view, seemingly swamped by burst after burst of flak. In disbelief, Harrison watched the Hampden emerge apparently unscathed and fly on steadily until it was again swallowed up, this time by the darkness as it broke free of the blinding beams. He, in the meantime, had had the presence of mind to take advantage of his unknown compatriot's predicament to press home his attack while the gunners below were busy and his bombs were soon added to the conflagration below. With no more than a few holes punched through the tail plane, Harrison's Hampden headed home with all on board thankful for a comparatively easy flight and mindful of the capriciousness of fate.

Many of the crews struggled to find their targets in the poor flying conditions. Of the ten Whitleys from 58 Squadron assigned to Magdeburg and Hanover, for example, half failed to locate any target at all and returned still fully loaded. One of these was piloted by Sgt Hughes who, ploughing through unbroken cloud, spent some time over where Magdeburg was, searching diligently for a break in the cloud. Reluctantly, he gave it up as a bad job and turned for Hanover, where conditions turned out to be somewhat better. As he and his crew were trying to fix their position, their aircraft was suddenly lit up as if by bright sunlight. Almost immediately a number of cannon shells hit home as a twin-engined aircraft bored in to attack. Caught unawares, Hughes belatedly began to hurl the bomber around the sky trying to shake off both the persistent searchlights and the assailant. As the German came around for a second pass, it became visible in the lights and the rear gunner squeezed off four long bursts in its direction, causing it to break away. A few, long seconds later, the Whitley was plunged into darkness, made all the darker by the crew's loss of night vision, as it outran both the lights and the fighter. Uncertain as to what damage the Whitley had sustained in the sudden and brutal attack and of their actual location, Hughes decided discretion was the better part of valour and set a general course west; after an uneventful flight, bomb load intact, he eased the aircraft down on to the soil of Yorkshire at 04.35 with a far greater story to tell far beyond the recorded detail of 'failed to locate target'.

Their friends at 77 Squadron fared little better, with several crews reduced to Razzling unidentified areas of woodland having failed to find a target more worthwhile. One crew managed to locate a coal yard and some industrial units near Amsterdam, which were attacked with as much precision as possible as the crew were well aware of the Allied citizens below. Four fires were left burning in the target but as the bomber left the area, one engine began to splutter and soon after fell silent, leaving the crew to face the chilling prospect of a sea crossing on a single engine. Slowly losing height, the Whitley painfully slowly ticked off the miles and to the immense relief of the young men on board, crossed the English coast, low and slow but still airborne. RAF Bircham Newton was but a few miles away and the Whitley landed there safely.

It could all have been so very different, as another 77 crew found out. Once again, the primary target proved elusive but, after some time spent searching, Minden was identified and attacked as an alternative with a single stick of bombs, the remainder being retained against the possibility of a better target being discovered later. Unable to see anything in the difficult conditions, the diligent crew flew through the darkness over enemy territory looking for a break in the cloud and a suitable target.

A stretch of water came into sight and it was thought to be the Zuiderzee, so, mindful of their duty, the pilot swung around and headed east back into enemy territory for one last sweep. To the delight of the crew, an airfield hove into sight and was promptly attacked with the second stick of bombs. The bursts were clearly visible across the airfield and the jubilant crew were satisfied that their dogged persistence had paid off. The conditions en route home quickly improved, enabling the aircraft's location to be fixed with certainty and as this was being worked out it began to dawn on the airmen that a terrible and potentially catastrophic error had been made. The landscape unfolding beneath them was that of England. They had travelled much further west than they had imagined and the Zuiderzee was in fact the North Sea, the enemy airfield in northern Holland was RAF Marham in Norfolk and the bombs had in fact fallen on home soil. Tortured by guilt and horror-struck, the young men set course for home, landing safely a bare thirty minutes later to report the unfortunate series of events. To their immense relief, they were informed that their aim had been rotten and the bombs had exploded in open country adjacent to the airfield. Amid much leg-pulling, the young men turned in, chastened by the thought of what might so easily have been. Ten men would not return that night as one 50 Squadron Hampden was lost without trace, one 37 Squadron Wellington was shot down near Osnabrück at 00.34 hours by Oblt Greise of 1/NJG1 with the loss of all the men on board bar one and a 75 Squadron Wellington that had lost its way on the long flight back from Leipzig, ran out of fuel and crashed on Exmoor, killing Plt Off E.A. Jelley and injuring the remainder of the crew.

The last day of September marked a major watershed in the Battle of Britain. It turned out to be the last day upon which the Luftwaffe mounted massed daylight attacks upon Britain, with several sweeping towards London and across the south-west. It was also the day upon which Bomber Command was informed officially that the threat of imminent invasion had passed, though the longer-term menace remained. There was still every reason to press on with the anti-invasion attacks, as whatever damage could be done to the invasion forces before they were dispersed would take time to replace or repair. Although a lack of cloud cover once again put paid to the Blenheims' daylight reconnaissance and harassing raids, a total of thirty-four attacked the harbours of Calais, Boulogne, Dunkirk and Ostend by night to keep up the pressure. One especially large blaze in Calais was still visible like some ancient beacon from the south coast six hours later. It was also noted that the defences had again been strengthened and were now formidable. A handful of Hampdens were given the task of laying mines in the Elbe estuary and the bulk of the Command was over mainland Germany, including Berlin.

On this occasion, a very particular target was given, the Reichsluft fahrtministerium in the Leipzigstrasse. To locate and hit one building, albeit a very large one, in the heart of a blacked out and increasingly heavily defended urban area was optimistic in the extreme but on the back of the titanic battle being slugged out day after day over Britain, it was vitally important to demonstrate that the RAF could not only take whatever the Luftwaffe could throw at it but also dish it out too. Some seventeen crews claimed to have located the vast office complex and aimed their bombs at it. Certainly, the newspapers were full of the Berlin raid the following Tuesday and Wednesday mornings, noting that bombers had been over the city for more than five hours and that several power stations and railway stations had been targeted and sustained damage. The *Evening Standard*'s headlines trumpeted, 'The RAF gave Berlin its largest raid during the night', before noting that much of the activity was focused upon the outskirts of the city. The Berlin correspondent of *The New York Times* also added that the AA fire appeared desultory and that none was heard from the newspaper's central office. More ominously, the correspondent also added that he could only confirm the detonation of a single bomb in the city centre. Although hindsight has placed the correspondent pretty close to the truth with only a half a dozen or so bombs recorded as exploding in the city, that is not how it appeared to those overhead. No. 37 Squadron, for example, reported being on the receiving end of a great deal of both heavy and light flak though, 'this was extremely ragged and inaccurate, causing

One of the Many who failed to return.

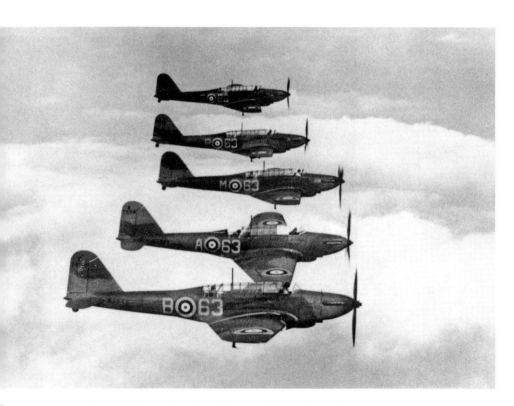

The obsolescent Fairey Battle suffered terrible casualties in the Battle of France but was pressed into service once more later in the summer of 1940.

The Hampden proved a robust yet nimble bomber and was popular with its crews.

Dunkirk, 19 September 1940. The threat of invasion was all too real and Bomber Command played a crucial and long-undervalued part in thwarting it.

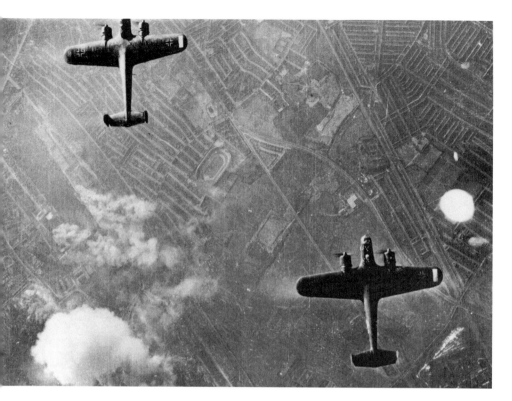

he bomber will always get through. Dorniers over West Ham on 7 September 1940.

he of the most chilling photographs of the war. Goring and his entourage view Britain, only a ndful of miles away across the English Channel.

Ground crews working on the rear turret of a Whitley. Thousands of men and women toiled long hours day after day to keep the aircraft in the air. Little glamour or glory came their way.

It looks pleasant enough on a summer's day but conditions on the wind-swept airfields could be bleak.

no great inconvenience. It is thought that this is probably due to the fact that a very large number of aircraft were operating in the area at the same time which tended to confuse the defences', a point later taken up by the adoption of the bomber stream as a regular tactic.

Extremely ragged and inaccurate or not, the defences of Berlin were not to be taken lightly. They were enough to unsettle veteran WopAg Larry Donnelly, though, to be fair, he had just been told that this would be his last operation before his tour expired. It was with a potent and heady mix of anticipation and trepidation that he climbed aboard T4143 at 18.00 hours, settled into his usual position and began to check his equipment. A few minutes later, the Whitley began to throb to the rhythm of its engines and climbed away into the gathering gloom. Passing south of Wilhelmshaven, the crew received a salutary reminder of what could happen to an aircraft over enemy territory. The sky unexpectedly erupted into an enormous firework display over to one side as a searchlight beam locked on to a bomber, drawing all of the flak in the area towards it like a magnet. A while later, it was their turn as the navigator map read his way to the final run-in to Berlin. Flying straight and level at 11,000ft, the Group's gunnery officer, Flt Lt Clarke, kept up a commentary of the scene in front of him, the pitch of his voice rising in direct correlation to the proximity of the flak bursts. After what seemed an eternity, the welcome cry 'bombs gone' was heard and with that Flt Lt Tomlinson thrust the Whitley's nose down to extract each precious ounce of speed to take the aircraft out of range. The bomber flew steadily through the night sky and landed safely at RAF Watton, having been diverted from Leeming; Donnelly's triumphant return home had to wait for a few more hours.

For 10 Squadron, though, it was not the best of nights. Of the ten aircraft assigned to Berlin, two failed to return. One fell to the guns of Oblt Streib of 2/NJG1 at 23.19 hours over Bad-Bergen, with the loss of two of the five men on board. The other aircraft was lost in more unusual circumstances. As the clock ticked on, in the absence of news from Fg Off L.D. Wood's N1483, those in the squadron began to fear the worst. Then at 04.43 a signal came in asking for a positional fix; when it was plotted, it was thought that an error had been made – the Whitley appeared to be well out over the Irish Sea. No more was heard for more than an hour when the bomber was, at best, at the very limits of its possible endurance; this time it was an SOS, sent prior to an emergency ditching. Wood succeeded in putting the bomber down on the waves off Waterford and, better still, within sight of a trawler, which scooped up the crew and landed them more or less intact at Holyhead a few hours later. It had been a near-run thing and underlines the wartime adage 'Only owls and bloody fools fly at night'. Landing was not always that much safer either; Fg Off De Mestre of 61 Squadron, a battle-hardened pilot, had attacked Berlin's Klingenberg power station without undue problem but misjudged his landing at Hemswell and ripped off one leg of the undercarriage on the boundary fence. Just a matter of feet in the air, there was nothing he could do. The Hampden's other wheel almost immediately touched the ground and the bomber toppled over with the opposite wing gouging its way through the earth until it finally ran out of momentum and ground to a halt; the crew was uninjured and had a good tale to tell later.

Another tale of outstanding bravery was unfolding at RAF Wattisham. Blenheim 6191 of 107 Squadron was ready and waiting about 20.30 hours for its sortie to the Channel coast with pilot Sgt Merrett and his crew on board. They went through the routine checks, started up and made their way to take off. For reasons unknown, the fully loaded light bomber crashed almost immediately on take-off and quickly turned into a raging inferno still within the boundary fence. Wg Cdr Laurie Sinclair, CO 110 Squadron, who was not flying that night, heard what had happened and hurried out of the mess to investigate. Realising the crew would be trapped within the wreckage and that time was of the essence, he sprinted towards the blaze. Just then a pair of 250lb bombs went off, scattering debris far and wide. Undeterred and aware of the likelihood of the remaining bombs following suit at any moment, Sinclair plunged straight into the fiery, tangled metalwork and managed to free gunner Sgt Walters and drag him clear. Even with the fire crews on hand, there was nothing that could be done for the other two on board and, sadly, little more for Walters, who died of his injuries shortly afterwards. For this magnificent display of selfless courage, Sinclair was awarded the George Cross and, at his investiture on 24 May 1941, became the first RAF officer to be presented with this decoration by King George VI. He went on to have a very successful career, retiring as AVM Sir Laurence Sinclair GC KCB CBE DSO.

For others, the night marked the beginning of a far less glamorous career. Plt Off 'Mac' Maclean was at the controls of 38 Squadron's Wellington Q Queenie as it roared down the flarepath, gathered speed and lurched into the air over RAF Marham. Although Maclean was a relatively recent addition to the crew, the four sergeants on board, Williams, Gammon, Hamilton and Tipping, were old hands, each with more than twenty operations under their belts. For Plt Off William Mathieson, however, this trip as rear gunner was to be his first. Only recently appointed the squadron's armament officer, he felt he needed operational experience and was delighted to be granted permission to join the crew. They were in for a long haul to the synthetic oil Leunawerke near Leipzig and they knew that they had little margin for error in their fuel tanks. As it happened, that was not the problem. About 10 miles from the Dutch–German border, the Wellington encountered a mass of very active searchlights, which efficiently picked up the bomber and blinded all on board. Almost immediately shells and bullets from an unseen assailant began shredding the fuselage and wings. Maclean lost no time in throwing the bomber into a series of violent manoeuvres in a bid to shake off the night fighter. The attempt failed and it made a second attack from the rear, raking the bomber from end to end and wounding Mathieson in the legs. With both wing fuel tanks well ablaze, the flames fanned by the slipstream, there was no option but for Maclean to give the order to abandon the doomed aircraft. As wireless operator Vic Gammon made his way to the hatch, he looked up to see Maclean still at the controls, struggling to keep the aircraft steady to enable his friends to escape. While Gammon fell out into the cool, peaceful night air to safety,

Maclean realised that badly wounded Mathieson would be unable to do likewise and, courageously, decided to remain with the blazing bomber and attempt a forced landing. That decision, as he almost certainly knew it would, cost him his life but it did save Mathieson's. He was pulled out of the wreckage by German soldiers, badly injured but alive, taken to hospital, where he had both legs amputated, before being transferred to Oflag IXA/H at Spangenberg.

In one of those curious moments of war, Vic Gammon, who had been captured within minutes of landing, was taken to Venlo, now a Luftwaffe night fighter base, and led into the officers' mess. There an immaculate, white-jacketed orderly was sent to find Oblt Streib, who had enjoyed a most successful night, claiming three kills, the first pilot to do so in a single night sortie. Somewhat surreally, the oddly matched pair amicably discussed the episode they had in common over a cup of coffee before going their separate ways. In the RAF man's case it was to a cell, where he met Ron Mogg, the navigator of a 115 Squadron Wellington also based at Marham, likewise shot down by Strieb and witnessed from the ground by Gammon in the moments before his capture. In total, Bomber Command had lost seven aircraft on the last night of September, very nearly 7 per cent of the force operating; fifteen airmen had lost their lives and another ten their liberty.

It was becoming clear that the Luftwaffe's daylight focus was shifting to hit-and-run fighter-bomber raids and smaller-scale attacks, reserving its major effort for the night raids on urban centres. On the other side of the coin, Bomber Command's response was gathering momentum, seeking out more and more targets in the German heartland. It was not yet an equal struggle in terms of numbers and destructive capacity but the Command had set itself the task of hitting back as hard and often as it could. On the first night of October, a mixed force of Blenheims, Wellingtons, Hampdens and Whitleys, just shy of 100 strong, set off to bomb oil plants, marshalling yards, airfields, power stations, munitions factories and docks the length and breadth of Germany; no one could fail to be aware of its presence. Once again, Berlin came under attack, this time the focus was on the Elgemeine power station and giant Siemens works. The aircraft were overhead for more than two hours and one pilot reported the whole sky as being lit up by an enormous, brilliant white flash that dazzled and temporarily blinded his crew. One of 9 Squadron's aircraft failed to make it back to Honington, crashing into the sea off Lowestoft, probably as a result of battle damage; there were no survivors. No. 78 Squadron's Whitleys were in action in fairly clear conditions over the Sterkrade oil plant, where they were faced with an intense flak barrage supported by a large number of searchlights. Some of these were now believed to be radar guided, a recent and potent innovation in anti-aircraft defence. These were also beginning to be used in conjunction with night fighters and it was this novel and potent combination that was thought to have accounted for the loss of the squadron's P4964 with all on board shortly after midnight. In return, the crews reported several fires burning fiercely in the target area, with one large building observed to disintegrate in a particularly large and violent explosion.

Sqn Ldr Tom Sawyer was in a Whitley V bound for an oil target but this one was adjacent to the River Rhine, just south of Cologne. He and his crew had benefited from a trouble-free flight to the target area and had no trouble at all in the clear conditions in picking out the river from 10,000ft. There was some activity ahead of them but as Sawyer began his final run guided by his navigator all seemed as calm as could be in such extraordinary circumstances. Unexpectedly, a searchlight switched on and locked on to the bomber, quickly joined by several others, starkly illuminating the aircraft against the dark sky. Within seconds, the beams had been joined by deadly flak and inside the aircraft both the noise and blast of the bursts were all too apparent to the shaken young men. Cruising straight and level at just 130mph, the Whitley offered perfect live target practice for the sweating gunners working feverishly below and it seemed only a matter of time before it would be smashed to pieces. Sawyer pushed the nose down, willing the Whitley to gain speed and shake off the dazzling beams of light; his wishes were not entirely granted and with 230mph on the clock, the wings flapping visibly under the unaccustomed strain and the controls stiffening alarmingly, all he had succeeded in doing was bringing the still illuminated bomber within range of the light flak, which was now opening up to add to the mass of explosives already coming his way. Realising this, he heaved on the controls and, little by little, he managed to bring the Whitley's protesting nose up, roaring over the city at just 1,000ft before using his speed to gain some height. Now out of range and back in the protective darkness, Sawyer's heart rate began to slow and he brought the bomber around in a broad sweep, taking stock of the situation. He then noticed that the crew had not uttered a single word throughout the hair-raising, Earth-bound plunge and they remained in stunned silence as he lined up for a second pass. Curiously, this time the flak was desultory at best but, the words 'bombs gone' in his ears were never more welcome. Some ground mist began to form and this meant that Sawyer was unable to locate the Dutch coast but this was not too unusual and silence still reigned supreme as he droned his way serenely across the North Sea, turning over in his mind what he should do if he should ever be coned over a target again. Some time later, it dawned on him that he had not seen the English coast either, especially now that the mist was thinning a little. With alarm bells beginning to ring, he sent the second pilot back to drop a couple of flares and asked the wireless operator for a positional fix, which was then passed on to the navigator. Only sea was visible beneath the aircraft, which should by now have been taxying on Yorkshire soil. Fearing he could have overflown England entirely and be out over the Irish Sea, Sawyer turned about and began a search pattern, keeping a close eye on the sinking fuel gauge. The navigator could offer no advice, saying he could make no sense of the fixes given and had not got the foggiest idea where they were. Increasingly anxious, a long dark line began to take shape on the horizon and as it drew nearer a wave of relief washed over the pilot; ahead was Scarborough Castle. From there, he had no difficulty in setting course for Leeming, where he landed well overdue twenty minutes later. A quick inspection in the early morning light revealed thirty or so holes of various sizes along the fuselage and wings, made by shrapnel, light flak and even machine gun bullets. Further investigation of what had gone awry revealed that no fewer than six fixes had been sent to the aircraft, placing it clearly over the North Sea, heading towards the coast. The wireless operator had passed them all on to the navigator, who had been unable to do anything constructive with them being as he was in a state of shock following their terrifying ordeal. There were no recriminations over this as a quick and simple check also revealed that the Whitley had returned with its bomb load intact. In the heat of that extremely stressful moment, the navigator had forgotten to press the release button and nobody else, including Sawyer, had had the presence of mind to notice or check. It was a salutary lesson to all on board as to just how powerful an effect combat can have upon even well-trained and experienced men. Sawyer and his crew learned and lived but Sgt H. Day of 44 Squadron did not as his aircraft plunged into the North Sea on the way back from Cologne; two bodies were washed ashore by the tide a few days later. The cruel and harsh hand of fate was not respectful of previous achievements, however great. Flt Lt Learoyd VC of 44 Squadron was crossing the Dutch coast when, for no apparent reason, one of his engines cut out, leaving him little choice but to release his bombs as quickly as possible and turn for home. A row of four white, flashing lights beneath caught his attention so he turned towards them in the belief they were connected to an airfield and, therefore, constituted a legitimate target. The bombs were dropped near Outsdorp and Learoyd then turned for home, anxiously listening to the rhythm of the remaining engine and willing it not to follow suit with its defunct partner. Luckily for him, it did not and he returned to land safely on one engine.

Several other Hampdens spent much of their night out over the sea, being tasked to mine the waters in the Gironde area. Such a sortie required a good deal of navigational skill and precision, and was not without its dangers. However, it lacked the appeal or satisfaction of other types of operations, even though mining was often combined with nuisance raids. One report read:

An uneventful trip. We crossed the Channel and flew around the coast to the first landmark. Set course and located the second landmark and laid the mine in the appointed place. The journey home was uneventful and steered course inland and carried out a diving attack from 4,000ft, releasing bombs at 1,000ft and striking the south-west corner of hangars on the east of an aerodrome.

Although notoriously difficult to quantify, mining operations often proved effective in restricting traffic, if not actually sinking ships, and proved the bane of the navy on both sides.

The next morning came bright and sunny, a lovely autumn day and the Luftwaffe seemed determined to make the most of the fine conditions, mounting six major incursions into British airspace, one of which made it as far inland as south London. Six Blenheims carried out a routine sweep of the North Sea but, as was becoming usual, both sides waited until nightfall to unleash their main efforts. By then, the clear conditions had given way to cloud, patchy over Britain but increasingly dense and menacing over the Continent. As a result, the Luftwaffe had a good night, attacking targets from Scotland to London with relative ease. It was a very different picture for the RAF.

No. 105 Squadron had spent the previous day on an army cooperation exercise working with the 129th Infantry Brigade on an advance from Saffron Walden to Hawkspur Green in response to an invasion scenario. Now, however, it was back to the real war. A trio of Blenheims set off in mid-evening for an attack upon a busy marshalling yard at Gremberg in Belgium. They flew straight into low, dense, ice-bearing cloud and, unable to locate their target or indeed anything else, returned with their loads intact. In the meantime, another pair had taken off and set course for Calais harbour, where conditions were only marginally better but, based on the location of the searchlights and previous experience, the crews released their bombs, even if in hope rather than anything else. One aircraft failed to return, coming down south-west of Calais; the three dead men, Sgts Lord,

Bundock and Dunbar were highly experienced 'old sweats', having been with the squadron since February 1939. No. 101 Squadron fared equally badly. Plt Off Brown had taken off from West Raynham at 23.31 hours and soon ran into the ubiquitous ten-tenths cloud, which extended from almost ground level to 15,000ft. Unable to see anything and with the aircraft's surfaces icing heavily and responding very sluggishly to the controls, Brown turned for home, a sensible decision shared by many of the crews. Conditions over much of western and central Germany were little better. No. 37 Squadron's Wellingtons were assigned to a number of oil and transportation targets but the crews soon found the patchy clouds gathering to form an impenetrable blanket that smothered much of eastern Holland and western Germany. Billowing up to 25,000ft, beyond the operational ceiling of a Wellington, these dark, ice-bearing clouds were a formidable barrier to the aircraft. None of the crews bound for the oil plant at Bottrop located it but Sgt Anierton, working on ETA, did release his bombs on a group of searchlights he thought might be defending the target. Sgt Elstub gave cruising around up as a bad job and dropped down to 5,000ft to search for his secondary target, the industrial mass of Essen. The log records rather doubtfully, 'He is of the opinion that he reached his target and bombed it,' some flashes from the bomb bursts were at least visible. Sqn Ldr Golding also jacked in and ended up trundling along at just 2,000ft, picking out Schiphol airfield on his return journey; his bombs 'fell in the vicinity of the runways and buildings'. Sgt Palmer-Lambourne did not get as far as his primary or secondary target area before severe icing made it imperative he jettisoned his bomb load; a group of searchlights made a convenient target as he turned for home. Four other crews gave up the ghost and returned fully loaded. Three more aircraft were assigned the vast railway depot at Hamm as their target; none could find it. It was not, however, for the want of trying and all the crews spent some considerable time stooging around over hostile territory in dreadful conditions searching for a worthwhile destination for their bombs. Plt Off Heugh, for example, circled in the vicinity of Hamm for half an hour before making his way south to the

Ruhr. A railway line came into view through the clouds and on the basis that it was better than nothing, he decided to attack it; only a single 250lb bomb was released – the result of the explosion was not observed – the others being held back in case a better target presented itself later. As it turned out, this was the dedicated crew's only opportunity of the night.

Conditions further north were better and the mainly Hampden crews assigned Hamburg had a much better time of it. Guy Gibson was leading one of these crews. He recalled spending two hours cruising over the city dropping an individual bomb at intervals in order to prolong the dislocation and disruption below. 'Needless to say,' he later wrote, 'we came back dithering wrecks. Never had so many guns fired at so few', and he might have added 'for so long'. The contrast with the enormous bomber streams pushed over a target in a matter of minutes later in the war could not be more marked. Plt Off Thwaites of 50 Squadron was one of those who had cause to regret the time spent over Hamburg that night. Having taken off from RAF Lindholme at 18.40 hours, he had no difficulty in locating the city and releasing his bomb load. Matters, however, took a turn for the worse when one of his Bristol Pegasus engines suddenly packed up, possibly the result of a near miss. The cause was immaterial and Thwaites reacted immediately, turning for home in order to cover as much distance as possible before the inevitable occurred. The Dutch coast laboriously came and went and the hopes of the anxious crew soared with the passing of each eternity-like minute. The fuel situation became increasingly parlous as the overworked remaining engine struggled to keep ahead of gravity. Shortly before 02.00 faint lights were spotted on the horizon and as the bomber inched closer, to the delight of the young men on board, the lights transformed themselves into a flarepath. Thwaites at once prepared to land and it was not until the very last minute that he realised that all was not as it should be; he was attempting to land at a 'starfish' decoy site near Dunbar. Too low to do anything about it, Thwaites was fully committed to setting the Hampden down. Suddenly a tree loomed out of the darkness and the bomber smashed into it with a sickening crunch, skidding across the open ground beyond. Amazingly, the only casualty was the gunner, Sgt E. Smith, who sustained a broken leg and was taken to Edinburgh hospital for treatment. Reports of the raid itself were positive, with claims that several individual fires had joined to form a substantial conflagration, visible some 60 miles away. A pall of thick, black smoke was left hanging over the whole dock area.

For the next forty-eight hours the weather really clamped down as driving rain, cloud and fog combined to make flying even more perilous and accurate bombing all but impossible, especially at night. If anything, the conditions further east over Europe were expected to be worse and Bomber Command had to restrict itself to daylight coastal raids on 3/4 October. The weather did its best to thwart these too and the majority of the Blenheims sent out were forced to abandon their sorties, having seen nothing except cloud and general murk throughout. A few pressed on to attack a small convoy off Dunkirk without any visible effect and a couple more released their bombs over Dutch coastal targets, again without visible effect. On the 4th several more penetrated as far as western Germany but despite these determined efforts, failed to locate their targets through the dense ice-laden clouds; one crew recorded 20 degrees of frost. There was precious little to show for the airmen's brave efforts in the face of diabolical conditions.

The weather had ameliorated a little by Saturday 5 October and, although the crews had enjoyed and benefited from their enforced rest, the Command was keen to get back to business. Another group of eight Blenheims was ordered to attack oil and aluminium production targets in western Germany but all returned early because of a lack of cloud cover; the irony of the situation was not lost upon the hard-pressed crews. Half a dozen more carried out another routine sweep over the North Sea and this time picked up two small ships of the Kriegsmarine, just south of Utsine Island, achieving only near misses. By evening the conditions were deteriorating once again, making the main effort of the night fall upon the Hampdens of 5 Group. Eight were sent out to have yet another go at the busy marshalling yards at Hamm, Soest and Cologne and a further dozen to the equally popular oil plant at Gelsenkirchen. Fires were reported as being raised at all locations but nothing more specific than that. Ten more were allocated to mining operations in the approaches to the Elbe estuary. This did not appeal much to Stan Harrison of 61 Squadron, knowing that both Hamburg and the naval base at Cuxhaven were in the vicinity and were heavily defended, not only on land but by heavily armed flak ships that lurked unseen along the coast. Working with his navigator 'Jimmie' James, he planned to approach at 8,000ft and once he had got a locational fix on the small islands flanking the Elbe approaches to throttle right back and make as silent an approach as possible, gliding down to just 1,000ft to lay the mine. Then it would be full throttle and away back home. Everything went according to plan and, although a light flak battery on Neuwerk Island did open fire briefly, the Hampden was in and out quickly and efficiently. Perhaps it was the overwhelming feeling of relief washing over him that caused him to commit a cardinal and very nearly lethal error. Droning steadily west over the North Sea, he nodded off into a deep sleep. The bomber gradually adopted a nose down attitude, losing height steadily. At first, the crew thought nothing of it but as the angle of descent continued to steepen, mild puzzlement turned to concern and then to alarm. Oblivious to it all, Harrison slumbered on. The first he knew of the situation was when James was waggling and thumping his right leg vigorously. Coming to with a jolt, he momentarily wondered why his navigator was reaching through from his position towards him and knocking hell out of his leg. A second later, he worked it out and yanked the nose up while pouring out a stream of heartfelt apologies to those with him.

The Hampdens fared badly that night, losing five, a shocking 17 per cent of those committed to battle. One from 50 Squadron was lost without trace on the Cologne raid, another from 144 likewise from the same mining operation as Harrison. Upon his safe return, it became apparent that his squadron sustained a loss on the Elbe mining run. The Hampden of Plt Off D'Arcy-Wright had drifted north on his return and in poor conditions ploughed into the high ground of the unseen North Yorkshire moors, not far from RAF Leeming, with the loss of all on board. Two more crashed attempting to land in the stormy conditions. Sqn Ldr Lerwill of 144 momentarily lost control as he came into land at Hemswell in near gale force winds. The bomber flopped down hard, ripping off the entire undercarriage and eventually grinding to a jarring halt on its belly; fortunately, the crew sustained only minor injuries. No. 83 Squadron's Sgt Hawkes had encountered severe icing on route to Gelsenkirchen and, fearing the Hampden had sustained severe damage as a result, broke off his sortie and headed home to Scampton. His fears proved well founded as the aircraft crashed in rotten weather shortly before 21.00 hours near Hemswell. Hawkes and two others sustained serious injuries and the navigator, Sgt C.A. Sherwood, lost his life. No. 5 Group had paid a heavy price for its decision to operate in marginal conditions.

Only four other aircraft operated that night, all Wellingtons, their targets being the Dutch ports. Plt Off Nobby Clarke of 37 Squadron was assigned the dockyards at Rotterdam and from 8,000ft they were clearly visible as he brought his bomber in for its final approach. The bombs were duly released and the eighteen 250lb bombs were seen to explode across the dock area. No sooner had the bomb doors been closed when a near miss beneath the aircraft caused it to rear up sharply and stall, spinning earthwards to the right. Clarke pushed the throttles open and gave it full left rudder in a desperate attempt to regain control. Benny Goodman, still gaining experience as a second pilot, heaved himself across the cockpit against the force of the spin, hurled himself bodily at the rudder bar and began to haul for all he was worth on the right rudder. The combined effort was enough to move the controls and with a great shudder, the Wellington shook itself out of the spin. They were not out of the woods yet, however. Flak soared up towards them from all sides as the aircraft flashed over the harbour at low level, lurching wildly as Clarke struggled to master the damaged controls. When things calmed down a little, he and Goodman gingerly tested the controls and discovered that something was seriously awry with the elevators and, without the use of the flaps, their landing at Feltwell was nowhere near as smooth as usual. Inspection the following morning revealed that the elevators on the tail plane had been wrenched from their fittings and were simply dangling uselessly. It had been a terrifying ordeal and one that nobody on board, especially the two pilots, wished to repeat. Sometime later when Goodman was an instructor at 15 OTU at Harwell in Oxfordshire, the topic came up in discussion in the mess. Goodman's flight commander, a pre-war old hand, could not see any problem in bringing a Wellington out of a spin and, ignoring Goodman's pleas, decided to prove his point one day in the air. He did not and the Wellington failed to recover and came to ground just outside the airfield.

Another Wellington attempted to outwit the defences by gliding in to attack the docks at Flushing. The plan, as the young New Zealand pilot later explained, did not work.

We were fairly low when they opened up. I have never seen anything like it – it did not seem worth trying to dodge the flak, there was so much of it. I thought 'goodnight, nurse', put the nose down and hoped for the best. The inside of the aircraft was reeking with cordite. Nobody said anything. Frankly, I thought we weren't going to get out of it and I think the rest of them thought that too. The searchlights were holding us all the time. I kept my eyes on the instruments and on the docks. If one had looked around, one would have been blinded. As we went over, the bomb aimer made certain all the bombs had gone. We dropped them and they landed right in the centre of the dock buildings. Immediately we were thrown up to 600ft. There were tremendous explosions. The second pilot was standing beside me and his knees buckled underneath him and he fell to the floor. I just concentrated upon trying to keep the aircraft in the air and to get away. There was a curtain of fire on all sides and we went through. The ships opened fire on us as well as the guns on the shore. They seemed to have a ring of flak ships around the harbour. The machine gun tracer was making spirals in the air. They were using quick-firing guns too and flaming onions by the dozen. The sky was absolutely full of it. We scooted away along the edge of the sea. I could see the breakers quite clearly. By this time, I was fighting with the stick. We sent out an SOS that we were likely to be coming down. I knew that we'd been hit. I felt the shells smack into the plane and I couldn't hold the aircraft properly. Frankly, I never thought we'd make it home. There were heavy clouds and I was flying on instruments all the way. It was raining most of the time. My arms were aching and seemed tied up in knots from the strain of holding the aircraft. Finally, though, we got home and I landed safely.

The other two Wellingtons did too.

The stormy conditions had barely abated by morning, though daylight did offer marginally increased chances of success and a force of twenty-one Blenheims was sent to attack various targets in western Germany. Not one of them succeeded in locating their primary target and they reluctantly gave it up as a bad job and returned early, although some did lob bombs at what they could just about discern below them in the regular haunts of the Channel ports. The highlight was the confirmed destruction of a Me 109 by one jubilant crew over Calais. By the time they had landed only the most adventurous of birds were flying and, consequently, all operations for the night were called off. There were few complaints.

When it became light the next morning, the sleepy young men scanned the cloudy sky and instinctively knew that operations would be on. No. 2 Group staff were putting the final touches to their plans for a dozen Blenheims to range far and wide over occupied Europe and western Germany. As is the capricious way of the weather, the sky began to clear soon after leaving British airspace and within minutes the light bombers were flying in full view of all and sundry through a sunlit, cloudless heaven. Ten turned about on reaching the enemy coast but two managed to put in hurried attacks, having located barge concentrations at Goes and Sommelsdijk on the Dutch coast before they too scooted off low across the North Sea, keeping a wary eye out for roving fighters on patrol or returning home from sorties over Britain.

As if trying to make up for the cancellation the previous night, the Command from staff officers to armourers was working flat out to launch 140 bombers against selected targets, including forty-two Wellingtons and Whitleys to a dozen individual targets in Berlin. There were few major towns in western Germany or ports along the Channel coast that did not hear the throb of British engines droning overhead that night as, in penny packets, the bombers criss-crossed the dark sky over enemy territory. The Hampdens focused upon railway targets in Germany, although several attacked the large Fokker factory in Amsterdam and laid mines off the coast of Lorient before scattering bombs over the dock area for good measure. That port was also on the target list for the Blenheims, which put in a series of attacks over their regular haunts, the Channel airfields and harbours. None of either type was lost but a Blenheim from 110 Squadron crashed and burnt out on its return to Wattisham. It was air gunner Mike Henry's tenth operation but his first with Flt Lt H.J. Lyons, who was on his maiden sortie. At 23.40 hours, all preparations and checks having been made, Blenheim L9310 set off down the flarepath and into the darkness bound for the harbour at Boulogne. For the three men on board it was as near to ordinary and routine as an operational flight can be and Henry up in his turret was considering a job well done when at 02.15 the bomber began its long, sweeping, low approach to Wattisham. About a mile out, Lyons switched on the landing light set in the port wing and Henry was able to see through the wispy ground haze that the aircraft was a little lower than he would have expected and drifting off the line of the flarepath. Lyons abruptly caught on too and a little belatedly gunned the engines to go around again. Streaking low over the boundary fence at 100mph, Henry could clearly see the grass flashing past just feet below him. He instinctively sensed the port wing dipping a fraction and the next thing he knew he was standing in his turret with flames licking around his feet. Amid the mangled debris, he noticed by the orange light of the flames, a hole in the fuselage, not quite big enough for him to squeeze through. Not being at all deterred by this knowledge, he rammed his head and arms through and kicked and heaved until he fell out on to the damp grass, his thighs and shins torn by the jagged metal and bleeding like a stuck pig. With ammunition and oxygen bottles exploding in the heat, he was grabbed bodily by two burly men and half carried, half dragged from the danger zone and placed rather more gently in a waiting ambulance. Quickly assessed as having sustained only superficial injuries, Henry was taken to the station sick quarters but Lyons and Hardwick were taken to Ipswich hospital for treatment for concussion and broken bones. Once he was cleaned up, Henry was questioned by the CO, Wg Cdr Sinclair, and an engineer officer as to the details of the crash, which they had witnessed and judged serious enough to reckon all on board would be dead. By 04.00 hours, Henry was tucked up in bed, thanking his lucky stars for his near-miraculous escape.

The night also saw the first of a series of watery escapes for Fg Off Henry Young of 102 Squadron. Several Whitleys were on temporary secondment to Coastal Command and since late August had been operating out of both Prestwick and Aldergrove in Northern Ireland under the command of Sqn Ldr O.A. Morris. The Whitleys droned out over the Atlantic day after day on convoy escort duties, scanning the grey water for any sign of predatory U-boats. Very little of excitement occurred on the long flights and the repetitive routine dulled the crews' appreciation of the substantial risks in making these flights. These were brought into sharp focus for the young American and his crew when the engines of P4995 first began to play up and then spluttered and died. Far out to sea or not, there was nothing else for it but to send out distress signals and ditch upon the inhospitable Atlantic waves. Young pulled off the first of several perfect landings in his brief wartime career and the men were able to clamber into the dinghy more or less unhurt. It was to be their refuge for the next twenty-two hours, a tiny and vulnerable inflatable dinghy, tossed around by the relentless rising and falling of the waves. As their hopes of rescue were beginning to fade, HMS *St Mary* crept into sight and a sharp-eyed look-out spotted the stranded crew and brought them once again to terra firma. Young earned the epithet 'Dinghy' and went on to become a highly skilled and decorated pilot; Sqn Ldr Henry Young DFC lost his life with 617 Squadron on the Dams Raid in May 1943. His was the squadron's only loss on the secondment and on 10 October the seven remaining crews re-joined 102 Squadron in North Yorkshire.

The crews of 51 Squadron were over Amsterdam from shortly after midnight to 02.00 hours and with little effective AA fire and, only moderate searchlight activity, they took take their time to make an accurate attack on the Fokker works. Passing over at 7,000 to 9,000ft, Sqn Ldr Hollack's crew claimed to have observed clearly a series of direct hits upon the factory. Danger, however, lurked not far away and Plt Off Millson reported becoming engaged in a deadly 60-mile-long game of cat and mouse between the clouds with an enemy night fighter out over the North Sea. It was a very different story over Berlin where, according to Plt Off J.R. Denny of 78 Squadron, a veteran of previous attacks on Berlin, Kiel and the heavily defended Channel ports, the flak at 10,000ft was intense and as bad as anything he had yet encountered; Sgt G. Samson made similar statements regarding the highly effective and abundant searchlights, the glare of which he found blinding as he came over at 10,000ft. The lethal combination certainly put paid to a 38 Squadron Wellington, which came down near the capital with the loss of all on board. Nevertheless, all reports suggested that the crews were well on track to achieve the Command's stated aim to 'cause the greatest possible disturbance and dislocation both to the industrial activities and to the civil population generally in the area' by 'attacks on sources of power serving the city'. Thus the thirty Wellingtons of 3 Group and the twelve Whitleys from 4 Group, of which thirty-three claimed to have attacked their primary targets and a further seven other industrial or transportation targets, headed for the main power stations. Six Wellingtons attacked those in the Moabit district, causing fires and explosions visible up to 70 miles away. Four more started fires around the West power station and witnessed a series of large and colourful explosions in the area. The same number went for the Wilmersdorf power station but missed, their bombs fortuitously falling amid the nearby marshalling yards and railway junctions at Charlottenburg. The Whitleys headed for the city centre to attack the symbolic heart of the regime, the Reich Chancellery but, although several fires were ignited, nothing else could be observed. Further attacks were carried out on the Rummelsburg and Schonenburg railway yards, the BMW aero engine plant, the Victoria chemical works, a Siemens cable factory and the airfield at Bahrenfeld. Fires and explosions were noted and recorded in detail by the crews and faithfully reported to and scrutinised by Intelligence officers awaiting their return. The evidence of success was overwhelming, although a trial experiment that night did at least cast a modicum of doubt. A single Wellington had been fitted with a new night-time camera to take photographs as the bombs were dropped over the target. The crew reported a successful attack on an industrial target on the outskirts, executed as ordered, but the photograph, upon close inspection, revealed nothing more than a large wood. Hardly statistically valid, the simple piece of evidence was easily swept away by the veritable torrent of individual eyewitness statements from skilled professionals, each independently corroborating the other and supported by extensive and cross-referencing analysis. It was easy to explain away the photograph – aircraft travel very quickly, the target had been on the outskirts of the city, the camera angle might not have been exact and so on – but it was decided, nevertheless, to persist with such photographic trials as everyone agreed that hard evidence was essential to carry out this logical and progressive strategic offensive effectively.

Such thoughts were far from the mind of Plt Off Alec Cranswick, a Wellington pilot with 214 Squadron based at Stradishall. He had his hands full keeping F-Freddie in the air and on track over Berlin. He had already spent the best part of forty-five minutes cruising over the city, circling lower and lower until he was satisfied that his target had been accurately identified before making his attack. Within seconds a large bump rocked the bomber accompanied by an audible, dull thump. A decent-sized lump of shrapnel had passed through the wing, tearing a hole in one of the fuel tanks in the process. It was going to be a long and slow flight home at best and Cranswick could offer his crew no guarantee of making it in any case. Throttled right back, the long miles were gradually ticked off, first over Germany, then occupied territory and finally over the North Sea, the watery graveyard of many a lame bomber. To compound the gravity of the situation, the wireless set packed up and resolutely defied all attempts to coax it back into the land of the living and the weather had closed in, greatly reducing visibility. When it was calculated that the bomber should have reached the British coast, Cranswick let the aircraft sink lower and lower with each member of the crew anxiously scanning the fog for any sign of the countryside they hoped was below. There was a cry of delight as one picked up the light of a beacon, quickly verified by another. The beacon flashed the letter K, much to the puzzlement of those on board. Still, with the reassuring glow of a flarepath taking shape ahead and the fuel gauges reading flat zero, there was neither time nor inclination to consider the significance of the unfamiliar signal. The pilot could not discern any particular ground detail but lined up obediently on the flarepath and eased the bomber down for landing. Within seconds the belly of the bomber tore through several trees, smashing branches on all sides, before it struck the ground hard, rearing up into the air, before flopping down once again, skidding and grinding to a halt amid showers of dirt and debris. Amazingly, none of the crew sustained anything more serious than cuts and bruises, though the same could not be said about the Wellington, which was well and truly written off. A couple of airmen came running to the crash scene and the crew were taken aback by the absence of a full rescue team, the sound of one coming or indeed of any other sound. Their astonishment increased as they discovered they had landed in an ordinary field of turnips adorned with a flarepath of wooden poles with lanterns attached to them and a beacon that flashed letters at random; the decoy airfield had certainly done its job. Cranswick and his crew had not even been aware of the existence of such sites and eventually came to see the funny side of it all. Such sites were a vital part of the Command's defences against intruders, one of which accounted for a 99 Squadron Wellington that night.

In spite of the autumnal weather, there could be no let-up in Bomber Command's effort but such were the conditions the following morning that only a pair of Blenheims could be sent out on an armed reconnaissance over the Channel coast from Boulogne to Ostend. One gave it up as a bad job but the other pressed on to find conditions over Boulogne marginally better and released its load of light bombs over the harbour, where approximately twenty ships were seen to be moored. The crew did not hang around to see what, if anything, happened next. Meanwhile, throughout the day, more than 100 bombers were made ready. The weather worsened during the day and was predicted to worsen further that night and, as a result, take-off was brought forward, with, for example, 44 Squadron's Hampdens leaving Waddington for the *Tirpitz* at Wilhelmshaven as early as 17.00 hours. In the event, the attempt to beat the elements failed and few crews on targets as far afield as Calais, Boulogne, Le Havre, Hamburg, Bremen, Mannheim and Amsterdam met with any great success. By the time 37 Squadron's ten Wellingtons were ready at tea time, it was raining steadily from clouds a bare 2,000ft above the ground with visibility rated as poor. By the time the crews were passing over the coast near Great Yarmouth, the cloud was to all intents and purposes a solid block from 1,000 to 8,000ft and the situation remained unchanged all the way to the oil tanks at Hamburg. Some crews made their approach from the sea, hoping to follow the course of the Elbe to the vicinity of the port. All released their loads but did not observe anything at all. The squadron log rather optimistically offers the explanation that 'it is possible that the reason for the lack of fire may have been due to the fact that the oil storage tanks had been drained.' The crews probably had other explanations.

Plt Off Clark led the only crew from the squadron scheduled to attack the marshalling yards at Mannheim. Having encountered ten-tenths cloud for more than 50 miles on his approach to the city, he realised the futility of carrying on with the attack, turned around and set about searching for an alternative. The best he could find was an airfield near Charleroi and his bombs were seen to burst just short of the flarepath. Sgt Bedlow found himself in a similar situation on his way to the railway yards at Gremberg. He elected to stick with it and spent some considerable time over the target area trying to pick out some ground features below. Satisfied that the aircraft was in the right place and that all that could be done to carry out an accurate attack had been done, Bedlow released his bombs from 11,000ft and noted several flashes and incipient fires. However, still focused on making every one of his bombs count, he retained one for use against a suitable target on route home. This turned out to be a fully illuminated airfield at Eindhoven. Given that both Clark and Bedlow reported significant defensive fire had been directed against their aircraft, their determination to carry out an effective sortie can only be judged as highly commendable. Several aircraft were lost that night and the poor flying conditions certainly played a part. Two Blenheims from 82 Squadron returning from Calais crashed within ten minutes of each other at their airfield at Bodney, one crew emerging from the wreckage unscathed, the other all sustaining injuries. A Whitney of 77 Squadron, one of the night's latest returners at 03.55 hours, crashed into a tree with the loss of all on board near Snape, not far from its base at Topcliffe; amongst them was a young Royal Navy midshipman by the name of Haddington, attached to the crew to gain combat experience. It had not been a great night for the Command but the lack of success was not down to the efforts of the young men concerned, rather to the inclement weather and the dearth of equipment to counter it.

Perhaps the only silver lining to the rotten weather was the fact that it had caused almost as much trouble for the Luftwaffe, even though the distances involved were far shorter. As usual, the weather was moving from west to east and was due to improve over Britain during the day before another front slid in later. Eight Blenheims of 2 Group attempted to sneak in an attack while they could, heading for what was hoped to be the clearing skies of northern France and western Germany. Once again, it did not quite work out that way and three abandoned their sorties due to the adverse weather conditions. One pressed on as far as Homburg, where the crew claimed a direct hit upon an oil storage tank that burst into flames and belched out a column of thick, black smoke high into the sky. The remaining four restricted their operations to the Channel ports, notably Boulogne where several barges and a bridge were among the targets hit.

The met reports for the whole of Europe were so bad that 2 and 4 Groups called off all operations but 3 and 5 Groups decided it was worthwhile to carry on. Although eight obsolescent Battles managed to attack Calais harbour and a half a dozen Hampdens managed to complete their minelaying sorties off Lorient, those Wellingtons and Hampdens heading further east really struggled in the awful conditions. Nos 61 and 144 Squadrons formed the bulk of the twenty-strong force on 9/10 October bound for the massive Krupps works in Essen, the heart of the heavily defended Ruhr valley. By the time the crews reached the Frisian Islands, it had become clear that the already pessimistic weather forecast was in fact considerably over-optimistic. They were confronted by a solid mass of cloud, impenetrable beneath them and towering high above them. Very soon, the Hampdens began to buck and bump as they forced their way through the dense cumulus and cumulonimbus clouds. More ominous still was the sudden appearance of a film of ice creeping across the windscreen like an opaque skin and encasing the wings and tailplane in a deadly white coating. As the control surfaces stiffened and the weight of the heavily laden bomber increased, it became more difficult to keep the aircraft straight and level. The only solution was to lose altitude in search of warmer air but on such a stormy night over enemy territory, that in itself was fraught with danger. All but three of the Hampdens gingerly turned about and set course for Lincolnshire, setting about the thankless task of rooting out a suitable alternative target through the clag beneath them.

One that did manage to do so was 144's Sgt King, who had taken the most direct route home and discovered the cloud had begun to break up along the enemy-held coast. Dropping down as low as he dared, the crew picked up the Scheldt estuary and located the port of Flushing. As the flak opened up and whistled and banged all around them, it became clear that they were over an important area and the bombs were released, as best as could be judged from the bursts, in the vicinity of the harbour. The flak chased the Hampden out to sea but the crew could discern the dull glow of fires beneath the thinner low-level cloud. By the time the weary crews reached Lincolnshire, the night sky was all but clear – a perfect night for bombing as far as the Luftwaffe was concerned. The good conditions at least gave the crews some respite and for that they were grateful. Only a single aircraft, a Wellington from 149 Squadron, failed to return, lost without trace on its sortie to Herringen.

As day dawned, the conditions worsened again as the next front piled in and all Bomber Command focused upon preparing for the night ahead; no fewer than 157 bombers of all types were serviced, fuelled and bombed up ready to strike. Some headed to the oil targets at Leuna and Gelsenkirchen, while others maintained the pressure on the major ports of Hamburg, Kiel and Wilhelmshaven. One of the key targets was the *Tirpitz*, rapidly approaching completion, then in a massive floating dock. Whilst no hits were claimed, the harbour area was said to have been hit hard and significant fires were seen blazing along the quayside. The dangers of flying over enemy territory were increasing remorselessly and more crews reported encounters with night fighters over most of the targets. It was not all one-way traffic in these skirmishes and Sgt Atkins, in a 44 Squadron Hampden, when attacked took immediate evasive action and was reassured to hear his rear gunner steadily returning fire; within seconds, there was a loud cheer as the crew saw their assailant spiralling earthwards out of control, tracing a bright and fiery arc through the darkness. Nearer home, Benny Goodman, after several sorties as a second pilot, was on his first as captain with 37 Squadron. It was a quick in and out job over Eindhoven but as he closed in on the target under a clear sky, he spotted several night fighters aggressively patrolling the area. Deciding discretion was the better part of valour, he turned away and bombed an alternative target – the docks at Flushing. In spite of the good visibility, no particular results of his attack could be observed and the crew continued their journey westwards satisfied that they had at least made a positive contribution to the war effort.

Once again, however, the main focus of the attacks was upon the Channel coast, some of the results of which were clearly visible from the south coast of England. Indeed, it could be felt too as several of the German long-range batteries opened up in reply, lobbing shells at the Kent coastline. It was far worse on the other side of the water, especially at Cherbourg where a heavy combined RAF and Royal Navy bombardment was executed. Under the auspices of Admiral Sir Martin Dunbar-Nasmith VC, Western Approaches Command, a force of seven destroyers and six MGBs, led by the battleship HMS *Revenge*, slipped out of Plymouth and headed towards Normandy. Launched in the early years of the previous war, the 28,000-ton veteran still packed a formidable punch, armed with eight 15in and fourteen 6in guns. The log of 15 Squadron records the plan which was 'in cooperation with the Navy' and its part in it was, 'The first 10 crews bombed Cherbourg to create a diversion to allow the Navy to get within range and also to start fires for them to aim on. The remaining 2 crews went to bomb the shore batteries which attempted to reply.' The plan was considered to have been 'very satisfactorily carried out'. The Royal Navy stated, 'The excellent cooperation of the RAF made it possible to carry out the operation according to plan. A very large fire was started in the target area, which the Navy subsequently enlarged.'

This succinct account does not provide the full intensity of this whirlwind bombardment, which was all over in twenty terrifying minutes. As the naval forces stealthily approached through the darkness, the near horizon was suddenly lit up by dazzling searchlights probing the sky accompanied by brightly coloured flak bursts and, a minute or two later, by the first bomb blasts. A turn to port brought the ships into position and, scant seconds later, all hell broke loose as every heavy gun on the ships opened fire simultaneously. Jets of flame flashed out and clouds of smoke billowed from the enormous barrels as they hurled shell after shell towards the target. The dazed and bewildered shore batteries managed to fire a few desultory star shells in an attempt to locate their unseen assailants, followed by a handful of shells, more in hope than anything else; none of the ships sustained any damage. The short but sharp attack was soon over and the naval squadron turned for home, anxious to be back in home waters by dawn. As it came, two fighter squadrons appeared overhead to ward off any unwelcome intruders but there were none and all ships made port without interference. A signal was sent to all ships: 'The flotilla carried out last night's operation well.' The eyewitness accounts released shortly after were a little more effusive. One wing commander crowed in an interview, 'They didn't know if it was Christmas or Easter! The searchlights went quite drunk and waved aimlessly about the sky; some of the guns went on firing but goodness knows what at!' He concluded by asserting the fires were still visible from the aircraft as they crossed the English coast some 80 miles away. Another pilot used the flames started by the early crews as a homing beacon, picking them up about 100 miles from the port. He described the patchy clouds as being silhouetted against the white glow of the flares dropped by his colleagues in other aircraft as they illuminated the harbour beneath:

> We were over the target area when suddenly the Navy let fly. It was like 500 thunderstorms rolled into one. Every cloud flamed a bright amber colour and we could see the bursts of the first salvo plumb in the docks. Until then the ground defences had been blazing away at us but that sudden blast from the sea foxed them absolutely! There was complete chaos down below. I said to my crew when we landed, 'I have seen a few Fifths of November but what about October 11?'

For once the damage was real enough and the Bassin Napoleon, Bassin Charles and the Gare Maritime areas were hard hit. So was the confidence of the German naval commanders, who realised all too well that the long autumn and winter nights would enable their opponents to repeat such assaults well at will and with devastating results. It was becoming increasingly clear on both sides of the Channel that the golden moment for invasion had well and truly been and gone and would not return for a half a year at best.

After a busy and successful night without loss, Bomber Command approached the new damp day weary but with a renewed sense of purpose. As the Luftwaffe mounted no fewer than seven major raids, the bombers now outnumbered by their fighter escort, a half a dozen Blenheims took to the air to carry out uneventful routine sweeps over the North Sea. As the men and women beavered away to get everything ready for the night's operations, the routine training and test flying carried on apace. Even this was not without danger in wartime. A Wellington of 214 Squadron was gathering speed for take-off at Stradishall and nobody paid any particular attention to this training flight until a loud bang reverberated around the airfield, accompanied by the sound of grinding metal and a rising plume of dust and smoke. For reasons unknown, the pilot had lost control, veered off course and had smashed into a hangar at speed, killing four and injuring those in the aircraft.

As night fell, the sky over southern England throbbed with the sound of aero engines as the Luftwaffe ranged far and wide to pound cities all over the country and eighty-six British bombers took off to return the destructive compliment over Wilhelmshaven, Hamburg and Kiel. Both sides began their work earlier than usual, mindful of a forecast that predicted a deteriorating situation in the early hours, with dense fog becoming a widespread hazard. For both sides, conditions were far from conducive to effective bombing, with most crews being compelled to bomb alternative targets or seek targets of opportunity through the emerging clag. Perhaps the only saving grace for the frustrated crews scouring north-western Germany was that the foul conditions made life every bit as difficult for the defences, which were rendered just as blind and ineffective as the air crews. Nevertheless, Plt Off Gilbert and his 61 Squadron crew endured a nerve-shredding experience. Cruising over Hamburg at 7,500ft in search of the docks, the Hampden came under heavy and accurate fire, buffeted and blasted from all sides. The force of one particularly near miss, which burst just beneath the aircraft, flipped it right over and into a vicious spin. Twizzling out of control, the altimeter unwound first hundreds, then thousands of feet. Gilbert wrestled feverishly with the controls while the others on board could do little more than hang on grimly and wait. After dropping the best part of a mile, despairing of the situation, the pilot gave the order to attempt to abandon the aircraft. Sgt Neville, best placed to do so in the nose, clawed his way to the hatch and hurled himself out into the tranquillity of the night. As the others attempted to follow, the Hampden began to show signs of recovery and, mindful of the proximity of the German soil beneath them, Gilbert renewed his frantic efforts and, with a felicitous mix of skill and good fortune, he levelled out with scant seconds to spare, shrieking across the landscape at just a couple of hundred feet. Gingerly, he experimented with the controls and, finding nothing amiss, tried to take stock of the situation. In the absence of his navigator, he set course generally west, gradually easing the bomber up towards the safety of the clouds. Those same clouds, however, did little to aid navigation and once he judged he was over the North Sea, he let the bomber down little by little until the waves came into sight; the remainder of the crew then set about searching for any sign of land. After some time, to their relief and astonishment, the coast came into sight and with it proof that they were on track over Lincolnshire. Flying low, Gilbert picked his way back to Hemswell, where the Hampden, distinctly battle scarred, safely touched down – the battle of one crew amongst many that night. Although a dozen Hampdens had carried out mining operations according to plan, the night could hardly be judged successful, thwarted in the main by the might of the forces of nature.

No sooner had the fog started to clear than a half a dozen Blenheims set out on their routine armed reconnaissance flights. A single Blenheim had been detailed to mount an attack on the synthetic oil plant at Homburg but, perhaps to the relief of the crew, ran into clear blue sky that made it all but suicidal to carry on; the remainder had an equally unproductive time. All seemed set fair for the night raids when a large force of 138 aircraft were scheduled to attack the usual mix of German and coastal targets. However, the weather once again intervened and it was a force of just ninety-three that struggled into the murky air and set course. A mixed force of Blenheims and venerable Battles made their way to Le Havre, Dunkirk and Amsterdam to attack the ships at anchor in the harbours. These attacks, which left several fires burning in their wake, were the last sizeable ones mounted as being specifically anti-invasion and, thereafter, there would only be occasional small-scale nuisance intruder raids as the focus gradually shifted towards the full strategic offensive envisaged in the pre-war plans. No. 105 Squadron's Blenheims carried out its first night assault upon the Ruhr, their specific focus being the vast railway yards at Hamm, then the most attacked target in Germany. Familiar territory it might have been to many airmen but it was all new to Sqn Ldr Key as he lifted his light bomber off the ground at Watton, followed at forty-five-minute intervals by Flt Sgt Houghton and Flt Sgt Philips in order to lengthen the duration of the attack and increase the disruption and dislocation caused to the busy railway network. The crews found their view of the ground hampered by a low-lying mist but managed to pick out and follow the myriad rivers and canals leading to this heavily industrial area. After that, the flak and searchlight activity provided an accurate homing beacon and they were able to release their load of four 250lb bombs on target and start several fires, which in turn acted as beacons for those following on. All the crews returned safely.

Several Hampdens ventured further east to the equally industrial town of Kassel on the river Fulda. Stan Harrison, now a veteran pilot, almost did not go on this sortie. As his name had appeared on the top of the ops board that afternoon, he and his crew set about carrying out the routine flying tests in preparation for their night's work. Several minor faults and niggles were identified and passed on to the ground crews on landing. The problems were so bad that the bomber was still not ready by take-off. The squadron had no spare aircraft and neither, it turned out, did the neighbours – 144 Squadron. It looked as if the young men would be having a night off until some bright spark thought of contacting 83 Squadron, which operated Hampdens out of nearby Scampton. Luckily, 83 Squadron did have an aircraft available and ready and Harrison and his crew soon found themselves bouncing along in the back of a truck in full flying kit towards Scampton. The 10-mile journey gave them plenty of time to ponder their futures; operations in an unknown aircraft away from home were never a popular option as trust in the sound preparation of the aircraft by a known ground crew was considered an essential prerequisite. Take-off was soon after their arrival and as the Hampden flew smoothly across the North Sea a degree of optimism began to take hold on board. This strengthened as the target, a factory making components for U-boats, was located with greater ease than usual and, given the comparative absence of flak and searchlights, with greater accuracy. Three 500lb bombs and a 400lb canister of 4lb incendiaries were observed to explode in the target area before Harrison turned for Scampton, arriving safely after an uneventful flight; things had turned out rather well after all.

Other Hampdens carried out attacks upon the Fokker works at Amsterdam and the sprawling Krupps works in Essen, which was fast becoming one of the most visited targets in Germany. Plt Off Romans, who had been forced to ditch twice during the summer, had released his load over the industrial city to no visible effect and so as he passed over Texel airfield, he dropped down low to enable his gunners to loose off a couple of hundred rounds at the buildings and hangars, disappointingly to no visible effect once again. His 44 Squadron colleague Sgt Kneil did likewise over Vught and at least had the satisfaction of seeing several lights go out, although the causes of this remained a topic of hot speculation amongst those on board.

Although there were also attacks on oil plants in Cologne and Hanover, the Dortmund–Ems canal and the aluminium works at Heringen, the headline-grabbing raid was the one to Berlin. As the Whitleys were not flying that night, it fell to a handful of Wellingtons and Hampdens to make the long haul to the Reich capital. Ranging at will over the city for more than an hour, several military and industrial targets were attacked, notably the power station in the Moabit district, which was reported as well ablaze by the end of the night. In reality the damage was slight but with London under nightly attack and many other cities suffering repeated raids, the headlines did a power of good; so did the announcement that no aircraft had been lost.

There was, however, little room for unfettered optimism. Sunday 13 October saw more than 300 Luftwaffe aircraft mount four major daylight assaults, supplemented by more that night on cities across the nation; in this campaign of aerial attrition, the scales remained heavily weighted against the British. It was not for want of trying as Air Marshal Sir Richard Peirse, like his predecessor Sir Charles Portal, regularly committed well over half of the bomber forces available to battle night after night. Some aircraft, such as the Fairey Battle, were already obsolete and others, including the Blenheim, were fast approaching that status. Nevertheless, they remained in use and indeed, twelve Battles were over Calais on that very night, two of them crashing on their return; Plt Off Stevenson and his crew escaped unhurt as they parachuted to the ground when their 142 Squadron Battle's fuel tanks ran dry over Lincolnshire but Fg Off Gebiki's crew became the newly operational Polish 300 Squadron's first fatalities when their Battle crashed near Nottingham on its way back to RAF Swinderby.

The eighty-three Wellington and Hampdens focused upon the oil plant at Gelsenkirchen and the ports of Kiel and Wilhelmshaven. No. 61 Squadron, for example, were after the *Tirpitz* once again but conditions were far from helpful with heavy cloud smothering the entire area, turning the world beneath the crews into an amorphous, featureless mass of cotton wool. Accurate bombing was clearly out of the question but many of the crews doggedly attempted to carry out their orders. Sgt Loadsman recorded spending some forty-three minutes under fire while searching for the target he knew to be somewhere beneath him. To his disgust, no gap in the cloud manifested itself and he reluctantly set course for home, determined to locate a suitable target of opportunity. When this too proved impossible, he jettisoned his bombs over the North Sea and returned to Hemswell dejected and weary. By chance, Plt Off Webb, making his operational debut, did manage to find that elusive gap and had just enough time to drop his bombs into the general harbour area before the breach sealed itself; he was the only one of the seven pilots from 61 Squadron to do so.

For once, the Air Ministry communique released for publication on Tuesday 15 October made no bones about it, turning the lack of success into a brave struggle against the elements. It recorded that many crews had been forced to fly blind through dense cloud, electrical storms and sub-zero temperatures for almost the entire route only to find that the cloud had shown none of the expected tendency to break up and totally obscured the target area; the situation over Wilhelmshaven had been exacerbated by blinding snow storms. Although it went on to mention that several bombers did manage to locate the target, no results were observed. One aircraft was reported as lost over Wilhelmshaven. It took little imagination on the part of the reader to work out that it had not been the best of nights.

Throughout the war the centuries-old processes and niceties of diplomacy went on. In a meeting with Italian ministers on 14 October in Berlin, Hitler is reported to have dismissed British claims to be carrying on regardless during what was already widely reported as the Blitz. 'Let them announce what they will,' he declared, 'the situation in London must be horrific. Let's wait and see what London looks like in two or three months from now! If I cannot invade them, at least I can destroy the whole of their industry!' The people who worked in that industry too, he might have added. By the end of the week, 1,567 citizens had lost their lives under the bombs, 1,388 in London alone. The following week was no better and, depressingly, there was no sign of even a glimmer at the end of the tunnel. The only consolation to most was that the Germans were getting a taste of their own medicine as night after night Bomber Command went out to deliver Britain's defiant response.

Of the dozen Blenheims despatched to make daylight raids, three-quarters returned in the clear conditions; one 139 Squadron aircraft failed to return from an anti-shipping strike, the only trace of its crew being the badly decomposed body of Sgt D. O'Neill, the WopAg, identified only by the serial number on his parachute harness, which washed ashore some time later. By the time darkness fell, cloud once more dominated the picture and rain lashed the aircraft ready and waiting on airfields across eastern England. No. 37 Squadron was assigned two main targets, one a more attractive proposition to the crews than the other, the harbour in Le Havre and the other the oil installations in Bohlen. The four crews bound for Le Havre discovered that the murky conditions cleared somewhat over the Channel. The Wellingtons had little difficulty in identifying the port from 10,000 to 12,000ft and were able to release their loads on target in spite of fierce defensive activity. Several fires were left blazing as they headed back out to sea. The eight crews bound for Bohlen also recorded a significant improvement in flying conditions once they crossed the coast at Lowestoft. Even so, navigation and bombing by night even in good conditions is a difficult and tortuous process and Sgt Gillanders was carrying out a grid pattern search over the eerily silent, blacked out town, when he noticed his fuel was running low. He immediately broke off the search and turned for home, releasing his bombs from 7,000ft over an airfield identified as Nordhausen; they were seen to burst across the airfield and several lights were immediately extinguished. The novel German defence of complete non-reaction appears to have paid off as, although bombs were released, none of the crews were confident that they had located let alone hit the target accurately.

Although all 37 Squadron's aircraft returned safely from these targets, the raid on Le Havre did claim an unfortunate victim. Sgt D.R. Wright and his crew had taken off from Leeming at 17.31 hours and successfully located and bombed the port. By 20.00 hours they were flying in clear conditions with no reported problem over Weybridge to the west of London but, for reasons unknown, the Whitley was flying very low and came into contact with a balloon cable tethered to Site 21 in defence of the Brooklands aircraft factory, which had been damaged in a raid on 4 September. The cable did its job well and the resulting debris was scattered over a wide area;

although the main body came to rest and exploded at Hangar Hill near the railway station, one wing fell in Weybridge park and the tail unit, complete with rear turret, smashed into Elgin Lodge, where 81-year-old Boer War veteran Thomas Dickinson and his wife lived – both escaped serious injury. An investigation concluded that some incendiary bombs had ignited inside the bomb bay but it was impossible to ascertain whether this was before or after the impact. In any case, there were no survivors. It was, in fact, a bad night for 4 Group losses as the already marginal conditions over its Yorkshire bases had, if anything, deteriorated further in the hours since take off. Flt Lt Tomlinson of 10 Squadron had taken off a few minutes before Sgt Wright bound for Stettin. After almost eleven hours in the air, his fuel gauges reading zero, unable to pinpoint his position through the low-lying cloud and autumn fog, and acutely aware of the proximity of the high ground of the beautiful dales and moors, Tomlinson concluded the cards were stacked against him and gave the order to abandon the aircraft in an orderly fashion. He and two others, Sgts Byrne and Somerville, did so and floated safely to Earth near Thirsk at 04.30 hours but Plt Off Dickinson and Sgt Neville for some reason remained on board and shared its messy fate. Sqn Ldr Ferguson, also of 10 Squadron, had managed to keep his Whitley in the air even longer before, faced with the same circumstances, he made the same decision. All five men parachuted to safety at 05.20 hours near Bellingham in Northumberland, some 60 miles from Leeming. Fg Off B. Brooke failed to find 58 Squadron's base at Linton and shortly before 05.00 hours, while he still had the fuel to make a controlled and powered landing, he managed to identify a stretch of open farmland near Driffield and set the bomber down. Although the starboard wing was ripped off by the impact, the crew clambered out of the remainder pretty much intact. Sgt T.E. Coogan and his 77 Squadron crew fared less well. Visibility was practically nil, but after several attempts, Coogan had managed to catch sight of their base at Topcliffe and, shortly before 04.30, hauled his Whitley around in a tight circuit, trying to keep his eyes fixed on the airfield and the tantalising promise of safety. Coming in low, he undershot slightly and when a tree loomed out of the gloom, had no time or room to take evasive action. In the following seconds, Sqn Ldr G.R.H. Black lost his life and the other men sustained multiple injuries.

The crews based further south did not face such difficulties but the casualties kept coming. No. 44 Squadron was among a number assigned to attack Berlin, in particular the Danziger gas works, rail junctions and Tempelhof airport. Once again, several large fires were reported but nothing more specific. Sgt L.J. Burt had carried out his attack and had already turned for RAF Waddington when his Hampden came under shocking and devastating fire from a night fighter piloted by Lt Hans-Georg Mangelsdorf of 2/NJG1. The brutal encounter, which took place just after 03.00 hours, only lasted seconds but resulted in the bomber coming down a few miles north-east of Wolfsburg. Sgt D. Windle DFM was the sole survivor of this experienced crew, another of which, Sgt J. Baldwin, also held a DFM, a rare distinction at this stage of the war. Within minutes, another Hampden, this time from 50 Squadron, was brought down by Hauptman Werner Streib, commander of 1/NJG1; Sgts Hurrel and Lee survived, the latter being repatriated later in the war on account of the severity of his injuries.

The success of the night fighters continued as the night of 14/15 October turned into one of the most costly nights Bomber Command had yet experienced. Oberfeldwebel Herzog, also of 1/NJG1, successfully stalked and shot down a 9 Squadron Wellington to the north-west of its target, Magdeburg, killing all on board. It was the only loss sustained by those attacking the oil installations in the city and for some it was a quiet and uneventful trip. Sgt Woods was flying as a gunner in Sgt Con Curtis' 144 Squadron Hampden, even though he was a qualified navigator, and he took a professional interest in the route as he crossed the coast at Mablethorpe and headed out towards the Frisian Islands. Loaded with four 500lb and two 250lb bombs, the bomber proceeded serenely over the enemy coast and on to Magdeburg, which was located easily by the flak and searchlight activity and fires burning. Looking down through the widely dispersed patches of cloud, Woods could see the ground detail quite clearly between the lights and flashes of gunfire and watched as the bombs burst in the target area. Banking hard and diving to gain precious speed, Curtis guided the Hampden into more tranquil sky and pointed it towards the North Sea and the flat Lincolnshire countryside beyond. Two crews, one target and two very different experiences.

In spite of the losses – about 12 per cent of the aircraft committed and the lives of twenty-two trained airmen – Bomber Command spent most of the following day preparing for the night's onslaught in a systematic routine that would develop but not significantly alter for the next four and a half years. The Luftwaffe's attacks started early at 18.30 hours, not long after night fell, and several hundred raiders ranged far and wide over several industrial cities, notably Birmingham and London. A little later, the first of 134 RAF bombers began to take off and head the other way over the English Channel and North Sea. More than half of the force was directed to the major naval base and docks at Kiel and Hamburg in an attempt to neutralise the increasingly potent threat to British supply routes. No. 37 Squadron, for example, began to take off at 18.45 and half an hour later all the designated aircraft were in the air making their way through a thick layer of rain-bearing cloud that hung over eastern England and well out over the North Sea. Conditions for the crews barely improved and many reported the target areas to be blanketed by ten-tenths cloud. Sqn Ldr Collard, Plt Off Lax, Fg Off Baird-Smith and Sgts Thomas and Bedlow did their best to follow orders, making timed runs towards the target from any prominent landmark that they were able to discern; none of them, however, held any hope for an accurate attack. Only Sgt Gillanders fared any better when his approach coincided with a small break in the cloud over the dock area. Picking up the *Gneisenau* in the floating dock, he quickly released his bombs from 12,000ft but could not observe any results as the clouds merged once more beneath him. The cloud did not, however, prevent the ground defences pumping up shell after shell at the aircraft overhead and, though firing essentially blind, the gunners managed to cause the crews significant discomfort. The returning crews did receive the welcome news that conditions at home had improved markedly and were now cloud and fog free. Many other crews paid a visit to Calais and Boulogne, more now to keep the pressure on the light naval forces that were beginning to harass shipping in the Channel than to dislocate the preparation for invasion. Amongst these were nine Fairey Battles on what turned out to be the last operational flights of this type under the auspices of Bomber Command. Once again, fires were left burning in both harbours. Three mine-laying sorties off Kiel and a few to oil installations completed the roll call of targets for the night. By chance and by contrast to the previous night, there were no losses, although a Hampden from 83 Squadron made a successful, if unorthodox, landing on the beach at Southwold in Suffolk, having run out of fuel. The four men emerged from the lightly damaged aircraft easily enough only to have to pick their way gingerly through the anti-invasion paraphernalia under the watchful gaze of the local Home Guard on duty.

The Blenheims set out again that morning but all but one, which attacked a coastal convoy off Gravelines, returned early in accordance with orders because of a lack of cloud cover. Ironically, the meteorologists predicted a glut of cloud towards evening and the topic of weather, always popular in Britain, was being discussed at the highest levels. After a detailed discussion, the Cabinet decided that if poor weather conditions made it impossible to bomb specific targets accurately and effectively, Bomber Command should be authorised to attack large cities in general, especially Berlin. It was a pragmatic and far-reaching decision, based on an imperative to act upon the situation as it stood; the onset of winter, the widespread desire and obvious military and political need to respond to the apparently indiscriminate onslaught perpetrated by the Luftwaffe over Britain night after night and to clarify current practice in line with the incipient but dawning realisation that all was not well with the precision-bombing campaign. It was largely to maintain public confidence in the latter aspect that it was agreed not to make the decision public. Besides, it was patently absurd and intolerable in a major war situation to have young men risk their lives over enemy territory searching for specific targets but returning with their bombs on board if they failed to find them. Equally, very few people in the know in the autumn of 1940 cared much about the consequences of the decision upon the German people as a whole; had the public known, the cheers might well have been heard in Berlin.

The young men who climbed into their readied aircraft had a bad night ahead of them; almost 20 per cent of the seventy-three aircraft would come to grief one way or another and more than thirty of them would not live to see the dawn the following day. Benny Goodman of 37 Squadron on his third operation as skipper was very nearly the first casualty of the night. His was the first Wellington lined up for take-off at RAF Feltwell and all seemed to be running smoothly as he gunned his twin engines, released the brakes, gathered speed and became airborne. Almost immediately, he realised that the bomber was not responding properly and was struggling to maintain let alone gain altitude and speed, even on full power. Worse still, any reduction in power caused it to stagger and lose some of the precious 500ft gained so far. Gingerly, he began to turn the Wellington around, wracking his brains as to the cause of the problem as he circled slowly, nervously waiting for the rest of the aircraft to take off. Finally given the all clear, Goodman set about the risky business of landing a fully loaded bomber that was wobbling all over the sky and barely under control. Too low to bail out, the young crew had their hearts in their mouths as Goodman gently eased the bomber round on to the correct line but as soon as he backed off the throttle, it dropped like a stone, the force driving the undercarriage right up through the wings and causing it to belly flop and skid crazily to a halt. Fortunately, this did not trigger an explosion or fire and the crew leapt out and sprinted off to put as much distance as possible between themselves and thousands of pounds of bombs and aviation fuel. Later investigation revealed that this near fatal episode had been caused by a simple oversight; the petrol caps on both wings had been left unlocked and had opened in the airstream, acting as spoilers and reducing the lift under the wing. On such slender threads hung the lives of men.

For 49 Squadron, the night was little short of disastrous, all the more unexpected given that most of the Hampdens were engaged in what was considered the relatively routine and safe task of gardening. Sgt Ball had left Scampton a little earlier than the other pilots at 18.45 for the long flight south to the busy River Gironde near Bordeaux. The crew had no difficulty in locating the river and released the mine at the appropriate spot, before passing over the dock area to release their small additional bomb load. Within a couple of minutes, the Hampden shuddered violently as an unseen night fighter bored in to attack from the rear. In those few shattering moments, the top of the rudder was shot away, the tail plane as a whole and one of the wings were shredded by machine gun bullets. Fortunately, the fighter lost contact, leaving Ball to assess the damage as best as possible in the dark and face a long flight home. Nothing vital appeared to have been hit and Ball set the bomber down at RAF Marham at 03.30 hours. Sgt D.S. Imbers' Hampden fared less well after being hit by flak over the target area, crashing with the loss of all on board 6 miles north-east of Bordeaux. Plt Off Evans and his crew found themselves running perilously short of fuel as they eventually crossed the English coast low over Kent, well off track. With little choice in the matter and even less time, they began to search the patchwork fields and often wooded landscape of Kent for a suitable place to land, quickly electing a stretch near Lenham, a few miles north-west of Ashford. The landing was a bumpy one and by the time the bomber had slewed to a halt, it was well ablaze, trapping the wireless operator Sgt R. Potter and condemning him to a death amid the flames. Evans and the others were injured but managed to extricate themselves to join the rear gunner, who had been thrown clear on impact. Sgt G.M. Bates was also short of fuel as he steered his Hampden back from Bordeaux. Making up his mind to land at the first airfield he came across, he put down at RAF Abingdon but, unfamiliar with it, overshot and ploughed through the boundary fence, fortunately causing more damage to the aircraft than those on board. The same could not be said for the final 49 Squadron aircraft lost. At 05.20 hours, after well over ten hours in the air,

Fg Off C.D. Pitman's Hampden finally ran out of fuel and crashed in the fields near Andover, still 150 miles short of Scampton; there were no survivors.

No. 44 Squadron, based at RAF Waddington a few miles away, came off only marginally better from its attacks on the oil plants at Leuna and Merseburg. Flt Lt Ogilve had taken off at 18.40 hours and had had no difficulty in locating and bombing his target. Crossing the complex from south-east to north-west, his four 500lb bombs were seen to burst amid the buildings, quickly followed by a very large explosion and a sustained, dull red glow. On his way back from this textbook attack, however, the weather clamped down over the North Sea and by the time the bomber had reached the English coast, conditions were dreadful and Ogilve thought it touch and go to make a safe landing. Having made several circuits to locate his airfield, he finally guided the bomber down at 03.25 but as he did so clipped a hangar with his tail unit, damaging both but, fortunately, not the men on board. Facing the same conditions and equally keen not to be diverted to another base, Sqn Ldr H.P. Broad also ploughed into the same disused hangar but this time with less luck on his side. In the subsequent crash, Broad suffered serious head and leg injuries, his navigator, Sgt Hammond, injuries to both knees and the aircraft was burned out. Sgt Jimmy Kneil, like Ogilve and Broad, had little difficulty in delivering his 500lb bombs to the oil plant at Leuna and met with the same murky conditions over the North Sea and Lincolnshire. Having been given fixes by radio, Kneil and Sgt Hedley Hazelden, also up front, knew they were somewhere near their airfield and twice began their final approach, searching for any recognisable ground feature below. Unable to see a thing, Kneil turned away and climbed on both occasions. Preparing for a third nerve-shredding attempt, he brought the Hampden down low, groping his way gently and blindly towards the ground, well aware of the likely result of hitting the deck in the wrong place or colliding with any large object on the ground at speed. Suddenly, Hazelden, standing behind his pilot, picked out a flashing light and thumped Kneil's shoulder hard, screaming at him to climb on full power. Without wasting a moment, Kneil did so and watched in horror as

Waddington's water tower flashed by scant inches below. After this episode, ground control advised diverting to Bircham Newton and Kneil lost all interest in arguing. Upon arrival in Norfolk, he discovered the conditions there no better and, with fuel running low, he was diverted again to RAF Mildenhall. After five minutes of trying to work out a new course calmly and carefully, the Hampden flew straight into clear, moonlit conditions and things began to look up for the beleaguered crew. However, with cruel timing, the port engine began to splutter and seconds later died as the petrol supply dried up. At just 800ft and losing height steadily, it became apparent that Mildenhall was out of the question, leaving a forced landing as the only card left on the table. Kneil selected an open stretch of land ahead and throttled back as much as he dared, barely managing to keep the wallowing bomber under control. Committed fully, he guided the bomber down. The port wing smashed through the top branches of an unseen tree and the impact flipped the aircraft on to the starboard wing and then onto a more even keel, the belly of the bomber slithering across the fields at around 90mph and shooting clean over a 12ft wide water-filled drainage dyke, eventually grinding to a halt in a field of sugar beet near the quiet village of Ramsey St Mary's. Incredibly, all four men emerged unscathed and after a few minutes to gather their thoughts and take stock of the situation, they trudged wearily through the moonlit muddy fields, blundering into ditches and fences until they reached a cottage, the fearful but hostile occupant of which initially believed them to be German invaders. Another trudge across the soggy fields brought them to a farm, where a telephone call was put through to Waddington; arrangements were made to pick up the disgruntled and bone-weary quartet and they were taken to RAF Upwood, near Huntingdon, which they finally reached in time for breakfast.

The casualty count for the Hampdens continued to rise further. No. 144 Squadron lost two aircraft on the Merseburg raid. Sgt J.H. Brown sent a signal to note he had completed his attack but nothing more was heard beyond a distress call that placed them off the Frisian Islands; Brown's body was washed ashore on the Danish coast on 3 December 1940.

Plt Off T. Dawson was on his way back to Hemswell when he too flew into the lousy conditions and failed to find a place to land. When the bomber ran out of fuel, the crew abandoned the aircraft successfully near King's Lynn but Sgt J. Jackson lost his life. Sgt Cowan of 61 Squadron, also based at Hemswell, had taken off at 18.19 bound for Leuna. All had gone well until an intercom failure over the target led to a late release of the bombs, which were observed to explode at least 500 yards west of the plant. Frustrated by this, the crew set about their journey home and all appeared to be going well until, passing over the Zuiderzee, a Me 110 put in a devastating attack. With no intercom system to give him a warning, the first Cowan knew about it was when he felt the aircraft shudder and smelled the cordite from the gunner returning fire. Instinctively, he banked sharply and put the Hampden's nose down, the gunner maintaining a steady rate of fire. Their adversary had anticipated this move and followed him down, pouring an accurate stream of bullets and shells throughout. Keeping the nose firmly down, Cowan dropped more than 10,000ft, only pulling out when the ground was clearly visible just 600ft below. By then, under intense return fire, the Me 110 had broken off the engagement, perhaps judging the nose-diving bomber to be doomed. It was not quite but it had taken a pasting. The rear gunner had been hit in the foot and the wireless operator had had a miraculous escape, his water bottle and Mae West being holed, leaving him uninjured. In spite of considerable damage, Cowan managed to get the bomber home safely, although diverted to another airfield on account of the conditions. Many other weary crews did likewise and, like Stan Harrison, after the obligatory debriefing, settled into an armchair in an unfamiliar mess to snatch a couple of hours sleep before breakfast and a late return home.

The heavy losses that night were not confined to the Hampdens; the attack on Kiel claimed another five aircraft, although only one was lost to enemy action. The raid began at 21.00 hours and lasted for almost four hours, raising large fires and causing several enormous, multi-coloured explosions. Plt Off B. Landa belonged to 311 Squadron, based at

East Wretham, which had been formed in July 1940 as the first Allied and only Czech squadron to operate in Bomber Command. His Wellington was crossing the Zuiderzee on route to Kiel when it came under attack from a night fighter based at the nearby Deelen airfield. Landa and three others were killed as the bomber came down near Oosterwolde, near Apeldoorn. Flt Lt Josef Šnajdr fared a little better and bombed Kiel but his aircraft suffered a radio failure over Holland on its way back. Normally, this would have been little more than a minor inconvenience but with conditions becoming as bad as they were, it became a matter of critical importance. Roaming the sky over Britain with little clue as to where they were, the Czechs watched with growing anxiety as time and fuel ebbed away. When they blundered into heavy ice-bearing cloud, Šnajdr decided their position was untenable and gave the order to abandon the bomber, pretty confident that they were somewhere over England. Both the aircraft and its crew came to ground near Blidworth in Nottinghamshire about 03.20 hours. There, in a most regrettable but understandable incident, Plt Off Miloslav Vejražka's Czech accent was mistaken for that of a German and he was shot dead by a member of the local Home Guard.

The dreadful conditions and lack of local geographical knowledge also contributed to the loss of Sqn Ldr J. Vesely's Wellington. Another radio problem, compounded by a defective compass, led this experienced flyer to stray far off course as he headed home and by the time he realised, he was well and truly lost. Flying as low as he dared in the hope of picking up any landmark, his Wellington clipped a balloon cable near Fighter Command HQ at Bentley Priory in Middlesex. The impact ripped the wing from the fuselage and within seconds the bomber plunged to earth, killing five of the six airmen. The sole survivor, Sgt František Truhlář, suffered severe burns and was taken to East Grinstead Hospital, where he had the dubious distinction of being one of the early guinea pigs treated by the plastic surgeon pioneer Sir Archibald McIndoe. Truhlář underwent several painful operations but eventually regained his flying status and retrained as a fighter pilot, serving with 312 Squadron. In another cruel twist of fate, he was attempting to land in thick fog on 11 June 1944 after a patrol over the Normandy beaches when he came in a little too low, clipped the boundary hedge and crashed on to the airfield. The aircraft immediately burst into flames and Truhlář once more endured severe burns before help arrived.

Native knowledge, however, did not provide a cast iron guarantee either. Plt Off J.E.S. Morton had left Mildenhall at 18.20 to take his 75 Squadron Wellington to Kiel. By 03.30 hours he was flying blindly somewhere over England, completely ignorant of his position. With his fuel supply dwindling rapidly, Morton decided there was no better option than to abandon the aircraft and, with the pilot holding the aircraft steady to the last, all managed to do so in textbook fashion. On landing, they discovered they were a few miles north of Penrith on the eastern fringes of the Lake District, well over 200 miles from their Suffolk base. Sgt Bevan of 9 Squadron also became lost, having been diverted to Abingdon in Oxfordshire on his return from Kiel. Flying low to avoid the worst of the murk and to attempt to map read his way across England, the Wellington collided with a tree and crashed into a sandpit near Toddington in Bedfordshire, injuring all on board. Whilst the attacks themselves had gone pretty well as planned, the rotten weather conditions had wrought havoc among the crews on their return and reminded all concerned of the dangers of flying on the edge in wartime.

The same weather at least brought some respite for it caused the cancellation of all but one of the daylight sorties planned. The sole Blenheim gamely put in an attack on De Kooy airfield in marginal conditions that did not allow the observation of any results and, this was, as it turned out, the only offensive action undertaken by the Command on 17 October. In fact, the next forty-eight hours saw the majority of the crews grounded by the conditions and enjoying the welcome respite from the remorseless strain of operations. The morning of the 18th barely dawned but 2 Group decided to send a single Blenheim through the clag to the extensive Blohm and Voss shipyards in Hamburg; in accordance with Sod's Law, the cloud vanished entirely over the North Sea leaving the lone raider horribly exposed as it approached enemy territory. Realising this, the sortie was abandoned and the aircraft returned to the murky conditions, which continued to prevail over England throughout the daylight hours and beyond. Nevertheless, twenty-eight 4 Group Whitleys and 5 Group Hampdens, the marginal conditions notwithstanding, were despatched to bomb a number of naval and transportation targets, notably the docks at Hamburg, the aluminium works at Lunen and the railway yards in Dortmund, Osnabrück and Schwerte. The heavy, slow-moving cloud had drifted eastwards and now hampered all the attacks to the extent that no results were observed at any of the targets. If this was not enough to call into question the decision to carry out the sorties, the immense problems facing the returning crews were. By 05.30 hours, Plt Off K.T. Hannah had notched up more than eleven hours in the air on his sortie to Lunen and was still at the controls desperately searching for somewhere to land. As the engines began to splutter, matters were taken out of his hands and he gave the order to abandon the aircraft. All five men did so and landed safely a few miles east of Rotherham. The same fate befell Sgt J.G. Loveluck's 83 Squadron Hampden on its return from Hamburg. Unable to locate Scampton or indeed any other airfield and with the fuel situation critical, he too gave the order to bail out, with both the crew and the Hampden coming down a few miles from Malton in North Yorkshire. Luckily no lives were lost, but two aircraft were, seemingly for very little gain.

Bomber Command had made good use of the past couple of days to ready a major force of 151 aircraft for Saturday night's assault, buoyed by the prospect of improving weather conditions. In the event, this failed to materialise and the force was scaled right back to just a pair of Whitleys and a single Hampden. Berlin remained undisturbed as its would-be assailant returned early with mechanical problems, while another did mount an attack on Osnabrück, leaving several large fires burning brightly. The third aircraft failed to locate its primary target but released its load over an airfield in the Hague, having chanced upon its beacon flashing through the murk. Hardly great results but a whopping 192 aircraft were scheduled to operate the following night.

In the event, unexpectedly poor conditions cut this total back to 135 aircraft tasked to attack targets as far afield as Milan and Pilsen. The Blenheims were on the short coastal runs with 101 Squadron, for example, fielding nine aircraft, each armed with four 250lb bombs. Most carried out the raids as planned but one returned early when the pilot fell ill and was unable to continue and another failed to locate any worthwhile target even after spending twenty minutes flying up and down the coastal strip searching for any sign of life beneath the cloud. Unfortunately, heading home proved tricky and several crews struggled to locate West Raynham, even though the station had deployed additional glim lamps and fired flares periodically to guide the crews in. There was considerable anxiety among those on the ground for the last two Blenheims as both were heard overhead for some time criss-crossing the area. After a while, the sound of engines throttling back and approaching could be heard and both light bombers broke through the cloud simultaneously barely 50 yards apart, each oblivious to the presence of the other. No. 105 Squadron faced similar conditions at RAF Watton after their sorties to the airfield at Hingene and the docks at Antwerp. It was on the way back from the latter that Flt Sgt Richardson wandered off course in the continuous low cloud and fog. Staring out into the murky darkness, Richardson caught a glimpse of something looming out of the gloom and a second later, the Blenheim lurched to starboard accompanied by a short and sharp screeching sound as metal tore through metal; the wingtip had collided with a barrage balloon protecting the port of Harwich. By remarkably good fortune, the aircraft avoided the rest of the forest of cables and continued to fly more or less normally, enabling him to set down at Watton at 21.55, shortly before the station was declared closed on account of the foul conditions. Hemswell followed suit, as did several others, and many crews found themselves diverted to unfamiliar airfields, adding flying time to their sorties and condemning most to a quick drink of tea and an uncomfortable snooze in the mess before dawn.

Others had a far longer flight that night. The Whitleys of 51 Squadron split their efforts between Ostend, where they were over the target between

20.00 and 21.00 hours, and Milan and Turin, which took several more hours to reach. Crossing hundreds of miles of enemy territory including the Alps in a slow, heavily loaded bomber with little space to move was no easy or quick matter and even the desultory and ineffective defences over the Italian cities failed to endear such a flight to the crews. It was shortly after midnight by the time the bombers located the giant Fiat works and major steel plant at Aosta and lined up for run in. In clear conditions, the crews had no difficulty in identifying the industrial complexes and soon several large fires were raging beneath them, still visible for the first part of their long journey home. Although topped up at Wattisham on the outbound leg, the crews had very little margin for error, a tense situation made worse by the increasingly adverse conditions they now encountered. Sgt Wright and his crew ploughed straight into ten-tenths cloud in the later stages of his flight and soon became hopelessly lost. Throttled right back to conserve fuel and flying as low as he dared in the hope of breaking free of the cloud or at least finding a hole in it large enough to identify a landmark, Wright cruised on and clocked up a gruelling twelve hours in the air. When they finally did emerge from the cloud, to their great dismay, they discovered they were over water and facing the prospect of a ditching. As the engine began to splutter, Wright ordered his crew to take up their positions and set the bomber down on the water in textbook manner. Scrambling into the dinghy, the wet and cold young men could do little but wait for daylight. When it came, they discovered they were in the Irish Sea, a few miles north of the River Mersey; help arrived within a couple of hours.

The 58 Squadron Whitleys assigned Pilsen met with similar problems. The vast Škoda armament works was turning out enormous quantities of effective weapons for the German war effort and was an obvious, if distant, target for Bomber Command. Several crews did manage to push through the poor conditions to release their bombs in the target area, while others gave up and attacked secondary targets in Germany, in both cases without visible effect. Flying conditions had deteriorated further by the time of their return flights, causing severe problems. Plt Off Wilding simply used more fuel as he wandered across the Continent and had to ditch within sight of the Norfolk coast; fortunately, the sturdy Whitley lived up to its reputation of ditching well and floating for some time and the uninjured crew was soon picked up by the lifeboat *Foresters' Centenary*. Fg Off B. Brooke found himself in a similar position, being forced to ditch off the mouth of the Humber at 05.40 hours after little short of twelve hours in the air. Several of the crew suffered injuries; for Brooke and Sgts Halley (RAAF) and Henderson, it was less than a week since they had run out of fuel and crash-landed near Driffield on their way back from Stettin. Their squadron colleague, Plt Off Ernest Brown, also did not quite make it home that night. By 06.15 hours, the Whitley was finally back over Yorkshire and a mere handful of miles from RAF Linton when, as the heavily fatigued crew began to relax, out of the blue, the aircraft came under vicious attack and sustained critical damage. The pilot and two others died as the aircraft came down near Ingleby on the slopes of the Cleveland Hills; Sgt Green died of his injuries two days later, leaving Sgt Langfield the only survivor. This successful intruder sortie was carried out by Hauptmann Hulshof of 1/NJG2 who wrongly identified his victim as a Hereford, a bomber a generation older than the Whitley, and went on to add many more to his tally over the coming months.

The largest single force of the night, some thirty Hampdens, made for Berlin, the first arriving overhead from 22.00 hours and the last departing several hours later to increase disruption. The moonlight enabled the crews to pick out considerable ground detail through the thin and patchy cloud and many claims were put in for successful attacks. One sergeant pilot was over the city around midnight and remained there for twenty-five minutes in an attempt to pinpoint his target:

> We were doing turns to get the full benefit of the moon. You could see lots of buildings and roadways if you got the right angle. The ground defences were firing heavily from one corner of the city. Then from another corner, they started peppering us heavily and the searchlights got on to us.

Once the navigator had confirmed the location of the target, the pilot put the bomber into a shallow dive:

> We were diving down at a good speed and the target was getting bigger and bigger all the time. Then I shouted 'Let them go!' and the bomb aimer pressed the button. After we bombed, the defences really did let us have it. The sky seemed alive with flak. I put the aircraft into a vertical bank turn to get away and out we went. I was swinging all over the place.

The unnamed pilot concluded the interview by noting:

> Then suddenly, I saw a balloon go up in flames. Fire from the guns on the ground must have got it. There was a flash and the whole thing was ablaze. At first, I thought it was another aeroplane, then I saw the cable quite clearly. Some of the burning fabric came sliding down the cable. It fell in our direction and seemed to be following us. That put the wind up us for a bit. It was several seconds before we got clear. Just after that I asked the navigator to give me a course for home.

The Hampdens crew had it no easier than the others that night. The first to be lost was 44 Squadron's Sgt C.W. Hartop, all the crew perishing as it came down at Hasenheide near Berlin, having been hit by flak. The same squadron lost the aircraft captained by Sgt A.R. Atkins, which force-landed successfully in fields near Colchester after running out of fuel. Two men were injured when a 49 Squadron bomber followed suit near Veryan, a few miles from Truro, well off track on a flight to Scampton. Although this time the balance sheet was a little more even in terms of the damage inflicted, it had been another costly night for the Command. Of the seven aircraft lost, only two had been the direct result of enemy action, the rest falling victim, in one way or another, to the conditions.

Dawn came but slowly the following morning to reveal a dark, dank and miserable day, the sun's feeble light barely penetrating the thick, low cloud and fog that was smothering much of the country. Nevertheless, a dozen trusty Blenheims were assigned St Omer airfield as their target. Seven gave up in the appalling conditions and the rest went for whatever they could find along the coastal strip, a couple having some luck over Boulogne harbour. Flying conditions did not improve as the day wore on and only 3 and 4 Groups decided to mount operations that night. The force of eleven Whitleys was split between oil targets in Cologne and an aircraft component factory in Stuttgart, the thirty-one Wellingtons between an oil refinery in Reisholz and Hamburg, where the *Bismarck* was in residence. Its sister ship *Tirpitz* in Wilhelmshaven was the alternative and failing that in the poor conditions expected, any SEMO. No. 37 Squadron's Wellingtons were among those ready for take-off around 18.00 hours in spite of the low cloud and restricted visibility. Nothing much changed as they crossed the coast at Great Yarmouth and pushed on over the sea but as they approached the target area things quickly began to look up and the ground became visible, enabling the crews coming in at heights ranging from just 3,000 to 18,000ft to locate and release their bombs over their targets. Numerous fires and explosions were clearly observed and extant German reports confirm that the raid was far more effective than most, counting a dozen separate fires, two-thirds of which were classified as large by the authorities. By the time the crews were approaching Britain conditions were less than the marginal they had been and Sqn Ldr Collard, who was over Feltwell at 01.00 hours, described visibility in the autumn fog and general murk as virtually non-existent. Sgt Gillanders was the last to sneak in at 01.15 just before the airfield was declared closed.

Flt Lt C.L. Gilbert was not so lucky when his 75 Squadron Wellington was diverted to RAF Methwold, where conditions were deemed just about viable. Not familiar with his surroundings, he misjudged his approach and ploughed into a small copse at 23.20, 2 miles or so north of the airfield, writing off the aircraft and injuring all inside. The foul conditions had caused Fg Off R.P. Elliott, also in 75 Squadron, to wander off his projected route and out of the blue he blundered into a barrage balloon cable, protecting some unknown point. Fortunately, the damage appeared slight but it was enough to add even more urgency to the need to find a place to land. Stumbling across RAF Manston, the nearest RAF station to occupied territory, at 00.30, he immediately set about landing. Things did not go smoothly and by the time the Wellington had slithered to a halt on its belly, it was a sorry sight; its crew escaped with only minor injuries. The only other loss for the night was the result of enemy action. Flt Lt A.S. Phillips DFC had only recently returned to duty with 10 Squadron having recovered from injuries sustained in a forced landing near Needham Market in Suffolk on his return from an operation to Homburg. Flying with a new crew, he had left Leeming at 17.56 hours for Stuttgart to attack an aircraft factory there. For reasons unknown, the aircraft failed to return but the bodies of all the crew now rest in the Commonwealth cemetery at Durnbach. This meant a loss rate approaching 7 per cent for the night, an unsustainably high level in the long term.

Autumn was well and truly in charge as the next morning dawned wet, misty and miserable. Only one Blenheim took to the sky, directed to attack targets in Amsterdam. Instead, the crew chanced upon a cargo ship 3 miles north of the Hook of Holland and, deciding a bird in the hand was worth two in the bush, went in straightaway for a low-level pass. One of the bombs was clearly observed exploding on the ship but beyond this, nothing else could be claimed with certainty. It was the Command's only sortie in the twenty-four-hour period as all other operations were scrubbed. The rotten weather continued the following day but, this time, eight Blenheims were readied to mount offensive reconnaissance sorties along the coastal strip of occupied Europe. Most crews gave up after fruitless searches but three managed to locate targets in Ostend harbour, a ship off Walcheren and an unidentified factory in St Nicholaas in Belgium. No results from these opportunistic attacks could be seen. By evening, the conditions were at least no worse and a total of seventy-nine aircraft were bombed up for attacks across Germany on oil, naval, rail and aircraft targets. The largest single force of the night, twelve strong, went for the docks at Emden in two main waves. The first aircraft were over the city by 01.30 hours and remained overhead for over half an hour; the second arrived two hours later to extend the disruptive effect and catch the defences by surprise. Having endured ten-tenths cloud across the sea, the three aircraft from 37 Squadron were pleased to see the cloud well broken over the target, though a low mist combined with glare from the searchlights to hamper clear observation of ground detail. Sgt Goodman failed to locate the docks but released his load on to a searchlight concentration, igniting three separate blazes, which were clearly visible and gaining ground. Sgt Paul fared better, locating and bombing the docks from 9,000ft, causing several fires. Fg Off Curry had a more frustrating time cruising back and forth over the area, often under fire, catching tantalising glimpses of the ground beneath but too briefly to act with any degree of certainty. Eventually, he was forced to fall back upon a best guess approach, based on sightings and known courses; no results were observed. Nevertheless, all crews reported large, concentrated fires burning and thick, dark smoke towering 5,000ft over the target area. Conditions deteriorated again as the crews headed west and Fg Off D. W. Donaldson, who had left 149's base at Mildenhall at 23.24 hours to join the second raid, went off track and had little idea of where he was. By 07.30 hours the situation was critical and, unable to locate an airfield, he dropped down as low as he dared and gave instructions to his crew to scour the murk for any sign of an open space on which he could put the Wellington down. In the uncertain light of dawn, such a sighting was made and without further ado, Donaldson carried out a perfect emergency landing and all on board clambered out of the wreckage more or less intact; they discovered they were a couple of miles west of Clacton in Essex, not too far from their base in Suffolk.

Eleven aircraft took on the long journey and strong defences of Berlin, the twenty-second time the Command had attacked the city. The target was always more popular with the public than the crews but there was a certain satisfaction to be had in hitting back for the attacks on London. Reports in the press noted:

Bad weather stopped the RAF bombing operations over Germany during the previous night but conditions improved during the day so that after nightfall Berlin got a further taste of the medicine which Germany thought she alone could administer. Many military objectives were attacked there.

It did not appear so clear cut to the young airmen facing both poor conditions and powerful defences. Assigned specific targets, such as the Potsdam station, the Siemens complex and the Berliner power station, the crews often had to spend prolonged periods searching, all the while particularly vulnerable to the defences. Several managed to carry out their orders and left fires burning in their wake but others had more of a struggle. Plt Off Lax of 37 Squadron ran into severe icing just short of Berlin and broke off his attack; now ice-free, he began to search for a suitable target, eventually coming across Eelde airfield, where he left a number of fires in his wake. Two more aircraft overshot their target by some 40 to 50 miles, one eventually bombing the marshalling yards at Frankfurt am Oder, the other doing likewise, having been attracted by the fires. The last of those over Berlin did not leave until almost 04.00 hours, well aware that the last part of their long flight home would be just about in daylight, significantly adding to the risks threatening the crews.

Press reports quoted a pilot as commenting:

The ground defences were wide awake and over the city itself searchlights and AA fire were intense. We arrived about 03.00 and spent a half an hour over the city. The searchlights were on us but I don't think they could see us. We picked up a position and the bomb aimer brought us over the target and let his bombs go. This stirred up the AA again and we had to zig-zag our way out.

Another, not identified for the wartime readership, added:

The barrage was pretty heavy and several times I saw a long line of shells bursting in front of us. We picked up the Potsdamer railway station and from there got a straight run over the target. Someone else put a flare down for us at just the right moment. We attacked straight and level. About 15 seconds after dropping our own bombs, four fires sprang up making it evident that our target had been hit.

The target was not the only thing hit; Plt Off R.M. Sanderson's 75 Squadron Wellington failed to return. It had probably been damaged by flak and the wireless operator sent out a distress signal as it re-crossed the enemy coast. The message sparked an unusually strong response at Mildenhall and Plt Off 'Spanky' McFarlane's crew took off to carry out a search of the area as soon as an aircraft could be made ready. Swanning around in daylight off the enemy-held Dutch coast was a risky business but the crew were cheered by the sight of a dinghy bobbing on the sea in the distance. As the Wellington turned towards it, their heady mixture of anxiety and euphoria evaporated as it became apparent that it was empty. A series of low-level passes left the crew in no doubt that there was nobody in the sea nearby and reluctantly McFarlane turned for home. The body of Plt Off F.B. Cleak was washed on to the Danish shore a few days later but the chilly North Sea held on to the bodies of the other men, one of whom, Sgt Bill Hitchmough, had just turned nineteen.

Daylight revealed a typically still and lifeless mid-autumn morning, the tranquillity largely unbroken even by enemy activity. A handful of Blenheims set off for the usual passes along the coastal strip and North Sea, all of which were as uneventful as the weather. Not that there was a lack of activity on the ground on either side. Even a small group of Italian bombers were being readied for their maiden raid over the UK that night. By evening, more than 100 RAF bombers stood poised for the sorties that would range far and wide over the Reich. For Plt Off Richard Pinkham the night got off to an inauspicious start. A pilot with 77 Squadron who had been moved to RAF Topcliffe on 5 October, he had spent much of the past three weeks on standby before being stood down for one reason or another. On this night, he was allocated Kiel as his target and was already in his seat in his Whitley when word came through that there was an intruder in the vicinity. Keyed up and unwilling to depart from the scheduled scheme of things, he continued with the take-off procedure but without the benefit of any ground lights bar the faintest of glim lights dimly marking the runway. Also without the benefit of his navigation lights, Pinkham was gingerly taxying his bomber around the perimeter when there was a sharp bump and loud screech of tearing metal; he had collided with an unlit stationary aircraft. Although the damage to the aircraft was quite minor, the unfortunate episode put paid to his night's work and, he feared, the rest of his flying career. A short and unpleasant, largely one-sided conversation with the station commander, Gp Capt Hunter, followed and a little later, a formal admonishment was delivered by a rather more sympathetic Air Commadore Cunningham. Nevertheless, his logbook was endorsed in damning red ink 'Taxying accident 24/10/40 due to carelessness', forever a stark reminder of his night of misfortune and embarrassment.

It was far worse for Plt Off A.G. Davies and his 102 Squadron crew. They had barely been airborne for more than a couple of minutes and had only just finished retracting the undercarriage when they came under devastating fire from a roving Ju 88 intruder flown by Feldwebel Hans Hahn of 3/NJG2, based at Gilze-Rijen in Holland. The lumbering Whitley did not stand a chance and plunged to the ground only a few miles from Linton. Only Davies, though wounded, survived the attack, the rest probably becoming the victims of the intruder Pinkham had been warned about. Sgt Douglas Mourton later recalled that as he reported to 102 Squadron B Flight Commander Sqn Ldr Maxie Beare on arrival at the station, he was immediately assigned to the funeral party of this crew. He never forgot the anguish and grief of one man's young wife and parents at the service, nor his sobering introduction to the harsh realities of life and death on an operational squadron.

As ever, the giant machine that was Bomber Command ground onwards remorselessly, apparently oblivious to the human elements within. There was a war to be fought and little time for overt displays of sympathy.

No. 18 Squadron's Blenheims were set to attack the railway yards in Haltern in the industrial Ruhr valley. Take-off from Great Massingham was a little later than usual and it was 22.40 when Dinty Moore's twin engines powered him down the runway and into the air. The conditions were relatively clear and the crew had no problem in locating the target area, drawn if by no other means by the heavy flak pouring into the sky acting like an unintended beacon. They added their contribution to the fires raging on the ground and turned for home without undue difficulty. Two hours later, as they were all but home, WopAg Moore received the chilling message that intruders were active in the area and to be especially vigilant. The Blenheim landed without mishap but as if to underline the stark presence of this increasingly common threat, Great Massingham and nearby West Raynham did come under attack three nights later from a small force of Ju 88s; one Blenheim was written off, eleven more were damaged, four RAF personnel were killed, seven more were wounded, three seriously. It was clear that their raids on Germany were having an effect and had provoked a significant response from the Luftwaffe; there would be no respite for the crews from take-off to landing.

Eric Woods had taken off from Hemswell a little earlier and had given his skipper a course for Hanover. As the 144 Squadron Hampden approached the Dutch coast it came under steady and unnerving fire but this was just the warm-up act for Hanover itself. There was little need for accurate navigation as the target area was self-evident from miles away, with the clearly visible mass of red and orange fires on the ground being matched by the vividly coloured explosions and dazzling, probing fingers of white light stretching high into the sky. Peering between the swaying beams, Woods managed to locate the engineering works that was his target and then guided his pilot round to begin the final run-in. As he came in, Woods caught sight of a cone of searchlights with a brilliantly illuminated cigar shaped object in the middle of it, all but enveloped by bright orange flashes, another aircraft under heavy fire. Forcing himself to tear his eyes away from this horrifying sight and turn back to the job in hand, Woods saw a dense black mass directly in front of the Hampden and, instantly recalling what had been said at the briefing, screamed 'Balloon!' There was no time to take evasive action, yet no collision; Woods had picked out a black cloud of a very near miss. Passing straight through the harmless smoke, Woods steadied himself and released his load as intended. As it turned for home, he realised that the pair of 250lb bombs on the wings were still in place. Rather than go around again through the flak, it was decided to continue westwards and to find a target on route. There was no sign of life beneath them for some time but eventually the faint lights of an airfield came into view. Identified as De Kooy, the bomber carried out a textbook approach and released both bombs without a hitch; minutes later it was out over the sea and racing for home.

Stan Harrison from 61 Squadron had left the station it shared with 144 at a similar time and made his way to the same city. Crossing the enemy coast near Leiden and skirting heavily defended Osnabrück, he too had no difficulty in homing in on the inferno that was Hanover. Such was the intensity of the dazzling flak, lights and fires, however, that the crew struggled to identify much on the ground. Searching for as long as they dared, they released their bombs over an industrial area and poured on the power to get clear of the highly active defences. With 200 miles over enemy territory ahead, Harrison warned the crew to stay alert, especially as the conditions were just about perfect for night flying. As it turned out, nothing amiss happened and Harrison remembered his twenty-second return flight as both tranquil and beautiful, a reminder of why he had fallen in love with flying.

Although conditions were not quite so good over Hamburg, a strong force of Wellingtons hit the port hard that night. The crews themselves could report little but the fact that enormous fires had been seen blazing in the target area; nevertheless, what they could see appeared conclusive to them. German records agreed with their conclusions, noting the raid left thirteen fires burning, five of which were classified as large, and damage was caused to the tune of 3 million Reichmarks. They also recorded accurately that the defences had accounted for a Wellington and its crew. Berlin was hit for the second night in succession. The raid was deliberately staggered and it was not until 07.00 that the all clear was finally sounded, although by then the aircraft were well on their way home. Several fires were ignited and, although a long way from the wholesale destruction wrought by the Luftwaffe on London, the bleary-eyed inhabitants of Berlin certainly knew they had been under attack. International press reports and photographs revealed bomb damage to the city centre and recorded the continued evacuation programme for the city's children. The battle of urban attrition, unequal as it was at this stage, was well under way.

Friday 25 October saw the Luftwaffe step up the pace once again, with an estimated 440 aircraft over Britain in the shortening daylight hours and nocturnal raids. In reply 2 Group launched its regular North Sea sweep and a further six aircraft headed to attack the shipping in the northern ports of Bremen, Wilhelmshaven, Hamburg and Kiel. However, the complete absence of cloud cover compelled all of them to abandon their sorties. The Blenheims were more effective that night as they roamed the Channel coastal strip, with several putting in attacks on the massive gun emplacements at Cap Gris Nez. No. 105 Squadron fielded six fully loaded Blenheims under the command of Sqn Ldr Key. While five experienced a fairly trouble-free sortie, Plt Off Murray had a rather more torrid time of it, with his starboard engine playing up while over the sea. Breaking off his attack on his primary target, Murray spotted the coastal airfield at Étaples, easily located by its distinctive estuary and shoreline, and decided to give it a going over. The official record went on, 'After this attack, the starboard engine seized up completely and the airscrew and reduction gear broke away and fell, it is hoped, on some legitimate target in Occupied France. Plt Off Murray succeeded in piloting his aircraft back to England on one engine and made a successful landing on Debden aerodrome.' The Blenheim was repaired and Murray was reunited with it less than three weeks later on 14 November for a low-level attack on Boulogne harbour. No. 101's Blenheims were also in action over Cap Gris Nez, as much to cause annoyance and disruption as anything else given the increasingly strong protection being provided for the long-range guns. The squadron's log succinctly laid out the attack, 'All aircraft located the gun positions and dropped their bombs. The attack was carried out for its nuisance value and the squadron aircraft were over the target for 30 minutes and released their bombs singly. If the object was to arouse the enemy, it succeeded admirably.'

Germany's northern ports also faced heavy attacks, though the dense cloud over Bremen vitiated any realistic chance of an accurate bombardment. The Hampdens over Kiel fared a little better in their attacks on the docks and their mining of the offshore waters. Even so, when Sgt R.J. 'Con' Curtis of 144 made his final approach, he smiled ruefully at the favourable forecast confidently given by the met officer a couple of hours earlier. Beneath his aircraft was an almost unbroken layer of thick cloud, smothering all signs of offensive and defensive activity below. After searching for a break for some time, Curtis decided to head towards the naval and seaplane base on the island of Borkum in the hope that he might do better there. He did not and so, seeing no point in wasting his bombs, he set course for home and, after an uneventful flight, X2998 joined the landing circuit at Hemswell a minute or two after midnight. Then, as Curtis came in low, the flarepath lights suddenly went out, a sure sign that there was an intruder in the vicinity. By now manning the lower rear turret or 'tin', Eric Woods saw the treetops flashing by, soon followed by an almighty bang, sparks, lumps of metal and earth flying through the air at great speed and in all directions. The bone-shattering bumps and tearing sounds gradually faded to leave complete silence. As Woods' brain began to clear, he realised he was trapped in the wreckage, with at least one leg broken, and the ominous glare and crackling sound of flames penetrated his jumbled senses. Desperation really set in when he remembered the bomb load was still on board but heave and strain as he might, he could not break free. A voice suddenly penetrated his all-absorbing personal battle for survival, shouting, 'One of 'em's alive!', swiftly followed by hands clearing a path for Woods to drag and squeeze himself through. As he was hauled through the blazing side of the fuselage, he received burns even through his bulky sheepskin flying jacket but, in spite of the pain from being man-handled, he began to shout at the top of his voice that there were still bombs on board. His courageous and unknown saviours took little notice and continued to drag him clear of the inferno that had so nearly been his funeral pyre. Once comfortably ensconced in hospital in Lincoln, he was delighted to discover that all the crew had survived the crash on Cuckoo Farm near Hemswell. It would be some time before Woods was operational again. That was something Sgt H.C. Loadsman and his 61 Squadron crew would never be, having been lost without trace on the Kiel raid.

Given that nobody knew what had happened to Loadsman's Hampden, permission was unusually given for a couple of crews to carry out a search over the North Sea, concentrating on the most likely flight paths. Conditions were not at all promising with grey skies, moderate visibility and eight-tenths cloud with a base at 4,000ft. Plt Off Massey flew a series of box searches, right to within 3 miles of the Dutch coast, but without success. Almost back over the English coast a while later, Massey spotted an He 115 floatplane, either on a mine-laying sortie or similar mission to the Englishman. A twenty-minute battle through the cloud ensued as the two lumbering aircraft did their best to emulate their fighter pilot comrades. Eventually, the Hampden inflicted sufficient damage to cause the He 115 to make an emergency landing at sea, partially breaking up in the process. As the elated Massey and his crew circled overhead, they watched the German airmen climb out and squat disconsolately upon the wreckage. Perhaps mindful of the fact that the wet, cold and shocked young men adrift in the wintry North Sea could so easily have been them, Massey ordered the Hampden's dinghy to be dropped as he made a low pass; it washed ashore on the Norfolk coast some twenty-two hours later, with those on board no doubt grateful for the generosity of spirit shown to an enemy.

The squadron was back in action that night, providing part of a seventeen-strong force of Hampdens attacking a variety of targets in Berlin. Weather conditions were quite poor and certainly blunted the effectiveness of the bomber force, some of which flew at low level over the city in the hope of identifying and hitting their targets. Five more Hampdens were assigned to mine-laying in the mouth of the River Gironde. Although four completed the mission successfully, Sgt J.G. Loveluck of 83 Squadron was lost without trace, probably brought down by the increasingly strong defences now in place to thwart such regular flights.

Several oil and communication targets were attacked but, perhaps, the most challenging one was at Politz, near Stettin. Almost 660 miles from their North Yorkshire bases, it was towards the limit of a Whitley's bombed-up range and all the crews were well aware that they would have very little margin for error of any kind. Travelling at not much more than 120mph, it was going to be a long night. The Whitleys, each making their own way to Politz, came under fire from several defended areas, such as Hamburg, but had little option but to hold course and preserve fuel. Plt Off J.S.G. Crawford had taken off from Linton at 17.27 and had duly reached, located and attacked his target and was well on the way home when a coastal flak battery suddenly opened up and turned his starboard engine into a mass of twisted metal. Struggling to keep the stricken aircraft under control and in the air, Crawford tried to use his remaining and now overworked engine as effectively as possible, eking out the petrol as the bomber reluctantly limped across the sea with agonising slowness. The first sight of the English coast coincided with the first ominous splutterings of fuel starvation from the port engine. Unable to visually confirm their position or locate an airfield, Crawford gave the order to abandon the aircraft while he attempted to keep it steady. Following his crew out, Crawford landed safely near both his crew and his aircraft a few miles from Pickering and not too far short of Linton.

The Blenheims were out and about as usual the next day, oblivious to the fact that it was a traditional day of rest. In addition to the routine sweeps of the North Sea, a further nine were sent off to harass several naval dockyards, though in the poor conditions only one was able to put in an attack, having stumbled across minesweepers at work off Terschelling; no claims were made for hits. The Blenheims were busy that night too as they formed part of an eighty-two-strong force striking at targets across Europe. No. 15 Squadron contributed five aircraft to the proceedings, though one never quite made it off the ground. Sgt Dove had almost reached take-off speed when his port tyre unexpectedly burst, the severe shock causing the undercarriage to collapse. Immediately transformed into a bomb- and fuel-laden toboggan careering out of control, the three men on board could do nothing to guide the hand of fate. The fuel tanks ruptured, spewing out petrol liberally, which miraculously did not ignite, and as soon as the battered aircraft slithered to a halt, the uninjured crew scrambled out and sprinted away from the immediate area with alacrity. The incident was all over in a handful of hair-raising seconds. The other four pressed on to the Ruhr to find swathes of cloud all but scuppering their chances of bombing their targets with any degree of accuracy. Duisburg and Krefeld were hit as best they could but Sgt Garrioch could not locate his target. Flying as low as he dared, the pilot spotted a large building north-west of Cologne that was showing a few lights. Reckoning he would not find anything better and keeping his eyes glued to the spot, he went in to attack. His bombs were observed to explode on and all around the structure, whatever it might have been; the light bomber then scooted off home safely.

The Blenheims of 18 Squadron were also over Germany and as Fg Off Douch groped his way to the marshalling yards at Hamm, he could find little polite to say about the flying conditions. Cruising high above the plateau of cloud in clear, moonlit air, he warned his crew to keep an eye out for night fighters, which were now found regularly over frequently visited targets. Following the instructions given by the observer, Sgt Parr, Douch began a gradual descent through the clouds towards the estimated location of the target. With his eyes firmly fixed on the unwinding altimeter, Sgts Parr and Barrett peered out into the murk enveloping them, scanning all around for any sign of flak, fire or the ground. Douch was down to just 1,000ft before the Blenheim poked its nose out of the cloud, leaving scant seconds as a margin of error. The rain lashing the aircraft did little to help things and Parr had a terrible job attempting to match what he could see of the ground flashing by with the map in front of him. Suddenly, Barrett reported that a deadly layer of ice was rapidly forming all over the surfaces and estimated it to already be a half an inch thick on his turret. Almost simultaneously, Parr identified a railway line and called for Douch to turn right to follow it. He did so only to discover that there was nothing he could do to stop the Blenheim from going into a steeper and steeper turn, eventually flipping right over and heading earthwards with only a few seconds air time beneath them. Just as suddenly, the controls became responsive as the ice broke off and the Blenheim lurched back on to an even keel. With loose objects flying around the interior of the aircraft, Douch made a gentle climb to gain vital height but ran straight back into ice-bearing cloud, which reduced visibility to nil as it latched on to his windscreen. The aircraft alternately sank and rose as it became coated with and then shed its white, lethal blanket. It took quite some time before the aircraft broke out into the clear air above the cloud and when it did Douch decided to call it a day and headed home, his bomb load intact.

No. 110 Squadron was operating closer to home, harassing the Luftwaffe airfields in northern France. Plt Off Bennett was operating in the Lille–Douai area and was becoming increasingly irritated by the thick belt of cloud shielding the ground below. Realising that to attack a target as small as an airfield effectively he had to be able to see it, he began a cautious descent though the murk. It was not long before ice began to smother the aircraft, rapidly increasing its rate of descent. Then, reaching warmer air, chunks of it began to break off and slam into the fuselage, each lump making an unnerving bang commensurate with its size. By 1,500ft, the Blenheim was cloud-free but being pelted by torrential rain as it trundled over the dark French countryside. Ahead of them, pinpricks of light came into view through the rain-splattered windscreen and bit by bit transformed themselves into a fully illuminated and active airfield; those in the control room had clearly mistaken the intruder as a friendly aircraft on a routine approach. Several large aircraft, each with full navigation lights shining, were in the circuit to land; it was an ideal position for the Blenheim crew to be in. In his turret Sgt Henry was just lining up on a four-engined aircraft, perhaps a Ju 90 or Fw 200 Condor, when the navigator released part of the bomb load prematurely, missing the airfield entirely. Immediately, the airfield doused its lights, swiftly followed by the aircraft and darkness once more reigned supreme, even more so because of the deleterious effect of the lights on their night vision. To cap it all, light flak began to be hurled in their direction. The golden opportunity had been squandered and it was a very disgruntled crew that spent some time scouring the area for another suitable target for the rest of their bombs before heading for home, ruefully pondering what might have been.

Other types were busy putting in all manner of attacks. No. 61 Squadron's Hampdens were ordered to lay mines in Artichoke, the code name for the area off Lorient, an area now well defended by shore AA batteries and roving flak ships. Stan Harrison selected a longer route, staying out at sea and approaching from the north-west rather than passing over the Brittany peninsular and risk blundering into the defences around Brest. It was a wise decision as his sortie would be completed without interference but, on his return flight, still looking for a suitable recipient for his pair of 250lb bombs, he was momentarily tempted to make a swift pass over the docks in Brest. A grandstand view of the defences opening up on someone who was doing just that soon changed his mind and he opted for a quiet flight back to Lincolnshire after all, easily persuading himself he might find a target somewhere else. The other Hampdens also maintained a naval theme, with 49 Squadron assigned the sprawling dockyards in Hamburg as their target. By the time they left, there were several large and distinct fires blazing and spreading across the area. The Hampdens escaped unscathed but ran into a deadly and increasingly common problem on return – intruders. Plt Off Green was over Lincolnshire at 01.40 when his aircraft was suddenly raked by accurate fire from an unseen assailant; considerable damage was caused in those few seconds, most importantly to the tyres, but Green was able to carry out a emergency landing safely on the airfield shortly afterwards. Plt Off J.R. Bufton was not so fortunate. Returning a little earlier at 00.30 hours, his Hampden was over the coast when it came under attack from Lt Volker of 2/NJG2. This brief encounter brought the Hampden down into the sea barely 800 yards off Skegness; all on board were lost, although three bodies were recovered some time later.

The boot was sometimes on the other foot. Sgt Bovingdon had taken his 51 Squadron Whitley all the way to Gelsenkirchen to attack the large oil plant only to discover that he could not find a damned thing because of the ten-tenths cloud. Heading back home after his fruitless search, he was still bloody-mindedly on the lookout for something worth bombing and decided to try his luck at Schiphol airfield, which was more or less on his path home. Miraculously, the cloud began to break up and at 04.35 he passed over the blustery airfield, releasing five 250lb and two 500lb bombs in one stick. A half a dozen aircraft could be discerned, some with full navigation lights on ready for take-off; one, identified as an Me 109, was destroyed by a nearby bomb burst and the rest of the bombs were seen to explode within the boundary fence. At once, but already too late, the searchlights and AA kicked in, lighting up the sky well behind the bomber, which was already pushing out over the North Sea.

Other aircraft headed further afield to the giant Škoda works in Pilsen, Czechoslovakia. As the press reported, 'The onslaught on the giant Škoda works is the first and shows once more that distance is no object to the British air arm.' Perhaps by a fortuitous coincidence, it was the twenty-second anniversary of the founding of that state and an opportune moment to demonstrate the unshakeable resolve and determination of the British government to prosecute the war as vigorously as possible. A massive works, said to employ 50,000 workers, it was now turning out vehicles and weaponry of all types for its new German masters. It was a very long haul indeed for the crews, a round trip of 1,500 miles, most of it in hostile airspace. As if that was not bad enough, the weather conditions were poor and worsened as the target area came up on the horizon. Having got that far, many of the crews set to finding the works with a bloody-minded determination, fully cognisant of the risk they ran for each minute spent searching. Eventually their persistence was rewarded and a couple of crews managed to pick out the vast industrial complex against the snow-covered ground and released a series of flares. The other crews trundling steadily through the sky turned towards the area and released their loads, with several making multiple passes to ensure as accurate an attack as possible. A number of fires were observed taking hold and the red–orange glow was reassuringly visible to the crews from some distance away. Set for essential economic cruising, the bombers embarked upon their long homeward leg, each crew constantly calculating and recalculating the distance to fuel remaining ratio. For once, luck was with them and all the aircraft made it home safely, though in most cases by the slenderest of margins. The message sent out to the enemy was as stark as it was clear; Bomber Command intended to carry the fight to the enemy to the utmost of its ability.

Cloud remained the order of the day as the new working week got under way. The Blenheims were set to work over the North Sea as usual and several made good use of the patchy cloud cover to put in attacks on the Channel ports, with one executing a highly effective surprise pass over Berck-sur-mer airfield. The light bomber squadrons formed a significant component of the ninety-plus force launched to cause destruction and dislocation to targets ranging throughout Germany, Holland and Belgium. The benefits of concentration were still not recognised. In fact, the Blenheims did not fare well that night, with the Watton-based 105 Squadron losing two aircraft and all six crewmen. The unlucky pair had taken off just five minutes apart around 18.30 hours with Sqn Ldr Granum bound for the oil plant at Homburg and Plt Off I. Prosser for the marshalling yards at Ehrang. Prosser was part of a three aircraft strike force that diverted to a similar alternative target in Koblenz when they encountered an impenetrable sheet of cloud stretching over the target area. It is presumed he completed the attack before heading for home; for reasons unknown, the Blenheim came to ground at Cranmer Hall in Norfolk, not too far from RAF Bircham Newton. Sgt A.F. Dallas, a New Zealander, survived the impact but died of his extensive injuries in hospital. Sqn Ldr Granum had been leading an assault trio as B Flight commander. A man of considerable standing and experience, he had been with 105 since its time in France, what seemed like a half a lifetime ago. In the previous eight weeks, he had completed a dozen operational sorties and, the official records states, 'had exhibited a high degree of dash and initiative'. His WopAg Sgt Greenwood was another Battle of France veteran and such losses of old hands always hit hard and were keenly felt. They disappeared without trace, experienced or not, alongside a relative newcomer, observer Plt Off N.A. Knight. Less than forty-eight hours later, the squadron was notified that it was to leave Watton and transfer to RAF Swanton Morley, a new station near East Dereham.

The main thrust of the night was directed towards the north German ports, Bremen and Hamburg, and there were further losses. Whitley P5082 from 102 Squadron left Linton for Bremen shortly before 19.00 hours with Flt Lt R. Barnwell at the controls. All went smoothly and a signal was received from the aircraft confirming a successful attack but the next one was an emergency signal, giving the bomber's position as 20 miles east of Aberdeen, well to the north of its expected flightpath. No trace of the aircraft was found. The other crews returned safely but it had been a hard night. They had watched with growing dismay as the cloud attained ten-tenths status as they flew east, stretching unbroken right up to 8,000ft. Within thirty minutes' flying time of the ports, however, it broke up rapidly, enabling the crews to bomb from a higher and therefore slightly safer altitude than normal, in some cases from 16,000ft. Even so, the reception they got was vicious and several aircraft sustained flak damage. The destruction wrought was greatest, though by no means severe, in Hamburg, with fires and explosions observed in all the dock areas.

High cloud dominated the sky the next morning, spreading like an off-white bedsheet for hundreds of miles eastwards from the mid-Atlantic. A half a dozen Blenheims carried out the customary sweep of the North Sea but only a single crew was sent out on an overtly offensive sortie to attack Rotterdam. The crew followed their orders to the letter but were not able to see the fruits of their perilous labour. As dusk fell, another half a dozen set out to carry out a new series of spoiling attacks intended to disrupt the increasingly frequent and effective Luftwaffe intruder sorties; four busy airfields were selected, Dieppe, Giessen, Bercq and Antwerp, where a direct hit on a hangar was observed. Whether it made an appreciable difference is a matter of conjecture as the Luftwaffe was certainly out in force over the south-east and Midlands for much of the night but at the very least, such attacks, though small scale, can have done little for the morale of the increasingly weary German airmen who had now been in the vanguard of the German war machine for several months.

Again, on a smaller but gradually expanding scale, the ordinary citizens of the Third Reich were beginning to feel the pinch. Just shy of 100 British bombers were overhead, ranging right across the country, searching for targets in the northern ports, Ruhr and Berlin. No. 18 Squadron's Blenheims paid a visit to the 'Happy Valley', which was already carving out a reputation as an area protected by fearsome defences. The sortie would take a little under four hours if all went well, although of the key railway yards at Krefeld there was precious little sign amid the cloud, industrial smog and blinding searchlights and vivid flak bursts. No. 15 Squadron contributed seven Blenheims to the attack on an oil refinery in Hamburg where the cloud was less prevalent but the protective shield of dense haze was not. The frustrated crews released flare after flare in the hope of sighting the target below; one crew reported no fewer than ten burning at one point. Several crews made the decision to do the best they could and released their loads on a best estimate of the location and at least had the satisfaction of seeing a dull red and orange glow filtering up through the murk.

The Whitley force was sent into battle in penny packets. Plt Off Richard Pinkham of 77 Squadron was on his eighteenth sortie bound for Magdeburg, though it might just as well have been the North Pole for all he saw of the ground, let alone the city or his target. The weather was atrocious, with dense cloud, electrical storms, snow squalls and icing presenting themselves as potentially lethal obstacles along the rocky flightpath to the city. Even the flak had to fire blind as the searchlights failed miserably to pierce the murk. Bomb loads were dropped at ETA and after four hours in the air, there was no real way of ascertaining exactly where they fell to earth. Plt Off G. Franklin of 78 Squadron failed to locate his primary or secondary targets, eventually releasing his load in a single stick over what was tentatively identified as an airfield between Cologne and Dusseldorf. Sgt A.J. Mott resorted to his second target, the oil plant at Sterkrade, but was so uncertain of his position that he released only a couple of his bombs in case he should come across a better target on his way back; the harbour in Ostend ended up with the winning ticket and several fires were left burning in Mott's wake. Plt Off Harriott could not see any results of his efforts over Merseburg, nor Plt Off J.R. Deny over the Dortmund–Ems canal, nor Sgt W.C. Wilson over Osnabrück, nor Plt Off M.L. Stedman over Texel, nor Flt Lt D.S. Robertson over Nordhausen, nor Plt Off W. Gasquoine over Leipzig. Only four of the thirty Hampdens and Wellingtons bound for Berlin actually located and attacked the city. The tortuous flight endured by Plt Off C.J.R. Walker and his 50 Squadron crew is not untypical. The bomber lifted off the runway at RAF Lindholme at 17.56 bound for the Danzigerstrasse gas works in Berlin. Walker quickly encountered the rotten and worsening weather conditions and a severe snowstorm completely disorientated the crew about a half an hour's flying time short of the city. There was little to do but push through the storm and once clear Walker spent some time cruising around as all on board searched for some concrete evidence of the aircraft's position. When none was forthcoming and, mindful of the fuel situation, Walker reluctantly decided to give up and asked for a course for home. A general heading west was the best that could be provided so he followed that, encountering further storms and ice-laden clouds on his way. It was not until well after 04.00 hours that they staggered over the English coast but exactly where they were not sure. By 04.30 the fuel situation was critical and with ice forming on all of the surfaces, Walker gave the order for his crew to jump to safety, with himself being the last man out. They and the aircraft came down in open country, not too far from RAF Linton-on-Ouse.

Others did not fare even this well in the dangerous conditions prevalent over Britain that night. Flt Lt K.T.A. Harvey's Newmarket-based 99 Squadron Wellington had also endured the long and arduous flight to Berlin only to become equally disorientated and lost upon its return. More than 200 miles off track to the north, the Wellington smacked straight into the unseen high ground near Otterburn in Northumberland, killing one airman. Plt Off M.E. Sharp and his crew at least had the advantage of being well supported by the rescue services when their 51 Squadron Whitley abruptly came into contact with Mother Earth. With almost ten hours on the clock, there was little option for the pilot to get the aircraft down as soon as he could, in spite of the squally conditions. Caught by a particularly strong and sudden crosswind as it approached the exposed runway at RAF Dishforth, the Whitley lurched over, collided with the ground and ploughed into a field in spectacular fashion; Sgt J.R. Brown lost his life and the other crewmen sustained injuries. Perhaps the luckiest escape of the night belonged to a 10 Squadron crew led by Plt Off W.E. Peers. It had left the runway at RAF Leeming a little earlier than some at 16.58, bound for the oft-hit naval harbour and docks at Wilhelmshaven. The attack itself fared little better than many others that night and an accurate pinpoint strike was out of the question in the atrocious conditions. On their return to the rainy and stormy English airspace, the wireless operator picked up a message warning the crews of the presence of enemy intruders in the vicinity and advising them to hold off to the north-west. After about twenty anxious and interminable minutes, the very weary and impatient crew received the all clear signal and set course for Leeming. Within seconds there was a violent bang that shook the whole aircraft. Glancing quickly at the altimeter, which showed a steady 2,000ft plus, Peers was heard to say that the bomber must have struck a balloon cable before his voice was lost beneath the deafening tearing and shrieking sound of metal tortured by a tremendously powerful impact. Incredibly, in the pitch darkness, the five young men on board, groped and crawled their way out of the twisted wreckage, emerging into steady, torrential rain that reduced visibility to practically nil. The only injuries of any seriousness, a broken wrist and badly cut left arm, were sustained by gunner Sgt George Dove, ironically on his thirty-first and final operation before being screened. Convinced that an outbreak of fire was unlikely and distinctly unimpressed by the rotten weather, the five men clambered back into the wreckage and eked out the contents of an unbroken flask of coffee until the grey light of dawn began to reveal their whereabouts. Not that there was much to be seen. They had come to rest on the edge of a precipice with an 80ft drop, in the middle of nowhere in the high Pennines on the bleak and inhospitable Co. Durham, Cumberland and Northumberland borders. A few more feet might well have spelled disaster rather than uncomfortable inconvenience. It was a long walk back to civilisation. Two more aircraft, a Hampden from 106 Squadron on a mining sortie to the Baltic and a Blenheim from 144 Squadron carrying out an attack on Le Havre, were lost without trace that night, making it an expensive night for the Command; six aircraft lost with precious little to show for it.

As the month headed inexorably towards its close, the weather clamped down once again, as if confirming the end of the ancient campaigning season. It was now beyond doubt that there would be no invasion in 1940 and the Blenheim sea sweeps were called off for the winter. Not that the crews were kept idle; for most, night operations beckoned but, for some, hit-and-run nuisance raids along the enemy coast became the staple diet. Amid the persistent rain and low cloud, six Blenheims roared towards the Normandy coast at low level and some 20 miles off Cherbourg, one surprised several E-boats searching for unwary Channel traffic. Immediately, the Blenheim went into the attack, hurtling through the maelstrom of light flak hosing up towards it. The brief encounter proved indecisive with neither side knowingly scoring any hits. Another roving Blenheim spotted a small, three-ship convoy off Barfleur, making the most of the poor visibility and conditions; again, the outcome was inconclusive. The remainder put in attacks on Cherbourg harbour, now a crucial and heavily defended enemy-occupied port, leaving fires raging in their wake.

Although the rotten weather put paid to most of the Command's nocturnal sorties, several more Blenheims were among the twenty-eight aircraft that did manage to mount operations that night. The efforts of 2 and 3 Groups were fairly evenly split between German targets, such as Duisburg and Emden, and the Channel ports. Not that the prevailing wet and cloudy conditions aided the crews much; the wonder was that they achieved anything and returned, although a 101 Squadron crashed a few miles north of Scunthorpe for reasons unknown, killing all on board. No. 37 Squadron's Wellingtons encountered dreadful conditions over Emden, where the cloud base was barely 1,000ft. Plt Off Clark was dawdling along at 110mph at 11,000ft, scouring the dark clouds beneath for any break that would give him the chance of establishing his location, when he decided that he must be somewhere near his target area and turned around to continue his search. A few seconds later, his apparent tranquil isolation was shattered by a startlingly close shell burst that flipped the aircraft up and over, then nose down earthwards. Stunned by the sudden change of circumstances, Clark wrestled with the unresponsive controls as the Wellington plunged headlong through the inky, black sky. The bomber dropped more than a mile before the sweating pilot managed to regain a semblance of control and put the aircraft back on an even keel. Taking stock and unaware of what, if any, damage had been sustained, Clark decided to jettison his bomb load some way south of where he thought the target area was and set course for Hemswell, landing there without further incident.

A total of eighteen Wellingtons, equally divided, turned their attentions to the much closer targets of Antwerp and Flushing. These short incursions into heavily-defended hostile airspace were not without their dangers. An unnamed tail gunner gave an account of one such sortie to the press on his return. Isolated from the rest of the crew, he had seen little but cloud from his rain-splattered turret since leaving the ground, even though his pilot had tried to climb above the worst of it. Suddenly, the rain turned to hail and:

Whack! Whack! Whack! I knew what it was, ice flying off the airscrews and rattling down on the fuselage. Something flickered close to us. Were we over the target with flak coming up at us already? It flickered again and again. 'I don't like lightning,' I heard somebody say at the front. Then a strange thing happened. From the barrels of my four guns, little sparks began to shoot backwards with a thin, dry, crackling noise. Lightning shimmered in front and behind us and thunder bellowed all around. Our flying became very bumpy. We rose and fell at incredible speeds. I lurched about my turret, holding on tightly, wondering whether the next bump would knock me out of the roof. All the time, those flickering sparks shot out of my guns. The rain flicking off from the tail planes carried blue flames away with it, little blue flames of electricity blowing behind us. Then came one enormous bump when we must have dropped 500ft, then a pause. Then a purple flash filled the whole of my turret and there was a deafening report. I found myself completely blind. The aircraft rocked crazily. Not a sound came from those in the front. After a bit, light filtered back into my eyes; I was not blind after all. What was more, we were out of those clouds and my guns had stopped firing off sparks. I could see that their several thousand cartridges had not gone off in my face as I had suspected. At last a voice came to me, bringing me but little comfort. 'The plane has been struck by lightning,' the captain said, 'Have your parachute ready.' I took once glance at the cold sea gleaming below, opened the turret doors and reached for my parachute.

As it turned out, the anonymous gunner did not need it but it had been a terrifying ordeal and one that underlined the inherent dangers of flying in the face of the hostile forces of nature.

A pilot identified only as a New Zealander provided a lively account for the press of flying in the face of the hostile forces of Germany. Tasked to attack Flushing, his aircraft broke through the heavy cloud just south of the harbour but spent a further twenty minutes cruising up and down the coastline, attempting to identify the target positively through the thick murk beneath. Once this had been achieved, he intended to make a gliding attack across the docks and began his approach towards an ominously silent target area. Suddenly, the gloom was rent by countless dazzling and multi-coloured explosions and brilliantly white searchlight beams. 'Goodnight, nurse,' was the pilot's understated and laconic response and he pushed the nose down to gain speed:

The inside of the aircraft was reeking of cordite. Nobody said anything. Frankly, I thought we were not going to get out of it and I think the rest of them thought that too. I remember it flashing across my mind that if they did bring us down, the aircraft would make a pretty good bomb load to land on them – I don't mean anything heroic but even if it all was up, we were going to hit the docks anyway. The searchlights were holding us all the time. I just kept my eyes on the instruments and on the docks. If one had looked around, one would have been blinded. As we went over, the bomb aimer made certain all the bombs had gone. We dropped them and they landed right in the centre of the dock. Immediately, we were thrown up to 600ft. There were tremendous explosions. The second pilot was standing beside me. His knees buckled underneath him and he went down on the floor. I was just concentrating on keeping the aircraft in the air and to get away. More or less automatically, I pushed the nose down, the throttles forward and hoped for the best. There was a curtain of fire on all sides. We went through. I bet the Germans thought they'd got one aircraft down alright. The ships opened fire on us as well as the guns on the shore. They seemed to have a ring of flak ships around the harbour and by this time, I was fighting with the stick. We sent out an SOS that we were likely to be coming down as I knew we had been hit. I had felt the shells smack into the plane and I couldn't hold the aircraft properly. We said we would have a crack at getting home and we told them by wireless. I told the second pilot to have a look at all the control cables and keep an eye on the petrol gauges to see that the petrol tanks weren't leaking. The front gunner came out of his turret to operate the floatation gear in case we had to land on water. At 15–20 miles out, we could still see the flashes of explosions from the docks. Frankly, I never thought we'd make home. The aircraft was kicking like a bucking bronco. There were heavy clouds and I was flying on instruments most of the time. My arms were aching and seemed tied up in knots from the strain of holding the aircraft. Finally, we got home and I landed safely.

As in so many cases, it could so easily have turned out differently. The young men from 2 and 3 Groups went through the usual debriefing process and wearily made their way through the damp night to their quarters and bed.

Within a couple of hours, the airfields were humming with life and activity as the final day of October dawned, misty, dull and damp. Even in the unpleasant and unfavourable conditions, eleven Blenheims were made ready for sorties along the Channel coast and as far away as Duisburg. Although all made it into the air, only two judged it worthwhile to carry on with their attacks, one hitting the railway yards at Soesterberg and the other two E-boats, which it chanced upon near the mouth of the River Somme; no positive results could be seen from these attacks. When the crews landed in dribs and drabs, shut down their engines, clambered stiffly out of their cramped aircraft, stretched their legs on the damp grass and gulped in the cool, clear air, they were unaware that these were the last operational sorties completed by Bomber Command during the officially designated Battle of Britain. For, as the daylight raids mounted by the Luftwaffe continued to dwindle and fade like winter light, 31 October was later deemed to be the end of the most vital battle in Britain's long line of battles. Although it was obvious to all in Fighter Command that the campaign was entering a new and less frenetic phase, for those in Bomber Command the relentless grind continued seamlessly, without pause or respite, day after day, night after night. It would do so for another four and a half years.

Chapter 6

The Many

The summer of 1940 lies buried deep in the British psyche, even more than seventy years on. The events of those tumultuous months have shaped how many British people define themselves and their country. The heroism of The Few is inextricably linked to momentous days when the outcome of the war and the very existence of Britain and her Empire hung in the balance. Their finest hour is our finest hour, a reflected glory still worthy of celebration. Churchill, who had an uncanny knack for coming up with a cracking phrase, undoubtedly hit the nail on the head with the words, 'Never in the field of human conflict was so much owed by so many to so few.' The airmen of Fighter Command deserve their fame for they changed the course of the war and enabled Britain to fight on undefeated.

However, 'The Many' were there too. Air warfare was still in its infancy when the concept of a strategic air offensive was devised. A bold and innovative scheme, originating as a response to the static slaughter of the trenches, it aimed to weaken an opponent's capacity and will to fight by striking far beyond the battle line. For those with experience of the

1914–18 war, it had much to recommend it. Largely untested at the end of the war, this modern concept became a mantra of the inter-war RAF and the shadow of the bomber loomed large over servicemen, politicians and the ordinary man in the street. This annihilating rapier of a weapon would transform the face of warfare in the modern, industrial and technological age. Bomber Command, therefore, was intended to be placed right at the heart of Britain's armoury, able to strike offensively with devastating power at a distant enemy, thereby preventing or certainly reducing any similar assault upon this country. It became an accepted fact that the bomber would always get through, making the strategic offensive the cornerstone of Britain's defence. In many ways, Fighter Command was a late adjunct to Britain's long-held defence policy, an auxiliary and secondary defence against direct attack. However, like many new policies, the scheme would gobble up copious amounts of scarce funding and required considerable modification and adjustment in the face of actual circumstances.

Expectation, fuelled and heightened by service self-interest, was high and, put simply, well beyond the capacity of Bomber Command to deliver. The inter-war years were ones of parsimony in military expenditure and though bomber aircraft development fared slightly better than other areas, it hardly prospered, leaving capability far adrift of theory. Nor was there significant investment in terms of personnel training and new technology; airborne navigation, for example, remained rudimentary, an obvious and serious problem that was compounded when the failure of gunnery and the demise of the heavy cross-fire bomber self-protection theories in late 1939 compelled the termination of most operations in daylight. Even basic bombing practice was limited, neglected and nearly always confined to daylight, and then, generally, only on days where conditions were nigh-on perfect. Group Captain 'Hamish' Mahaddie, later a stalwart of the Pathfinder Force, summed it up years later, 'We started with a very small air force of quite experienced people – but experienced in the basic flying sense, not to any degree in wartime flying. So, we had to learn from the very first day and this was a very expensive business in aircrew and aircraft.'

Even a cursory glance through the preceding pages will reveal the single, dominating problem facing the aircrews in the execution of a strategic air offensive – the weather; and that, in the summer of 1940, contrary to popular myth, it was not all blue sky and sunshine. Sir Arthur Harris, later AOC Bomber Command, put it bluntly:

> People talk a lot about picking out targets and bombing them, including small targets – in the European climate? I've come to the conclusion that people who say that sort of thing not only have never been outside but they've never looked out of a window … how many occasions, looking out of a window or walking out in a garden, could you see up to 18,000–20,000ft? On how many occasions can you guarantee that you could see down through it 400–500 miles away at the other end of Europe? That was the situation – there was no possibility of hitting industrial targets consistently until we'd got the navigational, electronic aids that would show these targets up in the dark or through clouds.

The first year of the war, particularly from April 1940, did not go well for Britain, and Bomber Command performed no better and no worse than most of the other branches of the armed forces. Experience is a helpful but often brutal teacher. Doubts about the effectiveness of Bomber Command and its much-vaunted strategic air offensive, a lynchpin of Britain's offensive and defensive planning, surfaced early in the war, rumbled on through the summer of 1940 and came to a head the following winter. By October 1940, Sir Richard Peirse estimated that, in normal conditions on short-range operations, one crew in three managed to attack the primary target and on longer-range operations, this fell to one in five. The Butt Report of August 1941, which reviewed a large number of operational reports, summaries and photographic evidence, where available, came to some damning conclusions; of all the aircraft recorded as having attacked the primary target, only a third were within 5 miles of it. There were many factors involved in such a calculation, the weather conditions, the efficacy of the enemy's defences, the range and location of the target to highlight but a few. Over the Channel ports, he raised this total to two-thirds, while over the Ruhr, where industrial haze was prevalent and defences formidable, it fell to just a tenth. In good conditions and with the light of the moon, Butt estimated two-thirds of crews were within the 5 miles boundary but without the bounty of nature, the figure was just one fifteenth. The evidence that Butt relied on was, as was admitted, not always secure but as Churchill told Sir Charles Portal, Chief of Air Staff, it was 'a very serious paper and seems to require your most urgent attention'.

It was not, however, as completely at odds with the reports emanating from the squadrons as is often portrayed. An equally cursory glance at the preceding pages will reveal crew after crew reporting immense difficulties in locating, let alone hitting, target areas and their strenuous efforts to do so. The crews and all those involved were very much aware of the huge challenges facing them and, perhaps, this makes their determination to overcome them all the more impressive and creditable.

Bomber Command's campaign in the summer of 1940 has often been entirely overlooked, dismissed cursorily or compared unfavourably with that waged by the Luftwaffe. There is no doubt that the Luftwaffe had several crucial advantages; shorter ranges, particularly when targeting London, a greater understanding and application of the concept of concentration and more effective navigational technology stand out. Although it did have a number of spectacularly destructive and deadly successes, such as the raid on Coventry in November 1940, it also had many occasions when the raids were far from effective. Certainly, the general public believed that the bombing was not highly precise but was general and indiscriminate. The Luftwaffe too greatly underestimated the immense force required to break or seriously hamper the war effort of a major industrial power. It was several months before the penny dropped at Bomber Command and calls were made for a colossal force of 4,000 heavy bombers to do the job properly. Nevertheless, Bomber Command's achievements were by no means inconsiderable and, given the timing of them, proved crucial to the defence of Great Britain and its ability to carry on the war. For Churchill, this sole, major offensive arm was a godsend. Pugnacious by character, he knew very well the absolute importance of not only 'taking it' but also 'dishing it out', both for his domestic and global audiences. In the same months as he laid the foundations of the Special Operations Executive and the Commandos, he lost no opportunity to laud the role of Bomber Command in his major speeches, though these sections are often edited out nowadays. As part of his 'Finest Hour' speech of 18 June, he was keen to warn the public of the bombardment to come and to ameliorate the unpalatable truth with the promise that it would be no better for its German counterpart, 'There remains the danger of bombing attacks,' he began in his characteristic growl, 'which will certainly be made very soon upon us by the bomber forces of the enemy. It is true that the German bomber force is superior in numbers to ours but we have a very large bomber force also which we shall use to strike at military targets in Germany without intermission.' A couple of months later, that promised onslaught was under way and in his state of the war speech delivered on 20 August in the House of Commons, but with one eye over the Atlantic, he boldly stated:

> I have no hesitation that this process of bombing the military industries and communications of Germany and air bases and storage depots, from which we are attacked, which will continue upon an ever increasing scale until the end of the war and may in another year or two attain dimensions hitherto undreamed of, assures me of the surest, if not the shortest, of all roads to victory.

In this, one of the most famous speeches in British history, delivered at a particularly crucial period of the Battle, Churchill went out of his way to emphasise the importance of the air war and the critical role of the RAF. History and the public consciousness have bestowed immortality upon one pithy and succinct sentence in particular – 'Never in the field of human conflict was so much owed by so many to so few.' It is inextricably linked to the immensely courageous young pilots of Fighter Command who were fighting so magnificently day after day to deny the Luftwaffe control of the sky over Britain. The speech, however, continued:

> All hearts go out to the fighter pilots whose brilliant actions we see with our own eyes day after day but we must never forget that all the time, night after night, month after month, our bomber squadrons travel far into Germany, find their target in the darkness by the highest navigational skill, aim their attacks, often under the heaviest fire, often at serious loss, with deliberate careful precision and inflict shattering blows upon the whole of the technical and war making structure of the Nazi power.

Fighter Command is not mentioned again but the public recognition of Bomber Command continues:

> On no part of the Royal Air Force does the weight of the war fall more heavily than on the daylight bombers who will play an invaluable part in the case of invasion and whose unflinching zeal it has been necessary in the meantime on numerous occasions to restrain ... Even if the Nazi legions stood triumphant on the Black Sea or, indeed, upon the Caspian, even if Hitler were at the gates of India, it would profit him nothing if at the same time the entire economic and apparatus of German war power lay shattered and pulverised at home.

While this does not dull the lustre of The Few, it does demonstrate the level of faith and expectation placed in their comrades in the bombers and that its dual offensive and defensive role was widely understood and reported. Indeed, at the beginning of September, Churchill took the unusual step of making public a note from the War Cabinet to Bomber Command in which he consciously echoes his earlier speech, concluding, 'It is very satisfactory that so many tons of British bombs have been discharged with such precision in difficult circumstances and at such great distances and that so many military objectives in Germany and Italy have been so sharply smitten.' A month later, on 8 October, once more addressing the House of Commons, Churchill described in moving terms the humbling kindness with which he had been greeted by ordinary men and women who lived in the bombed-out areas, 'On every side,' he recounted, 'there is a cry "We can take it" but there is also a "Give it them back!" ... Our object must be to inflict the maximum harm on the war-making capacity of the enemy. That is the only object that we shall pursue.' If it was good enough for Churchill, most people reasoned, it was good enough for them.

The Secretary of State for War, Sir Anthony Eden, later recalled:

Winston rightly called it our finest hour and it was true but it was also our grimmest hour, without question. And there must have been moments for all of us – there certainly was in my mind – when I did not see how we were going to find a way through, just couldn't see it. There were moments when I thought the only thing that might be left for us to do would be to take a German with us into the other world.

The need for that was all too apparent and there were few in Britain that summer who did not expect an invasion. The preparation for it was an open secret around the world, reported in the press and discussed at dinner tables around the globe; it was a question of when, not if. Whatever the difficulties were or the outcome might have been, endlessly debated by historians, one thing stands clear: the immense scale of the preparations that were made. Moreover, they were not of the type made without specific and determined intent. As Hitler's Chief of Operations, General Jodl, wrote in August 1940, 'It is imperative that no matter what might happen, the operation does not fail.' The prestige of the Nazi regime, already sky high, was riding on it. Within the context of 1940, following the occupation of Norway, Holland, Denmark, Belgium and France with a matter of weeks, the successful invasion of Britain was all but inevitable and any and all problems or doubts would simply be washed aside by an unstoppable wave of martial prowess and public euphoria.

While The Few denied vital air supremacy to the Luftwaffe over the invasion area by day, The Many denied the Kriegsmarine the opportunity to concentrate and marshal the invasion fleet and forces. Naval Headquarters Group West reported to Berlin on 16 September, for example, 'The RAF are still by no means defeated; on the contrary, they are showing increasing activity in their attacks on the Channel ports and in their mounting interference with assembly movements.' The following day, a further signal added:

> The very severe bombing together with the bombardment by naval guns across the Channel makes it necessary to disperse the naval and transport vessels already concentrated on the Channel and to stop further movement of shipping to the invasion ports. Otherwise, with energetic enemy action, such casualties will occur in the course of time that the execution of the operation on the scale previously envisaged will in any case be problematic.

It is generally estimated that Bomber Command destroyed about 12 per cent of the invasion fleet, a significant but not overly substantial amount of shipping. The key point is that the Command showed no sign of letting up in its efforts. It was clear that the Luftwaffe had no means of preventing or thwarting such attacks and that such a steady rate of attrition would inevitably prove fatal to the plan. Little by little, right the way through the summer, autumn and into the winter, Bomber Command kept up the pressure and by an aerial blockade of sorts, denied full and effective use of the ports to the enemy. Without secure bases for the marshalling of men, materials and, crucially, the maintenance of supply to the invasion force, there could be no invasion.

The conduct of the strategic air offensive in the summer of 1940 was not without its brighter spots, even though its successes were fewer and further between than anticipated. It focused, in the main, upon targets that would reduce the offensive capacity of the enemy, thereby supporting in very real terms the defence of Great Britain: oil production and storage, shipping naval and merchant, transportation and the aircraft industry. They were wise choices and a couple of years later, when technology, tactics and sheer scale more or less matched aspiration and intention, they remained at the heart of the offensive that did much to wreck the German war machine and contain and undermine its capacity to wage war effectively. Reports from neutral sources increasingly painted a similar picture of dislocation and disruption, for example, to the rail network. An account emanating from Bucharest told of a traveller having to change fifteen times on a journey from Leipzig to Vienna. The inland waterway system, vital to the German economy and movement of war materials, was also hit; the crucial Dortmund–Ems canal sustained serious damage on several occasions, confirmed by photographic reconnaissance. Normal dockyard activity in many of the Baltic ports suffered too; an eyewitness report from a neutral source in mid-October claimed there were at least five sunken or badly damaged ships in Hamburg harbour and only seven of the seventy-five or so cranes were able to work at full capacity. Sea traffic was undoubtedly disrupted too by the mining campaign, although it is difficult to quantify by exactly how much; at the very least, considerable effort had to be expended to maintain the safety of the shipping lanes into the major harbours.

Industrial production was not without its problems; power stations, gas works and factories did sustain damage and the crews did hit targets on occasions, though there were few spectacular successes. Damage was, for example, caused to the Henschel aircraft works at Schonefeld, the Arado works at Babelsberg, the Daimler-Benz works at Genshagen, the vast Siemensstat complex, the Deutsche Werke in Kiel and the Oderwerke in Stettin. Put bluntly, the weight of bombs dropped on targets, spread across the enormous and still under-mobilised German industrial economy, was way too small to cause anything more significant than localised and temporary inconvenience, but at least that was achieved on many occasions.

Nevertheless, such raids were immensely popular with the hard-pressed general public in Britain. The press was keen to both build up and make use of this bulldog determination to keep fighting and strike back. With the aerial battle overhead approaching its peak, on Tuesday 13 August, the *Daily Mail* had 'Biggest Air Raids of All' as its headline, going on to describe the heaviest German raids of the war so far upon Britain. Its sub headline was a more reassuring and gratifying one 'and WE did this to them'. Such press coverage could have a highly significant impact abroad. The British Purchasing Mission in the USA, for example, had been struggling earlier in the summer to find anyone willing to invest and do business in Britain, then perceived as a sort of failing company, but found doors beginning to open to it as the RAF began to hit Germany, buoyed by headlines such as that in *The New York Times* on that same Tuesday 'Blitzkrieg on Britain: 500 planes raid Britain. RAF hits back at the Reich'. By October, the mood in America had changed sufficiently for Roosevelt to state in an election speech in Dayton, Ohio, 'Our course is clear … We will continue to help those who resist oppression and those who now hold the aggression far from these shores. The men and women of Britain have shown how free people defend what they know is right.' Radio too played its part and throughout the summer the BBC made use of the men and women in the front line to lend additional authority to its accounts and bring the drama of war right into the homes of the civilians, now very much in the front line themselves. One such speaker was Flt Lt J.C. Macintosh, a bomb aimer with operational experience on Hampdens. He vividly recounted an attack on an oil refinery during which the crew endured three separate sweeps under heavy fire while Macintosh methodically scanned the ground below. On the fourth, he continued, 'There it was. The dim outline of an oil refinery, wonderfully camouflaged. It was getting more and more in the centre of the sights. I pressed the button and my stick of bombs went hurtling towards Germany's precious oil. The rear gunner watched the bombs burst and in a very few seconds, those thousands of tons of valuable oil became hundreds of feet of black and acrid smoke.'

Once the ball was rolling, the cries to hit back became increasingly strident. The well-known detective writer Dorothy L. Sayers noted in a piece in *The Daily Telegraph* in August that there was a practice, a worthy practice, whereby newspapers around the Empire had run campaigns to raise money to buy aircraft for the RAF. Building upon Lord Beaverbrook's notional figure of £5,000 to purchase a Spitfire, the readers of *The Gleaner* in Jamaica, for example, had raised the huge sum of £20,000 and those of the *Singapore Strait Times* no less than £25,000. To Sayers, the object of their magnificent fundraising was misguided for 'Defensive attitudes and defeatist mentality be hanged', she wrote, '… there are many good, human sentimental reasons why Hurricanes and Spitfires should have caught the public's imagination [but] we must not, in our excitement, appear unappreciative of the work of Bomber Command. I enclose £5 towards a bomber and feel sure your critical correspondents will subscribe lavishly.' She was right and the money poured in, quickly amassing the £20,000 to 'buy' a bomber. Perhaps the most emotive story of any such donor belongs to Lady Rachel MacRobert. By 1941 she had lost all three of her sons while serving with the RAF, one whilst training, one attacking a German airfield and another on a sortie to search for a bomber crew downed in the chilly waters of the North Sea. The indomitable Lady wrote to the Secretary of State for Air, Sir Archibald Sinclair, asking him to use the enclosed cheque for £25,000 to purchase a Stirling bomber to be known as 'MacRobert's Reply', adding, 'If I had ten sons, I know that they would all have followed the path of duty and may the blows you strike with her bring us nearer to victory.' There were many other heartbroken but proud parents like her, less well-off but equally determined to do their bit, to honour their sons and hit back.

The Home Intelligence Reports for the summer of 1940 compiled by the Ministry of Information logged the opinions prevalent throughout the country on a daily basis. The basic imperative to hit back as well as to take it is a common theme, both in areas directly affected by the Luftwaffe blitz and in those not. A report from Reading on Saturday 14 September, for example, concluded: 'There is a feeling in some quarters that there is too much emphasis placed on damage [in the UK] by press photographers and the attitude that "we can take it", which rather suggests our ability to suffer rather than our power to hit back.' Another from Tunbridge Wells two days earlier noted, 'There is still some grumbling over the fact that the RAF bombers sometimes return from Germany without unloading their bombs'; on the same day, almost 300 miles away in Leeds, a report stated, 'Many people still believe that the civilian population in Germany should be bombed.' Indeed, the public did want Germany to be bombed and they wanted to know all about it too. From Nottingham on Friday 6 September came the message, 'Many people are asking for a quicker and more complete news service of RAF activity. The opinion is expressed in Rutland that we should retaliate for German indiscriminate bombing.' A report a few days earlier in Bristol commented, 'War in the air excludes almost all other topics; there is a strong demand for the bombing of Berlin and offensive action against Italy,' and on the same day from Belfast, 'The extension of the British air offensive over Germany and Italy is welcomed.' As the residents of Birmingham bluntly summed it up on 30 August, 'The bombing of Berlin has caused great satisfaction.'

There was far less satisfaction for this turn of events among Berliners. Berlin was not the first German city to experience the horrors of air attack that summer; that dubious honour fell to Mönchengladbach on 11 May when four civilians died, including one resident British woman. The first raid in August was played down by the regime and, as one American reporter, Fred Oechsner, wrote, 'laughed it off as a fluke'. A few weeks later in October he added, 'What the Nazis had originally tried to laugh off as a joke has now become a serious matter.' Another American reporter, William Shirer, famously wrote, 'The Berliners are stunned. They did not think it could happen. He [Goring] boasted that no enemy planes could ever break through the outer and inner rings of the capital's anti-aircraft defence. The Berlinners are naïve and simple people. They believed him. Their disillusionment today, therefore, is all the greater.' He later added,

'The main effect of a week of constant British night bombing has been to spread great disillusionment among the people here and to sow doubt in their minds.' Initial official tours for neutral journalists to highlight damage done to civilian and cultural aspects of the city's life were quickly cancelled as the air attacks became more frequent and the damage caused more widespread. The raid on 7 October, for example, began early at 22.00 and lasted for several hours. The 200 high explosive bombs and hundreds of incendiaries that fell on the city killed thirty-one, injured ninety-one and caused significant and very obvious damage to the Lehrer and Stettiner stations. With the death toll mounting, though by no means as high as in London, there was no way to keep the lid on the information. An internal report by the SD, the regime's security service, revealed that alarm bells were beginning to ring:

> The attacks on Berlin have aroused considerable interest across the Reich, as people were wholly convinced that not a single aircraft could reach the city centre. The population is thereby reminded of announcements which claimed that enemy aircraft would be unable to attack Berlin. However, as it has recently been shown that it is possible for the English even to linger over the capital and drop their bombs without suffering appreciable losses, the expectations for the capital's defence have clearly not been fulfilled.

Goebbels, an astute observer and manipulator of public opinion who, unusually for a senior member of the Nazi hierarchy, frequently toured the bombed areas of Berlin and other cities, confided in his diary on 26 October, 'Report on morale from the Sicherheitsdienst … things are none too rosy. We absolutely must do more to keep morale high. The continued air raid alerts are making people nervous. We must be careful.'

The effect was out of all proportion to the damage caused. Goebbels noted, 'Late at night the usual air raid warning. Two aircraft scuttle over Berlin. And for that a city of 4½ million people must take to the shelters. Berlin is a tired town.' Worse still for a regime apparently invincible and at the peak of its powers, the view was shared abroad. On 27 September, for example, the Italian Foreign Minister Count Galeazzo Ciano, architect of the Rome–Berlin Axis signed in October 1936, wrote in his diary that the people of Berlin were looking tired and ill, adding, 'Bomb damage is slight, nervousness is very high.'

Nor was the problem confined to Berlin as numerous cities had been attacked over the length and breadth of the large country; Hamburg, Kiel, Wilhelmshaven, Stettin, Cologne, Hamm, Essen, Hanover, Mannheim, Leuna, Osnabrück, Gelsenkirchen, Leipzig and many more. Damage and casualties might well have been light but the British bombers were there, always there, night after night. It was impossible to predict where or when they might strike next. The regime had to be seen to respond to this unexpected and unwelcome turn of events and did so with totalitarian efficiency. Highly effective, if costly, schemes to care for, rehouse and compensate bombed out citizens were rapidly introduced, as were large rapid response damage clearance parties. On 10 October an emergency programme was begun to provide bomb-proof shelters in seventy-nine German cities; by the following summer more than 5 million cubic metres of concrete had been used. The Reichsluftschutzbund was set up to train volunteers to carry out air raid precaution and rescue duties. A blackout was rigorously enforced, with severe penalties for infringement of regulations being introduced. Monstrous and demonic posters appeared everywhere warning 'Der Feind sieht dein licht –Verdunkeln!', which translates as 'The enemy sees the light – blackout!'

On 26 September, in a week that saw Berlin bombed on four consecutive nights, Hitler met with Baldur von Schirach, the Reich Youth Leader, to discuss an evacuation programme for children. The following day, the Kinderlandverschickung (KLV) programme was announced to evacuate 'young people who live in areas which are subject to repeated air alarms … to other areas of the Reich', a tacit admission both of the inability of the regime to defend its urban population and to defeat Britain for some time to come. Not even the instruction to officials to use the phrase 'despatch to the countryside' rather than evacuation could disguise the gravity of the situation and an SD report for 30 September noted, 'that the rumours of evacuation are causing serious and growing disquiet among the population'; Goebbels in his diary agreed, stating that, 'The plan has created enormous discontent.' The plan was to begin on 3 October and by the end of the month over 15,000 had left Berlin, with a further 42,000 leaving the following month as the scheme gathered momentum. By the end of the war, some 5 million children would be involved in the KLV programme. Nor was all of the effort passive.

General Josef Kammhuber was appointed to reorganise and expand German night air defences, which already by the autumn of 1940 deployed 2,600 heavy AA guns, 6,700 medium and light weapons, 2,300 searchlights and 160 aircraft. It was the beginning of a deleterious and draining process to respond to Bomber Command's constant and ever weightier pressure, which would in time significantly blunt Germany's offensive capabilities, skew its war economy and production and lead to its ultimate demise.

The Nazi regime had throughout the 1930s created and skilfully cultivated an aura of grandeur and invincibility. The party had brought about an astonishing transformation of Germany's fortunes and, importantly, national psyche. The events of the first months of the war confirmed beyond all doubt that Germany was everything the Nazi Party had said it was – and more. It was the dominant power on the planet, an unstoppable military force, capable of achieving anything it set its sights upon. The conduct and outcome of the Battle of Britain revealed with stark clarity that reality is not the same as belief, however passionately held. The very fact that Britain, so obviously battered, bloodied and on the point of collapse, could not be beaten into submission and finished off, shattered forever the myth of invincibility upon which the Nazi regime was built. The Nazi leaders had feet of clay too.

The Battle of Britain, like all the other campaigns of 1939–40, took place beyond the borders of the Reich, known to the German public through stringently controlled newsreels, newspapers and radio reports.

The Other Battle of Britain took place over Germany and was known and experienced by the people themselves, immediately, personally and at first hand. Night after night, throughout the summer and autumn of 1940 and into the months and years ahead, the German people, huddled in claustrophobic, dank, overcrowded shelters, emerging into the grey dawn to a charred, changed and uncertain landscape, were reminded of their failure to beat Britain and stand victorious. The presence overhead of the aircraft of Bomber Command was eloquent and increasingly devastating testimony to that failure. It was equally eloquent testimony to the world, especially the United States of America, that Britain remained unbowed and unbeaten, still capable of defending herself and taking the fight to the enemy. The Many deserve to stand shoulder to shoulder with The Few. Their summer should remain forgotten no longer.

Bibliography

Bishop, P., *The Battle of Britain* (London: Quercus, 2010).

Bungay, S., *The Most Dangerous Enemy* (London: Aurum Press, 2009).

Cheshire, L., *Bomber Pilot* (St Albans: Goodall Publications, 1988).

Chorley, W., *Bomber Command Losses* (Leicester: Midland Publishing, 2013).

Clayton, T. & Craig, P., *Finest Hour* (London: Hodder and Stoughton, 1999).

Donnelly, L., *The Whitley Boys* (Worcestershire: Air Research Publications, 1991).

Donnelly, L., *The Other Few* (Worcestershire: Red Kite, 2004).

Gibson, G., *Enemy Coast Ahead* (London: Pan, 1956).

Harris, A., *Bomber Offensive* (London: Frontline Books, 2015).

Hastings, M., *Bomber Command* (London: Pan Military Classics, 2010).

Henry, M., *Air Gunner* (St Albans: Goodall Publications, 1997).

Middlebrook, M. & Everitt, C., *Bomber Command War Diaries* (Leicester: Midland Publishing, 1985).

Neillands, R., *The Bomber War* (London: John Murray, 2004).

Overy, R., *Bomber Command* (London: Collins, 1997).

Overy, R., *The Battle of Britain: Myth and Reality* (London: Penguin, 2010).

Overy, R., *The Bombing War* (London: Allen Lane, 2013).

Richards, D., *The Hardest Victory* (London: Hodder and Stoughton, 1994).

Sawyer, T., *Only Owls and Bloody Fools Fly at Night* (St Albans: Goodall, 1985).

Thorburn, G., *Bomber Command 1939 – 1940* (Barnsley: Pen and Sword, 2013).

Thorburn, G., *The Squadron that Died Twice* (London: Metro Publishing, 2015).

All station and squadron logs are available to the public at the National Archives AIR files, along with operational plans, directives, combat and casualty records.

Abbreviations

AA	Anti-aircraft
AASF	Advanced Air Striking Force
AFC	Air Force Cross
AOC-in-C	Air Officer Commanding-in-Chief
AVM	Air Vice-Marshal
ARP	Air Raid Protection
C-in-C	Commander-in-Chief
CO	Commanding Officer
Cpl	Corporal (Ger rank)
DFC	Distinguished Flying Cross
DFM	Distinguished Flying Medal
DSO	Distinguished Service Order
Fg Off	Flying Officer
Flt Lt	Flight Lieutenant
Flt Sgt	Flight Sergeant
Gp Capt.	Group Captain
HE	High Explosive
IFF	Identification, Friend or Foe
Lt	Leutnant (Ger. rank)
MC	Military Cross
MGB	Motor Gun Boat
MOPA	Military Objectives Previously Attacked
Oblt	Oberleutnant (Ger. rank)
OM	Order of Merit
OTU	Operational Training Unit
Plt Off	Pilot Officer
RAFVR	Royal Air Force Volunteer Reserve
RFC	Royal Flying Corps
RNZAF	Royal New Zealand Air Force
Sgt	Sergeant
SEMO	Self-evident Military Objective
Sqn Ldr	Squadron Leader
Sub Lt	Sub Lieutenant
VC	Victoria Cross
WopAg	Wireless Operator/Air Gunner
Wg Cdr	Wing Commander
WO	Warrant Officer
W/T	Wireless Telegraphy